Noah's Curse:
The Biblical Justification
of American Slavery

STEPHEN R. HAYNES

OXFORD UNIVERSITY PRESS

NOAH'S CURSE

Recent titles in
RELIGION IN AMERICA SERIES
Harry S. Stout, General Editor

Saints in Exile: The Holiness-Pentecostal Experience in African American Religion and Culture
Cheryl J. Sanders

Democratic Religion: Freedom, Authority, and Church Discipline in the Baptist South, 1785–1900
Gregory A. Wills

The Character of God: Recovering the Lost Literary Power of American Protestantism
Thomas E. Jenkins

The Revival of 1857–58: Interpreting an American Religious Awakening
Kathryn Teresa Long

Taking Heaven by Storm: Methodism and the Rise of Popular Christianity in America
John H. Wigger

Encounters with God: An Approach to the Theology of Jonathan Edwards
Michael J. McClymond

Evangelicals and Science in Historical Perspective
Edited by David N. Livingston, D.G. Hart, and Mark A Noll

Methodism and the Southern Mind, 1770–1810
Cynthia Lynn Lyerly

Princeton in the Nation's Service: Religious Ideals and Educational Practice, 1868–1928
P. C. Kemeny

Church People in the Struggle: The National Council of Churches and the Black Freedom Movement, 1950–1970
James F. Findlay Jr.

Tenacious of Their Liberties: The Congregationalists in Colonial Massachusetts
James F. Cooper Jr.

In Discordance with the Scriptures: American Protestant Battles over Translating the Bible
Peter J. Thuesen

The Gospel Working Up: Progress and the Pulpit in Nineteenth-Century Virginia
Beth Barton Schweiger

Black Zion: African American Religious Encounters with Judaism
Edited by Yvonne Chireau and Nathaniel Deutsch

Religion and Sex in American Public Life
Edited by Kathleen M. Sands

Transgressing the Bounds: Subversive Enterprises among Puritan Elite in Massachusetts, 1630–1692
Louise A. Breen

The Church on the World's Turf: An Evangelical Christian Group at a Secular University
Paul A. Bramadat

The Universalist Movement in America, 1770–1880
Ann Lee Bressler

A Republic of Righteousness: The Public Christianity of the Southern New England Clergy, 1783–1833
Jonathan D. Sassi

Noah's Curse: The Biblical Justification of American Slavery
Stephen R. Haynes

NOAH'S CURSE

The Biblical Justification of American Slavery

STEPHEN R. HAYNES

OXFORD
UNIVERSITY PRESS

2002

OXFORD

UNIVERSITY PRESS

Oxford   New York

Athens   Auckland   Bangkok   Bogotá   Buenos Aires   Cape Town
Chennai   Dar es Salaam   Delhi   Florence   Hong Kong   Istanbul   Karachi
Kolkata   Kuala Lumpur   Madrid   Melbourne   Mexico City   Mumbai   Nairobi
Paris   São Paulo   Shanghai   Singapore   Taipei   Tokyo   Toronto   Warsaw

and associated companies in
Berlin   Ibadan

Copyright © 2002 by Stephen R. Haynes

Published by Oxford University Press, Inc.
198 Madison Avenue, New York, New York 10016

Oxford is a registered trademark of Oxford University Press, Inc.

Library of Congress Cataloging-in-Publication Data
Haynes, Stephen R.
Noah's curse : the biblical justification of American slavery /
Stephen R. Haynes.
p.   cm.—(Religion in America series)
Includes bibliographical references and index.
ISBN 978-0-19-531307-9
1. Bible. O.T. Genesis IX–XI—Criticism, interpretation, etc.
2. Slavery—Justification.   3. Ham (Biblical figure)   4. United States—
Church history.   I. Title.   II. Religion in America series (Oxford University Press)
BS1235.2 .H357 2001
222'.1106—dc21   2001021800

Printed in the United States of America
on acid-free paper

Preface

My interest in the book of Genesis as a source for American racial discourse was piqued about 1990, when, in an informal conversation with erstwhile colleague Valarie Ziegler, I learned that Benjamin M. Palmer (1818–1902)—the "father" of Rhodes College—was a vociferous advocate of slavery who relied on the so-called curse of Ham to justify the South's peculiar institution. When I indicated my desire to learn more about Palmer and his proslavery worldview, Valarie suggested I consult the "Palmer Memorial Tablet" that hangs in a dimly lit corner of Palmer Hall, the oldest and most prominent building on the Rhodes campus. Finding the tablet, I read these dedicatory words:

> To the Glory of God
> and
> In Grateful Recognition
> of the generosity of the peo-
> ple of New Orleans by whom
> this building was erected
> In Memory of
> Benjamin Morgan Palmer
> for forty five years pastor of
> The First Presbyterian Church
> of New Orleans
> Born in Charleston, SC 1818
> Died in New Orleans 1902
>
> The father of this institution
> which was the first to place the

Bible as a required textbook in its
curriculum and which through all
the years continues to enshrine
this ideal of Christian education

A Patriot, A Scholar, An Educator
an Ecclesiastical Statesman
and a pulpit Orator unsurpassed.[1]

Reflecting on this tribute to Palmer's legacy, I began to form a question: What "ideal of Christian education" has Palmer bequeathed to my college, and to what extent is it separable from his use of the Bible to sanction slavery, secession, segregation, and genocide? Though I have not arrived at a conclusive answer to this question, it continues to exercise my mind and soul. This book is a public attempt to place it in larger historical, theological, and cultural perspective.

In this sense, Benjamin Palmer occupies a central place in this study for reasons that have much to do with the author. For the man provokes in me complex urges of hostility and desire, just as his portrait on my office wall is an object of awe and repulsion alike. As I have struggled to come to terms with my own identity as a Southerner, a Presbyterian, and a clergyman, Palmer has been my wrestling partner. For years we have grappled over the Bible he read, the ideas he espoused, and the institutions to which he was dedicated. One of those institutions is Rhodes College, my first and only home as a professional academic. Founded in 1848, Rhodes was reorganized under Palmer's leadership in 1875 as Southwestern Presbyterian University. Until his death in 1902, the institution remained extremely dear to him.

Just one document from Palmer's hand has been preserved in the Rhodes College archives, but it typifies his great fondness for the place. In May of 1889, Palmer wrote from New Orleans to inform Chancellor C. C. Hersman that lingering illness would prevent him from making the trip to Clarksville, Tennessee, to attend SPU's commencement. Though he would live for another thirteen years, chronically poor health and failing eyesight convinced Palmer that the days of his association with the university were numbered. He lamented that he would be "compelled to decline reappointment" to the board of directors. "In this prospective severance of my relations with the Directors," Palmer wrote, "permit me to say to them that, during a long life, no association has been more pleasant or profitable than with my Brethren of the Board . . . And the tears blind me, as I write these lines of farewell to Brethren whom I have learned to love in Christ Jesus. . . ."[2]

It is not surprising that Palmer wept as he contemplated the termination of his service to Southwestern Presbyterian University. The establishment of a viable Presbyterian institution of higher learning in the Old Southwest had been one of his preoccupations since he arrived in the region in 1855. This hearty and active man had outlived his wife and all but one of his five children, he had survived the Civil War as a refugee and fugitive, and he had bravely ministered to victims of New Orleans's yellow fever epidemic in 1858. His stature as a religious leader was unsurpassed in the region. But now, through some inscrutable movement of Providence, failing health forced him to sever official ties with the institution he helped bring to life just as it entered its heyday.

Given that Palmer probably composed thousands of letters during his adult life, it is strangely appropriate that this one alone is preserved on the campus of his beloved college. Not only does it offer a personal glimpse of the man honored as the institution's "father," but its reference to sightlessness is eerily prophetic. For in the succeeding years physical blindness would disable Palmer and ultimately hasten his death. According to eyewitnesses, Palmer never saw the streetcar that struck him down in 1902 while he attempted to cross the rails near his New Orleans home. The image of blindness invoked by Palmer in 1889 was prophetic in another way as well. A century after his death, it is impossible to ignore Palmer's theological myopia. In fact, any honest reckoning of Palmer's legacy must conclude that despite the respect and recognition accorded him during his lifetime, he was profoundly nearsighted in matters relating to race. Specifically, his worldview lacked utterly the baptismal vision of Christian unity that has been the church's ideal since Paul proclaimed to the Galatians, "There is no longer Jew or Greek, there is no longer slave or free, there is no longer male and female; for all of you are one in Christ Jesus" (Gal. 3:28). Even if the apostle failed to keep this goal in sight, it marks the acme of his ascent toward Christ's kingdom. Palmer is guilty of ignoring the vision of unity at the heart of the gospel and of replacing it with a myth of racial hierarchy. The infusion of Christian anthropology with racial or national myths has always spelled apostasy, as it did in Palmer's case.

Graciously, Palmer was afforded a final opportunity to correct his flawed vision. His biographer relates that after being struck by a streetcar near the intersection of St. Charles and Palmer Avenues, a group of Negro laborers "hurried to the scene, took up the bruised form of the venerable old man and bore him tenderly back to his home."[3] If Palmer's story were to be written in the tragic vein, this episode of "reversal"—the Chosen Race's venerable priest is rescued by "sons of Ham" who may have been former slaves—would issue in a scene of "recognition." Just before his death, the black men's humane deed would move the white victim to an epiphany of the rainbow people of God. But Palmer's biographer offers no evidence of such a recognition, forcing us to conclude that Palmer's fate, physically and spiritually, was blindness. The American religious and cultural forces that have obscured the Christian ideal of community rooted in creation are the subject of this study.

Secondary literature on the religious justification for slavery is voluminous. Two studies were particularly helpful as I began to explore the so-called curse of Ham and its role in American racial discourse. The first is *Illusions of Innocence,* in which Richard T. Hughes and C. Leonard Allen analyze the way Noah's curse functioned for Southern proslavery intellectuals as a "world-defining myth" whose appeal was based in part on Noah's traditional association with the invention of agriculture and his role as the patriarch of the first postdiluvian family.[4] The second work is Thomas V. Peterson's *Ham and Japheth in America,* which traces the contours of the curse in the collective mind of the Old South and elucidates the ways it functioned to sustain the worldview of antebellum Southerners when their peculiar institution came under attack after 1830.[5] Peterson clarifies the "mythic" quality of the curse by carefully noting the cultural functions of Genesis 9:20–27 in the Old South. Drawing on the work of anthropologists Clifford Geertz and Claude Lévi-Strauss, Peterson defines myths as shared cultural symbols that uphold a social order. According to this definition, the story of Noah and his sons functioned mythically in the Old South inasmuch as the characters and actions it narrated symbolized Southern cultural beliefs, institutions, and attitudes, successfully bringing together whites' "racial stereotypes, political theories, religious beliefs and economic realities."[6]

As will be evident in the pages that follow, I am deeply indebted to Peterson's fine study. By exploring the curse in the light of symbol, myth, and sacred history, he clarifies how Noah's malediction became a pivotal element in the biblical argument for slavery. Peterson also cites a great many works by proslavery intellectuals, many of which are referred to in this study. Nevertheless, this project expands on Peterson's work in important ways: by placing American readings of Genesis 9 within the long history of Western biblical interpretation; by attending to texts dealing with Nimrod (Genesis 10:6–12) and the Tower of Babel (Genesis 11:1–9), without which the role of Noah's curse in American history cannot be properly understood; and by analyzing the way Genesis 9 and its cognate texts were employed in American racial discourse after the demise of slavery, when white Southerners found themselves more in need than ever of biblical sanctions for the inferiority of blacks, the evil of miscegenation, and the necessity—or at least permissibility—of racial segregation.

This study is thoroughly and unapologetically interdisciplinary. It incorporates methodologies associated with history, biblical studies, literary criticism, the history of interpretation, theology, and anthropology. In part because academic forces at the professional and institutional levels mitigate against this sort of interdisciplinary scholarship, I have made an effort to transgress traditional boundaries of scholarly inquiry. One of the book's goals, in fact, is to foster dialogue between scholars who work in separate corners of academe and who too often are unaware of others' labors. Our immature scholarly understanding of Noah's curse and its role in American history is due in part to the disciplinary isolation that discourages students of American culture and history from interacting with scholars of the Bible. This study seeks to over-come this isolation by exploring the intersection between racial readings of Genesis 9–11 and the history and cultural patterns that have influenced them.

Finally, because this book treats biblical texts that have been objects of exten-sive historical-critical analysis, it is necessary to defend its focus on the history of biblical interpretation—that is, on how Genesis 9–11 *has* been read, rather than on how it *ought* to be read. Modern scholars have been keen to employ critical tools to defuse the pernicious social influence of the Bible in Western history. But doing so does not alter the textual forces that have encouraged misinterpretation or the penchant of Bible readers to read in self-justifying ways. Among the unifying themes of this study are the convictions that read-ers—whatever their qualifications, background, or official status—make meaning of biblical texts and that the meanings they make, however foreign they appear to minds conditioned by biblical literalism or the historical-critical method, are significant in their own right. They demonstrate how personal, theological, and social forces affect every act of interpretation.

John Sawyer has recently lamented biblical criticism's studied ignorance of the history of interpretation: The concern of most modern biblical experts, he notes, "has been with the original meaning of the original text: anything later that that is rejected as at best unimportant, at worst pious rubbish. If anything, they want their main contribution to the study of the Bible to be a corrective one, explicitly rejecting what people believe about it: 'Ah, but that is not what the original Hebrew meant!' "[7] Studies of Noah's curse by Bible scholars confirm Sawyer's observation. Many seek to recover the prehistory of Genesis 9:20–27 as a way of limiting the parameters of valid interpretation. In opposition to this narrow interest in uncovering original meanings, how-ever, the method of analysis employed here foregrounds postbiblical data.[8] As Sawyer argues, this approach is "no less historical or critical" than the historical-critical method, because "there is just as much evidence for what people believe the text means, or what they are told to believe it means, as there is for what the original author intended, and this can be treated with just the same degree of sensitivity and scientific rigor as a reconstructed orig-inal Hebrew text or any other ancient near eastern text." Sawyer adds that "what people believe a text means has often been far more interesting and important, theologically, politically, morally and aesthetically, . . . than what it originally meant."[9]

The focus on Bible readers will be evident throughout this study. Genesis 9–11's history of interpretation is explored in detail in part I. Part II analyzes the distinctive ways Noah's curse was interpreted and expanded in antebellum America. Part III deals with the role played by Genesis 9–11 in the theological and social thought of influential Presbyterian divine Benjamin Morgan Pal-mer. And part IV revisits the history of interpretation, focuses on traditions of counterreading, and offers a redemptive interpretation of Noah's curse.

Acknowledgments

A variety of people and institutions have contributed to this project. Much of the research that informs the study was conducted during a sabbatical leave from Rhodes College during the 1995–96 academic year. Lilly Endowment Inc. provided funding that made possible a full year's leave from teaching. Annette Cates of Rhodes's Burrow Library supplied access through interlibrary loan to many of the primary texts cited here. Timothy Huebner of the Rhodes History Department was an important conversation partner as the project evolved. James Vest and Lawrence de Bartolet of the Rhodes Department of Foreign Languages and Literatures translated the French texts cited here. Their assistance was invaluable.

Several scholars at other institutions made important contributions to the book as well. Erskine Clarke of Columbia Theological Seminary served as my first conversation partner an Southern religion. Danna Nolan Fewell of Drew University deserves much credit for encouraging the project to completion. Following my presentation on Benjamin M. Palmer at the 1996 American Academy of Religion–Society for Biblical Literature annual meeting in New Orleans, Danna suggested I explore the American hermeneutics of race more generally. I began to do so, and the result is a study that is considerably broader and more historically informed than would have been the case without her input. She and Fred Burnett of Anderson University read the manuscript at an early stage and made valuable suggestions. Eugene D. Genovese, Bertram Wyatt-Brown, and Walter Brueggemann also read and commented on early versions of the manuscript. Their support and guidance have been tremendously valuable.

Benjamin Braude of Boston College became an important conversation partner as this project developed. Working on a similar topic, Ben graciously shared ideas and resources. Thee Smith of Emory University proved to be a helpful interpreter of Girardian theory. Julia O'Brien of Lancaster Theological Seminary read portions of the manuscript and made helpful suggestions. Finally, Cynthia Read of Oxford University Press is responsible for seeing promise in a rough manuscript. Her vision and support are much appreciated.

Permission is gratefully acknowledged to use material that was originally published in two scholarly journals. A version of chapter 4 appeared in the January 2000 issue of *The Journal of Southern Religion,* and a version of chapter 7 appeared in the Summer 2000 issue of *The Journal of Presbyterian History.* All Bible quotations are from the New Revised Standard Version, unless otherwise noted.

While this book was in process, my personal life underwent unexpected and difficult changes. Family members and close friends have been extraordinarily supportive. I am particularly indebted to my parents, Jean and Ronald Haynes, and to Kenny Morrell, Anne Davey, Stephanie Bussey-Spencer, Mark Weiss, Mary Allison Cates, John Kaltner, John Carey, Harry Smith, Palmer and John Jones, Bunny and Jeff Goldstein, Stephen and Gwen Kinney, Kim and Eric Schaefer, and especially Alyce Waller. To these remarkable friends, this book is lovingly dedicated.

July 2001   S. R. H.
Memphis, Tennessee

Contents

1. Setting the Stage, 3

PART I. CHARACTERS IN THE POSTDILUVIAN
         DRAMA

2. A Black Sheep in the (Second) First Family: The
   Legend of Noah and His Sons, 23

3. Unauthorized Biography: The Legend of Nimrod and
   His Tower, 41

PART II. HONOR AND ORDER

4. Original Dishonor: Noah's Curse and the Southern
   Defense of Slavery, 65

5. Original Disorder: Noah's Curse and the Southern
   Defense of Slavery, 87

6. Grandson of Disorder: Nimrod Comes to America, 105

PART III.   NOAH'S CAMERA

7. Noah's Sons in New Orleans: Genesis 9–11 and
   Benjamin Morgan Palmer, 125

8. Honor, Order, and Mastery in Palmer's Biblical
   Imagination, 146

9. Beyond Slavery, Beyond Race: Noah's Camera in the
   Twentieth Century, 161

PART IV.   REDEEMING THE CURSE

10. Challenging the Curse: Readings and
    Counterreadings, 177

11. Redeeming the Curse: Ham as Victim, 201

12. Conclusion: Racism, Religion, and Responsible
    Scholarship, 220

    Notes, 223

    Bibliography, 299

    Index, 314

NOAH'S CURSE

1

Setting the Stage

IN MAY 1999, the National Broadcasting Corporation telecast its widely anticipated TV version of *Noah's Ark*. Commentators claimed that the production had taken liberties with the biblical text; they were silent, however, about aspects of the Bible's history of interpretation that were retained in the television miniseries. For instance, the movie linked Noah's son Ham with Africa (by casting a woman of African descent as his wife), with unrestrained desire (by including scenes in which Ham makes sexual overtures toward his fiancée), and with rebellion (by depicting Ham as the instigator of mutiny on the ark).

In April 1999, National Public Radio aired a report on the legal barriers to interracial marriage that persist in a few Southern states.[1] The report noted that although residents of South Carolina had voted the previous November to nullify that state's antimiscegenation law, nearly 40% of votes cast were in opposition to repeal. To illustrate the religious basis for Southern resistance to intermarriage, the report included a sound bite in which State Representative Lanny F. Littlejohn (Rep., Spartanburg and Cherokee counties) declared that interracial marriage was "not what God intended when he separated the races back in the Babylonian days." Littlejohn acknowledged that his perspective on the question probably stemmed from his Southern Baptist upbringing.[2]

In October 1998, James Landrith of Alexandria, Virginia, inquired of South Carolina's Bob Jones University concerning possible enrollment at the institution. Because Landrith was forthright about his marriage to an African American woman, the university's community relations coordinator was obliged to explain that Landrith's marital status presented a barrier to his

3

admission. In a letter from the university, Landrith was informed that "God has separated people for His own purpose. He has erected barriers between the nations, not only land and sea barriers, but also ethnic, cultural, and language barriers. God has made people different one from another and intends those differences to remain." The letter went on to explain that "Bob Jones University is opposed to intermarriage of the races because it breaks down the barriers God has established. It mixes that which God separated and intends to keep separate."[3] While conceding that no Bible verse "dogmatically says that races should not intermarry," the letter did invoke a specific text:

> The people who built the Tower of Babel were seeking a man-glorifying unity which God has not ordained (Gen. 11:4–6). Much of the agitation for intermarriage among the races today is for the same reason. It is promoted by one-worlders, and we oppose it for the same reason that we oppose religious ecumenism, globalism, one-world economy, one-world police force, unisex, etc. When Jesus Christ returns to the earth, He will establish world unity, but until then, a divided earth seems to be His plan.[4]

In a spectator culture that is titillated by bizarre expressions of religiosity, people briefly wonder at such stories and then push them out of their minds. However, as this study seeks to demonstrate, these are only recent examples of a perennial American tendency to apply stories from the postdiluvian chapters of Genesis to the problem of "race" relations. In fact, each of these news items—BJU's defense of segregation based on the Tower of Babel, NBC's embellishments on the story of Noah, and Representative Littlejohn's cryptic reference to racial separation in "Babylonian days"—are unconscious expressions of an American interpretive tradition rooted in Genesis 9–11.

Dispersion and Differentiation

What is the content of these chapters that conclude the primeval history of Genesis? Chapter 9 completes the biblical flood narrative by relating the Lord's instructions to the human survivors, the establishment of a covenant with their leader, and the tale of Noah's drunkenness (vv. 20–27). Genesis 10 offers a detailed genealogy of Noah's offspring, framed by the statements "These are the descendants of Noah's sons, Shem, Ham, and Japheth; children were born to them after the flood" (v. 1), and "These are the families of Noah's sons, according to their genealogies, in their nations; and from these the nations spread abroad on the earth after the flood" (v. 32). Genesis 11 relates the cautionary tale of the tower before extending the postdiluvian genealogy to Abram.

These folktales and genealogical lists may be viewed as literary stage props for the entrance of Abram in Genesis 12. But a handful of crucial passages have led careful Bible readers to ascribe theological and social import to this section of scripture. These are 9:20–27 (the story of Noah's drunkenness), 10: 8–12 (the brief description of the "mighty hunter" Nimrod), 10:25 (which indicates a "division" of the earth in the days of Peleg), 10:32 (with its reference to the "spreading abroad" of nations), and 11:1–9 (the story of the tower, culminating in the "scattering" of the builders). Under the influence of these texts and the cultural forces explored in this book, readers of Genesis have construed chapters 9–11 as a thematic whole, reflecting the themes of *dispersion* and *differentiation*.

In modern European and American racial discourse, Genesis 9 has been regarded primarily as a story of *differentiation* among Noah's sons Shem, Ham, and Japheth. Triggered by some transgression on the part of Ham, Noah prophesies the distinct destinies his sons' descendants will assume in the corporate development of humankind. In part because it conforms to notions that humanity is comprised of essential "racial" types, this passage has shown a remarkable capacity to elucidate the nature of human difference. For instance, according to a modern Christian tradition, the magi who trekked to Bethlehem to honor the newborn messiah represented the three races (white, red, and black) stemming from Noah's sons. The racial motif in depictions of the magi apparently emerged in the fifteenth century[5] and survived into the twentieth.[6]

But prior to the racialization of Noah's sons in the modern period, Genesis 9 was read as a prelude to the chronicle of human *dispersion* in chapters 10 and 11. Early Bible readers noted that the story is prefaced by the observation that "from [Shem, Ham, and Japheth] the whole earth was peopled" (vv. 18–19). The dispersion implied in the Masoretic text became explicit in the Septuagint ("from there they were *dispersed* upon the whole world") and Vulgate ("from them each race of man was *dispersed* upon the whole world") renderings of the passage.[7] This subtle shift in emphasis between the Hebrew, Greek, and Latin versions of Genesis 9 no doubt influenced Bible readers to link Genesis 9 thematically with chapter 10, where dispersion is the leitmotif.

In the so-called Table of Nations in Genesis 10, Bible readers have discovered both a catalog of Noah's descendants and a description of the earth's repopulation following the Deluge. Readings of Genesis 10 as a divinely directed dispersion are reinforced by a variety of textual prompts—"From these the coastland peoples spread" (v. 5); "From that land [Nimrod] went into Assyria" (v. 11); "Afterward the families of the Canaanites spread abroad" (v. 18); "To Eber were born two sons: the name of the one was Peleg, for in his days the earth was divided (v. 25)—as well as by orthodox assumptions regarding the historicity of Genesis.[8] The familiar connection of Noah's sons with Europe, Asia, and Africa (the three regions of the Old World) developed only "slowly and tentatively" in the first centuries of the common era. What became the conventional "three son, three continent view" was elaborated by Alcuin (732–804) and refined in the twelfth century by Peter Comester (ca.

1100–1179). But these medieval associations were unstable, and the assignment of Ham to Africa, Shem to Asia, and Japheth to Europe was not inscribed on the European mind until the Age of Exploration.⁹ By the nineteenth century, the same intellectual and social forces that contributed to the racialization of Noah's prophecy came to bear on Genesis 10, which was consistently read as an account of humanity's racial origins and as proof that "racial distinctions and national barriers proceed from God."¹⁰

The Tower of Babel story in Genesis 11 has been read as a reiteration of dispersion and differentiation alike; indeed, both themes are implicit in the text. Dispersion is evident in the builders' justification of their project as a defense against being "scattered abroad upon the face of the whole earth" (v. 4), and the narrator's statement that "the LORD scattered them abroad from there over the face of all the earth" (v. 8). Differentiation emerges when, in response to this brazen attempt to reach the abode of God ("Come, let us build ourselves a city, and a tower with its top in the heavens," v. 4), the Lord purposes to distinguish the divine and earthly realms and to divide human beings by confusing "their language there, so that they will not understand one another's speech" (v. 7). Thus, whether dispersion or differentiation is emphasized, the Tower story may be read as confirming the thematic unity of Genesis 9–11.

Another interpretive force linking these chapters is the legend of Nimrod. The enduring association of Nimrod with the Tower of Babel is a classic example of what contemporary literary critics call intertextuality. References in Genesis 10 to Babel and Shinar ("The beginning of his kingdom was Babel, Erech, and Accad, all of them in the land of Shinar," v. 10) led early Bible readers to cast Nimrod as the antagonist in the drama of the Tower. This interpretive move linked a character without a narrative to a narrative without identifiable characters¹¹ and contributed to the reception of Genesis 9–11 as a textual unit. Particularly when he was racialized by nineteenth-century pro-slavery authors, this grandson of Ham came to embody the curse uttered in Noah's original act of postdiluvian differentiation. The chapters that follow indicate how the perceived unity of Genesis 9–11 has affected both the history of biblical interpretation and the logic of American racial discourse.

Noah's Curse

The evolution of the so-called curse of Ham as a biblical justification for racial slavery is, of course, an essential part of our story. The tale itself—related in Genesis 9:20–27—most likely reflects conditions in the tenth century B.C.E., specifically the enslavement and debasement of "Canaanites" by the Israelite monarchy. Only in the third and fourth centuries C.E., however, was the biblical story read to emphasize a perennial curse on "Hamites." What are the origins of this pernicious use of Genesis 9 to connect Ham with slavery and blackness? In recent years, much ink has been spilled in scholarly attempts to answer this question; here a brief summary must suffice.

The modern association of Genesis 9 with black servitude is adumbrated in works by church fathers and rabbis alike.[12] For instance, Origen (ca. 185–254) wrote that by "quickly sink[ing] to slavery of the vices," Ham's "discolored posterity imitate the ignobility of the race" he fathered.[13] Augustine (354–430) saw the origins of slavery in Ham's transgression,[14] Ambrose of Milan (339–397) opined that Noah's malediction applied to the darker descendants of Ham,[15] and Ephrem of Nisibis (d. 373) is said to have paraphrased Noah's malediction with the words, "accursed be Canaan, and may God make his face black."[16] Several notorious rabbinic glosses on the biblical text that appear to link Ham's descendants with dark skin and other negroid features have been identified as wellsprings of antiblack sentiment. But these texts and their relationship to slavery and racism are the subject of intense controversy.[17]

One medieval rendering of Christ's genealogy has been interpreted as racializing some of Ham's descendants through Cush.[18] Yet at least one scholar who has reviewed the relevant evidence concludes that no medieval Christian source explicitly connects Ham, sex, and blackness.[19] Even if they do adumbrate modern racism, medieval Christian and Jewish interepretations of Genesis 9 may reflect the emerging reality of racial slavery as effect rather than cause.[20] It was in the Muslim Near East world that slavery was first closely allied with color, that black Africans first gained a "slavish reputation," and that the so-called Hamitic myth was first invoked as a justification for human thralldom. In fact, it appears that race and slavery were first consciously combined in readings of Genesis 9 by Muslim exegetes during the ninth and tenth centuries, though these authors claim to draw on rabbinic literature.[21]

In western Europe prior to the modern period, the curse was invoked to explain the origins of slavery, the provenance of black skin, and the exile of Hamites to the less wholesome regions of the earth. But these aspects of malediction were not integrated in an explicit justification for racial slavery until the fifteenth century, when dark-skinned peoples were enslaved by the Spanish and Portuguese, and the European slave stereotype was stabilized.[22] Thus, only with the growth of the slave trade and the increasing reliance on sub-Saharan Africa as a source for slaves did the curse's role as a justification for racial slavery eclipse its function as a scriptural explanation of either "blackness" in particular or servitude in general.

As this summary indicates, it is not clear when to date the fateful conjunction of slavery and race in Western readings of Noah's prophecy. The constitutive elements in the application of Genesis 9 to New World servitude—the conviction that the story narrated the origins of slavery, association of Ham's offspring with the continent of Africa and with dark skin, and the notion that Noah's words represented a prophetic outline of subsequent human history—were present in some of the earliest readings of Genesis 9 among Jews, Christians, and Muslims. Yet the application of the curse to racial slavery was the product of centuries of development in ethnic and racial stereotyping, biblical interpretation, and the history of servitude.

Nevertheless, by the early colonial period a racialized version of Noah's curse had arrived in America. In fact, the writings of abolitionists indicate that by the 1670s the "curse of Ham" was being employed as a sanction for black enslavement. In 1700, when Samuel Sewall and John Saffin squared off over the rectitude of human thralldom, the efficacy of Ham's curse figured in the debate.[23] It is significant that Saffin, whose tract carries the distinction of being "the earliest printed defense of slavery in Colonial America,"[24] was reluctant to make the dubious identification of Africans with Ham (or Canaan). But as white servitude declined and racial slavery came under attack, the curse's role in the American defense of slavery was increasingly formalized. By the 1830s—when the American antislavery movement became organized, vocal, and aggressive—the scriptural defense of slavery had evolved into the "most elaborate and systematic statement" of proslavery theory,[25] Noah's curse had become a stock weapon in the arsenal of slavery's apologists, and references to Genesis 9 appeared prominently in their publications.

Honor, Order, and the American Biblical Imagination

This study devotes particular attention to the American legacy of Noah's curse, beginning with a careful examination of its role in the antebellum proslavery argument. By locating American readings of Genesis 9 within the history of biblical interpretation, the distinctive features in proslavery versions of the curse are clarified. Overwhelmingly, these reflect two concerns that pervaded antebellum slave culture—honor and order.[26]

Over the past half-century, much has been written about Southern honor. Even today attempts to explicate the "Southern mind" rely on the concept. Social scientists design experiments to demonstrate that honor is indeed constitutive of the Southern male character, and commentators find honor useful for explaining hostile behavior on Southern highways.[27] Yet despite decades of attention to honor's links with Southern history, few have attempted to explore its role in the religious defense of slavery, even though the solid scholarly consensus is that "on no other subject did the [antebellum] Southern mind reveal itself more distinctly than on the institution of slavery." Because part II considers the place of honor in proslavery readings of Genesis 9, it will be useful to review the evolving scholarly understanding of honor's place in the Southern mind.

Among the first to hazard an explanation of the distinctive Southern character was Mark Twain. In *Life on the Mississippi,* Twain employed the sort of insightful hyperbole that became his trademark when he identified the roots of the Civil War in the type of literature favored by Southern readers:

> Sir Walter [Scott] had so large a hand in making Southern character, as it
> existed before the war, that he is in great measure responsible for the war.
> It seems a little harsh toward a dead man to say that we never should have
> had any war but for Sir Walter; and yet something of a plausible argument
> might, perhaps, be made in support of that wild proposition. . . . [The South-
> ern] character can be traced rather more easily to Sir Walter's influence than
> to that of any other thing or person.[28]

This reference to the immensely popular British author of historical romances
has been dismissed as "probably the wildest passage in all Mark Twain's literary criticism."[29] But when Twain connected the novels of Scott, the code of
honor inscribed in them, the antebellum South, and the American Civil War,
he was composing a prelude to the twentieth-century scholarly quest for the
lineaments of the Southern character. The quest was officially launched in
1941 in W. J. Cash's impressionistic but influential reading of honor as a
dimension of the Southern mind that survived the Confederacy's defeat. In
1949, Rollin G. Osterweis argued in a classic study that romanticism was a
constitutive element of Old South culture.[30] In *The Militant South* (1956), John
Hope Franklin initiated a new era in scholarly study of the South by emphasizing the centrality of honor to Southern history and explicitly linking slavery
and the Southern character. According to Orlando Patterson, Franklin was
the first to show "a direct causal link between the southern ruling class's
excessively developed sense of honor and the institution of slavery."[31]

For the past forty years, scholars of the American South have emulated
these pioneers by exploring the effects of Southern chivalry and honor on the
region's distinctive identity. The resulting vast literature features such notable
studies as Clement Eaton's "The Role of Honor in Southern Society" (1976),
Bertram Wyatt-Brown's *Southern Honor* (1982) and *Honor and Violence in the
Old South* (1986), Orlando Patterson's *Slavery and Social Death* (1982), and
Kenneth Greenberg's *Honor and Slavery* (1996).[32] Of particular interest for
these second-generation scholars has been the nexus between white Southerners' cult of honor and their advocacy of slavery. In a variety of insightful ways,
they interpret the Old South's attachment to slavery as a function of its commitment to a strict timocratic code. In the 1980s, Wyatt-Brown articulated the
emerging consensus when he declared that honor must be seen as "greater,
longer and more tenacious than it has been viewed before, at least in relation
to the slaveholding South."[33]

This study takes up Wyatt-Brown's charge by investigating the dynamics
of honor and shame in antebellum readings of Noah's curse intended to defend the institution of slavery. On the basis of this investigation it will be
argued that proslavery readings of the curse were rooted in a pair of crucial
premises: that slaves are debased persons and slavery a form of life without
honor and that as the eponymous ancestor of Africans, Ham embodies the
dishonorable condition of black slaves. Accordingly, the themes of honor,
dishonor, and social death are pivotal for comprehending the cultural significance of antebellum American readings of Genesis 9.

Following an examination of honor in the biblical proslavery argument, is an exploration of the passion for order that pervades American readings of Noah's curse. Although order was not a distinctively Southern feature of antebellum culture, it served as a thematic link between racist readings of Genesis 9–11 before and after the Civil War. Precisely because Noah's curse was so clearly applicable to the question of slavery, its postwar relevance was not selfevident. But American Bible readers soon discovered that the curse could function as a condemnation of the Hamite penchant for disorder, an inclination embodied in Ham's grandson Nimrod. Over time, the builder of Babel's tower became the chief representative of a Hamite character typified not by dishonor but by disorder and rebellion. Thus, when studied chronologically, American readings of Genesis 9–11 reveal a development in the biblical imagination: from Ham, the lecherous and dishonorable son who is fit only for servitude, to Nimrod, the rebel-king who tyrannizes his fellows, usurps territory allotted to others, and thwarts God's purposes for humanity.

Like other American stereotypes of the Negro, these biblical types are complementary as well as contrasting. According to John W. Blassingame's classic study of plantation life, two conflicting slave stereotypes existed side by side in the antebellum mind. One was "Sambo," the docile, deferent, helpless, and ultimately harmless slave. The other was "Nat," the slave who might *appear* harmless but was in fact incorrigibly rebellious.[34] Sambo, "combining in his person Uncle Remus, Jim Crow, and Uncle Tom, was the most pervasive and long lasting of the . . . literary stereotypes. Indolent, faithful, humorous, loyal, dishonest, superstitious, improvident, and musical, Sambo was inevitably a clown and congenitally docile." Nat, by contrast, was "the rebel who rivaled Sambo in the universality and continuity of his literary image. Revengeful, bloodthirsty, cunning, treacherous, and savage, Nat was the incorrigible runaway, the poisoner of white men, the ravager of white women who defied all the rules of plantation society. [He was] subdued and punished only when overcome by superior numbers or firepower."[35]

Blassingame's vivid rendering of these stereotypes indicates the ways they are reflected in American readings of Genesis 9–11 before and after the Civil War. In fact, the dichotomous depiction of the Negro slave in Southern literature appears to correspond to a bifurcation in the American biblical imagination between the mischievous Ham and the rebellious Nimrod. On one hand, antebellum readers of Genesis 9 consistently described Noah's youngest son as a sort of Sambo figure. For his lack of honor and a tendency toward mild but annoying disorder, Ham was condemned to servitude, no doubt for his own good. On the other hand, American portraits of Nimrod have tended to fit the Nat stereotype in the white mind. Depicted as a cunning leader with empire as his goal, Nimrod is savage rebellion personified. No doubt the merging of these biblical archetypes and slave stereotypes was enhanced by the subtle linguistic affinities between *Ham* and *Sam*bo, *Nat* and *Nim*rod. As we shall see, these enduring literary and cultural stereotypes outlived the institution of slavery to achieve a permanence in American racial discourse.

The Curse Reconsidered

Antebellum abolitionists were keenly aware of Genesis 9's prominent role in proslavery rhetoric, a fact reflected in Theodore Weld's oft-cited observation that "this prophecy of Noah is the *vade mecum* of slaveholders, and they never venture abroad without it."[36] But some contemporary scholars have doubted what was self-evident to antislavery activists. In fact, the curse's role in the proslavery argument has been questioned recently on several grounds, including the claim that it was "largely passé among intellectual elites,"[37] the supposed difficulty literal interpreters of the Bible would have in applying Noah's malediction to Ham, and the assumption that biblical proof-texts are in fact post hoc justifications for positions adopted on other grounds. But the most substantial argument of this kind is that proslavery Bible readers knew that Genesis 9 was not concerned with race and thus could not accept it as a convincing justification for black servitude.

This case against the curse's pivotal role in American proslavery thought has been articulated by Eugene D. Genovese, a leading scholar of Southern culture. Relying on his voluminous knowledge of the slaveholders' Weltanschauung, Genovese concludes that manifest difficulties in applying Noah's curse to racial thralldom limited its utility in the proslavery rhetorical arsenal. Genovese contends that "before the War the [Southern proslavery] divines had not rested their case on race. They had explicitly declared slavery scripturally sanctioned and ordained of God regardless of race. True, many divines did invoke the Noahic curse and the supposed black descent from Ham in an ideology that took deep root among the people, but [some] . . . prominent divines, regarded it with suspicion since neither the Bible nor science demonstrated that the blacks descended from Ham."[38]

Genovese's challenge raises a series of questions regarding the role of Noah's curse in antebellum America: How central was the "Ham myth" to the proslavery argument? Was it purely "popular," effective only at "the level of propaganda and mass consciousness"?[39] Should references to the curse in the works of proslavery intellectuals be read as concessions to popular credulity or palliatives for a guilty Southern conscience?[40] Did most Southern divines regard the curse with suspicion because they could not "demonstrate" blacks' descent from Ham? Could the curse adequately sanction racial slavery without proving too much—that is, the possibility of white slavery? And, given the problems of applying Noah's curse to racial servitude, why do we not find more explicit attention to "race" in antebellum works that invoke the curse?

Thomas Peterson illumined these questions more than two decades ago when he showed that because the curse so conveniently "framed the ethos of plantation life within a sacred history," it assumed a *givenness* among antebellum slavery advocates.[41] According to Peterson, Noah's curse "became symbolically persuasive because it reinforced prevalent attitudes about the nature of government and the planters' image both of themselves and of the ideal

Southern plantation."[42] Did the curse's mythic givenness in the Old South mean that its application to racial slavery was also taken for granted? This is where the cultural motifs of honor and order prove so helpful. These aspects of Southern slave society operated in symbiosis with the biblical text itself to encourage "racial" readings of Genesis 9 in which Ham's essential "blackness" was evident not in his descent so much as in his character and behavior: By comporting himself as a dishonorable or disorderly son, did not Ham embody the very traits that distinguished the slave population? W. E. B. Dubois was not far off in describing the process by which Genesis 9 was "racialized" in the minds of America's slavery advocates: "'Cursed be Canaan!' cried the Hebrew priests. 'A servant of servants shall he be unto his brethren.' With what characteristic complacency did the slaveholders assume that Canaanites were Negroes and their 'brethren' white? Are not Negroes servants? Ergo!"[43]

Undoubtedly, this sort of racial thinking was largely unconscious; but by contemporary standards it was far from irrational. In fact, in the antebellum intellectual milieu, Ham's affinity with the Negro could be defended within the realms of tradition (the long genealogical convention that linked Ham with Africa), history (the Table of Nations was widely accepted as a reliable account of the world's repopulation following the Deluge), and social thought (Genesis 9–11 was believed to contain a veritable constitution for postdiluvian societies). During the heyday of slavery in America, a racial understanding of Genesis 9–11 was so much a part of cultural common sense that defensive arguments were no longer required. The significance of Noah's curse in American slavery debates cannot be appreciated until we grasp the way Genesis 9 provided the implied racial context that other biblical arguments lacked.

Even if we assume that Christian advocates of slavery knew the Bible lacked any explicit justification for the "enslavement of Africans, and only Africans, in particular,"[44] this only confirms the central role of Noah's curse in the proslavery argument. The curse became indispensable precisely because, according to culturally sanctioned views of the Bible, history, and society, it could be regarded as providing the justification for black enslavement missing from other biblical texts. If the majority of antebellum proslavery intellectuals failed to emphasize the racial dimensions of Genesis 9:20–27,[45] it is not because they were embarrassed by their inability to prove that Ham was the ancestor of black slaves. Rather, they considered Ham's negritude to be as self-evident—as given—as Noah's identity as the first planter patriarch or the Bible's applicability to American society.

Noah's Camera

Because it traces the lingering influence of Genesis 9–11 after the Civil War, this study implicitly challenges another of Genovese's claims regarding the place of race in Southern religious discourse. According to Genovese, the reluctant acknowledgment that the Bible did not sanction racial slavery led Southerners to abandon their professed theological orthodoxy by succumbing to the attractions of secular ideologies such as scientific racism and American imperialism.[46] Genovese argues, in other words, that the racist bridge often assumed to link the Old South with the New obscures the significant disjunction between the intellectual and moral justifications provided for antebellum slavery and postbellum segregation. These chapters reveal, however, that American reliance on Genesis 9–11 as a source for discerning God's will in racial matters is responsible for significant continuities between the proslavery and prosegregation arguments.

Many examples of this continuity will be gleaned from the life and letters of Benjamin Morgan Palmer, one of the South's preeminent clergymen during the second half of the nineteenth century. In the late antebellum period, Palmer employed Noah's prophecy as a sanction for chattel slavery, and following the war he analyzed the South's recent past—and its future—by using the lens provided by Genesis 10 and 11. As a leading Presbyterian divine, Palmer's influence was considerable between the mid-1850s and his death in 1902.[47] In sermons from the pulpit of New Orleans's First Church—arguably the most prestigious Presbyterian post in the South—Palmer "raise[d] the function of the clergy as ennobler and defender of Southern traditions to perhaps its highest level."[48]

Despite the attention given to Palmer by historians and scholars of religion, his reliance on Genesis 9–11 as a divinely revealed blueprint for human societies has been ignored. For instance, in a recent study entitled *Gospel of Disunion,* Mitchell Snay confirms Palmer's significance in reflecting and influencing the antebellum Southern mind but fails to note Palmer's privileging of Genesis 9–11 as the biblical foundation for Southern secession.[49] Snay observes that many clergymen utilized biblical history to elucidate the sectional conflict, but he overlooks the mythic power in Palmer's invocation of the primeval history in Genesis. Pre-Israelite themes such as Noah's drunkenness, the dispersion of nations, and the Tower of Babel were more universal in scope and application than stories from Hebrew history. The postdiluvian Adam and his descendants possessed a timeless relevance that was not lost on Palmer or his auditors.[50]

A careful examination of Palmer's evolving interpretation of Genesis 9–11 is useful for evaluating Genovese's arguments regarding the role of race in the proslavery argument and the purported discontinuities between antebellum and postbellum Southern discourse. First, unlike many of his Old School Presbyterian (and thus orthodox Calvinist) coreligionists, Palmer had no qualms about appealing to Noah's prophecy as a justification—indeed, *the* biblical justification—for Negro slavery, despite the fact that many of the Presbyterian intellectuals who mentored Palmer rejected Genesis 9's application to American slavery.[51] Second, Palmer's reading of the text thoroughly troubles Genovese's assumptions about the American reception of Noah's curse. Genovese contends that because proslavery divines understood that the story of Noah and his sons concerned slavery but not race, the curse died a natural death following emancipation. But Palmer represents a tradition of American interpretation in which Noah's "prophecy" (he never used the word *curse* with reference to Genesis 9) applies to race relations in general rather than to slavery per se. Before and during the war, Palmer referred obliquely to Hamite "servitude" without forcing American slavery into the mold of Genesis 9. After the war, however, he invoked Noah's prophecy with greater frequency, arguing that it contained a normative picture of the relationship between the world's three great "races." The American message in Noah's prophecy, Palmer implied, was not that blacks had to be enslaved, but that their essential character befitted servitude. Because subservience could take many forms, this message might be heeded under a variety of social conditions. Yet no historical contingency could alter the fundamental relationship of the great "nations" foreseen by Noah.

Third, in that Palmer's career spanned the five decades between 1850 and 1900, he provides an excellent case study for judging Genovese's contention that the postbellum South forsook the proslavery worldview and the orthodox theology that sustained it. As we shall see, Palmer both confirms and troubles this claim. His writings following the Civil War contain just the sort of accommodation between theology and rational racism discussed by Genovese. But while Palmer was influenced by secular images and idioms, he continued to regard Genesis 9–11 as the basis for reliable knowledge concerning the world's "races." As one who successfully assimilated racism and imperialism to a theology ostensibly rooted in scripture, Palmer represents an important strand of continuity between prewar and postwar Southern ideology. Fourth, Palmer reveals that the religious continuity in Southern racism was aided by the easy transition from Ham to Nimrod in applications of the Bible to American history. In Palmer's evolving interpretation of Genesis 9–11, we perceive how these biblical "Negroes" were made to reflect not only the dichotomous perception of blacks symbolized in slave stereotypes but also whites' shifting perceptions of themselves and their status in the world.

The key to comprehending Palmer's enduring reliance on Genesis 9 is "Noah's camera,"[52] an image he used repeatedly to symbolize the centrality of Genesis 9:25–27 to his theological vision. Like many Southerners who survived the war between the states, Palmer watched helplessly as a new world came into being. Despite his confident assertions that the South's lost cause would be vindicated at the tribunal of history, Palmer's sight had been trained in the Old South, and he had difficulty finding his intellectual bearings in the postwar world. Under these circumstances, the sure perception of "Noah's camera" promised to illumine a worldview sustained by the perfect vision of God.

Other Chapters in the Genesis of Race

This is not a comprehensive treatise on the Bible's utilization to support racist social agendas. In fact, several prominent instances of racial exegesis in the book of Genesis are ignored: the use of Genesis 2–4 in creating a two-seedline version of human origins, most recently by the theorists of so-called Christian Identity; interpretation of the Genesis Flood story (chapters 6–8) as a divine judgment upon "race mixing"; and employment of passages from Genesis 10 and 11 to construct a theological rationale for South African apartheid. Because these episodes in the history of modern racist biblical exegesis overlap in varying degrees with our subject, they are briefly reviewed here.

Pre-Adamism

One of the oldest traditions of racist Bible reading focuses on the creation story in Genesis and explicates the existence of various human races by postulating separate acts of creation. Pre-Adamism, as this tradition has come to be called, was introduced as early as the tenth century, though it received systematic exposition only in the seventeenth. In 1655, French scholar Isaac de la Peyrère purveyed his pre-Adamite theory as an answer to the age-old question regarding the identity of Cain's wife: If Cain was the first descendant of Adam and Eve, with whom did he continue his line after being banished to the land of Nod. During the European Enlightenment, pre-Adamism was embraced as a challenge to the biblical account of human origins, and in the nineteenth century it was welcomed by advocates of white superiority. While "scientific" racists embraced "polygenesis" as proof of nonwhites' inferiority, religious writers such as Dominick M'Causland and Alexander Winchell sought to correlate pre-Adamism with both scripture and empirical knowledge.[53]

Pre-Adamism has given rise to a number of interpretive schemes involving the early chapters of Genesis, all of them racist in some degree. One involves the idea that Cain left his family to master an inferior tribe described alternately by pre-Adamite theorists as "nonwhite Mongols," "Black Races," or "beasts of the field." The suggestion that Cain's mark was blackness was advanced in eighteenth-century Europe and was popularized a century later in America by Joseph Smith, the founder of Mormonism. In the early twentieth century, writers such as Ellen Bristowe and Charles Carroll gave Cain's traditional association with evil distinctly racial dimensions when they claimed that he married a black wife or that he had black skin. These shifting images of Cain—as a white Adamite who deigned to associate with inferior beings or as the first black—give some sense of the protean role he has played in readings of Genesis concerned with racial difference.

Eve and the Serpent

The early chapters of Genesis are also at the center of a racist mythology forged by the leaders of the Christian Identity movement in America. As Michael Barkun has shown in his masterful account of the intellectual origins of this movement, contemporary Identity has its roots in the tradition of biblical interpretation known as British-Israelism. British-Israelism evolved among mid-nineteenth-century English Protestants and within a few decades had spread to North America. Migrating from New England to the Midwest and finally to the West Coast, American British-Israelism gradually lost its ties to England, and following World War II was fully Americanized in nascent Christian Identity. Leading Identity theorists published their seminal tracts during the 1960s, and in the 1980s Identity adherents were making news in dozens of antigovernment and racist groups across the country. In the 1990s, Identity was linked to a series of violent acts against minorities and attacks on the federal government, including the Oklahoma City bombing.

Identity's most distinctive teaching casts Jews and other "nonwhite" peoples as literal descendants of Satan. Barkun summarizes the doctrine this way: "Either the Devil himself or one of his underlings had intercourse with Eve in the Garden of Eden. Cain was the product of this illicit union. Hence Cain and all his progeny, by virtue of satanic paternity, carry the Devil's unchanging capacity to work evil. These descendants of Cain became known in time as 'Jews.' "[54] In this inventive reading of Genesis, Eve is seduced by the serpent, by a pre-Adamite "beast of the field," or by the Devil himself. In each case, the product of this ill-fated dalliance is Cain, whose demonic seedline links Satan with Canaanites, Edomites, Shelahites (descendants of Judah and his Canaanite wife), and modern Jews. Significantly, Ham is included in this satanic seedline that links Cain with his putative Canaanite descendants.[55] Some Identity advocates highlight Ham's place in this chain of infamy by arguing that he took a Cainite wife (a view that would appear to explain how tainted Cainite blood endured the destruction of the Deluge). In another version of this racist doctrine, the descendants of Cain and Ham produce Hittites and Edomites.[56]

Even when they locate Ham in the ignominious seedline that has yielded modern-day Jews, Identity believers virtually ignore Genesis 9:20–27. Identity exegesis does intersect with Genesis 9–11 in oblique ways, however. One is the belief that Ham wed a descendant of Cain, thus harboring Cainite evil through the Flood. Another is the view that Canaanites (descendants of Ham, according to biblical logic) are actually "children of Cain." More intriguing, though, are the parallels between Identity's Cain and the traditions surrounding Nimrod in American biblical interpretation. Descriptions of Cain by Identity theorists and their predecessors bring to mind the traditional portrait of Nimrod the arch-rebel, despot, and idolater.[57] In fact, the similarities between the Cain of Christian Identity and the Nimrod of racist exegesis may explain why so few Identity theorists feature Ham and his descendants in their explanations of primordial evil.[58]

The Nephilim and the Flood

According to Genesis 6, God flooded the earth in order to punish human "wickedness" or "violence." Understandably, early Bible readers sought textual clues for a more explicit understanding of the transgression that precipitated this cleansing of the world. Many seized on Genesis 6:1–5, which contains mysterious references to "sons of God" who "took wives for themselves" from among the daughters of men (v. 2) and adds, "The Nephilim were on the earth in those days—and also afterward—when the sons of God went in to the daughters of humans, who bore children to them. These were the heroes that were of old, warriors of renown" (v. 4). Characterizing Jewish and Christian glosses on the Flood story, James L. Kugel writes that ancient readers found in these verses

> a hint that the immediate cause of the flood (and perhaps other ills) had been the mating of the "sons of God" (generally interpreted to mean some sort of angel or heavenly creature) with the "daughters of men." The flood must have come about, directly or indirectly, as a result of this union. Perhaps it was because of some sort of sexual profligacy implied in this passage, or because the mating of these two groups brought about a new race of beings who were given over to sinfulness, or because, through their contact with the humans, the angels had passed along a knowledge of secret things that led to the humans' corruption. All three traditions are found intermingled even in the most ancient writings of the period.[59]

Distant reflections of this interpretive tradition appear in Euro-American readings of Genesis that regard the cataclysm as a localized flood brought about when wicked Adamites engaged in the heinous sin of racial intermarriage. Americans Alexander Winchell, John Fletcher, "Ariel" (Buckner H. Payne), and Charles Parham were among nineteenth-century adherents of this view. William Potter Gale and Wesley Swift, both influential leaders in Christian Identity circles, perpetuated the idea in the 1960s. According to Gale, God's original command to Adam and his descendants was a prohibition of miscegenation. Satan tempted the Adamites to mongrelize themselves with pre-Adamites, and God visited a flood upon them as punishment for this transgression. The survivors, naturally, were those who resisted the temptation to intermarry.[60] This view of the Genesis Flood has become a staple of biblical thinking on the racist right. In 1986, Thom Robb, national director of the Knights of the Ku Klux Klan, applied the causal link between race mixing and apocalypse to America's near future:

> The Bible talks about the return of Christ. . . . Jesus said, "As it was in the days of Noah, so shall it become in the days of the Son of Man." And in the

days of Noah there was massive race mixing. Most churches teach that Noah was a righteous man and this is why he was preserved. But Noah was a man, according to the Bible, who was "perfect in his generations." The word "generations" means race. And so Noah was one of the few individuals at that time who was not racially polluted.[61]

Thus, just as did ancient Bible readers, contemporary interpreters of the Deluge seek textual clues wherever they can be found.

The Tower, Dispersion, and Diversity

"The land of Shinar," identified in Genesis 11:2 as the location for the Tower of Babel, has proved a fertile field for racist readings of the Bible. In modern South Africa, where Noah's curse has played a very minor role in white arguments for racial supremacy,[62] Genesis 10 and 11 have been used to locate the rationale for apartheid in the very mind of God. As the struggle over apartheid's theological status raged during the 1970s and 1980s, Genesis 11:1–9 became an interpretive crux for those in both the liberation and proapartheid camps.

The story's stature as the "cardinal text" in the Dutch Reformed Church's theology of race relations was confirmed in 1974, when representatives of the NGK (Nederduitse Geformeerde Kerk, the largest and most influential of the Afrikaner Reformed churches) responded to attacks on "separate development" in a document entitled *Human Relations and the South African Scene in Light of Scripture.* The authors inquired "whether the Scriptures give us a normative indication of the way in which the human race differentiated into a variety of races, peoples and nations," whether this diversity accords with the will of God, and "whether Gn. 11:1–9 can serve as a Scriptural basis for a policy of autogenous development."[63] Their response was instructive, if somewhat predictable.

While claiming that the genealogical tables in Genesis 10 teach the unity of humankind, the authors concluded that ethnic diversity "is in its very origin in accordance with the will of God for this dispensation."[64] Significantly, the authors conjoin the story of the Tower of Babel with the passages that precede it:

> It is important to note that the situation presupposed in Gn. 11:1–9 goes back beyond Gn. 10 and in reality links up with the end of Gn. 9. The descendants of Noah's three sons remained in the vicinity of Ararat for a few generations (Gn. 10:25) before they decided to move in an easterly direction to Babylonia (11:12). . . . These people clearly valued the unity of language and community because, apart from the motive of making a name for themselves, their city and tower had to serve specifically to prevent their being "scattered abroad upon the face of the whole earth" (v. 4). From the sequel to this history it is clear that the undertaking [the tower] and the intentions of these people were in conflict with the will of God. Apart from the reckless arrogance that

is evident in their desire to make a name for themselves, the deliberate concentration on one spot was in conflict with God's command to replenish the
earth (Gn. 1:28; 9:1, 7).[65]

Following a disquisition on the psychic and spiritual significance of human language (a discussion that recalls nineteenth-century romantic nationalism), the authors restate their contention that Genesis 11 communicates both
"man's attempt to establish a (forced) unity of the human race . . . [based in]
sinful human arrogance" and God's reassertion of the original command that
humanity split into separate *volke* with distinct languages and cultures. The
confusion of tongues and the diversity of races and peoples to which it contributed are therefore "an aspect of reality which God obviously intended for
this dispensation. To deny this fact is to side with the tower-builders."[66] Thus,
the scriptural solution for human disharmony is not "a humanistic attempt
at unity based on the arrogance of man (Babel!)," but God's promise of
spiritual unity. On the basis of these assertions, the authors conclude that the
policy of "autogenous development" (apartheid) is appropriate for governing
relations between differing racial and cultural groups.[67]

Other biblical proof-texts in the arsenal of apartheid's defenders include
Deuteronomy 32:8 ("When the Most High apportioned the nations, when he
divided humankind, he fixed the boundaries of the peoples according to the
number of the gods") and Acts 17:26 ("From one ancestor he made all nations
to inhabit the whole earth, and he allotted the times of their existence and
the boundaries of the places where they would live"). Like the passages explored in this book, these proof-texts have featured prominently in American
racial discourse over the last two centuries. There is no evidence that Americans or South Africans who have advanced these racial readings of the Bible
have done so in dependence upon one other or on a common source. Although this does not exclude the possibility of mutual influence, it is an
indication of the curious power exercised by certain scriptural texts over those
seeking warrants for racial separation or superiority.

I

CHARACTERS IN THE POSTDILUVIAN DRAMA

2

A Black Sheep in the (Second) First Family

The Legend of Noah and His Sons

Noah, a man of the soil, was the first to plant a vineyard.
He drank some of the wine and became drunk, and he lay
uncovered in his tent. And Ham, the father of Canaan,
saw the nakedness of his father, and told his two brothers
outside. Then Shem and Japheth took a garment, laid it
on both their shoulders, and walked backward and covered the nakedness of their father; their faces were turned
away, and they did not see their father's nakedness. When
Noah awoke from his wine and knew what his youngest
son had done to him, he said, "Cursed be Canaan; lowest
of slaves shall he be to his brothers." He also said,
"Blessed by the Lord my God be Shem; and let Canaan
be his slave. May God make space for Japheth, and let
him live in the tents of Shem; and let Canaan be his
slave."

Genesis 9:20–27 (NRSV)

BY TRACING Genesis 9's history of interpretation from the formative periods
of Judaism and Christianity through the twentieth century, this chapter establishes a context for recognizing the distinctive features in American versions of Noah's curse. As we shall see, themes that animated proslavery readings of Genesis 9—for instance, the beliefs that the story relates the historical
origins of slavery and confirms Ham's genealogical connection with Africa—
appear early and often in the history of interpretation. However, the perennial

tendency to view Ham's misdeed in terms of sexual depravity or assault is conspicuously absent from the writings of antebellum Americans. The significance of this discontinuity will be explored in part II.

As readers through the ages have encountered the story of Noah's drunkenness, gaps in the biblical text have given rise to a number of interpretive questions: Was Noah at fault in becoming intoxicated? What is implied by the statement that Ham "saw the nakedness of his father"? What does it mean that Noah "knew what his youngest son had done to him" when he awakened?[1] Does Noah speak for God when he announces a curse and blessings upon his sons? If Ham is the culprit of some evil deed, why is Canaan the object of Noah's malediction? Finally, what motivates Noah to announce the curse? Over time, answers to these questions assumed recurring patterns. Eventually, they crystallized into an orthodox interpretive paradigm that cast Noah as an innocent and righteous patriarch and his son Ham as culprit in some heinous act against him. We begin our survey of the history of interpretation with early Jewish readings of Genesis 9:20–27, construals that have been the subject of recent controversy.

Jewish Interpretation

The Rabbis

Rabbinic commentary on this passage is quite rich. Early Jewish interpreters assumed Noah was intrinsically righteous,[2] considered his condemnation of Ham justified, vilified Ham's Canaanite descendants as liars, thieves, and fornicators,[3] praised the exemplary behavior of Shem and Japheth,[4] and found in the story an explanation of Africans' distinctive color. However, they reached no consensus on the nature of Ham's transgression, characterizing it as everything from ridicule to sexual assault. The latter theme is featured in a variety of rabbinic glosses on the story. One of these affixes blame to Canaan, who "entered the tent, mischievously looped a stout cord about his grandfather's genitals, drew it tight, and unmanned him."[5] Observing the behavior of his son, Ham laughingly shared the account with his brothers. In a variant tradition, Ham himself is held responsible for Noah's castration: "Ham saw [Noah in his tent with his wife], and he told his brothers what he had noticed. [Ham then spoke] disrespectful words against his father. Ham added to his sin of irreverence the still greater outrage of attempting to perform an operation upon his father designed to prevent procreation."[6]

An alternative explanation for Noah's curse is located in Ham's conduct during the Flood: "During their sojourn in the ark, the two sexes, of men and animals alike, had lived apart from each other. . . . This law of conduct had been violated by none in the ark except by Ham, by the dog and by the raven. They all received a punishment. Ham's was that his descendants were men of dark-hued skin."[7] In Genesis Rabbah, Rabbi Hiyya claims that "Ham and a dog had sexual relations in the ark. Therefore Ham came forth dusky, and the dog, for his part, has sexual relations in public. . . ."[8] It is not clear whether this rabbinic tradition censures Ham for engaging in forbidden sex with his wife or with one of the animals. But the ambiguity may have given rise to the medieval Christian legend that Canaan was the offspring of Ham's liaison with a raven.[9]

Another rabbinic theme associates Ham's presumed sexual assault upon Noah with the condition and color of his descendants:

A. Said R. Berekhiah, "Noah in the ark was most distressed that he had no young son to take care of him. He said, 'When I shall get out of this ark, I shall produce a young son to take care of me.'

B. "When Ham had done the disgraceful deed, he said, 'You are the one who stopped me from producing a young son to take care of me, therefore that man himself [you] will be a servant to his brothers.' "

C. R. Huna in the name of R. Joseph: " 'You are the one who prevented me from producing a fourth son, therefore I curse your fourth son [corresponding to the fourth son I never had].' "

D. R. Huna in the name of R. Joseph: " 'You are the one who stopped me from doing something that is done in darkness, therefore your seed will be ugly and dusky.' "[10]

The connection between Ham's sin and the physical appearance of his descendants is featured in a notorious compendium of rabbinic comment on Genesis 9:

When Noah awoke from his wine and became sober, he pronounced a curse . . . upon the last-born son of the son that had prevented him from begetting a younger son than the three he had. The descendants of Ham through Canaan therefore have red eyes, because Ham looked upon the nakedness of his father; they have misshapen lips, because Ham spoke with his lips to his brothers about the unseemly condition of his father; they have twisted curly hair, because Ham turned and twisted his head round to see the nakedness of his father; and they go about naked, because Ham did not cover the nakedness of his father.[11]

Despite the temptation to trace later racial readings of Noah's curse to the rabbis, it must be emphasized that there is no definitive rabbinic interpretation of Genesis 9:20–27. Typical, in fact, is a Talmudic passage in which two third-century rabbis debate the meaning of Genesis 9:24, one arguing that Ham mutilated Noah, the other that he raped him, while the redactor harmonizes these opinions by suggesting that Ham first raped, then emasculated, his father.[12] But in the process of wrestling with the meaning of this difficult text, the rabbis did strike themes that would resonate through the history of interpretation.

Other Jewish Readings

Midrashic treatments of the biblical tale retell the story of Noah and his sons in imaginative ways. The *Sibylline Oracles*, a Jewish work from the late first century B.C.E., portrays Noah as a righteous preacher who attempted to warn fellow human beings of the coming deluge: "[Then Noah] entreated the peoples and began to speak such words: 'men, sated with faithlessness, smitten with great madness, what you did will not escape the notice of God.' "[13] *The Book of Jubilees* has Noah pass on to his sons the commandment to cover their shame and to honor father and mother.[14] In *The Book of Adam and Eve*, the episode is reshaped so that Noah becomes drunk and has sex with his wife, Ham sees Noah senseless, laughs and tells his brothers, and Noah's wife informs him of Ham's fault on the following day.[15]

According to Philo of Alexandria (ca. 20 B.C.E.–50 C.E.), Noah did not drink to excess but remained a wise and virtuous man. Indeed, his very name means "righteousness." When prophesying about his sons, he spoke under divine possession and thus should be considered a prophet. Ham's fault was casting shame upon his father by holding some lapse of his up to laughter and scorn. Ham compounded his guilt by broadcasting Noah's failure to others "outside" the family. In Philo's reading, Noah's sons represent the good, the bad, and the indifferent in nature. Ham is called the youngest because his temperament loves rebelliousness and defiance. Philo also connects Ham's name with "heat," a sign of vice in the soul: "Ham is vice in its quiescent state while Canaan is vice in the active state. The two represent a single object—wickedness."[16] Thus, although he read Genesis 9 through the lens of allegory, Philo nevertheless remained within the orthodox interpretive paradigm established by the rabbis.

In *Antiquities of the Jews,* Josephus (ca. 100 C.E.) echoed Philo in recording what was to become an influential rendition of the episode recorded in Genesis 9. After the flood, Noah offered his sacrifice to God, feasted and fell asleep drunk. Then,

> when his youngest son saw this, he came laughing, and showed to him his brethren; but they covered their father's nakedness. And when Noah was made sensible of what had been done, he prayed for prosperity to his other sons; but for Ham, he did not curse him, by reason of his nearness in blood, but cursed his posterity. And when the rest of them escaped that curse, he inflicted it on the children of Canaan.[17]

As we shall see, Josephus's remark that Ham laughed at his father—though a seemingly minor addition to the story—would become a leitmotif in the history of interpretation. Another distinctive aspect of Josephus's reading of Genesis 9 was his reliance on "Berossus the Chaldean" (a Babylonian priest of the third century B.C.E.). Berossus argued that in punishment for his transgression, Ham was "banished to the dark regions of Africa, forever carrying the taint of corruption."[18]

The *Zohar* (ca. second century C.E.) echoed this association of Hamites with darkness, explaining that

> Ham represents the refuse and dross of the gold, the stirring and rousing of the unclean spirit of the ancient serpent. It is for that reason that he is designated the "father of Canaan," namely, of Canaan who brought curses into the world, of Canaan who was cursed, of Canaan who darkened the faces of mankind. For this reason, too, Ham is given a special mention in the words, "Ham the father of Canaan," that is, the notorious world-darkener.... [19]

It is not apparent whether the phrase "world-darkener" refers to skin color or to the introduction of death, but it is clear that vilification of Ham and his descendants was a recurring theme in formative Jewish literature and that the link between Ham, sin, and Africa was forged quite early in the history of interpretation.

Christian Interpretation

Church Fathers

Although the New Testament contains no allusions to Genesis 9:20–27, the early Christian assessment of Noah is evident in the epistle to the Hebrews, where the patriarch is depicted as an exemplar of moral rectitude. When the church fathers considered Noah, they portrayed him, along with Abraham and Enoch, as paragons of human obedience. Lactantius (ca. 240–320), for instance, wrote that prior to the flood Noah "stood forth preeminent, as a remarkable example of righteousness."[20] But the Christian portrait of Noah featured distinctive themes, none more prominent that his depiction as a forerunner of Christ.

Once the bond between Noah and Jesus was established in the Christian imagination, pious commentators discovered typological symbols throughout Genesis 6–9. Justin Martyr (ca. 100–165) wrote that like Christ, who regenerated a new race "through water, and faith, and wood . . . Noah was saved by wood when he rode over the waters with his household." Justin also found import in the number of Noah's family who boarded the vessel. The eight were "a symbol of the eighth day, wherein Christ appeared when He rose from the dead. . . ."[21] Origen (ca. 185–254) so identified Noah as a type of the savior that he could refer to Christ as the "spiritual" and "true" Noah.[22] To many of the church fathers, the ark was a fitting symbol of Christ's church, in which the faithful are rescued from the tumults of a wicked world.[23] Typological perceptions of Noah and his ark pervade Christian art during the first five centuries of the common era. Because Noah is the emblem of the risen Christ, "the Ark must look like a gravechest, like a sarcophagus, the funeral box in which the body of Christ was laid."[24]

In keeping with the convention of viewing Noah christologically, many church fathers discerned in Genesis 9:20–27 both a recapitulation of Adıam's "fall" and a compelling anticipation of the gospel. The standard typological reading of the story regarded Noah's nakedness as a prefiguration of Christ's passion, Ham's treatment of his father as a type of "the Jews'" irreverence toward Christ's body, and the brothers as exemplars of worshipful reverence toward the crucified Christ.[25] A representative gloss on the story is Augustine's allegorical reading:

> "And he was drunken," that is, He suffered; "and was naked," that is, His weakness appeared in His suffering, as the apostle says, "though He was crucified through weakness." Wherefore the same apostle says, "The weakness of God is stronger than men; and the foolishness of God is wiser than men." And when to the expression "he was naked" Scripture adds "in his house," it elegantly intimates that Jesus was to suffer the cross and death at the hands of His own household, His own kith and kin, the Jews.[26]

As for the meaning symbolized by the fact that Ham "went out and published his father's nakedness outside, while Shem and Japheth came in to veil it,"[27] Augustine asserts that Ham represents "the tribe of heretics, hot with the spirit, not of patience, but of impatience, with which the breasts of heretics are wont to blaze, and with which they disturb the peace of the saints."[28] For Augustine,

> not only those who are openly separated from the church, but also all who glory in the Christian name, and at the same time lead abandoned lives, may without absurdity seem to be figured by Noah's middle son: for the passion of Christ, which was signified by that man's nakedness, is at once proclaimed by their profession, and dishonored by their wicked conduct. Of such, therefore, it has been said, "By their fruits ye shall know them."[29]

Typological interpretations of Genesis 9 could also embrace Noah's sons as a group. Hilary viewed them as illustrating three sorts of relationship to God: Shem symbolized those under the Law, Japheth those justified by grace, and Ham the pagans who mock the dead Savior and the nude body of God.[30] Far outlasting the convention of typing Noah as a Christ figure, in fact, was the tradition of casting his progeny as exemplars of distinct human groups. With a burgeoning interest in history and the origins of human diversity, Christian readers were instructed by the biblical claim that the post-diluvian world had been repopulated by Noah's descendants. The "T-O" map of Isidore of Seville (560–632) presents a tripartite division of the globe in which Asia is associated with Shem, Europe with Japheth, and Africa with Ham.[31]

If the story of Noah and his sons provided convenient explanations for human diversity and servitude, it also raised vexing questions. Particularly bothersome was a textual non sequitur, that Canaan received a curse for a sin committed by his father. In seeking to resolve this dilemma, Justin Martyr followed rabbinic exegesis[32] in arguing that "the Spirit of prophecy would not

curse the son that had been by God blessed along with [his brothers]."[33]
Chrysostom (347–407) supposed that Canaan was cursed because he had been
begotten on the ark. Ambrose concurred that Ham was unable to abide by
Noah's suspension of marital relations and suggested that Canaan is mentioned in Genesis 9 in order to highlight Ham's disobedience: Because he
would not obey his father, he was punished with a wicked son.[34] Irenaeus (ca.
130–200) opined that because he was guilty of impiety Ham received a curse
that involved his entire race.

Yet despite the textual logic that made Canaan the story's likely villain,
Ham became the church fathers' archetype of human depravity. Augustine
figured him as "the symbol of the man in isolation, the clanless, lawless,
heartless man who, like heathen ethnics, did not know God."[35] But the
Bishop of Hippo was only summarizing a Christian interpretive tradition that
for centuries had excelled in the vilification of Hamites. Lactantius believed
that after his fateful encounter with Noah, Ham "went into exile, and settled
in a part of that land which is now called Arabia; and that land was called
from him Chanaan, and his posterity Chanaanites. This was the first nation
which was ignorant of God, since its prince and founder did not receive from
his father the worship of God, being cursed by him; and thus he left to his
descendants ignorance of the divine nature."[36] Ham's other descendants fared
no better, according to Lactantius; those who occupied Egypt "were the first
. . . to adore the heavenly bodies" and later "invented monstrous figures of
animals, that they might worship them." Origen wrote in a similar vein about
the character of Ham's progeny. The Egyptians, he opined, were

> prone to a degenerate life and quickly sink to slavery of the vices. Look at
> the origin of the race and you will discover that their father Cham, who had
> laughed at his father's nakedness, deserved a judgment of this kind, that his
> son Chanaan should be a servant to his brothers, in which case the condition
> of bondage would prove the wickedness of his conduct. Not without merit,
> therefore, does the discolored posterity imitate the ignobility of the race.[37]

Clement (ca. 150–215) seems to be responsible for the view, widespread
in the Middle Ages, that Ham was the first magician. In his "Recognitions,"
Clement wrote that Ham "unhappily discovered the magical act, and handed
down the instruction of it to one of his sons, who was called Mesraim, from
whom the race of the Egyptians and Babylonians and Persians are descended."[38] Clement maintains that Ham developed magic in order "to be
esteemed a god" among his contemporaries. Though he was consumed by a
fiery miracle of his own creation, Ham's magic remains the source of "diverse
and erratic superstitions" that plague the world. In another place, Clement
traces most of the world's nascent evils to Ham and his posterity:

> In the thirteenth generation [after the creation], when the second of Noah's
> three sons had done an injury to his father, and had been cursed by him,
> he brought the condition of slavery upon his posterity. . . . In the fourteenth

generation one of the cursed progeny first erected an altar to demons, for the purpose of magical arts, and offered there bloody sacrifices. In the fifteenth generation, for the first time, men set up an idol and worshipped it.[39]

In Clement's litany of disgrace, Hamites are blamed for the existence of slavery, magic, idol worship, and aggressive war.

The writings of the fathers do not present anything like a consensus on the meaning of Genesis 9:20–27. There is disagreement regarding the nature of Ham's transgression—with some interpreters concluding that it was sexual assault (e.g., Chrysostom thought Canaan was born on the ark as a result of Ham's violation of the prohibition against copulation)[40] and others, notably Augustine, locating Ham's fault in his calling attention to Noah's nakedness— as well as on the significance, consequences, and longevity of the curse.[41] But as our survey demonstrates, the practice of stigmatizing Ham as an irredeemable archsinner was well established in the patristic era.

Medieval Christendom

The legend of Noah and his sons was a meta-text in the European Middle Ages. It was relied upon to explain the provenance of servitude,[42] the dispersion of human beings after the Flood, and the structure of medieval society. In fact, medieval exegetes did not so much interpret the story of Noah and his sons as mine it for clues to the origins of postdiluvian phenomena. John Cassian (360–435) claimed that Ham learned magic from the daughters of Cain, inscribing its secrets on plates that would survive the flood. Others linked Ham's descendants with Zoroastrianism (Gregory of Tours, 540–94), with the inhabitants of Sodom (Venerable Bede, ca. 642–735, following Genesis 10:19), with infidels (Rabanus Maurus, 776–856), and with unbelieving Jews (Augustine, Jerome, Rabanus, Bede, Hilary, et al.).[43]

While never doubting the historicity of Genesis, medieval interpreters accorded grand symbolic import to the Flood narrative. They discovered in Genesis 9 both the origins of servitude and the partition of humanity into distinct types. About 1125, Honorarius of Autun wrote that Ham, Shem, and Japheth represented society's three estates: "In Noah's time the human race was divided into three: into free men, soldiers and servants. The free are of Shem, the soldiers of Japheth and the servants of Ham." In the windows of Chartres Cathedral (1235–40) Noah's sons are portrayed as forerunners of those who pray (priesthood), those who fight (knighthood) and those who work (serfs and working classes).[44] The Cursor Mundi (ca. 1300) combined this social etiology with the older convention that assigned Noah's sons to dwell in separate regions of the world: "O sem freman, o Iaphet knytht/Thrall of cham the maledight . . . Asie to sem, to cham affrik,/ To Iaphet europ, pat wil-ful wike."[45] Hugo von Trimberg's Renner (1296–1313) combined a symbolic understanding of Noah's sons with a serious look at the text of Genesis 9. In

Hugo's view, the brothers' behavior was causally related to the condition of their descendants: The nobility typically ascribed to Shem's progeny stemmed from neither wealth nor descent, but from their ancestor's virtuous action. Conversely, if Ham had remained uncorrupted, his descendants would not have been condemned to servitude.[46]

Little concerned with the literal meaning of the biblical text, medieval exegetes nevertheless conformed to the orthodox interpretive paradigm bequeathed to them by the rabbis and church fathers. On one hand, they reiterated traditional conceptions of Noah's righteousness, often casting him as a progenitor of the Messiah. According to Dom Cameron Allen,

> In the allegorical accounts of the Middle Ages, Noah was always treated as one of the great precursors of the Saviour. Endless comparisons were made between the waters of the Flood and those of baptism, between the wood of the Ark and the wood of the Cross, and between the door in the Ark and the wound in Christ's side. So the story of Noah had as definite a sanctity as the story of Adam, Samson, David, and any other of the great adumbrators of the doctrine of grace. . . . [47]

In Dante's *Divine Comedy,* Noah is among the virtuous Hebrews who are rescued in Christ's harrowing of hell (*Inferno* IV:56), and his covenant with God is cited as the reason the world will never again be flooded (*Paradise* XII:17). Even Noah's shameful nakedness could be circumvented by imaginative interpreters. Peter Comestor inferred from the patriarch's condition that underwear had not yet been invented.[48] On the other hand, the medieval portrait of Ham recalled earlier affirmations of his craftiness, prodigious sexuality, and affiliation with magic and the Devil.

Both Noah's piety and Ham's villainy are reflected in the popular story of "Ham's Broken Oath,"[49] a thirteenth-century legend elaborating the rabbinic notion that Ham could not abstain from sexual intercourse on the ark. According to the version that appears as a marginal note in *Aurora* by Peter of Riga (d. 1209),

> Ham, younger son of Noah, trespassed against the continence proclaimed by Noah—that women should spend the night by themselves and men likewise. Ham, calling up a demon by magic art, crossed over to his wife and slept with her. The reason why the vehicle of the demon was used is that Noah had strewn ashes between them, by means of which he could observe the footprints of those crossing over to their wives. The others remained continent with their father; Ham alone through the service of the devil and the aid of his wife rendered himself to his wife's embraces. Because Noah persisted in his prayers the demon was unable to bring Ham back; blocked in his efforts by Noah's nocturnal orisons he fled. Ham therefore was compelled to walk back before daylight to the other brothers, and because of the scattered ashes he could not hide his guilt. Noah therefore detected his footprints, and he began to hate Ham for his disobedience. This is the reason Ham laughed at him after his intoxication.[50]

Riga's account of the legend may have been influenced by Peter Comestor's *Historia Scholastica*, which features a related tradition—the identification of Ham and Zoroaster, who is called "inventor magicae artis." According to Francis Lee Utley, the medieval association of Ham with magic "ultimately goes back to the feeling that someone had to carry on magic tradition from the antediluvian *fons et origo,* and that wicked Ham was the most likely candidate."[51]

Another source for gauging medieval perceptions of Noah and Ham is the popular fourteenth-century *Travels of Sir John Mandeville,* which purports to explain why the Khan of the Mongols is called the "Grand Ham":

> During the great downpour of long ago . . . this Ham was the one who saw the natural member of his father while he was sleeping uncovered. And he mocked him and pointed him out. And for this he was cursed. Japhet averted his glance and covered him. The three brothers took their entire lands. This Ham for his cruelty took the biggest eastern part. . . . And because of this Ham, all the emperors have since then been called Grand Ham and the son of nature and the sovereign of all the world. And thus he calls himself in his decrees.[52]

These medieval legends are intriguing inasmuch as they charge Ham with mocking or laughing at his father, an extrabiblical theme that is prominent in American versions of Noah's curse as well.

Reformation

Despite the emphasis on rigorous biblical exegesis that accompanied the Reformation, the parameters of the orthodox interpretive paradigm remained in force among Protestant commentators. In extensive remarks on Genesis 9: 20–27 in his "Lectures on Genesis," Martin Luther treats the episode in traditional fashion. Luther regards Noah as "just and perfect," adding that the patriarch's failure to beget children until he was five hundred years old was an indication of his "remarkable and almost unbelievable continence."[53] Luther perceives another model for pious readers in the behavior of Shem and Japheth, who refuse to let Noah's drunkenness "destroy the respect they owe their parent." The story's supreme message, however, is God's "terrible judgment" upon Ham's "horrible example."

For Luther, Ham's laughter at his father's nakedness is a serious offense indicating that Ham "regard[s] himself as more righteous, holier, and more pious than his father."[54] No doubt Ham would not have mocked his father "if he had not first put out of his heart that reverence and esteem which, by God's command, children should have for their parents. . . . This points to a heart that despises not only its parent but also the commands of God." Ham's misdemeanor, then, should not be regarded as childish mischief, but as an act reflecting "the bitter hatred of Satan." Because Ham had such contempt for his father, God "hates Ham with the utmost hatred."

Luther's conception of Ham's career following the episode with Noah seems to have been influenced by his reading of the church fathers. For instance, he suggests that Ham "later on filled the world with idolatry";[55] claims that after being cursed Ham traveled to Babylon, where he "engage[d] in building a city and a tower, and establish[ed] himself as lord of all Asia," and developed "a new government and a new religion";[56] and adopts Augustine's suggestion that Ham's name means "hot."[57] But Luther updates the tradition of Hamite vilification, writing that "because the pope's church condemns our doctrine, we know that it is not the church of Christ but the church of Satan and truly, like Ham, 'a slave of slaves.' "[58]

John Calvin also discusses this biblical tale, most notably in his commentary on Genesis. Although Calvin pays careful attention to the text of Genesis 9:20–27, his portrait of Ham falls squarely within the interpretive tradition. Calvin echoes Luther (and Clement and Josephus) in noting that "by reproachfully laughing at his father, [Ham] betrays his own depraved and malignant disposition."[59] He also concludes that Ham "must have been of a wicked, perverse and crooked disposition," "ungodly and wicked." It is significant, Calvin observes, that even in the hallowed sanctuary of the ark "one fiend was preserved." Why did Ham fail to show his father due respect? Calvin determines that Ham must have dishonored Noah "for the purpose of acquiring for himself the license of sinning with impunity." Does Ham's punishment fit the crime? Calvin reasons that Noah would not pronounce such a harsh sentence except by divine inspiration, and so "it behooves us to infer from the severity of the punishment, how abominable in the sight of God is the impious contempt of parents, since it perverts the sacred order of nature, however, . . . ' "[60]

Calvin departs from the interpretive tradition, however, in his refusal to exonerate Noah. He flatly rejects the excuse that Noah had "completed his labour, and being exhilarated with wine, imagines that he is but taking his just reward," countering that when Noah "in a base and shameful manner, [did] prostrate himself naked on the ground," he deserved to be laughed at because he defaced the image of God. Calvin adds that the weightiness of Noah's sin is reflected in his dishonor: For "shamefully lying prostrate on the ground," "God brands him with an eternal mark of disgrace"; his son's mocking was thus a punishment "divinely inflicted upon him."[61] For Calvin, Ham's chastisement reveals God's attitude toward the "impious contempt of parents, since it perverts the sacred order of nature. . . ."[62] Noah, for his part, acted "in a base and shameful manner," "shamefully lying prostrate on the ground."[68]

Though loathe to depart from the text or accept interpretive conjecture, seventeenth-century English Protestants freely borrowed from the tradition in delineating Ham's culpability. Andrew Willet is typical of biblical exegetes influenced by the Reformation. Willet "lets passe" the opinions of "some Hebrewes" that Ham castrated his father or "enchanted" his private parts. We need not exaggerate Ham's disobedience, Willet writes, for it was great enough: "he doth not ignorantly or by chance, but willingly gaze upon his fathers secrets. . . . Neither is he content thus to disport himselfe, but hee telleth his brethren, thinking to corrupt them also, to deride their father." Further, Ham rejoiced in his father's fall, "as the ungodly doe reioyce, at the fall of the godly." Despite this unremarkable gloss on Ham's offense, Willet lends credence to Berossus's view that Ham "was after this given over to all leaudnes, corrupting mankind with his evill manners: and taught them, by his owne example, approoving the same, that it was lawfull, as the wicked use was before the flood, to lie with their mothers, sisters, daughters, with the male, and bruit beasts. . . ."[64] Willet's Protestant sensibility regarding the primacy of Scripture notwithstanding, he seems unable to conclude that Ham was cursed solely for dishonoring his father.

Willet's contemporary, Scottish commentator Abraham Rosse, published *Exposition of the Fourteene First Chapters of Genesis* in 1626. Like Willet, Rosse casts a skeptical eye at the interpretive tradition, denying that Noah "was gelded by his son Cham as the Hebrews thinke, for this is fabulous."[65] Rather, Ham's sin consisted in a lack of reverence for his father, the fact that he took pleasure in "seeing those members, whereof all men by nature are ashamed," mocked his righteous father, told his brethren, and, finally, as a grown man himself, was not possessed of more "grace and discretion." Yet despite his Protestant attention to the letter of scripture, Rosse reveals the influence of the interpretive tradition. In Rosse's typological reading, Ham is "the type of wicked children, and in Sem and Iapheth [we find] a patterne for good children," who are careful to honor their earthly father.[66] Rosse even associates Ham with "witchcraft, malice, contempt of religion, leacherie and other vices."[67]

Early Modern Period

Although Hamites had long been linked with southern regions of the inhabited world, Ham himself was rarely racialized before Europeans explored West Africa in the fifteenth century. A German map reflecting the medieval European view of Noah's sons places Ham at the bottom of the world, as it were, near the continent of Africa. But it does not assign him a distinctive physiognomy.[68] Yet with increasing European involvement in the African slave trade came a growing interest in Noah's curse as an explanation for racial slavery. In his *Chronicle of the Discovery and Conquest of Guinea* (1441–48), Portuguese scholar Gomes Eanes de Azurara invoked Genesis 9 to justify the enslavement of Africans. According to Azurara, the servitude of non-Muslim "Moors" resulted from the curse, "which, after the Deluge, Noah laid upon his son Cain [*sic*], cursing him in this way:—that his race should be subject to all the other races of the world. And from this race these blacks are descended. . . ."[69]

Yet the European racialization of Hamites was neither consistent nor permanent.[70] For instance, although attempts to trace the human family's genealogy invariably placed blacks in the Hamite line, tokens of negritude could be introduced at many junctures—as early as Cush or as late as Dathan[71] (who, according to Numbers 16, participated in a revolt against Moses at Kadesh). Furthermore, early modern intellectuals retained a keen interest in Genesis 9:20–27 as an episode in "the legend of Noah," quite apart from its usefulness in justifying the slave trade. Historians, poets, visual artists, and dramatists treated the story of Noah's drunkenness, transmitting the history of biblical interpretation in the process. A prominent aspect of this history was Ham's sexual vilification, and among biblical commentators sexual versions of his "sin" became explanations of choice. According to Dom Cameron Allen, "the two most popular explanations [for Noah's curse] were that Ham had either castrated his father or rendered him impotent with a magic spell."[72] In *Purchas His Pilgramage* (1614), Samuel Purchas assigned to Ham a full catalog of sexual sins. He cited Berossus's view that "*Cham, the Sonne of Noah*, was by his Father banished for particular abuse of himselfe, and publike corruption of the World, teaching and practising those vices, which before had procured the deluge, as Sodomie, Incest, Buggerie; and was therefore branded with the name *Chemesenua*, that is, dishonest *Cham*"[73] Later that century, Hermann Von der Hardt extended the tradition of regarding Ham as a sex offender by theorizing that to "look on the nakedness" of one's father was to have incestuous relations with one's mother.[74]

How is this early modern resurgence of sexual readings of Ham's indignity to be explained? Winthrop Jordan notes that "with the onset of European expansion in the sixteenth century, some Christian commentators, or rather some commentators who were Christians, suddenly began speaking in the same mode which Jews had employed a thousand years and more before."[75] Like the convention of racializing Noah's progeny, the sexual theme in Genesis 9 was a dimension of the interpretive tradition that was well suited to the ideological climate of the Age of Exploration. Englishman George Best provides an excellent example of how race and sexuality converged in readings of the curse during this period. Following a sea voyage in 1577, Best seized on the biblical account of Ham's disobedience to explain Africans' skin color:

> The wicked Spirite . . . finding at this flood none but a father and three sons living, hee so caused one of them to disobey his fathers commandment, that after him all his posteritie should bee accursed. . . . Noah commaunded his sonnes and their wives, that they should with reverence and feare beholde the justice and mighty power of God, and that during the time of the floud while they remained in the Arke, they should use continencie, and abstaine from carnall copulation with their wives: and many other precepts hee gave unto them, and admonitions touching the justice of God, in revenging sinne, and his mercie in delivering them, who nothing deserved it. Which good instructions and exhortations notwithstanding his wicked sonne Cham dis-

obeyed, and being perswaded that the first childe borne after the flood . . .
should inherite . . . all the dominions of the earth, hee . . . used company with
his wife, and craftily went about thereby to dis-inherite the off-spring of his
other two brethren: for which wicked and detestable fact, as an example for
contempt of Almightie God, and disobedience of parents, God would a
sonne should bee borne whose name was Chus, who not onely it selfe, but
all his posteritie after him should bee so blacke and lothsome, that it might
remaine a spectacle of disobedience to all the worlde.[76]

Best utilizes the rabbinic tradition of Ham's incontinence at sea, the well-
rehearsed theme of disobedience, and the notion that the substance of the
curse was blackness and combines them all with the idea that Ham sought to
usurp the birthright of his brothers' sons. Although Ham's prodigious greed
was noted by other interpreters,[77] this was not a common theme in the history
of interpretation. As we shall see, the charge of tyranny over Noah's other
descendants was typically debited to the account of Ham's grandson Nimrod.

The nexus between blackness, sexuality, and the curse was revisited early
in the seventeenth century by Richard Jobson, a trader on the African coast,
who wrote that "the enormous Size of the virile Member among the Negroes
[was] an infallible Proof, that they are sprung from *Canaan*, who, for uncovering his Father's Nakedness, had (according to the Schoolmen) a Curse laid
upon that Part."[78]

Works of the imagination from this period were more concerned with
Ham's character than with his color or penis size. Nevertheless, they tended
to reiterate the orthodox interpretive paradigm: They cast Noah as an innocent patriarch whose naive experiment with viticulture goes slightly awry,
while depicting Ham as a sullen, impious, and lecherous lad whom the upright
Noah must patiently endure.[79] A veritable compendium of anti-Hamitism was
produced by sixteenth-century poet Guillaume De Salluste Sieur Du Bartas,
a Calvinist from the south of France who is probably best known for his
influence on Milton. In "L'Arche," an early section of Du Bartas's *La Seconde
Sepmaine,* Ham's irreverence is extended into the prediluvian age. As Noah
warns of impending doom, Ham is said to "nourish already within his breast
a blind root of profane atheism." In Du Bartas's vision, Ham's ultimate intention is to occupy God's place "in order to possess a magnificent temple
under the name of Jupiter amid the sands of Africa."[80] Ham meets the pious
Noah's concern for God's judgment with disdain: "Alas! I'm happy that these
servile fears—annoyances normally associated with low-spirited souls—take
hold of you! My father, do you want always to face the outrageous judgments
of a false Judge? . . . A barbarous hangman, who with a bloody sword menaces
night and day your criminal neck?" Ham goes on to call the Lord a tyrant
and a slaughterer of innocent beasts, "who, caught up with rage, exterminates
cruelly his own empire."[81]

Later, Du Bartas relates the episode narrated in Genesis 9:20–27:

Like the ravens that, with wind in their tailfeathers, pass over the perfumed
woods of happy Arabia, scorning its delightful parts and gardens whose

bright flowers perfume the skies, and stop—the gluttons!—at the dirty corpse of a criminal bludgeoned some time before, or like a painter crazy about a new palate-knife neglects the most beautiful part of a portrait and accentuates, highlights the ugliness of a deformity, big nose or lips, sunken eyes, or some other ugly trait—thus the treacherous sons of the father of the lie with ingratitude mop up with a sponge of forgetfulness the traits of virtue, and envious, throw upon the least sins the venom of their eyes . . . ; broadcasting in every age the peccadilloes of the greatest people, thus Ham, who allowed his impudent eyes to graze on the parental dishonor: and who bursting out in a profane laugh, shamelessly announces the miserable state of this drunken old man.

"Come, come, brothers" says he, "Come, run and see this controller who censured us wrongly, and so often, see how he messes up his bed, vomiting through the nose, the eyes, the mouth, governed by wine, and—the brute—leaving his genitals uncovered for all to see!"[82]

Du Bartas is equally graphic in describing the reaction of Shem and Japheth:

"Huh? you impudent piece of shit!" says each of the brothers, with just ire written on their brows: "Unnatural villain, pernicious monster, unworthy to see the beautiful torches of heaven, since we weren't here, you should have hidden with your mantle—and especially with your silence—your father, whom boredom, strong wine, and old age caused to slip this once; you yap on about him and, to build yourself up, make a center stage show of his shame." Having said this, averting their eyes, they cover the naked body of their venerable father.[83]

Du Bartas's poetic retelling of the episode represents the acme of Ham's defamation, at least until American advocates of slavery began to read the story.

John Milton also chronicles Ham's transgression, although in terms that are surprisingly mild, given Du Bartas's influence on him. In Book XII of *Paradise Lost,* the archangel Michael outlines for Adam and Eve the history of sin that will be written by their descendants: "Witness th' irreverent son/ Of him who built the ark, who for the shame/ Done to his father, heard this heavy curse,/ 'Servant of servants,' on his vicious race."[84] Although Milton does not attribute a peculiar stigma to the descendants of Ham, he does place the burden of postdiluvian corruption on Noah's "irreverent son": "Thus will this latter, as the former world,/ Still tend from bad to worse, till God at last/ Wearied with their iniquities, withdraw/ His presence from among them, and avert/ His holy eyes; resolving from thenceforth/ To leave them to their own polluted ways."[85]

Enlightenment

Between the early eighteenth and mid-nineteenth centuries there appeared a number of commentaries, dictionaries, and encyclopedias that cataloged traditional readings of Genesis 9. Though skeptical of the interpretive tradition, Pierre Bayle (1647–1706) transmitted many of the "unknown number of ludicrous stories" that had crystallized around the figure of Ham by the late seventeenth century.[86] In his landmark *Dictionaire Historique et Critique* Bayle summarized this catalog of infamy:

> It has been believed that since Ham had displayed such indiscretion toward his father, he was a cursed soul who had committed all sorts of abominations. He is said to be the Inventor of Magic and many things are told about this. It is claimed that he gave an example of unchastity not very edifying, that is to say that he made his wife pregnant in the ark itself. Some say that the offense which he committed against his father is infinitely more atrocious than the way in which it is represented in the Holy Scripture. Some believe that he castrated him; others say that he made him impotent thanks to some magical spells; others claim that he wallowed in incest with Noah's wife.[87]

Bayle approaches this litany of charges with a combination of Renaissance skepticism and pre-Enlightenment credulity. On one hand, he doubts that Ham castrated his father, commenting that "if such a painful operation as the one that is mentioned had been carried out on him, he would not have had to wait to awake from his drunkenness."[88] Bayle also discounts the possibilities that Ham reintroduced antediluvian sins following the Flood (a view he attributes to *Berrosus*) or that the words "Ham saw the nakedness of his father" mean that he engaged in incestuous relations with his mother. On the other hand, while denying that Ham invented magic (it was "the Angels enamored of sex who taught it to men"), Bayle does hold him responsible for preserving it through the Deluge. Bayle also considers it likely that Ham settled in Egypt and was posthumously worshiped there as Jupiter Hammon. Thus, although the Frenchman regarded Noah's "curse" as nothing more than a prophecy of Hebrew victories under Joshua and dismissed the notion that Ham became black as "a chimerical tale," his dictionary gave wide circulation to some of the more pernicious strands of European anti-Hamitism.

Augustin Calmet's (1682–1757) *Dictionary of the Holy Bible* was probably the most influential treatment of Ham and his curse to appear in the eighteenth century.[89] Published in France in 1722, by 1832 Calmet's dictionary had appeared in a seventh edition in America, where it promoted the idea that Ham's name means "burnt, swarthy or black." Calmet also perpetuated the notion that Ham "ridiculed" his father, a leitmotif in American readings of the curse. Furthermore, although European writers had previously cited Genesis 9 in relation to the African slave trade, Calmet appears to have been the first scholarly Bible commentator to link Ham with blackness and slavery.[90]

Another influential eighteenth-century interpreter of Noah's curse was Bishop Thomas Newton, chaplain to George II of Great Britain. In his *Dissertations on the Prophecies* (1759), Newton asserted that "Ham the father of Canaan . . . instead of concealing [Noah's] weakness, as a good-natured man or at least a dutiful son would have done, he cruelly exposed it." Ham's brothers, by contrast, "more compassionate to the infirmities of their aged father ... acted with such decency and respect, that 'they saw not the naked-ness of their father.' "[91] Newton's otherwise unremarkable comments on the biblical text nevertheless provided an original contribution to the history of interpretation. Confronted with the contradiction between Ham's offense and Canaan's punishment that had vexed earlier interpreters—and firm in the conviction that "such arbitrary proceedings are contrary to all our ideas of the divine perfections,"—Newton offered a text-critical solution to the prob-lem:

> Hitherto we have explained the prophecy according to the present copies of our Bible; but if we were to correct the text, as we should any ancient classic author in a like case, the whole perhaps might be made easier and plainer. *Ham the father of Canaan* is mentioned in the preceding part of the story; and how then came the person of a sudden to be changed into *Canaan?* The Arabic version in these three verses hath *the father of Canaan* instead of *Canaan.* Some copies of the Septuagint likewise have *Ham* instead of *Canaan,* as if Canaan was a corruption of the text.[92]

In Newton's endeavor to eschew logical inconsistency and affirm divine jus-tice, he eliminated the need to explain why Canaan had been cursed for Ham's transgression. In the process, he forged a useful weapon in the American struggle to justify the peculiar institution.[93]

Also noteworthy for its treatment of Genesis 9 is the one-volume Bible commentary of Matthew Henry (1662–1714), an English divine who enjoyed a considerable reputation in America as a Bible expositor. Henry's portrait of Ham was simultaneously conventional and inventive: Ham "pleased himself with the sight [of his naked father], *as the Edomites looked upon the day of their brother* (Obad. 12), pleased, and insulting. Perhaps Ham had sometimes been himself drunk, and reproved for it by his good father, whom he was therefore pleased to see thus overcome...." However, Henry differed mark-edly from other commentators by describing Ham's offense solely in terms of honor and shame:

> [Ham] told his two brethren *without* (*in the street,* as the word is), in a scornful deriding manner, that his father might seem vile unto them.... It is very wrong ... to publish the faults of any, especially of parents, whom it is our duty to honour. Noah was not only a good man, but had been a good father to him; and this was a most base disingenuous requital to him for his tenderness.... Disgrace is justly put upon those that put disgrace upon oth-ers, especially that dishonour and grieve their own parents.[94]

For Henry, as for Calvin, Noah contributed to his own dishonor through shameful drunkenness: "He was uncovered within his tent, made naked to his shame, as Adam when he had eaten forbidden fruit."[95] Still, Henry's con-clusion must have encouraged American readers of his commentary who sought a biblical sanction for slavery: "An undutiful child that mocks at his parents is *no more worthy to be called a son*, but deserves to be *made as a hired servant*, nay, as *a servant of servants*, among his brethren."

Nineteenth Century

Biblical expositor Adam Clarke appears to have exercised a peculiar influence on popular readings of Genesis 9. In his widely read *Commentary* (published between 1817 and 1825), the British exegete popularized Bishop Newton's textual solution to the problem of Noah's curse, even while admitting that "this [reading] is acknowledged by none of the other versions, and seems to be merely a gloss."[96] In other respects, Clarke reiterated the orthodox interpretive paradigm. He claimed that the conduct of Shem and Japhet was "such as became pious and affectionate children" and affirmed that Noah was "without the least blame."[97] Clarke's opinion that "Ham, and very probably his son Canaan, had treated their father on this occasion with contempt or reprehensible levity"[98] may have influenced antebellum American slavery advocates, who agreed that Ham had dishonored Noah by making sport of his nakedness.

Later chapters will explore the role of Noah's curse in the American biblical imagination. Next we turn to a survey of the interpretive tradition that developed around Ham's grandson Nimrod.

3

Unauthorized Biography

The Legend of Nimrod and His Tower

The descendants of Ham: Cush, Egypt, Put, and Canaan.
The descendants of Cush: Seba, Havilah, Sabtah, Raamah,
and Sabteca. The descendants of Raamah: Sheba and De-
dan. Cush became the father of Nimrod; he was the first
on earth to become a mighty warrior. He was a mighty
hunter before the LORD; therefore it is said, "Like Nimrod
a mighty hunter before the LORD." The beginning of his
kingdom was Babel, Erech, and Accad, all of them in the
land of Shinar. From that land he went into Assyria, and
built Nineveh, Rehoboth-ir, Calah, and Resen between
Nineveh and Calah; that is the great city.

Genesis 10:6–12

NIMROD'S PLACE in the landscape of modern racial discourse came to my
attention as I perused a reprint of Josiah Priest's influential *Slavery as it Relates
to the Negro or African Race* (1843). Priest's text includes two crude illustrations
of Ham's grandson Nimrod. One depicts a swarthy savage engaged "in battle
with a gang of wild beasts." The other portrays Nimrod in conversation with
Ham's brother Japheth in front of the Tower of Babel. According to the cap-
tion, we are witnessing an episode of primordial conflict between the eponymous ancestors of white Europeans and black Africans. Japheth is "finding
fault with Nimrod, on account of his project," the tower "built by the Negroes
of the house of Ham, under the direction of Nimrod."[1] These sketches present
a series of intriguing questions: Why is Nimrod—an obscure figure men-

tioned briefly in the Table of Nations in Genesis 10—of such importance to Josiah Priest, a New Yorker known for his frontier adventure stories, Indian captivity narratives, and "true" tales of the Revolutionary War?[2] Is Priest's conception of Nimrod original, or does he drawn on earlier depictions of this shadowy biblical character? And to what extent is Priest's picture of Nimrod based in the biblical text?

According to Umberto Cassuto's renowned Bible commentary,[3] the references to Nimrod in Genesis 10:6–12 indicate that he was "a famous ancient hero, and was a popular subject of Israelite epic poetry." In fact, the words "therefore it is said . . ." (v. 9) connote a proverb widely current in Israel and based on an epic poem in praise of Nimrod. Cassuto speculates that the biblical author borrowed from this epic, making vv. 6–12

> perhaps an excerpt from the very opening lines which indicated at the outset, in accordance with the customary practice in epic poetry, the subject of the poem. In the continuation of the poem, in so far as we can surmise, a detailed account was given of his mighty deeds in hunting beasts and monsters, of his military expeditions and conquests in the lands of Babylon and Assyria, and of the cities he built.[4]

Like Cassuto, modern commentators are interested in recovering the Nimrod who may lurk behind the text of Genesis 10. Our concern, however, is with the Nimrod who has taken shape in front of the text, as it were—the figure who has come to life in the imaginative space between the Bible and its readers. The historical Nimrod—and the epic chronicle of his deeds that may be reflected in the text of Genesis—are lost to us. But Nimrod's legend, woven by generations of Bible readers from scraps of text and tradition, is available for scholarly perusal in the history of interpretation. This chapter traces the contours of Nimrod's unauthorized biography from early Jewish midrashim to the speculative works of nineteenth-century Christian polemicists.

Jewish Contributions

The legend of Nimrod commences with postbiblical glosses on Genesis 10 authored and collected by the rabbinic sages. Not surprisingly, the Bible's gnomic description of this "mighty hunter before the Lord" piqued the midrashic imagination. Although Nimrod is mentioned in rabbinic texts that are quite diverse in provenance and genre, a brief summary of Jewish legend concerning Ham's grandson will provide a starting place for tracing his unauthorized biography.[5]

One rabbinic tale relates that following the Flood, the descendants of Noah's sons appointed princes to rule over them: "Nimrod for the descendants of Ham, Joktan for the descendants of Shem, and Phenech for the descendants of Japheth." Determined to "make bricks, and each one write his name upon his brick," Nimrod and the other princes undertake to build the tower described in Genesis 11. Twelve righteous men, among them Abram, dissent from the plan. When the twelve are brought before the princes, Nimrod and Phenech become enraged and resolve to throw them into the fire.[6]

In another version of the tale, Nimrod raises an army from the descendants of Shem and Ham in order to rout the Japhethites. The Hamites crown Nimrod king, and he vanquishes the Semites. Having achieved dominion over Noah's descendants, Nimrod builds "a fortress upon a round rock, setting a great throne of cedar-wood upon it to support a second great throne, made of iron; this, in turn, supported a great copper throne, with a silver throne above the copper, and a golden throne above the silver. At the summit of this pyramid, Nimrod placed a gigantic gem from which, sitting in divine state, he exacted universal homage."[7]

Jewish legends also feature descriptions of Nimrod's clothing: His "father Cush ... gave him the clothes made of skins with which God had furnished Adam and Eve at the time of their leaving Paradise." Intended for Shem, these garments were stolen by Ham from their father and passed on to Cush. Cush hid them until he could bequeath them to his son Nimrod, who received them at the age of twenty.[8] According to tradition, these garments had a wonderful property: "He who wore them was both invincible and irresistible. The beasts and birds of the woods fell down before Nimrod as soon as they caught sight of him arrayed in them, and he was equally victorious in his combats with men. The source of his unconquerable strength was not known to them. They attributed it to his personal prowess, and therefore they appointed him king over themselves. . . ."[9] After consolidating his power, Nimrod chose Shinar as his capital. "Thence he extended his dominion farther and farther, until he rose by cunning and force to be the sole ruler of the whole world, the first mortal to hold universal sway, as the ninth ruler to possess the same power will be the Messiah."[10]

In rabbinic legend, Nimrod's impiety keeps pace with his growing power. He fashioned and worshiped idols of wood and stone and, aided by his son Mardon, tempted his subjects to evil. The effects were sinister: "Men no longer trusted in God, but rather in their own prowess and ability, an attitude to which Nimrod tried to convert the whole world. Therefore people said, 'since the creation of the world there has been none like Nimrod, a mighty hunter of men and beasts, a sinner before God.' "[11] In some versions of Nimrod's legend, he wishes to "set himself up as a god" so that all nations will pay him divine homage.

According to the rabbis, Nimrod's iniquity climaxed in the building of the Tower of Babel, an enterprise that "was neither more nor less than rebellion against God." Nimrod said: "I will be revenged on Him for the drowning of my ancestors. Should He send another flood, my tower will rise even above Ararat, and keep me safe."[12] According to tradition, three sorts of rebels could be found among the tower's 600,000 builders: those who said, "Let us ascend into the heavens and wage warfare with Him," those who said "Let us ascend into the heavens, set up our idols, and pay worship unto them there," and those who said "Let us ascend into the heavens, and ruin them with our bows and spears." Upon completing the tower, the builders shot arrows upward. When these returned to them covered with blood, they cried, "We have slain all who are in heaven."[13] The builders "were punished according to the nature of their rebellious conduct." In addition to confounding their language, the Lord pelted them with bricks. "Some were turned into apes and phantoms, some were set against each other in combat, some were scattered over the earth."[14] Following the episode at Babel, Nimrod continued to rule and build cities, "which he filled with inhabitants, reigning over them in majesty."[15]

Other Jewish contributions to Nimrod's unauthorized biography concern his relationship to the Hebrew patriarchs, particularly Abram. These include the legend that Abram's father, Terah, commanded Nimrod's armies and that Nimrod's astrologers witnessed a comet at Abram's birth. According to this tradition, the wise men whispered to each other that Terah's son would be a mighty emperor, his descendants inheriting the earth and dethroning kings. Upon learning of this, Nimrod attempted to buy Abram, but Terah outsmarted the king by selling him the son of a slave woman. Abram he secured in a cave until he was ten years old.[16] In another legendary account of Abram's birth, Nimrod is an astrologer who discerns from the stars that a child will overthrow the gods he worships. His counselors advise him to slaughter every male child in his kingdom, which he does. Observing the slaughter, the angels cry out to God, "Have You not seen how Nimrod the blasphemer murders innocents?" But the unborn Abram is miraculously undetected in his mother's womb. He survives, grows to adulthood in twenty days, and instructs Nimrod on the nature of the true God.[17]

In another rabbinic tradition, the angel Gabriel magically spirits Abram to Babylon, where his father has fled with Nimrod. Abram enters Nimrod's palace, shakes his throne, and calls him a blasphemer, at which the king and his idols fall on their faces. In still another legend, Satan appears to Nimrod and offers to build him a catapult with which to heave Abram into a fiery furnace.[18] In a tradition involving Abram's grandchildren, we learn that at the age of 250 Nimrod was killed by Esau, "each having been jealous of the other's fame as a hunter." Esau derives strength from Nimrod's holy garments until Jacob steals them from his tent.[19]

Josephus warrants special attention, in that he is both a window on conceptions of Nimrod current among Hellenistic Jews and a conduit to the world of the Christian church fathers. In *Antiquities*, Josephus writes "concerning the Tower of Babylon, and the Confusion of Tongues" that God commanded the survivors of the Flood and their descendants to "send colonies abroad, for the thorough peopling of the earth, that they might not raise seditions among themselves." According to Josephus, the postdiluvians refused to comply with this command because they suspected God wished to divide them so they would be more easily oppressed. "Now it was Nimrod," Josephus contends, "who excited them to such an affront and contempt of God." He was

> a bold man, and of great strength of hand. He persuaded them not to ascribe it to God, as if it was through his means they were happy, but to believe that it was their own courage which procured that happiness. He also gradually changed the government into tyranny, seeing no other way of turning men from fear of God, but to bring them into a constant dependence on his power. He also said, "He would be revenged on god, if he should have a mind to drown the world again, for that he would build a tower too high for the waters to be able to reach; and that he would avenge himself on God for destroying their forefathers."[20]

Josephus recapitulates many features of the rabbinic portrait of Nimrod, including his association with the tower. But he also introduces themes that would influence later writers. One is his claim that Nimrod and "the multitude" in his train built the tower with "burnt brick, cemented together with mortar made of *bitumen*, that it might not be liable to admit water."[21] This idea, a corollary of the belief that the tower was designed to withstand another flood, was adopted by Milton in the seventeenth century. Another novel dimension of Josephus's commentary was his emphasis on the dispersion that followed the confusion of tongues at Babel. The survivors of the Flood feared that God's mandate to "send colonies abroad, for the thorough peopling of the earth" was intended to keep human beings divided and weak. According to Josephus, Nimrod led those who resisted this diaspora. But following the tower episode, the dispersion was more efficacious. The builders "went out by colonies every where; and each colony took possession of that land which they light upon, and into which God led them."[22] The motif of dispersion—based textually in Genesis 11:9 ("from there the LORD scattered them abroad over the face of all the earth")—would became quite prominent among Nimrod's American biographers.

It is possible to discern subtle evolution in the Jewish picture of Ham's grandson. If the rabbinic Nimrod is a portrait of arrogance, violence, and blatant rebellion, Josephus's Nimrod is craftier and more focused in his opposition to the divine will. He is, in fact, a sort of anti-Noah—not an exemplar of righteousness who builds an ark at God's behest, but a paragon of unrighteousness who presumes to thwart God's will and constructs a tower to ensure against the consequences. Nimrod is not yet the satanic figure he would become in the Christian Middle Ages, but his legend is clearly developing in that direction.

Considered as a whole, the Jewish tradition made several lasting contributions to the legend of Nimrod: (1) He governed the sons of Ham following the flood, choosing Shinar as his capital; (2) he was a universal ruler whose success was attributable to dark magic; (3) he was an irascible man prone to violence; (4) much like the fallen angels, he fomented rebellion against and within heaven;[23] (5) he demonstrated his penchant for defiance by building a tower with which he intended to avert a second deluge; (6) his contumacious character and belligerence toward God were reflected in the tower's builders; (7) he encouraged human self-sufficiency and introduced the worship of idols; and (8) he posed as a god and demanded that the nations pay him homage.

Christian Contributions

Church Fathers

Like the rabbis, Christian writers of the patristic period felt obliged to explain the arcane reference to Nimrod inserted into Genesis 10's Table of Nations. In the process, they made lasting contributions to his incipient biography. Among the fathers, Augustine's musings on Nimrod were probably the most influential. In Book XVI of *City of God*, Augustine attempted to clarify the Bible's sketch of Ham's grandson by translating Genesis 10:9 "[Nimrod] was a gigantic hunter *against* the Lord God."[24] This construal contained two elements that would have an impact on subsequent interpreters.

The first was the notion that Nimrod was of prodigious size. Among Christian writers, this idea can be traced to Filaster in the fourth century and to Tertullian in the second.[25] But ultimately it may be based in Jewish sources—either the Septuagint version of Genesis (which reads "And Cush begot Nimrod; . . . He was a giant hunter before the Lord God")[26] or 1 *Enoch*, an apocalyptic text from the third century B.C.E.,[27] which contends that the forbidden union between "daughters of men" and "sons of God" described in Genesis 6 yielded a race of giants. Because the description of Nimrod in Genesis 10:8–9 features the same word (*gibbor*, "mighty") used in Genesis 6: 4 to describe the inhabitants of the prediluvian world, early Bible readers assumed that Nimrod must have been "mighty" in this physical sense.[28] Whatever its provenance, Nimrod's herculean stature became an enduring aspect of the interpretive tradition when it was endorsed by Augustine.

Another notable influence on subsequent interpreters was Augustine's claim that Nimrod was a hunter *against*, rather than *before*, the Lord. It may be that Augustine followed Philo in reading the text this way.[29] In any case, having rendered the preposition in 10:9 to denote Nimrod's spiritual demeanor, Augustine was led to conclude that the noun *hunter* could "only suggest a deceiver, oppressor and destroyer of earth-born creatures."[30] Through a combination of translation and interpretation, Augustine portrayed Nimrod as an enemy of God and a foil to true humility: "The safe and genuine highway to heaven is constructed by humility," Augustine noted, "which lifts up its heart to the Lord, not against the Lord, as did that giant. . . ."[31] The supposition that Nimrod resisted God was intimately related in Augustine's view to the assumption that he, "with his subject peoples, began to erect a tower against the Lord, which symbolize[d] his impious pride":

The city which was called "Confusion" is none other than Babylon, whose marvelous construction is praised also by pagan historians. The name "Babylon" means, in fact, "confusion." Hence it may be inferred that Nimrod "the giant" was its founder, as was briefly suggested earlier. For when the Scripture mentions him, it says that "the beginning of his empire was Babylon," that is, Babylon was the city which had the pre-eminence over all the others. . . . [32]

Augustine opines that God's breaking of the human conspiracy by the confusion of tongues was a condign retribution for Nimrod and his underlings: "Since a ruler's power of domination is wielded by his tongue, it was in that organ that [Nimrod's] pride was condemned to punishment." As a consequence, "he who refused to understand God's bidding . . . was himself not understood when he gave orders to men."[33] This gloss on Babel may well have influenced Dante, who, as we shall see, portrayed Nimrod as a titan lacking intelligible speech.

Several patristic writers reinforced Nimrod's long-standing association with tyranny. For instance, Jerome (347–420) asserts that "Nimrod the son of Cush was the first to seize tyrannical power [previously] unused, over the people."[34] In his *Recognitions*, Clement elaborates this picture of Nimrod and his descendants:

> In the seventeenth generation Nimrod I reigned in Babylonia, and built a city, and thence granted to the Persians, and taught them to worship fire. In the nineteenth generation the descendants of him who had been cursed after the flood [Ham], going beyond their proper bounds which they had obtained by lot in the western regions, drove into the eastern lands those who had obtained the middle portion of the world . . . while themselves violently took possession of the country from which they expelled [its inhabitants].[35]

Clement's thumbnail sketch of the Hamite genealogy includes some leading features of Nimrod's legend as it would develop in the succeeding centuries. Nimrod is associated with city building and idolatry, and his descendants are said to emulate the tyrannous behavior for which he will become notorious. Clement also presents the idea—adumbrated in Josephus—that Nimrod led an insurrection against the postdiluvian allotment of territory among Noah's sons. Rejecting their assignment to "the western regions," the Hamites under Nimrod migrate "beyond their proper bounds which they had obtained by lot" and invade Shem's lands in Mesopotamia ("the eastern lands of those who had obtained the middle portion of the world"). Like Josephus, Clement charges Nimrod with opposition to God's plan for postdiluvian dispersion, an accusation that would become a leitmotif in the history of biblical interpretation.

Patristic interpreters assigned Nimrod symbolic as well as historical significance. His legendary role as hunter, tower builder, and tyrant made him a consummate symbol of human pride and rebellion. Ambrose cast Nimrod as the type of all who pursue earthly glory, thus contrasting him with Peter, the fisher of men for God's glory. In time, Nimrod came to represent "an excessive attachment to earthly things, a noble but ill-directed ambition, since its objective was not God but human goods."[36] Meanwhile, despite his legendary connection with Babylon, Nimrod's descent from Ham through Cush led patristic authors to regard him as an African. Some claimed that "in Hebrew Chus means Aethiops"; others that "Nembroth means Aethiops." In both cases, Nimrod and his tower were africanized through association with Ham.[37] The combination of spiritual and genealogical attributes that tradition ascribed to Nimrod led Ambrose to conclude that he was a personification of humanity's dark side: "Forced by his nature to live and act more like an animal than a creature of reason, Nimrod is an image of the guilty soul, 'Ethiopian, enemy of the light, deprived of brightness.' "[38]

Middle Ages

The legend of Nimrod continued to evolve during the Christian Middle Ages. Lineaments of the portrait rendered by the rabbis and church fathers remained intact, but there were many embellishments. For instance, Nimrod was increasingly associated with hidden knowledge, being credited with everything from composing a prophecy to inform the Magi of Jesus' birth,[39] to unlocking the mysteries of the stars, to mastering the knowledge of statecraft.

One medieval tradition connected Nimrod with the mysterious fourth son of Noah. *The Book of the Cave of Treasures,* composed in Syriac perhaps as late as the sixth century C.E., claims that Noah's fourth son, Yonton, (Jonathan) traveled to the east and encountered Nimrod.[40] There Jonathan taught the giant-king oracular wisdom—that is, legitimate astronomy.[41] According to *The Book of the Cave of Treasures,* Nimrod was a teacher as well. "The revelation of Nimrod" was thought to be a Christian messianic prophecy, the knowledge of which brought the Magi to Bethlehem.[42] Another medieval text in which Nimrod figures prominently is the so-called *Apocalypse* of Pseudo Methodius (Syriac, probably late seventh century C.E.). It relates a similar story regarding Yonton, begotten by Noah after the flood and sent to the east. A recipient of divine revelations that include astronomical knowledge, Yonton instructs Nimrod "in all wisdom," particularly statecraft.[43]

The medieval association of Nimrod and astronomy has been analyzed in a classic study by Charles Homer Haskins.[44] Haskins notes that in the twelfth century a mysterious figure—variously named Nebrot, Nebrod, Nebroz, Nembroz, or Nembroth—was cited as an "authority on astronomical and chronological matters of the same type as Bede, Helperic, Gerland, and Thurkil." Since no writer of this name is known to have existed in the Middle Ages, the probable reference is to the Nimrod of Genesis, "whose name has furnished a fruitful field for speculations and conjectures of orientalists."[45] By the sixth century, Nimrod had become an astronomer, "and an astronomer he remained to the men of the Middle Ages."[46] Haskins describes a medieval manuscript purported to be the treatise of Nimrod the giant on astronomy, which he dates to around 800 and places in Gaul.[47] This work features a drawing of Atlas and Nimrod, the two kings "whom classical and oriental tradition respectively make the founders of astronomy." According to Haskins, "Atlas is depicted standing on the Pyrenees and bearing on his shoulders the firmament with its stars, while Nimrod stands on the mountain of the Amorites and looks upward while he supports in his hands the heavens without stars."[48] The content of the treatise reflects another medieval theme in the legend of Nimrod, for it takes the form of a dialogue between Nimrod and Noah's fourth son, Jonathan.[49]

Despite Nimrod's mythic prominence, medieval writers never lost sight of his blood relationship to Ham. The fourteenth-century *Travels of Sir John Mandeville* emphasized this connection as it transmitted and embellished Nimrod's legend:

> From one of [Ham's] sons, Nimrod the giant was born, who was the first king in the world and who started to build the tower of Babel. And with him the fiends of the underworld would come frequently to lay with the women of [Nimrod's] descent and created various people, all disfigured, one without testes, another without an arm, a third with one eye, a fourth with the feet of a horse, and many others disfigured and misshapen. And from this generation of descendants of Ham came the pagan folk and the various peoples of the isles of Asia. And because he was the most powerful and none would dare oppose him, he was called the son of God and sovereign of all the world.[50]

Recalling that the same author calls Ham "the mightiest and most powerful" and regards him as the forerunner of Mongol emperors who call themselves "Grand Ham and the son of nature and the sovereign of all the world," we note that Nimrod's legend was definitely shaped by his connection with Ham. But this dynamic worked in the other direction as well. Nimrod's identity as the archetypal rebel and tyrant was often projected back onto his grandfather. In fact, perceiving Ham through Nimrod's lens promoted the paradoxical notion that the curse of Ham "led to cruelty, to mastery, to imperial power, even to becoming 'the son of God.' " It was no doubt this association that caused Luther to dub Ham "the lord of all Asia." Benjamin Braude has shown that the tradition of a masterful Ham grew directly out of medieval attention to Nimrod, who was, "after Noah himself, the most imperial figure, literally and figuratively, in the ancient and medieval imaging of the Bible."[51] The Hamite's association with rulership made him strangely attractive to Europe's imperial rulers, some of whom claimed descent from both Ham and Nimrod.[52]

Because of Dante's prodigious influence on the literary imagination in his own and in subsequent ages, Nimrod's treatment in *The Divine Comedy* deserves close attention. The aspects of Nimrod's evolving legend transmitted by Dante are his giant stature, his tyranny over humanity, and his responsibility for the confusion of language at Babel. Nimrod is mentioned in each section of *The Divine Comedy*, but by far the most important passage appears in Canto XXXI of *Inferno*. Dante discovers Nimrod in the region of hell inhabited by the giants of myth and legend, and describes him in terrible detail:

> I began now to distinguish the face of one [horrible giant], the shoulders and the chest and a great part of the belly and down by his sides both arms. Nature, assuredly, when she gave up the art of making creatures like these, did right well to deprive Mars of such executors; and if she does not repent of elephants and whales, one looking at it carefully will hold her the more just and prudent for it, for where the equipment of the mind is joined to evil will and to power men can make no defence against it. His face appeared to me to have the length and bulk of Saint Peter's pine-cone at Rome and the other bones were in proportion, so that the bank [of the pit in which Nimrod and the other giants are sunk], which was an apron to him from the middle down, still showed so much of him above that three Frieslanders would have boasted in vain of reaching his hair; for I saw thirty great spans of him down from the place where a man buckles his cloak.[53]

While Dante is marveling at the prodigious Nimrod, a strange sound reaches his ears: " 'Raphel may amech zabi almi,' began the savage mouth to cry, for which no sweeter psalms were fit; and my Leader towards him: 'Stupid soul, keep to thy horn and vent thyself with that when rage or other passion takes thee. Search at thy neck, bewildered soul, and thou shalt find the strap that holds it tied; see how it lies across thy great chest.' "[54] Virgil instructs Dante on the hideous behemoth's identity: "He is his own accuser. This is Nimrod, through whose wicked device the world is not of one sole speech. Let us leave him there and not talk in vain, for every language is to him as his to others, which is known to none." Significantly, Nimrod's only words are unintelligible murmurings. Other references in Dante's *Divine Comedy* emphasize Nimrod's responsibility for the tower and the resultant confusion of languages.[55]

By the end of the Middle Ages, the contours of Nimrod's legend were firmly established. He was Ham's grandson, a physical giant sometimes associated with disfigurement and the loss of human intelligence. He was the earth's first tyrant. He possessed astronomical and other types of esoteric wisdom. He was an archrebel "against the Lord," who refused to abide by Noah's postdiluvian allotment of lands. Migrating to the east, he settled on the plain of Shinar, where he became the builder of the infamous Tower of Babel. This project led directly to the dispersion of nations and the plurality of tongues.

Reformation and Renaissance

In his *Lectures on Genesis,* Martin Luther indicates just how close had become the association of Ham and Nimrod in the Christian imagination. Not only do the characters share a family resemblance; but they begin to merge when Luther ascribes to Ham significant aspects of Nimrod's legend. For instance, he places Ham in Babylon, where, "together with his descendants, he engages in building a city and a tower."[56] But Luther does not ignore Nimrod, who, "after setting up his power through tyranny, afflicts the godly descendants of Noah in various ways, establishes a kingdom for himself, and assumes sole sovereignty over it."[57] Like grandfather, like grandson. Just as Ham despised Noah's religion and doctrine by mocking his father and establishing a new government and new religion, so Nimrod "sinned against both the government and the church. He did not cultivate the true religion."

Following Josephus and the church fathers, Luther indicts Nimrod for practicing "unjust tyranny on his cousins, whom he expelled from their paternal lands."[58] Specifically, the Hamites under Nimrod invade the region delegated to Shem, "the heir of the promise concerning Christ." For such behavior, the Hamites are painted in demonic language: "Even though there is no written record of what they attempted against the true church, against Noah himself, the ruler of the church, and against his pious posterity, it can nevertheless be surmised by analogy if we carefully consider the actions of our opponents at the present time. For Satan, who incites the ungodly against the true church, is always the same."[59] As the enemy of Noah and his pious descendants, Nimrod invites identification with the evil one.

John Calvin's discussion of Nimrod in his *Commentaries* is brief but noteworthy. Despite his reputation as a careful biblical scholar, Calvin transmits many features of Nimrod's burgeoning legend. According to Calvin, Moses made special mention of Nimrod because as "the first author of tyranny" he was eminent in an unusual degree. For this distinction, Nimrod was "branded with an eternal mark of infamy," indicating how pleasing God finds "a mild administration of affairs among men." Calvin claims it was ambition that led Nimrod to seek high honor rather than to cultivate equality with his inferiors: "Nimrod attempted to raise himself above the order of men; just as proud men become transported by a vain self-confidence, that they may look down as from the clouds upon others." The description of Nimrod as a "mighty hunter" Calvin takes to mean that he was a "furious man, and approximated to beasts rather than to men." Nimrod was also an expansionist, who, "not content with his large and opulent kingdom, gave the reins to his cupidity, and pushed the boundaries of his empire even into Assyria, where he also built new cities."

Following the interpretive tradition and clues in the biblical text, Calvin affirms that Nimrod probably built the tower (though he is troubled by the fact that the name Babel, which presumably denotes the confusion of tongues, appears already in Genesis 10). On Nimrod's role in leading this project, Calvin surmises thus: "Solicitous about his own fame and power, [Nimrod] inflamed [his contemporaries'] insane desire by this pretext, that some famous monument should be erected in which their everlasting memory might remain." Like Luther, Calvin refers to the violent expulsion of Shem from the dwelling place allotted him under Noah.[60]

Once again, Du Bartas's *La Seconde Semaine* deserves a special place in our survey of the interpretive tradition. Although dependent on previous authors, Du Bartas brings Nimrod's legend to a new level of detail and psychological complexity:

> Nimrod has not even reached his twelfth year
> when he begins to act the tyrant among his peers,
> vaunting himself over his equals, and under that good sign
> establishes the foundation of his future grandeur
> and carries in his hand reeds for scepters,
> doing apprenticeship among the shepherds.
>
> Then, understanding that a lord who aspires
> to a powerful empire, presuming it his fate,
> must surpass his vulgar companions in deeds of renown
> or at least wear the mask of virtue,
> he doesn't spend the night on a soft mattress
> or the day in a heated room; so, the young man becomes accustomed
> to bad weather and good, taking, ambitious [as he is]
> a rock for his pillow and the sky for his bed linens,
> bows are his toys, sweat his delight,
> preferring hawks to sparrows, his hunting dogs are constantly
> with him
> and his preferred feast the flesh of a fine trembling buck
> that he has not finished flaying.
>
> Sometimes he challenges himself to mount in a single breath
> a steep rock outcropping that dominates a plain,
> to cross against the current a flooding river
> that in the rainy season has destroyed a hundred bridges
> and gallops and bounds
> across a narrow gorge
> to recapture a shaft [arrow or javelin] gone astray
> to take in fine chase either a doe or a buck.
>
> But at age twenty-five
> and proudly sensing his physique and his courage
> worthy of proud Mars, he seeks out here and there
> a tiger, a lion, a bear, a leopard,
> attacks it without fear, conquers it, slaughters it and
> displays its bloody hide on the high places.
>
> Then the common people—who see by his warlike hands
> the roads freed of inhuman assassins,
> the deep forests [cleared] of horrible groanings
> and the flocks [liberated] from fear—they like this liberator
> this evil-chasing Hercules, show him their favor,
> and call him father and savior.

Nimrod, grabbing fortune by the hair and striking while the iron
is hot, flatters, presses, importunes
now one, now another; hurrying along his good fate,
from a hunter of animals, he becomes a hunter of men.
Because, just as he used in his earlier hunts
birdlime, traps, birdcalls, [and] nets,
and in the end, against the wildest
maces, spears, arrows, and darts;
[so] he wins certain ones with promises,
others with presents, others by tricks,
and furiously tearing asunder the ties of equality,
seizes rule over the renascent world,
whereas before this the chief of each clan
commanded it separately, and the youthful audacity
of a frisky spirit, an ambitious upstart,
dared not put its sickle into the harvest of the patriarchs.[61]

Du Bartas goes on to describe Nimrod's career on the throne, accenting his violent and cruel nature. Nimrod insults the Almighty, waving his scepter in the Lord's face; he enslaves the people and forces them to construct a tower. Enough living in tents, he announces; let us build an edifice that will have its base in the depths and its head in the heavens, a tower that will stand as "an inviolable asylum and sacrosanct refuge from the wild inundation of a ravaging deluge."[62]

By illuminating new aspects of Nimrod's life and character, Du Bartas significantly expands the interpretive tradition. For the first time, Du Bartas offers depictions of Nimrod's childhood, his early aspirations for power, his asceticism, his training as a hunter and warrior, his tactics for gaining favor among the people, and his conniving methods for maintaining it. The composite portrait that emerges from Du Bartas's biography of Ham's grandson is one of alarming hubris; of a man who dares to "put his sickle into the harvest of the patriarchs," and of an illegitimate ruler who cleverly exploits human insecurity while flaunting his power before God. To the feudal mentality, Nimrod's ill-gotten rulership might appear liberating. But in Du Bartas's mind it is a bane to society that "furiously tear[s] asunder the ties of equality" and usurps the respect previously commanded by the patriarchs.

In Britain, as on the continent, Nimrod found prominence in a variety of learned works published between 1500 and 1700. Sir Walter Raleigh's (1554–1618) popular *History of the World* includes a lengthy discussion of Noah's descendants, with particular attention to Nimrod and his legend. Raleigh looks to the biblical account of human origins for a record of the world's repopulation following the flood. To the lineage of Noah, God "assigned and allotted to every son, and their issues, their proper parts."[63] According to Raleigh, Nimrod figured prominently in this initial dispersion: "All these people which came into Shinaar, and over whom Nimrod, either by order or strength, took the dominion, did, after the confusion of languages, and at such time as they grew to be a mighty people, disperse themselves into the regions adjoining to the said valley of Shinnar, which contained the best part of Mesopotamia, Babylonia, and Chaldea, and from the borders thereof in time they were propagated. . . ."[64]

Raleigh calls Nimrod the "establisher of the Babylonian monarchy," the first to reign "as sovereign lord after the flood." But did his rule derive from just authority? Raleigh is aware that "this empiry of Nimrod, both the fathers and many later writers, call tyrannical." However, he contends that Nimrod gained the reputation as a "bitter or severe governor, because his form of rule seemed at first far more terrible than paternal authority." He received the moniker "mighty hunter" because he "destroyed both beasts and thieves."[65] It appears to Raleigh that Nimrod did not usurp his rule but received it "by just authority." Like Caesar, Nimrod broke the "rule of eldership and paternity, laying the foundation of sovereign rule."[66] This discussion reveals an element of Nimrod's legend that was increasingly contested among European commentators: Whether Nimrod was the original tyrant and usurper of patriarchal authority, or a type of the monarch who governs with divine sanction.

John Milton's portrayal of Nimrod seems to have been influenced by his reading of Du Bartas, a fellow opponent of monarchy.[67] Book XII of *Paradise Lost* includes an extensive reference to the shadowy king and his tower. Milton has Michael prophesy of one who

> . . . shall rise
> Of proud ambitious heart, who not content
> with fair equality, fraternal state,
> Will arrogate Dominion undeserv'd
> Over his brethren, and quite dispossess
> concord and law of Nature from the Earth;
> Hunting (and Men not Beasts shall be his game)
> With War and hostile snare such as refuse
> Subjection to his Empire tyrannous:
> A mighty Hunter thence he shall be styl'd
> Before the Lord, as in despite of Heav'n,
> Or from Heav'n claiming second Sovranty;
> And from Rebellion shall derive his name,
> Though of Rebellion others he accuse.
> Hee with a crew, whom like Ambition joins
> with him or under him to tyrannize,
> Marching from *Eden* towards the West, shall find
> the Plain, wherein a black bituminous gurge
> Boils out from under ground, the mouth of Hell;
> Of Brick, and of that stuff they cast to build
> A city and Tow'r, whose top may reach to Heav'n'
> And get themselves a name, lest far disperst
> In foreign Lands thir memory be lost,

Regardless whether good or evil fame.
But God who oft descends to visit men
Unseen, and through thir habitations walks
to mark thir doings, them beholding soon,
comes down to see thir City, ere the Tower
Obstruct Heav'n Tow'rs, and in derision sets
Upon thir tongues a various Spirit to rase
Quite out thir Native Language, and instead
To sow a jangling noise of words unknown:
Forthwith a hideous gabble rises loud
Among the Builders; each to other calls
Not understood, till hoarse, and all in rage,
As mockt they storm; great laughter was in Heav'n
And looking down, to see the hubbub strange
And hear the din; thus was the building left
Ridiculous, and the work Confusion nam'd.[68]

This passage, based loosely on Genesis 10 and 11, catalogs most of the patristic and medieval themes in the developing legend of Nimrod. He is the archetypal tyrant ("not content/ with fair equality, fraternal state,/ Will arrogate Dominion undeserv'd/ Over his brethren, . . . With . . . Subjection to his Empire tyrannous . . .). He is a hunter of human beings ("and Men not Beasts shall be his game"; "A mighty Hunter thence he shall be styl'd").[69] He is builder of Babel's Tower[70] and responsible for corrupting human speech (God "sow[s] a jangling noise of words unknown/ Forthwith a hideous gabble rises loud Among the Builders"). His tower is both an expression of self-aggrandizement and a ploy to resist dispersion ("And get themselves a name, lest far disperst/In foreign Lands thir memory be lost"). But although echoes of Josephus, Augustine, and Dante are audible in Milton's text, novel chords are struck as well. These include the notion that Nimrod's name means "rebellion" ("And from Rebellion shall derive his name,/ Though of Rebellion others he accuse"). This idea seems to have been widespread during the Renaissance, but *Paradise Lost* was the conduit through which it entered modern literature.[71] Another innovative element in Milton's biography of Nimrod is his placement of the tower over the spot "wherein a black bituminous[72] gurge/ Boils out from under ground, the mouth of Hell." This nexus between Nimrod, the tower, and hell is a potent one: Milton portrays Nimrod as the first tyrant on earth, Satan as the first tyrant of all.[73]

Nimrod was also of considerable interest among British biblical commentators, who, despite their stated interest in the literal meaning of scripture, faithfully transmitted his legend. Writing in 1637, Gervase Babington deemed Nimrod the quintessential despot: "Nimrod a tyrant starteth up in this Chapter . . . ancient therefore are oppression and cruelty." In Nimrod's character, Babington perceives insight into sin's effects on human beings: If we continue to do evil, "at last it will be said of us as of *Nimrod*, that even before God we are become hunters, that is, we are growne to an impudency and boldness of sinning." Iniquity is so virulent, Babington observes, that every town has one or two Nimrods: "That is, a hard, cruell, a greedy, and covetous man, that grindeth the faces of his neighbours, till both skin and flesh being off, the bare bones doe onely remaine."[74] Babington's contemporary Abraham Rosse agreed that Nimrod was the original tyrant, interpreting the phrase "mighty in the earth" as indicating that he was "bloody and cruell." Nimrod was also an inventor of idolatry and builder of the tower. Like many Bible readers before him, Rosse linked Nimrod's sordid character with his descent from Ham.[75]

Andrew Willet was skeptical of the Hebrew "fables" that had attached themselves to the figure of Nimrod. Nevertheless, he transmitted many of them, including the notions that Nimrod was a giant, that he hunted men, that he spread contempt for God, that he brought idolatry into the world and taught men to worship fire, and that he clothed himself with the skins donned by Adam and Eve in the garden. The *scriptural* view, Willet contends ironically, is "that even in the sight and presence of God, without all feare of God, Nimrod practiced tyrannie and crueltie: so that it grew into a proverbe, to resemble a cruel tyrant and oppressor to Nimrod."[76] Willet thinks it likely that Nimrod was identical with Belus, the founder of the Babylonian monarchy.

The texts we have surveyed from the Reformation and Renaissance reveal that in an age when the divine right of monarchs and the religious authority of popes were contested, one's picture of Nimrod was determined to a great extent by one's attitude toward kings and bishops. Thus Andrew Willet perceives in the sinister Nimrod a symbol of papal despotism: "As old Babylon was the beginning of the kingdom of Nimrod . . . so Rome the second or new Babylon, is the head of the kingdome of Antichrist, the Nimrod of the world that hunteth mens soules, as the other did tyrannize over their bodies."[77] Similarly, Milton describes Ham's grandson as the sort of tyrant who "from Heav'n claim[s] second Sovranty."

Eighteenth and Nineteenth Centuries

At this point, we begin to consider texts that were published in America and that influenced conceptions of Nimrod there. As we have seen, Augustin Calmet was instrumental in shaping Ham's image in the American mind. Calmet's *Dictionary of the Bible* (1722) also provided a concise sketch of Nimrod's legend. According to Calmet, Nimrod

> was the first who began to monopolize power on the earth, and gave occasion to the proverb, "Like Nimrod, the great hunter before the Lord." His hunting was not only of wild beasts, but also to subdue men, to reduce them under his dominion. Ezekiel (xxxii.30. Vulg.) gives the name of hunters to all tyrants. The foundation of the empire of Nimrod was at Babylon; and, very probably, he was among the most eager undertakers of the tower of Babel.

He built Babylon at, or near, that famous tower, and from thence he extended his dominion over the neighboring countries, . . . when Nimrod had established the beginning of his empire at Babylon, and in the land of Shinar, he advanced towards Assyria, where he built powerful cities, as so many fortresses, to keep the people in subjection. . . . To Nimrod is imputed the invention of idolatrous worship paid to men.[78]

This recitation of traditions includes mostly familiar ideas:[79] Nimrod was the prototypical tyrant who invented idolatry and built a city and tower, around which he organized an expansionist empire.

In his *Commentary on the Whole Bible,* Matthew Henry transmitted even more of the interpretive tradition regarding Nimrod. According to Henry, Nimrod was

1. *A usurper:* "Nimrod was a violent invader of his neighbour's rights and properties, and a persecutor of innocent men, carrying all before him, and endeavoring to make all his own by force and violence."
2. *An idolator:* Like Jeroboam, Nimrod set up idolatry to consolidate his dominion. "That he might set up a new government, he set up a new religion upon the ruin of the primitive constitution of both."
3. *A hunter against the Lord:* "He carried on his oppression and violence in defiance of God . . . as if he and his huntsmen could outbrave the Almighty. . . ."
4. *A political sovereign:* He laid "the foundations of a monarchy, which was afterwards a head of gold, and the terror of the mighty, and bade fair to be universal. . . . See the antiquity of civil government, and particularly that form of it which lodges the sovereignty in a single person."[80]
5. *A cunning builder:* He was most likely the architect of Babel. When his project to rule the Noahides failed in the confusion of tongues, Nimrod left and built Ninevah.
6. *An object lesson in human ambition:* From Nimrod we learn that ambition is boundless, restless, expensive, and daring.
7. *A rebel:* "Nimrod's name signifies rebellion, which (if indeed he did abuse his power to the oppression of his neighbours) teaches us that tyrants to men are rebels to God, and their *rebellion is as the sin of witchcraft.*"[81]

Adam Clarke, the British divine who published his biblical commentary in the early nineteenth century, appears to have been another source for American versions of Nimrod's legend. Clarke reflects the conflicted attitude of Protestant commentators caught between text and tradition, writing that although the verses regarding Nimrod in Genesis 10 are not definite, "it is very likely he was a very *bad man.*" Clarke confirms that Nimrod's name derives from the Hebrew *marad*, "he rebelled"; that he was a warlike giant; that as an archrebel and apostate he was a principal instrument in the spread of idolatry; that his kingdom at Babel "appears to have been founded in apostasy from God, and to have been supported by tyranny, rapine and oppression"; and that Nimrod was among the tower's builders (perhaps assisted by giants like himself).[82] While failing to endorse Nimrod's entire legend, Clarke's text valorized the themes that animated the history of interpretation. And his portrait of Nimrod was painted with the broad strokes of condemnation that would characterize American versions of his legend. When this portrait is contemplated, there is only one response: "From the Nimrods of the earth, God deliver the world!"[83]

The strangest chapter in Nimrod's unauthorized biography is also the longest and most intricate. Its author is Alexander Hislop (1807–1865), a Scottish divine who in 1858 published *The Two Babylons, or Papal Worship Proved to be the Worship of Nimrod and His Wife*.[84] Hislop's goal in this exceedingly convoluted anti-Catholic tract was to demonstrate the "Babylonian character of the Papal Church" by uncovering the common "mysteries" uniting them. In Hislop's view, the Roman church had borrowed extensively from the "ancient Babylonian Mysteries," and in their chief objects of worship—the madonna and child—the two religions were virtually identical. On what basis does Hislop make this bizarre claim? First, he identifies Nimrod's father Cush with Bel the founder of Babylon and Nimrod himself with the Babylonian divine child Ninus. These associations are established on putative linguistic affinities, as well as the penchant for conquest shared by Nimrod and Ninus.[85]

And what sort of man was Nimrod? Hislop's answer draws to a great extent on the interpretive tradition he inherited. For instance, he contends that Nimrod led a band of "mighty ones," bent on invading neighboring peoples, and links him with Babylon and the Tower of Babel.[86] Nimrod's path to sovereignty is also quite familiar: Although he shattered the patriarchal system, Nimrod gained the loyalty of his subjects by taming and ordering the postdiluvian world:

> The amazing extent of the worship of this man indicates something very extraordinary in his character; and there is ample reason to believe, that in his own day he was an object of high popularity. Though by setting up as king, Nimrod invaded the patriarchal system, and abridged the liberties of mankind, yet he was held by many to have conferred benefits upon them, that amply indemnified them for the loss of their liberties, and covered him with glory and renown. By the time that he appeared, the wild beasts of the forest multiplying more rapidly than the human race, must have committed great depredations on the scattered and straggling populations of the earth, and must have inspired great terror into the minds of men. . . . The exploits of Nimrod, therefore, in hunting down the wild beasts of the field, and ridding the world of monsters, must have gained for him the character of a pre-eminent benefactor of his race. . . . [87]

Had Nimrod earned renown solely from his prowess as a hunter, all might have been well. But a pernicious effect on his fellows was soon evident in the religious sphere: "Not content with delivering men from the fear of wild beasts, he set to work also to emancipate them from that fear of the Lord which is the beginning of wisdom, and in which alone true happiness can be found."[88] His contemporaries came to view Nimrod as a great "Liberator" in that he had emancipated them from "the impressions of true religion"; in fact, however, he was an "Apostate" who led them in abandoning the primeval faith.[89] Nimrod convinced his followers to "put God and the strict spirituality of His law at a distance" and "to seek their chief good in sensual enjoyment."[90] It is no surprise to learn that Nimrod traveled with troops of women, accompanied by music, games, and revelries.

Hislop reports that in the midst of a "prosperous career of false religion and apostasy," Nimrod met a violent death. He was not crushed by his own tower, as some surmise, but slain by Noah's son Shem. With "resolution and unbounded ambition," Nimrod's wife Semiramis elevated him to a place in the Babylonian pantheon, and when his mystery cult was forced underground he was worshiped alternatively as Osiris, Tammuz, or Adonis. "Men were gradually led back to all the idolatry that had been publicly suppressed, while new features were added . . . that made it still more blasphemous than before."[91] When Nimrod's mystery religion of idolatry, prostitution, and human sacrifice emerged into the light of day centuries later, it took the form of Roman Catholicism.

Hislop's biography of Nimrod is distinctive in several respects. For instance, despite his interest in etymology, Hislop denies that Nimrod's name should be translated "to rebel." Although "there is no doubt that Nimrod *was* a rebel, and that his rebellion was celebrated in ancient myths," Hislop discounts the traditional derivation. Further, Hislop links Nimrod with the "Giants [who] rebelled against Heaven" (the *Nephilim* of Genesis 6?), identifying these behemoths with Nimrod and his party.[92] Hislop's drama is also notable for its casting of the members of Nimrod's family. Although he reveals little interest in Ham, Hislop does allege that he was "black . . . a negro . . . and the real original of the black Adversary of mankind, with horns and hoofs."[93] Meanwhile, Nimrod's father, Cush, ignored by the majority of commentators, is identified with Bel, the traditional founder of Babylon, and is assigned responsibility for fabricating the Tower of Babel, "the first act of open rebellion after the flood."[94] Cush is characterized as "a ringleader in the great apostasy," who had a "pre-eminent share in leading mankind away from the true worship of God."[95] Finally, Hislop pays considerable attention to Nimrod's consort Semiramis (associated with Diana, among others), whom he claims was deified in the Babylonian mysteries.

Conclusion

Briefly, let us sketch a composite portrait of Nimrod as he was imagined by European Bible readers through the middle of the nineteenth century. The dominant lines in this portrait appear in italics, the various subthemes as bullets:

Nimrod was a grandson of Ham through Cush.
Nimrod was a man of renown, stemming from:
- his prowess as a hunter
- his success as a leader
- his magical clothing

Nimrod was the first sovereign ruler:
- he was appointed by the descendants of Ham
- he usurped authority from the patriarchs
- he manipulated and intimidated common folk in order to introduce tyranny
- he assumed "just authority" under God's aegis

Nimrod was the world's first idolater:
- he introduced fire worship
- he established false religion
- he set himself up as a god
- he was taught esoteric knowledge by Noah's son Jonathan

Nimrod was a rebel:
- his name means "to rebel"
- he resisted God's wish that humanity disperse following the flood
- he rebelled against patriarchal authority

Nimrod built the Tower of Babel:
- over the mouth of hell
- as protection against a second flood
- as a means of ascending into heaven

Nimrod was responsible for the plurality of tongues:
- he was cursed with an inability to render intelligent speech
- he is an example of those who attempt to thwart God's will

Nimrod was "mighty":
- he was an imposing figure, perhaps a physical giant
- he may have been identical with ancient mythological figures, perhaps Bacchus, Osiris, or Hercules

Nimrod was a hunter:
- he was a warrior who fought wild beasts after the flood
- he "hunted" men, in the sense that he became a tyrant bent on conquest
- his success against wild beasts that threatened postdiluvian humanity contributed to his support among the people

Nimrod was a city builder:
- from his base in the plain of Shinar, he founded the major cities of Mesopotamia
- he was taught the art of statecraft by Noah's son Jonathan

Nimrod was an expansionist:
- he and his minions spread into areas reserved for others
- he invaded the territory allotted to Shem
- he thus became "lord of all Asia" and the archetypal imperial ruler

Nimrod symbolizes ill-directed ambition:
- his tower is a monument to human vanity
- he is an emblem of human pride and rebellion
- he is the type of all who pursue earthly glory

Nimrod was an agent of Satan:
- he defied God and led others to do the same
- he encouraged human beings to believe they were self-sufficient
- he created a mystery religion instigated by Satan
- he symbolizes the despotism of Rome, the new Babylon

Nimrod was black:
- his grandfather Ham was the first Negro
- his father Cush was the ancestor of Ethiopians
- he personifies human nature's darker side

American chapters in Nimrod's unauthorized biography are the focus of chapter 6. As we shall see, while American Bible readers utilized most of the themes in the portrait of Nimrod they inherited, they made their own contributions as well.

II

HONOR AND ORDER

4

Original Dishonor

Noah's Curse and the Southern Defense of Slavery

And Noah began to be an husbandman, and he planted a
vineyard: 21. And he drank of the wine, and was drunken;
and he was uncovered within his tent. And Ham, the father of Canaan, saw the nakedness of his father, and told
his two brethren without. And Shem and Japheth took a
garment, and laid it upon both their shoulders and went
backward, and covered the nakedness of their father; and
their faces were backward, and they saw not their father's
nakedness. And Noah awoke from his wine, and knew
what his younger son had done unto him. And he said,
Cursed be Canaan; a servant of servants shall he be unto
his brethren. And he said, Blessed be the LORD God of
Shem; and Canaan shall be his servant. God shall enlarge
Japheth, and he shall dwell in the tents of Shem; and Canaan shall be his servant.

Genesis 9:20–27

SO READS Genesis 9:20–27 in the King James Version of the Bible, the English
translation in which antebellum Americans encountered the story of Noah's
drunkenness. This chapter explores the various ways nineteenth-century
American advocates of slavery utilized the story to defend the institution of
slavery. It illumines the peculiar manner in which Genesis 9 was read by
proslavery intellectuals (particularly between 1830 and 1865). And it suggests
how this distinctive chapter in the history of biblical interpretation confirms

the centrality of honor in the white Southern mind. In the process, it prob-
lematizes the view that Old South racism was a projection of white sexual
fears and fantasies. Beginning with nineteenth-century abolitionists, who regarded the South as a modern-day Sodom in which "men could indulge their
erotic impulses with impunity,"[1] the proslavery argument has been perceived
as a rationale for dominance and sexual transgression. But careful study of
the way Genesis 9 was read in antebellum America indicates that proslavery
intellectuals were at least as deeply concerned with honor and dishonor as
with sex and power.

Noah's Curse and Southern Honor

Once light was shed on the role of honor in the Southern psyche, it was
inevitable that it would illuminate the institution the Southern mind sought
hardest to protect.[2] However, attempts to clarify the nexus between honor,
slavery, and its religious defense are conspicuously absent from scholarly discourse. Although it is acknowledged that the so-called curse of Ham was the
religious rationale for slavery invoked most frequently by antebellum Southerners,[3] scholarship has failed to explicate the curse's American reception.
Why have studies of American slavery ignored the link between antebellum
readings of Genesis 9 and Southern honor?

    One contributing factor has been disciplinary specialization. Just as his-
torians often reveal a superficial knowledge of the Bible or a tendency to
introduce extratextual assumptions,[4] scholars of religion are typically unaware
of the vast literature on Southern culture and its implications for interpreting
documents of the antebellum period. In addition, those in both groups have
failed to properly consider Genesis 9's history of interpretation and thus have
overlooked the distinctive ways antebellum advocates of the curse read the
story of Noah and his sons. Another explanation for the failure of academics
to thoroughly explore proslavery readings of Genesis 9 is the assumption that
doing so is wasted effort, in that anyone claiming to find a justification for
chattel slavery in the pages of the Bible must be of limited intelligence, grave
foolishness, or profound insincerity. This assumption is widely held among
scholars, even though it is contradicted by several known facts: Antebellum
advocates of the curse included respected professionals such as doctors, law-
yers, politicians, clergymen, and professors; these men were, relatively speaking, well educated; and although it is not possible to ascertain their motives
in writing about the curse, they appear to be as sincere on this topic as on
the others they addressed. These things were particularly true of proslavery
divines.[5]

    Whatever the reasons, scholars of history and religion alike have failed
to comprehend that proslavery Southerners were drawn to Genesis 9:20–27
because it resonated with their deepest cultural values. This chapter begins

with what is known—that for Southern proslavery intellectuals Ham's act of gazing on his father's nakedness and Noah's subsequent curse of the descendants of Ham and Canaan to be "servants of servants" were held to be definitive proof that the enslavement of black Africans was God's will—and it poses a heretofore unexamined question: Precisely how did proslavery men read this story, and why? The answer offered is that, almost invariably, white Bible readers understood the transgression as a violation of familial loyalty that marked Ham and his African descendants as utterly devoid of honor and thus fit for slavery. In other words, proslavery Americans were unconsciously drawn to the tale of Noah's drunkenness because it cast slavery's origins in an episode of primal dishonor.

Reviewing the History of Interpretation

Chapter 2 showed that vilification of Ham has been the leitmotif in Genesis 9's history of interpretation and that the interpretive imagination has known few limits in denigrating Noah's youngest son. This praxis of vilification is a function of clues within the text, as well as what readers have brought to it— namely, a desire to make Ham's crime fit the punishment meted out by his father and the conviction that humanity's sinful tendencies must have their origin in Noah's family. Thus, for over two millennia Bible readers have blamed Ham and his progeny for everything from the existence of slavery and serfdom, to the perpetuation of sexual license and perversion, to the introduction of magical arts, astrology, idolatry, witchcraft, and heathen religion. They have associated Hamites with tyranny, theft, heresy, blasphemy, rebellion, war, and even deicide. Benjamin Braude's observation that during the Middle Ages Ham was "an archetypal Other, the example of qualities not to be emulated,"[6] could be fairly applied to the entire history of interpretation.

Among the various forms of ignominy applied to Ham through the ages, sexual themes have dominated. Sexual commentary is invited by verse 24 ("And Noah awoke from his wine, and knew what his younger son had done unto him," KJV), a statement that, despite its ambiguity, "leads the reader to resolve that something sexual has transpired."[7] In response to this textual provocation, Bible readers have figured Ham's transgression as attempted rape or castration of his father, as incest with his mother (an act that produced Canaan, perhaps), as willful violation of Noah's policy of celibacy on the ark, or as some combination of these heinous acts. As was demonstrated in chapter 2 images of Ham "brimming with sexuality"[8] animate rabbinic comments, the writings of church fathers, medieval legends, Renaissance art and drama, and biblical commentary. Even modern Bible scholarship has contributed to the remarkable longevity enjoyed by sexual readings of Genesis 9. These are encouraged by historical-critical inquiry (which suggests that the story is an etiological tale explaining Canaanite sexual practices the ancient Israelites found abhorrent), as well as by canon criticism.[9]

Charges that Ham was guilty of filial disobedience, disrespect, or irreverence also appear throughout the history of interpretation. However, these themes rarely displace other forms of vilification. The same rabbis who allege that Ham spoke "disrespectful words against his father" also charge that he "added to his sin of irreverence the still greater outrage of attempting to perform an operation upon his father designed to prevent procreation." Likewise, Martin Luther, while condemning Ham's disobedience, attributes his filial disrespect to "a satanic and bitter hatred" and associates Ham with idolatry, tyranny, and rebellion. The conviction that Ham's trespass was failure to honor his father—and nothing more—was apparently first advanced in the sixteenth century by John Calvin. This reading of the story, which may reflect the Renaissance emphasis on personal honor,[10] was adopted by a number of European commentators between the sixteenth and nineteenth centuries. For instance, seventeenth-century English exegete Jeremy Taylor opined that God had "consigned a sad example that for ever children should be afraid to dishonour their parents, and discover their nakedness, or reveal their turpitude, their follies and dishonours." Similarly, Sir Edward Coke wrote that "Bondage or Servitude was first inflicted for dishonouring of Parents: For Cham the Father of Canaan . . . seeing the Nakedness of his Father Noah, and shewing it in Derision to his Brethren, was therefore punished in his Son Canaan with Bondage."[11]

Still, given the conscious and unconscious forces that impinged on antebellum interpreters of Genesis 9—the biblical text's invitation to view Ham as a sexual offender or voyeur, the need to identify a crime commensurate with Noah's punishment, and the prominence of sexual themes in the history of interpretation—we should expect a thorough sexualization of the story among Bible readers who wished to sanction the enslavement of Ham's putative offspring. Further, given the general propensity to view members of marginalized groups as sexual predators, a sexualized Ham would be doubly attractive to members of the Southern Bible-reading elite. Conversely, if the white minority's intellectual vanguard failed to exploit the sexual clues in the text and the interpretive tradition, it must be because they found some other explanation of Ham's iniquity more compelling, more damning, more intimately related to the condition of slavery.

Antebellum Readings of Genesis 9 and the Interpretive Tradition

Because American defenders of slavery rarely cited exegetical authorities, it is difficult to determine how much, if at all, they were influenced by the interpretive traditions that developed around the story of Noah and his sons. On one hand, they seem unaware and uninterested in specific traditions that cast Ham as sexual offender, heretic, blasphemer, magician, father of idolaters, archrebel, and friend of demons. And they are largely silent regarding Ham's conduct on the ark, his career following the Flood, his religious legacy, and his standing with God and Satan. On the other hand, proslavery readings of Genesis 9 adhere strictly to the paradigm of orthodox interpretation that had developed over the centuries. The parameters of this paradigm were Noah's exaltation as a righteous and obedient patriarch and Ham's deprecation as a worthless son, both of which were axiomatic in antebellum America. If anything, proslavery Southerners surpassed the interpretive tradition in venerating Noah, who in their eyes was not only God's regent in the postdiluvian world but also the patron saint of plantation life.[12] And because they strained to identify some behavior that merited a severe punishment among Ham's putative descendants, American proslavery intellectuals were quite at home in an interpretive tradition that had developed defamation into an art form.

Despite their interest in extending the chief trajectories of the tradition, however, proslavery Bible readers represent a conspicuous departure from the history of interpretation. Quite simply, one searches in vain among their comments on Genesis 9 for an explicit statement that Ham's transgression was in any way sexual.[13] Even as proslavery propagandists strain to identify a crime warranting eternal servitude, they inexplicably refuse to take refuge in the ignominy of sexual assault. A typical example is John Bell Robinson, who, while charging that "Ham's crime was a thousand times more flagitious [than Adam's]," does not give any indication how this heinous crime is to be understood.[14] The lone exception to this generalization—an exception that effectively proves the rule—is Josiah Priest, whose *Slavery as It Relates to the Negro or African Race* (1843) was widely read in America prior to the Civil War. Priest not only dwells on Ham's career and disposition but also serves up the seamy details of his crime against Noah, retrieving the early modern tradition that Ham's outrage may have been incest with his mother.

> It is believed by some, and not without reason, that [the crime of Ham] did not consist alone in the seeing his father's nakedness as a *man*, but rather in the abuse and actual violation of his own mother.
>
> This opinion is strengthened by a passage found in Levit. xviii. 8, as follows: "The nakedness of thy father's wife shalt thou not uncover: it is thy *father's* nakedness." On account of this passage, it has been believed that the crime of Ham did not consist alone of seeing his father in an improper manner, but rather of his own mother, the wife of Noah, and violating her.
>
> If this was so, how much more horrible, therefore, appears the character of Ham, and how much more deserving the *curse*, which was laid upon him and his race, of whom it was foreseen that they would be like *this*, their lewd ancestor.[15]

Priest's defamation of Noah's son extends beyond the charge of sexual impropriety; yet the incident is regarded as constitutive of Ham's character and predictive of Hamite destiny.[16] It is easy to understand why Priest portrayed Ham as a sexual reprobate, for this portrait was sketched in the biblical text and fleshed out in the history of interpretation. What is puzzling—especially considering the influence Priest enjoyed in the antebellum South,[17] white conceptions of the "lascivious African," and popular notions that blacks were more "sensuous" than intellectual, naturally lewd, and in possession of unusually large sex organs[18]—is that the proslavery tracts that proliferated in the 1840s and 1850s did not emulate Priest in exploiting the theme of sexual aggression.

Absent this theme and its powerful leitmotif of vilification, how did proslavery intellectuals sufficiently impugn the character they regarded as the father of the African race? The answer is hinted at in Priest's own reading of Genesis 9, which depicts Shem and Japheth as gentlemen who behave toward their father in a "delicate and thoughtful manner" before retiring in silence and refers to Ham's descendants as occupying "the lowest condition of all the families among mankind . . . [as] a despised, a degraded, and an oppressed race." The dynamics of honor and dishonor in Noah's family alluded to by Priest were reflected in dozens of proslavery publications during the second third of the nineteenth century.

Varieties of Interpretation in the Antebellum South

If we examine antebellum proslavery treatises in terms of how they treat Genesis 9:20–27, three categories of interpretation can be discerned. The majority cite the story (as both a biblical justification for slavery and a historical account of servitude's introduction in the postdiluvian world) but do not relate or analyze it. Texts in a second group cite the story as a rationale for slavery and in the process paraphrase or recount it, but they do not characterize the offense for which Ham or Canaan is condemned. A third collection of texts analyze or retell the story, in the process describing or intimating the nature of Ham's misdeed.

Texts in the first and largest category are of interest inasmuch as they confirm the central role of Noah's curse in the antebellum proslavery argument. Though many are secular in orientation, these texts confirm that the great majority of slavery's defenders felt obliged to invoke the curse, and they substantiate abolitionist Theodore Weld's oft-cited claim that "this prophecy of Noah is the *vade mecum* of slaveholders, and they never venture abroad without it." Representative of these tracts is James Smylie's *Review of a Letter from the Presbytery of Chillicothe, to the Presbytery of Mississippi, on the Subject of Slavery,* published in 1836. Introducing the Old Testament evidence for his scriptural proslavery argument, Smylie wrote that "it appears, from Genesis ix, 25, 26, and 27, that when there was but one family on the face of the earth, a part of that family was doomed, by the father Noah, to become slaves to the others. That part was the posterity of Ham, from whom, it is supposed, sprung the Africans."[19] Reflecting a similar lack of interest in the details of the story is an address delivered in 1818 by Senator William Smith of South Carolina, who averred that "Ham sinned against his God and against his father" but failed to describe the violation in any way.[20]

Texts in the second category—those that paraphrase or recount Genesis 9:20–27 without enumerating Ham or Canaan's offense—serve two functions. In addition to validating the curse's role in the defense of slavery, they reveal that proslavery authors did not feel obliged to delineate Ham's crime in order to commend the curse to American readers. Typical of texts in this group is *The Christian Doctrine of Slavery* (1857) by Virginia Presbyterian George D. Armstrong, who writes that "it was in consequence of sin, in part actually committed, and yet more foreseen in the future that the first slave sentence of which we have any record was pronounced by Noah upon Canaan and his descendants."[21] Even Baptist J. L. Dagg, author of a proslavery textbook prepared to rival Francis Wayland's *The Elements of Moral Science*,[22] does not offer a definite reading of Ham's offense. In exploring slavery's origins, Dagg observes that the "curse was denounced by the patriarch Noah, because of a crime committed by his son Ham, the father of Canaan. . . . [The words of Noah] are a denunciation of God's displeasure at the sin of Ham, and an explanation of the degradation which has fallen on his posterity."[23] Yet despite his stated goal of defending the *moral* rectitude of slavery, Dagg fails to identify Ham's "crime" or "sin."

Frederick Dalcho, whose *Practical Considerations Founded on the Scriptures Relative to the Slave Population of South-Carolina* appeared in Charleston in 1823,[24] is another advocate of the curse who remains mute on the nature of Ham's transgression. The Bible teaches, according to Dalcho, that human beings lost immortality through disobedience and sin. "And, perhaps, we shall find," he continues, "that the negroes, the descendants of Ham, lost their freedom through the abominable wickedness of their progenitor." Although this "abominable wickedness" is not further enumerated, Dalcho claims that Noah's malediction encompassed "Canaan's whole race . . . [who] were peculiarly wicked, and obnoxious to the wrath of God."[25] In 1852, Louisianan John Fletcher related the tale of Noah's drunkenness with a passing reference to "the ill-manners of Ham towards his father" but supplied no clues for interpreting this phrase.[26] A *Defence of Virginia*, published in 1867 by Presbyterian Robert L. Dabney, characterized Ham and his descendants as "wicked," "depraved," and "degraded in morals," referred to "the indecent and unnatural sin of Ham," and described slavery as God's "punishment of, and remedy for . . . the peculiar moral degradation of a part of the race." Still, Dabney's text fails to illumine the offense(s) for which it holds Ham responsible.[27]

It is texts in the third group—those that communicate the nature of Ham's indignity—that clarify the distinctive way Genesis 9:20–27 was read by

antebellum proslavery authors. The silver thread that ties together these readings of Genesis 9 is the assumption that in reacting to Noah's shame Ham
revealed a fundamentally dishonorable character. Renditions of the curse in
this category traffic in standard images of violated honor, including (1) the
statement or implication that Noah is deserving of honor, a fact unaltered by
his temporary disgrace; (2) the notion that by dishonoring or shaming his
father, Ham divulged his own dishonorable character; (3) the assumption that
Ham's dishonorable behavior constitutes a serious offense, the one for which
he (or his son Canaan) is cursed; (4) the contrasting of Ham's conduct with
the respectful and dutiful action of Shem and Japheth; and (5) the prediction
of future degradation or "social death"[28] for the descendants of Ham or Canaan, who are destined to reflect this condition through forced servitude until
the world is redeemed from the effects of sin.

Perhaps the most explicit honor-bound reading of Genesis 9 to appear
in antebellum America was published in 1860 in an anonymous pamphlet
titled *African Servitude*. Preparing readers for his discussion of the curse, the
pamphlet's author avers that "the family was instituted by God," who gave to
its head "great power and corresponding honor and responsibility." Following
the flood, Noah received from God "directions for the government of the
world." Then,

> Noah became a husbandman, planted a vineyard, and partaking too freely
> of the fruit of the vine, exposed himself to *shame*. The Scriptures do not
> state that he was guilty of anything more than an act of imprudence. In his
> exposed state he was discovered by his younger son, probably his grandson
> Canaan, who informed his father Ham, and one or both of them, so far
> from feeling or expressing grief for the dishonor of their parent, exultingly
> informed others of it, glorying in his shame, despising his power and au-
> thority, and his office as ruler and priest of God to them and the rest of
> their father's family, lightly esteeming also his parental blessing, as well as
> the blessing of God.
>
>   A true spirit of filial regard, love, honor and obedience moved Shem
> and Japheth to protect their father; just the reverse of that which influenced
> their brother Ham to dishonor him. On the part of the former, it was an
> act of faith; of the latter, unbelief. . . . [Ham] knew that God had chosen his
> father as the honored head of the human family, declaring him faithful, and
> communicating to him his designs. . . . In refusing to honor his parent, he
> refused to honor all governors, natural civil, ecclesiastical, human, and di-
> vine. The sin was a representative one, and, under the circumstances, it was
> no light one in Ham and his son. It manifested in them no love for their
> parent, but an evil heart of unbelief toward God.[29]

According to the author of *African Servitude*, Ham lost his position in the
great human family as a result of his "lack of faith, his sinful conduct of
defection." Ham "broke the first command on the second table, by scorning
and deriding his father, the legal consequences of which seems to be death of

his body, or the forfeiture of it for the benefit of others."[30] With the language of "honor," "dishonor," and "shame" and the contention that Ham's primal dishonor resulted in social death ("death of his body, or the forfeiture of it for the benefit of others") *African Servitude* inextricably links honor and slavery in its treatment of Genesis 9:20–27.

Another proslavery text that utilizes the vocabulary of honor in describing the relationship of Noah and his sons is *Dominion; or, the Unity and Trinity of the Human Race* (1858) by Tennessee clergyman Samuel Davies Baldwin.[31] In this five-hundred-page expatiation on Noah's prophecy (regarded by the author as a "divine political constitution of the world"), Baldwin expounds the divine plan for the three "races" that inhabit the earth. Ham has been condemned to endure "the humility of bondage," but for what reason? Baldwin notes "Ham's vile deportment toward his father," alleges that he was a "source of shame" to the patriarch, and intimates that Noah's curse befell him for the sins of "filial dishonor," "mocking or making light of a parent," and "base and shameless conduct." At one point, Baldwin pauses to remark on the perception that Noah's response is incommensurate with Ham's transgression:

> Filial dishonor is not regarded as a heinous offence by civil law; and many moralists, unconsciously governed by mere human statutes in their estimate of guilt, seem to look at Ham's wickedness as venial. Viewed, however, in the light of revelation, it is more obnoxious to censure and punishment than theft, forgery, or falsehood, and stands before them in importance in the graduated scale of the Decalogue.[32]

It may be debated whether Baldwin's standard for judgment is "revelation" or the interests of slave culture, but it is clear that his understanding of Genesis 9 hinges on Ham's presumed dishonor toward his father.

A similar reading of the biblical story is offered in *The Great Question Answered* (1857) by Mississippi Presbyterian James A. Sloan.[33] Sloan locates in Genesis 9 both the origin of human diversity and the basis for "the subordination of one portion of the human family to that of another." In recounting the biblical tale, Sloan censures Ham who,

> instead of concealing the matter [of his father's nakedness], as both decency and respect for his father should have directed, his bad disposition led him to give vent to his sinful feelings, and wishing his brothers to have a part of his unseemly enjoyment, he "told it to his two brothers without." Shem and Japheth did not enter into this improper and sinful sport of their brother, but took means to hide the shame of their father, and adopted a plan to accomplish that end which manifested the greatest respect for their parent, and at the same time, the feelings of refined delicacy toward their erring father. . . . [34]

The honor-bound character of Sloan's exegesis is indicated not only by his use of terms such as *decency, shame, respect,* and *refine*[ment] but also the

claim that Ham's dishonor warrants his social death. Sloan contends that
"Ham's conduct really deserved death. 'Honor thy father and thy mother, that
thy days may be long in the land which the Lord they God giveth thee.'—
Exodus XX:12. Such is the express law of God; and passages bearing on this
point are found scattered throughout both the Old and New Testaments. . . ."
In making death a meet punishment for dishonor and servitude an acceptable
substitute, Sloan elucidates the nexus between honor and the social death of
slavery.[35]

H. O. R., anonymous author of *The Governing Race* (1860), also proffers
an honor-bound reading of Genesis 9. H. O. R. notes that the "awful scene"
involving Noah and Ham is actually the third instance in Genesis where God
chastises a portion of the human race in retribution for sin. But what is the
nature of this outrage, "more wicked in its inception, more polluting in its
nature than the fratricide of Cain"? According to *The Governing Race,* Ham
is guilty of "dishonoring his father"; in contrast, Shem and Japheth exemplify
"chaste reverence and filial obedience" by refusing to succumb to Ham's
"wicked temptation of dishonoring . . . their father."[36]

Reading Honor

Recognizing the dynamics of honor and shame in antebellum readings of
Genesis 9:20–27 can aid us in interpreting proslavery tracts in the second
category—those that paraphrase or recount Genesis 9:20–27 but fail to describe Ham's transgression. Typical of texts in this group is Georgian Howell
Cobb's *A Scriptural Examination of the Institution of Slavery in the United
States* (1856), which argues that slavery was established as a penalty for the
transgression related in Genesis 9 but does not reveal what "sin" Ham committed. The nature of Ham's "reprehensible" conduct toward his father must
be inferred from Cobb's observation that "the text does not warrant the conclusion that Canaan participated in the mirth or contempt which the discovery
of Noah's condition occasioned." And thus, "The whole prophecy must be
taken together—Shem and Japheth had shown a virtuous regard for their
father; that virtue manifested itself in their posterity—it was that virtue that
was blessed. On the contrary, Ham's conduct was vicious (vice in his posterity
has ever been their most marked characteristic)—it was that viciousness that
was cursed, and which has been punished in so peculiar a manner."[37] Although
Cobb provides little evidence for characterizing Ham's "vicious" conduct, we
may conclude that his interpretation of the curse is honor-bound, because it
hinges on a contrast between Ham's "contempt" and his brothers' "virtuous
regard" for their father.

Once the central role of honor in proslavery readings of Genesis 9 has
been grasped, it is possible to make sense of otherwise puzzling treatments of
the story. Undeveloped comments—that Ham's waywardness consisted of "ex-

posing his father's shame"; that Ham "failed to cover his father. . . . This was the amount of his fault. The failure left Noah exposed to the gaze of others"; that Shem and Japheth "covered their father in a way that evinced ingenuity and delicacy in a very high degree"[38]—can be confidently read as intimations that Ham's crime was his failure to behave honorably toward his father.

The authors surveyed to this point are all Southerners. Yet honor-bound readings of Genesis 9 were common among proslavery Northerners as well. For instance, Pennsylvania Methodist John Bell Robinson alleged that Genesis 9 demonstrates "the duty of children to parents under every circumstance of this life"—that is, their duty to honor parents even if parents act dishonorably. In Robinson's view, Noah's curse represents God's judgment on Ham's crime against "the old patriarch, who was [his] temporal parent." Shem and Japheth, by contrast, acted "as every good child would. Therefore a blessing was pronounced upon them."[39] Robinson observes that among the story's lessons is that "children must be respectful to their parents in and under all circumstances in this life. One of the commandments says, 'Honor thy father and thy mother; that thy days may be long upon the land which the Lord they God giveth thee.'—Ex. xx.12. . . ."[40]

Robinson reveals the organic bond in proslavery thought between filial disobedience, dishonor, and slavery when he remarks that "if Ham and his son Canaan had been true to their father and grand-father, there would have been no slaves nor negroes in this world of ours."[41] He goes on to describe the consequences of Ham's dishonor as a sort of living death in which his descendants "are marks of the displeasure of the Divine being toward the disobedience of children to their parents, and they are this day moving, living, hearing and talking monuments of his displeasure towards disobedient children to parents."[42] For this honor-bound reader of Genesis 9, American slaves are emblems of God's displeasure, living embodiments of dishonor.

John H. Hopkins of Vermont is another Northerner whose reception of Genesis 9 is infused with the dynamics of honor.[43] Hopkins observes that "the first appearance of slavery in the Bible is the wonderful prediction of the patriarch Noah: "Cursed be Canaan . . ." (Gen 9:25)." Commenting on the story, he supposes that "Ham became disrespectful and irreverent toward his father, and trained his children in a course which, of all others, is most hateful in the eyes of that God, who commands that HONOR must be given to the father and the mother."[44] Although Ham's behavior was the immediate occasion for Noah's prophecy, its fulfillment was reserved for his posterity, "after they had lost the knowledge of God, and become utterly polluted by the abominations of heathen idolatry. The Almighty foreordained them to servitude or slavery . . . doubtless because he *judged it to be their fittest condition.* And all history proves how accurately the prediction has been accomplished, even to the present day."[45] Hopkins's reading is somewhat atypical for antebellum America, reflecting as it does the patristic tradition that Ham's posterity fell into "groveling idolatry." Nevertheless, it is honor-bound inasmuch as it depicts Ham's transgression as "heartless irreverence . . . toward his eminent parent," and connects slavery with the degraded "condition" to which Ham's descendants sank following the episode narrated in Genesis 9.

Perhaps the most notorious proslavery propagandist of the antebellum period was New Yorker Josiah Priest, whose *Slavery as It Relates to the Negro or African Race* (1843) was reprinted eight times during a five year period. Curiously, although Priest thoroughly sexualized Ham's offense, he nevertheless found in the story a serious violation of honor. For instance, Priest argued that "the Patriarch was deeply grieved on account of the reckless impiety of Ham" and concluded his rendition of the episode by remarking:

> On the subject of a child's treating its parents with intended disrespect, see the opinion of God himself, Deut. xxvii, 16, who, in that place says, "CURSED be he that setteth light by his father or his mother, and all the people shall say amen." This sin, the treating a father or mother disrespectfully, was, by the law of Moses, punished with death. See Deut. xxi, 18, 19, 20, 21. Consequently, according to this law, Ham was morally worthy of death.[46]

As if to cover all the bases in his vilification of Ham, Priest included many of the elements of honor-bound interpretation described previously.

Finally, there is evidence that even antebellum authors opposed to slavery instinctively viewed Genesis 9 through the lens of honor. The best example is Joseph P. Thompson's *Teachings of the New Testament on Slavery* (1856). While ostensibly treating the New Testament, this antislavery tract includes a three-page section on the "curse of Ham." Thompson takes pains to show that Noah's curse fell only on Canaan and was fulfilled in the Canaanites' subjection by Israel "900 years after." Still, he regards the encounter of Ham and Noah as an affair of honor: "You, my youngest son, have put me to shame before your brethren; you shall feel the punishment of this in the degradation of your youngest son; he shall be put to shame before his brethren, and his posterity shall feel in their bones the curse of their dishonored ancestor."[47]

The proliferation in antebellum America of honor-bound interpretations of Genesis 9 indicates that proslavery tracts from this period that fail to describe Ham's offense are not silent because their authors regarded his transgression as inconsequential but because author and implied reader alike assumed it to have been an egregious violation of honor. As the tale of Noah and his sons came to function as a myth of origins for slaveholding culture, honor was the spirit that animated antebellum reception of the curse. The influence of this dominant reading made it increasingly unnecessary for expositors to state the obvious.

Alternative Explanations

I have made the case that antebellum proslavery writers did not sexualize Ham's behavior because they instinctively viewed his "sin" as a violation of honor; that because these authors regarded Ham's shameful act with dreadful seriousness, they did not resort to other species of vilification; and that the charge of dishonor bore in the white mind a convenient relation to the social death of slavery. But perhaps there are other explanations for the distinctive way antebellum slavery advocates interpreted Genesis 9.

One alternative is that proslavery intellectuals eschewed sexualized readings of Genesis 9 because, unlike the rabbis and church fathers who developed and transmitted them, they felt obliged to interpret the biblical text as literally as possible.[48] The difficulty with this argument is that, as abolitionists never tired of pointing out, proslavery intellectuals did not read Genesis 9:20–27 in the literal sense. If they had, they would have been forced to acknowledge that Noah's curse was aimed at Canaan, not Ham, and that according to Genesis 10's Table of Nations Canaan had no connection to Africa. If their commitment to "literalism" did nothing to deter proslavery interpreters from assuming that Noah's curse applied to Ham, that Ham was the father of sub-Saharan Africans, and that the curse was perpetual, it is difficult to understand how it would deter them from vilifying Ham as a sexual offender.

Another possible explanation for the conspicuous absence of sexual themes in antebellum glosses of Genesis 9 is that proslavery authors feared contravening the Victorian sensibilities of white Bible readers. Although this argument seems plausible, it, too, is plagued by difficulties. For instance, earlier interpreters of the story had successfully avoided the details of Ham's nefarious act, while intimating its sexual nature.[49] Furthermore, nineteenth-century gentlemen frequently extended the bounds of good taste to exploit white fears of black sexual aggression. Scholars since W. J. Cash have noted Southern whites' phobic concern with slave insurrections and with the sexual violence they imagined would befall white women if slaves successfully rebelled. Southern Presbyterians, among the more genteel of the region's Protestants, went on record as opposing recognition of slave marriages because, as they put it, no legal remedies would control the "deplorable sensuality of our Africans."[50]

Finally, the "Victorian sensibility" argument would have to convince us that antebellum prudishness was sufficient to counteract the biblical, cultural, and historical factors that invited a sexual reading of Ham's offense. If the history of interpretation is any guide, textual cues alone have led many Bible readers to infer a sexual encounter between Ham and Noah. When we go on to consider the cultural forces that would impinge upon interpretation of this text in antebellum America—including the hoary tradition that cast Ham as a Promethean sexual force, a similar view of Africans widespread in the Old South, and the tendency for majority cultures to attribute deviant sexual practices to racial and ethnic minorities[51]—it is really quite remarkable that sex does not animate at least a minority of proslavery readings of Genesis 9. As Lillian Smith noted so forcefully in *Killers of the Dream*, the Negro, sex, and the body have been inextricably bound in the Southern mind.[52] The unlikelihood that fear of offending readers would completely obscure this bond in antebellum readings of the curse is underscored by the reappearance of sexual themes in twentieth-century invocations of Noah's curse among white Americans.

Genesis 9 and the Nature of Southern Honor

To this point, we have considered how antebellum advocates of Ham's curse *might* have read the story of Noah and his sons (by briefly reviewing Genesis 9's history of interpretation), and we have examined the ways they *did* read it (by carefully analyzing proslavery renditions of the curse). We turn now to explore *why* these men interpreted Genesis 9:20–27 in the manner they did. What factors, in other words, contributed to the predominance of honor readings of Genesis 9 among American proslavery intellectuals?

Based on our survey of the text's history of interpretation, we cannot rule out the possibility that some proslavery divines were directly influenced by John Calvin or his epigones. But, of course, not all advocates of the curse were Calvinists, nor can it be assumed that those who were knew Calvin's exegesis of this passage.[53] Further, although Calvin did read Genesis 9 from the perspective of honor, he neither invoked the passage to justify the enslavement of human beings nor made the dishonorable Ham a representative of his biological descendants. Another explanation is that the code of honor and shame inscribed in the Hebrew Bible determined the American perception of violated honor in Genesis 9.[54] As Julian Pitt-Rivers notes, in all cultures of honor "the private parts are the seat of shame, vulnerable to the public view and represented symbolically in the gestures and verbal expressions of desecration . . . as the means of procreation they are intimately connected with honor, for they signify the extension of the self in time."[55] Bertram Wyatt-Brown shows that in the vortex of the secessionist crisis, Southern clergy easily adopted an idiom of honor that was familiar in both the Hebraic and Christian traditions. This was in part, he argues, because of the affinity between ancient Israelite culture and their own. In particular, "the Old Testament rendering of honor endured among southerners accustomed to face-to-face, small-scale, family oriented usages that bore analogy with the pastoral society that produced the Holy Word."[56]

But a nuanced assessment of the forces driving honor readings of Genesis 9 requires that we consider not only Bible readers and their texts but also the world that shaped their reading. How does scholarship on Southern culture illumine proslavery intellectuals' identification with the culture of honor, and how this might have affected their reception of Noah's curse? First, this scholarship confirms the essential place of honor in the Southern mind. As John Hope Franklin wrote in 1956, "while the concept of honor was an intangible thing, it was no less real to the Southerner than the most mundane commodity that he possessed. . . . To him nothing was more important than honor. Indeed, he placed it above wealth, art, learning, and the other 'delicacies' of an urban civilization and regarded its protection as a continuing preoccupation."[57] Honor "entered the very texture of upbringing" as Southern males were socialized into "the most elaborate and deliberately articulated timocracy of modern times."[58] Clement Eaton observes that the Southern culture of honor flourished in the second quarter of the nineteenth century, precisely when the majority of proslavery treatises were published. It did so in response to "strong political and external forces . . . operating on the Southern psyche," including abolitionism, which led Southerners to idealize their society and portray slave masters as "paternal, high-minded and honorable gentlemen."[59] Thus, the abolitionist attack on the South's peculiar institution not only impelled Southerners to embrace moral and biblical justifications for slavery but also heightened their attraction to honor and thus increased the likelihood that they would interpret Genesis 9 in honor-bound fashion.

In addition, honor scholarship reminds us that many Southern slaveholders regarded themselves as patriarchs in the tradition of Noah, men who demanded filial respect from family members and slaves alike. As Charlestonian Christopher Memminger explained in 1835: "The Slave Institution at the South increases her tendency to dignify the family. Each planter in fact is a Patriarch—his position compels him to be a ruler in his household. . . ."[60] Michael P. Johnston writes that while "few families attained the patriarchal ideal, many approached it."[61] The patriarchal conception of slavery was "familial proprietorship, in which reciprocal, parent-child obligations and affections gave meaning to those involved." Southern men "championed a form of slaveholding that extended the protective authority of a loving father over the entire household of whites and blacks."[62] When we compass the fact that "Christian patriarchalism remained the keystone of proslavery thought,"[63] it is easier to appreciate the appeal of a biblical text in which agricultural life, the patriarchal family, and the imposition of slavery were believed to originate.

Honor scholarship also aids us in imagining how men of honor might have reacted to the shame associated with Noah's inebriation and disrobing. As Bertram Wyatt-Brown comments, the greatest dread imagined by adherents of honor was "the fear of public humiliation," especially when it involved "bodily appearance [that] was an outward sign of inner merit." Noting that cultures concerned with honor highly value appearance, Kenneth Greenberg adds that a momentous form of dishonor in the Old South was the shaming of an opponent through unmasking him "to identify an image as falsely projected and to show contempt for it." In light of these observations, we can imagine how men of honor might perceive Noah's shame: Just as Jefferson Davis was notoriously unmasked by Federal soldiers at the conclusion of the Civil War, Noah is figuratively stripped under Ham's gaze, while his brothers reclothe their father in an attempt to preserve his threatened honor.[64] We can also discern why Ham's broadcast of Noah's condition became a crucial part of the biblical story among proslavery interpreters. If in the Old South "an affront [to honor] depend[ed] upon being made public," naturally Ham's report to "his two brethren without" would be highlighted in honor-bound readings of Genesis 9.[65]

Furthermore, honor scholarship helps explain why antebellum Southerners were quick to overlook Noah's own shameful behavior. Kenneth Greenberg suggests that proslavery authors would have been significantly less concerned than previous interpreters with whether Noah had sinned when he became intoxicated: "When the man of honor is told that he smells, he does not draw a bath—he draws his pistol. The man of honor does not care if he stinks, but he does care that someone has accused him of stinking."[66] For readers formed by Southern honor, the point of the biblical story was not whether Noah had acted dishonorably but why Ham had discovered his shame and revealed it to others. As Orlando Patterson writes, "two persons may perform the same act, yet the behavior of one is considered honorable while that of the other is not. Acting honorably is not the same thing as being honorable; it is not enough to abide by a code of honor."[67] Because Southern proslavery intellectuals assumed that Noah possessed honor while Ham did not, their "dishonorable" actions took on profoundly different meanings.

Honor scholarship also illumines elements in the biblical text that may have encouraged proslavery writers to assess the story itself as an affair of honor. First, like the affair in the Old South, the biblical story features a conflict between men. Second, alcohol was a factor in the biblical tale, as it often was in affairs of honor.[68] Third, to avoid offense, Southern men approached each other carefully, often by means of deferential letters that assumed a standard form. Considering the biblical story through this cultural lens, we might say that the deferential letter is to the breach of honor between men what the brothers' carrying of the blanket is to Ham's gazing at and broadcasting his father's nakedness. In one situation, a man of honor is approached carefully and according to custom; in the other, custom is disregarded and honor is encroached upon. Thus it is the absence of deference—highlighted by the respectful behavior of Shem and Japheth—that invites an honor reading of Genesis 9.

In the Old South, affairs of honor could be precipitated by an inappropriate look. According to the code penned in 1847 by "A Southron," the man of reputation could not afford to disregard "the sneers and scoffs and taunts, the burly bullying look, the loud and arrogant tone, the thralldom so often coveted to be exercised by the physically strong over the physically feeble"; Wyatt-Brown adds that in the Old South "the eyes witnessed honor and looked down in deference or shame. Thus a steady gaze from a slave signaled impudence." In view of the look's importance in Southern culture, it is not surprising that a stare from the putative progenitor of the African race was viewed as a breach of patriarchal honor.[69] These analogies between the biblical story and the structure of antebellum affairs of honor help explain why proslavery readings of Genesis 9 place so little importance on precise descriptions of Ham's offense. If the story was read implicitly as an affair of honor between men, readerly focus would settle not on the nature of the "crime" committed but on the necessity of satisfaction.

Studies of Old South romanticism suggest another reason the unlikely story of Noah's curse so appealed to men of honor. According to scholars of the region, "there arose in the South between 1820 and 1861 a luxuriant romanticism of mind that formed the principal basis of Southern honor." In this region "powerfully influenced by myths," the stories generated by men of honor often became crucial to their identity: "Telling these stories about themselves, planter-class men renewed their belief in themselves, their explanations, and the institutional forms that served them so well."[70] Given the appeal of these personal myths, it is no wonder the story of Noah and his sons was widely told and retold in the Old South. Similarly, honor scholarship assists us in hearing Noah's "prophecy" the way it must have been heard by Southern ears.[71] As Greenberg writes, in the Old South "truth was a matter of assertion and force—and the master had it in his control." Wyatt-Brown notes that "the stress upon external, public factors in establishing personal worth conferred particular prominence on the spoken word and physical gesture as opposed to interior thinking or words and ideas conveyed through the medium of the page."[72] All this suggests that the cogency of Noah's curse must have been enhanced for Southern Bible readers if they assumed it was uttered by a man of honor, was stated forcefully, and had come to fruition in the history of Ham's putative descendants.

In elucidating the relation between honor, loyalty, and duty, scholars of the South indicate how the various attitudes of Noah's sons would be judged in a culture of honor. Wyatt-Brown writes that "from the earliest times in Western history, the cardinal principle of honor was family defense. To war against one's own family was a violation of law—a law that, unwritten and often unspoken, superseded all others." Franklin adds that in the antebellum period "loyalty was connected with the concept of honor which required every man of the South to profess a kind of fidelity to his nation, his state, his family, even to his slaves." According to Julian Pitt-Rivers, in honor societies "the family (and in some societies the kin group) and the nation" are the fundamental collectivities that define one's essential nature. Thus, "traitors to their fathers or their sovereigns are the most execrable of all."[73] Although Southerners felt acutely the conflict between honor and conscience, shame and guilt, both systems agreed upon the importance of deference to the older generation (cf. Ham and Noah), on which point "conscience and honor arrived at the same point from somewhat different perspectives."[74]

Honor scholarship also helps explain why, in the minds of the curse's advocates, slavery seemed an apt punishment for Ham despite the clear biblical precedent for executing those who dishonor parents. Orlando Patterson's groundbreaking cross-cultural work demonstrates that in timocratic societies slavery is defined as a life without honor, and thus worse than death. Greenberg, citing the writings of proslavery theorists Thomas Roderick Dew, William Harper, William J. Grayson, Edmund Ruffin, Iveson Brookes, and Samuel Cartwright, notes that "slavery was viewed in the [Southern] culture of honor as an alternative to and substitute for death."[75] Understanding that American slavery was the antithesis of honor and a substitute for death clarifies the instinctive connection drawn by proslavery writers between enslavement and African debasement. As Rev. George D. Armstrong related the "Scriptural theory respecting the origin of Slavery, . . . the effect of sin, i. e., disobedience to God's laws, upon both individuals and nations, is *degradation*."[76]

Finally, honor scholarship confirms that proslavery intellectuals who were not members of the aristocracy were nevertheless likely to identify with the values of the upper class. Following John Hope Franklin, Orlando Patterson argues that in the South "the notion of honor diffused down to all free members of the society from its ruling-class origins." Clement Eaton agrees: "What is remarkable about the Southern practice of honor as a code of conduct was that it was not confined to the upper class . . . , through a process of osmosis [it was] acquired by all classes of Southern society." Wyatt-Brown describes Old South honor as "a people's theology." And in a study with direct relevance to proslavery divines, Christine Leigh Heyrman has shown that in the early nineteenth century Southern Protestant clerics aggressively conformed to codes of white southern manhood in an effort to demonstrate "mastery" and "prove themselves men of honor in recognizably southern ways."[77]

In all these respects, scholarly analyses of Southern culture have the potential to illumine antebellum readings of Genesis 9. Initially, proslavery men and women may have been drawn to Noah's curse because it was located in holy writ and was believed to depict the normative relationship between the great races of humankind. But as they rehearsed and reflected on the story, they were grasped by the dynamics of honor and shame inscribed there. As the biblical story received compelling honor-bound readings in the early decades of the nineteenth century, its grip on the slaveholding imagination tightened, to the point where otherwise reasonable men and women, otherwise careful Bible interpreters, became oblivious to the manifest textual and historical problems with linking Noah's curse and American slavery.

God, Honor, and Noah's Curse

For proslavery intellectuals who were also devout Christians, Genesis 9 seems to have become an intellectual nexus where religion and honor commingled in support of a common cause. But this observation raises a question that has vexed students of Southern culture for decades: How did timocracy and Christianity coexist in the antebellum Southern mind? How did the ostensibly antithetical ethics of evangelical Christianity and manly honor function symbiotically? Our analysis of proslavery readings of Noah's curse does not solve this dilemma, but it does shed light on how the dissonance between honor and conscience was temporarily submerged in efforts to justify African servitude.

A widely accepted construction of the relationship of honor and evangelical Christianity in the Old South is offered by Ten Ownby, who writes that among Southern men evangelical behavior and the code of honor were "ever in conflict."[78] Ownby claims that although evangelical Christianity and "masculine sinfulness" operated simultaneously, "male culture and evangelical culture were rivals, causing sparks when they came in contact and creating guilt and inner conflict in the many Southerners who tried to balance the two. The two forces operated against each other in an emotionally charged dialectic, the intensity of each reinforcing the other."[79] Bertram Wyatt-Brown enumerates the same paradox when he observes that although "the Southern mind has always been divided between pride and piety," no scholar has yet succeeded in portraying "the tortured relationship between Protestantism and popular ethics."[80]

Wyatt-Brown's attempt to do so sketches honor and religion as "ideologies . . . in contention for mastery of the soul of the South." He contends that between 1600 and 1861 the balance of power between these ideologies slowly and fitfully shifted in favor of religion until the establishment of a Confederacy "based on a paradoxically dissonant union of honor and the cause of God."[81] Especially in the Age of Custom (1600–1760), "honor, not Christian practice, provided the psychological framework in an unreliable world." However, "the hard code of family-based honor gradually softened" during the Age of Fervor (1760–1840), "as piety became a prerequisite for the determination of respectability."[82] By the Age of Ambivalence (1840–1861) the church's power was sufficient to jeopardize the rule of honor, yet barriers to the Christianization of Southern culture remained. These are attested by the habits of violence that plagued the region and by the church's inability to transform popular attitudes on moral issues such as drinking and dueling. Wyatt-Brown concludes that while some honor-based Southern ideals were compatible with Christian doctrine and faith, others were "clearly anti-Christian." In the latter case, because the church was not in a position to challenge "the salience of honor and shame," it upheld the honor system by coexisting with it or by serving as guardian of the social order.

Wyatt-Brown maintains that the church's adaptation to—and ultimate embrace of—the Southern code of honor is evident in the language used by patriotic clerics to welcome secession from the Union:

> Because honor to God and honor to self in this southern discourse [of secession and war] were so closely bound together, it was possible for churchgoers to reconcile the traditional ethic and evangelical belief. Romantic heroism—the badge of the Confederate cavalier—and Christian dignity and zeal could be—and were—congenially united. Robert E. Lee, Stonewall Jackson, and Jefferson Davis were both Christian gentlemen and men of honor in the highest sense of those terms that southern culture could produce.[83]

But because neither honor nor evangelical religion triumphed by the time war arrived, "the South would have to live thereafter with a divided soul."[84]

Responding to Wyatt-Brown, Ownby, and others who underscore the enduring conflict of religion and honor in the Southern mind, Edward R. Crowther casts this troubled relationship in a new light.[85] He argues that historians have struggled to identify the interpretive thread running through the Old South because "students of the southern mind have placed religion outside the mainstream of forces that shaped both southern behavior and secession. According to these scholars, concepts of honor, not religious beliefs, directed the southern male, or at least those southern men who exerted real influence."[86] This is a false dichotomy, Crowther asserts, because the basis of the South's remarkable cohesion was essentially religious. He observes that

> by the time Abraham Lincoln was elected president, secessionists uttered their calls for action in language borrowing from and mixing together evangelical rhetoric and traditions of honor, creating a southern civil religious litany. Over time, many religious and secular ideals, which were not necessarily dissonant in their expression, had fused to produce a hybrid and distinctly southern value, a holy honor that drew on evangelical and martial traditions for its sustenance and animated and, for white southerners, justified southern behavior.[87]

Crowther contends that this "holy honor" was nurtured in the common ethos of preachers and planters (a commonality rooted in shared class anxieties), and the desire of evangelical Christians to redirect rather than destroy concepts of personal honor. He concludes that "by the mid-nineteenth century both sacred and secular values reflected and were helping to transform a common ethos, at least at the level of ideals."[88]

If Crowther is correct, and the antebellum South was infused with a holy honor that united planter and preacher in common perceptions of the world's order, then we would expect this vision to be reflected not only in the thought and behavior of Southern planters (as examined by Crowther) but also in the writings of proslavery apologists who identified with the planter class. To test this thesis, let us review some honor-bound renditions of Noah's curse, paying special attention to idioms of honor-shame and righteousness-sin. Many of these texts use the vocabularies of honor and faith interchangeably, as when James A. Sloan identifies "shame" with "sinful sport."[89] Others provide glimpses of the fusion of evangelical Christianity and timocracy Crowther calls "holy honor." For instance, the author of *The Governing Race* thoroughly integrates the languages of honor and morality in his portrayal of Ham's transgression. He characterizes Ham's affront as "dishonoring his father" and then classifies this misdeed as one of "three notable instances of laws in which our Creator imposed certain specified penalties for sin on certain classes of the human race." On one hand, Ham's dishonor has transmitted an "insensibility to shame" to his progeny; on the other hand, it was a "polluting depravity," "treason against nature and rebellion against God," an attempt to "overthrow and destroy the moral life of mankind."[90]

Similarly, in his description of Ham's villainy, the anonymous author of *African Servitude* conflates honor with faithfulness, respect with faith, disgrace with "the fall," and dishonor with "an evil heart of unbelief toward God." Although containing a very explicit honor reading of Noah's curse, the pamphlet is permeated with religious images: Hamite slavery is a result of "righteous judgment"; God "allowed the faith of the three sons of Noah to be tried, and Ham was found wanting"; Ham "broke the first command on the second table, by scorning and deriding his father." Occasionally, the vocabularies of honor and faith merged, as in the reference to Ham's "lack of faith, his sinful conduct of defection." A few Southern advocates of the curse sought to reduce the dissonance between religion and honor through linguistic baptism. Recall Samuel Davies Baldwin's claim that, viewed in the light of revelation, "filial dishonor . . . is more obnoxious to censure and punishment than theft, forgery, or falsehood, and stands before them in importance in the graduated scale of the Decalogue." Citing the fifth commandment ("Honor your father and your mother. . . ." Exodus 20:12; cf. Deuteronomy 27:16: "Cursed be anyone who dishonors father or mother"), Baldwin—along with Sloan and others—roots honor at Sinai rather than South Carolina.

In the process of embracing Noah's curse as a chief rationale for human bondage, antebellum proslavery intellectuals made a remarkable contribution to the development of "holy honor." Reflecting the influence of previous interpreters,[91] the dynamics of honor and shame inscribed in their Old Testament, and their own sensibilities as Southern gentlemen, they interpreted Noah's curse in a manner that made the ethics of faith and honor virtually interchangeable. These authors indicate the fluid boundaries that existed in the Southern mind between honor and faith, shame and unbelief, and they provide a unique glimpse of the proslavery imagination straining to alleviate the conceptual discordance between faith and timocracy. Bertram Wyatt-Brown has written that "without grasping the ancient, even pagan origins and continuities of honor, we cannot comprehend the endurance of racism as a sacred, intractable conviction, or the approach of civil war, or the desperate commitment of Southern whites to hold black Americans forever in their power."[92] We should add that without grasping the "continuities of honor," it is not possible to comprehend the way antebellum proslavery intellectuals read the biblical text they regarded as containing both the origin and the justification for African slavery.

Epilogue: Resexualizing Ham's Transgression

Given the usefulness of Genesis 9:20–27 in defending American slavery, it is not surprising that Noah's curse was rehabilitated during the 1950s and 1960s

by white Christians seeking to buttress the religious case for legalized segregation. Naturally, American segregationists are regarded as the intellectual
grandchildren of antebellum slavery advocates. But this assessment ignores
the facts that Civil Rights–era segregationists who invoked Noah's curse departed from the proslavery legacy—by failing to interpret Ham's transgression
in terms of familial honor and by reclaiming the presumption of innate sexual
perversion in the "Negro" descendants of Ham.

In *Place of Race*—a short work published in 1965 to explicate the biblical
mandate for racial segregation outside the church—C. E. McLain refers
plainly to "the sensual sin of Ham." This outrage, McLain suggests, reveals
"the germ of sexual sin which was to permeate the Hamitic tribes."[93] Similarly,
in a published sermon titled "God the Original Segregationist," Baptist minister Carey Daniel associates the episode in Genesis 9 with the destruction of
Sodom and Gomorrah. In a sly reference to popular conceptions of black
sexuality, Daniel writes that "anyone familiar with the Biblical history of those
cities during that period can readily understand why we here in the South are
determined to maintain segregation."[94] Later in the same sermon, Daniel
frankly links the curse and sexual impropriety: "The Bible clearly implies that
the Negroes' black skin is the result of Ham's immorality at the time of his
father Noah's drunkenness. For example, in Jeremiah 13:23 we read, 'Can the
Ethiopian change his skin, or the leopard his spots? Then may ye also do
good, that are accustomed to do evil.' Here the black skin of the Negro is
obviously a symbol of evil."[95]

American Segregationist readings of Genesis 9–11 will be discussed in
more detail in chapter 6. At this point, we note only that references to the
story of Noah and his sons among twentieth-century segregationists conspicuously lack the theme of honor that is so distinctive in antebellum readings
of Genesis 9.[96]

5

Original Disorder

Noah's Curse and the Southern Defense of Slavery

> When Ham had been within the tent, and had seen the
> condition of his father, he was noticed by them to rush
> out in a state of very great excitement, yelling and explod-
> ing with laughter. . . .
>
> Josiah Priest, *Slavery as It Relates to the*
> *Negro or African Race*

THE PREVIOUS CHAPTER probed the relations between Southern honor, the
American proslavery argument, and the biblical text most often relied upon
to sustain that argument. This chapter continues the investigation of the distinctive ways Genesis 9 was read to support American slavery, arguing that
antebellum readings of the story of Noah and his sons reflect both the penchant for disorder believed to exemplify the "Negro" character and the necessity of preserving order in the ideal society. Though expressed in a variety
of ways, the order dynamic in proslavery commentary on Genesis 9 can be
described quite simply: The servitude of Ham's descendants functions to protect the social order from the sort of disorderly conduct that Ham brought
to the postdiluvian community. Subordination is necessary, in other words,
to restrain the rebellious Negro character so accurately depicted in Genesis 9:
20–27.

Long before they were embraced by American Bible readers, concerns for
order appeared throughout Genesis 9's history of interpretation. In fact, one
of the tradition's enduring motifs is the threat to social harmony associated
with Ham and his descendants. Examples include rabbinic comments that

conjoin Ham with theft, fornication, prevarication, and hatred for masters, and the medieval *Zohar*, in which Canaan is given the appellation "notorious world-darkener." It was left to Christian writers, however, to fully conceptualize the Hamite predilection for disorder. Recall that in Clement's genealogy of human corruption, Hamites are responsible for slavery, demon worship, idolatry, the practice of magical arts, and violent conquest. Transmitting and embellishing Ham's legacy as the patriarch of chaos, Luther claims that after receiving Noah's curse, Ham developed a new government and religion and filled the world with idolatry. This chapter explores how antebellum interpreters of Genesis 9 extended this tradition of Hamite disorder in response to the peculiar needs of the American slavocracy.

Order and the Southern Mind

As was noted in chapter 1, Mark Twain is credited with the audacious claim that the character of the Old South could be understood as an outgrowth of the region's penchant for the novels of Sir Walter Scott. Although most interpreters regard Twain's comment as tongue-in-cheek social commentary, in the 1960s James McBride Dabbs revisited the issue by arguing that Scott's popularity could indeed shed light on the formation of Southern character. In an essay entitled "Sir Walter Scott and the Civil War," Dabbs contended that the underlying aim of the Waverly novels was to "present the primary purpose of the social order, especially as bound up with the institution of property." "Scott created two types of heroes and heroines: the proper, or passive, hero who defended law and order, reason, prudence, and the accepted values, especially property; and the dark hero, who acted for the individual against these values, and in a spirit of passion and disorder. Though perhaps he lived more richly, the dark hero always came to a disastrous end, in failure, exile, or death."[1] In Dabbs's view, the essential though unconscious message for Southerners in Scott's novels was "the value of social order over freedom and of prudence over passion." The Southerner embraced Scott's romances because he identified himself in the passive hero who was defender of law, order, and property.[2] If there is truth in Dabbs's analysis, and antebellum Southerners were attracted to stories in which the "passive hero" represented order and the "dark hero" passion and disorder, we should not be surprised to discover similar dynamics in their readings of biblical narratives. But first let us consider evidence of order's centrality to the proslavery imagination.

The integral link between order and African servitude is discernible in many aspects of the proslavery weltanschauung—the aristocratic conservatism common among Southern intellectuals,[3] a widespread perception that the only reliable social constitution was to be found in the Bible, and the notion that slavery was necessary to control "Africans' predisposition to lascivious and socially disruptive behavior."[4] Americans on the proslavery side also assumed that God's careful structuring of the natural world was evident in racial hierarchy. As Howell Cobb maintained in the 1850s, "the great Architect . . . framed [blacks] both physically and mentally to fill the sphere in which they were thrown, and His wisdom and mercy combined in constituting them thus suited to the degraded position they were destined to occupy."[5] In 1862, Joseph C. Addington applied this apperception of racial gradation to the destiny and character of Noah's sons, writing that "the White or Japhetic race is first in position. The Red or Shemitic Race, is second. . . . The Black or Hamitic race, is last in position. . . ."[6] Rooted in creation and providence alike, this hierarchy had to be upheld for whites to fulfill the great work of civilization to which they were called. This conviction was dramatized in a fictional dialogue between representatives of the Japhetic and Hamitic races published in the *Southern Literary Messenger* in 1855. The son of Japheth warns his cousin that "you may not mingle your blood with ours, you may not participate in our counsels . . . for you may not be permitted to thwart by your incompetence the great scheme in which we are engaged and on which so much depends."[7] According to the proslavery mind-set, the organization of the world both justified and required black servitude.

Another dimension of American slave culture that reflected the intellectual kinship between servitude and order was the perception of blacks as perpetual children in the human family. Thought to combine adult strength and childlike judgment, slaves were considered susceptible to disorder in a variety of forms.[8] White infantilization of African Americans was fostered by the popular sentiments that blacks were naturally unintelligent, morally underdeveloped, and imitative and by the supposition that whites were obligated to care for and protect the semisavages in their midst. It was also nourished by assumptions regarding the biblical pattern of "domestic slavery," in which wives, children, slaves, and other relatives were considered members of an extended patriarchal family. Thus, ironically, the conception of slaves as puerile beings was encouraged by religious reformers who insisted that American slavery meet the "Bible standard." Among them was Presbyterian James A. Lyon of Mississippi, who in 1863 opined that the relationship of slave and master was "equal, in all respects, to that of parent and child," the only difference being that "a slave is a minor for life."[9]

Corollary to the image of slaves as dependents in the patriarchal family was the expectation that order and hierarchy structure every domestic relationship. In 1857, Fred A. Ross asserted that husband-wife and parent-child relations ought to reflect "the world-wide law that service shall be rendered by the inferior to the superior." Ross did not hesitate to "run a parallel between the relation of master and slave and that of husband and wife."[10] Although some proslavery ideologues were uncomfortable linking slavery and wifely submission, others found the analogy too compelling to resist. Samuel B. How sought a middle ground, denying that "the relation between husband and wife is similar to that which exists between the master and the slave," but affirming that both could be traced to the Garden of Eden. In God's response to human transgression, How perceived "the origin of [man's] subjection to labor" and thus the incidental cause of slavery. And because Eve was the vehicle for sin's entry into paradise, her subjection to Adam was coeval with the origin of servitude—of man to man, and man to earth.[11] Although not always visible in proslavery literature, the ligament between slavery and women's oppression was obvious to radical abolitionists such as Sarah Grimké.

Systematic proslavery thought developed after 1830 in reaction to the abolitionist assault on human servitude, and, of course, the specifics of that attack determined the character of the proslavery response. Because abolitionists wished to portray thralldom as barbaric and hopelessly out of step with modern religious, political, and social principles, slavery's defenders were obliged to portray the institution as a cornerstone of the good society. In fact, the claim that slavery was essential for producing and maintaining societal order pervades the writings of proslavery intellectuals, religious and secular alike. South Carolinian William Harper called slavery a "Great Wall" that protected every white man, woman, and child.[12] John C. Calhoun stressed that Southern bondage was the best system of control for maximizing societal peace and the happiness of whites and blacks alike.[13] Rev. Leander Ker boasted that Southern slaves were "ten times more polite, mannerly, genteel, intelligent, and moral, than those dogged impudent, insolent, profane and filthy creatures that swarm about the towns and cities of the North"[14] William Henry Hammond contended that slavery was less abusive than so-called free labor. Responding to the plight of workers in the British Empire, Hammond wrote to an English abolitionist: "To alleviate the fancied sufferings of the accursed posterity of Ham, you sacrifice by a cruel death two-thirds of the children of the blessed Shem—and demand the applause of Christians—the blessing of heaven!"[15]

And what of the charge that because slaves would naturally seek their freedom, bondage increased social insecurity? William Gilmore Simms responded that the danger of insurrection did not arise in "the natural movements of the servile mind . . . [but were] instigated from without."[16] Charleston, he observed, was plagued by neither mutiny nor revolt and had less need for police protection than New York or Europe. Thomas R. Dew concurred: American blacks had been so civilized under slavery that "nothing . . . but the most subtle and poisonous principles, sedulously infused into [the slave's] mind, can break his allegiance, and transform him into the midnight murderer."[17] In "Professor Dew on Slavery," Dew argued that slavery prevents social chaos by strengthening the bonds of mutual affection among members of two otherwise incompatible and antagonistic races. Furthermore, he opined, "there is nothing but slavery which can destroy those habits of indolence and sloth, and eradicate the character of improvidence and carelessness, which mark the independent savage."[18] Because in Dew's mind blacks were peculiarly drawn to immorality, slavery was a suitable vehicle for controlling their sinful predispositions. Further, human bondage was a boon to peace and order, in that it mitigated the frequency and horrors of war and destroyed "that migratory spirit in nations and tribes, so destructive to the peace and tranquility of the world."[19]

The proslavery compulsion to associate human subjugation and civic harmony is quite evident in the writings of Virginian George Fitzhugh, the most respected slavery apologist in the decades prior to the Civil War. In two books published during the 1850s—*Sociology for the South, or the Failure of Free Society* (1854) and *Cannibals All! or, Slaves Without Masters* (1857)—Fitzhugh assailed the foundations of democratic society while establishing an intellectual basis for slavocracy. Fitzhugh regarded the preservation of societal order as among the chief benefits of human thralldom, declaring that "at the slaveholding South all is peace, quiet, plenty and contentment. We have no mobs, no trade unions, no strikes for higher wages, no armed resistance to the law, but little jealousy of the rich by the poor. We have but few in our jails, and fewer in our poor houses."[20] This was no coincidence: Because blacks so clearly required masters, racial slavery was "the most necessary of all human institutions," an "indispensable police institution."

In Fitzhugh's view, abolitionists sought nothing less than the reorganization of American society. They wished "to abolish . . . or greatly to modify, the relations of husband and wife, parent and child, the institution of private property of all kinds, but especially separate ownership of lands, and the institution of Christian churches as now existing in America."[21] If they are successful, Fitzhugh warned, government, law, religion, and marriage would be among the casualties. Just as abolitionists could not recognize the South apart from its support for human servitude, Fitzhugh perceived Northern social ills as by-products of a free society, whose principles were at war with "all government, all subordination, all order."[22] If slavery is wrong, he reasoned, then all human government is wrong. Because opposition to slavery threatened society's very survival, Fitzhugh cast abolitionist William Lloyd Garrison as the "Great Anarch of the North" and abolition itself as a precursor to "Anarchy, Free Love, Agrarians, &c., &c."[23]

In Fitzhugh's mind, the spread of abolitionism could not be considered apart from the scourge of infidelity. Claiming that organized opposition to slavery contributed to universal skepticism, Fitzhugh embellished the truism that abolitionists were "commonly infidels":

> It is notorious that infidelity appeared in the world, on an extensive scale, only contemporaneously with the abolition of slavery, and that it is now limited to countries where no domestic slavery exists. . . . Where there is no slavery, the minds of men are unsettled on all subjects, and there is, emphatically, faith and conviction about nothing. Their moral and social world is in a chaotic and anarchical state. Order, subordination, and adaptation have vanished; and with them, the belief in a Deity, the author of all order.[24]

According to Fitzhugh, social reform was animated by "a universal spirit of destructiveness, a profane attempt to pull down what God and nature had

built up and to erect ephemeral Utopia in its place."[25] The North was home
to a thousand superstitious and infidel-isms, a land that evinced "faith in
nothing, speculation about everything." In opposition to these taproots of
disorder and chaos, Fitzhugh placed family, hierarchy, and subordination.

In the antebellum period, the concern for order was paramount not only
for secular slavery apologists like Fitzhugh but also for clergy intellectuals,
who promoted "Bible slavery" and decried abolitionist "fanaticism" and "atheism." These Southern divines offered a concerted moral defense of "social
inequality, class stratification, male supremacy, and the subordination of the
laboring classes to personal authority."[26] For instance, in an address before
the General Assembly of the Presbyterian Church in the Confederate States
of America in 1863, James A. Lyon asserted that the patriarchal relation (an
emblem of Bible slavery) had to be tempered by absolute authority, in part
to mitigate the tendency to insubordination. Lyon commended the religious
instruction of slaves by noting that the irreligious servant was harder to govern
and that intelligent slaves were "less likely to engage in insurrectionary and
unlawful enterprises." Finally, Lyon referred to black thralldom as Providence's scheme for subjecting an inferior to a superior race. Slavery would be
necessary, then, until Christianity gained such ascendancy "as to bring the
entire race under the absolute and delightful control of the spirit and principles of the Gospel."[27] James H. Thornwell, another Presbyterian reformer,
connected "insurrection, anarchy and bloodshed, revolt against masters, [and]
treason against States."[28] Such religious perspectives on the relation of slavery
and societal order were well suited to white Southerners' images of themselves
as humane masters devoted to Christianizing the heathen African, benevolent
patriarchs who cared for slaves as family members, and reformers who, if
spared antislavery agitation, would perfect their peculiar institution.

Remarkably, the association of slavery and order in the Southern mind
survived the Civil War and the Emancipation Proclamation. Particularly when
the trauma of defeat and occupation began to subside and "home rule" was
reestablished, there was renewed stress on maintaining social equilibrium.
Wistful recollections of slavery's role in upholding the old order highlighted
the need for separation and subordination in the postwar world. As Charles
Reagan Wilson observes, before segregation became an accepted substitute for
servitude around 1890, Southern clergy associated with the Lost Cause proclaimed that slavery had been a civilizing institution essential to the peace
and welfare of prewar society. These priests of the Lost Cause believed strongly
that "slavery had brought essential order, discipline, and morality in Negro
life."[29] Proof of slavery's edifying effect on the Negro was found in the faithful
behavior of slaves during wartime and the decline in Negro morality following
emancipation. Some ministers even explained the emergence of the Klan as a
response to the "condition of total lawlessness" that prevailed in the absence
of slavery.

An instructive example of the postbellum perception of slavery as a sta-
bilizing influence on the black community appeared in an 1877 *Southern Pres-*

byterian Review article, "The Colored Man in the South." The article compared the behavior of black American Christians to that of their African relatives and concluded that whatever civilization could be found in the Negro church was a product of slave discipline. The author expressed surprise that attendees at a recent black church convention had conducted themselves "in an orderly manner, under the control of [an efficient] moderator," in a fashion that is "sensible," "practical," and "systematic." If there is any governability in the Negro character, any possibility of improvement for the race, he concluded, it is thanks to slavery, which did a "wonderful, beneficent work" in converting "hopeless barbarians into citizens." Absent the assistance of slavery in making the African savage "docile, industrious and subordinate," the white South was now forced to identify new methods for imposing authority, obedience, and discipline on its dark brothers.[30]

Having documented the concern for order that animated the world view of white Southerners before and after the Civil War, we are prepared to further explore the distinctive meanings assigned to the tale of Noah's curse by proslavery Bible readers. We will see that proslavery interpreters reflected their interest in preserving societal harmony by reading Genesis 9:20–27 as an episode of primal disorder.

Order and Paradise

The symbolic meaning of Ham's offense can be gauged only if we note the setting of his encounter with Noah in the postdiluvian utopia. Proslavery interpreters of Genesis 9:20–27 emphasized that following the great watery purge, Noah and his family resided in a pristine world where they lived out the agrarian ideal in the shadow of Mount Ararat. Drawing on these utopian images, antebellum Bible readers depicted Noah as a second Adam who enjoyed unmediated communion with God. In the words of Virginian Robert L. Dabney, when he uttered the curse, Noah acted "as an inspired prophet, and also as the divinely chosen, patriarchal head of church and state, which were then confined to his one family."[31] Leander Ker was another proslavery author who carefully placed the biblical story in its primordial context:

> This crime of Ham was the first transgression recorded after the flood, and probably the first committed; and you must remember, in the next place, that Noah now was to the world what Adam was, when created—the official head—the Viceregent of Heaven—and, therefore, the first deliberate and willful offence, as in the case of Adam, according to the moral government of God, must be punished with the utmost rigor of law.[32]

Other slavery apologists described the Edenic paradise that awaited Noah's family as they disembarked after the flood:

> The place [Noah] selected, was doubtless, in the great vale which stretches out southeasterly from the foot of the mountain, where the Ark grounded,

some twenty miles, presenting to the eye an ocean of green foliage, which had but newly grown, after the receding of the waters, and presented to the voyagers a rapturous sight. . . . Broad savannas, abounding with all kinds of beasts, and fowls—the waters with fishes, and the wilderness with berries, fruits, roots, and esculent herbs. Nuts of all trees, spices, gums, aromatics, and balms, frankincense, myrrh, cinnamon, and odors, wild honey, grapes and flowery regions, with perpetual verdure, could but captivate the hearts of these pioneers. . . . [33]

Given his utopian description of the postdiluvian world, it is hardly coincidental that the author locates Noah's settlement "near the head waters of the Euphrates," one of the rivers flowing out of Eden (Gen. 2:14).

No doubt the textual parallels between Genesis 9 and Genesis 2–3—the divine charge to "be fruitful and multiply," the placing of a man in paradise to till the ground, nakedness, servitude, and the imposition of a curse[34]—brought the creation story to mind as proslavery Bible readers reflected on the tale of Noah's drunkenness. These parallels reinforced their perceptions that Noah was entrusted with humanity's second chance and that the events leading to Ham's curse were a narrative of the second "fall."[35] And because his behavior precipitated the end of orderly existence, Ham could be blamed not only for the ruination of the postdiluvian paradise but also, in much the same way as Eve, for the world's fallen state. These associations with cosmic order and disorder provided the background against which antebellum order-bound readings of Noah's curse developed.

Ham, Laughter, and Slave Impudence

The most common order theme in antebellum American readings of Genesis 9:20–27 was laughter. Whence originated the extrabiblical notion that laughter was an essential aspect of Ham's contumacy? Although neither asserted nor implied in the text of Genesis 9, the image of Ham laughing at his father emerged quite early in the history of interpretation. The ultimate source for the laughter theme appears to be Josephus, who in *Antiquities of the Jews* summarized the encounter between Noah and Ham this way:

> Noah, when after the deluge, the earth was resettled in its former condition set about its cultivation; and when he had planted it with vines, and when the fruit was ripe, and he had gathered the grapes in their season, and the wine was ready for use, he offered sacrifices and feasted, and being drunk, he fell asleep, and lay naked in an unseemly manner. When his youngest son saw this, he came laughing, and showed him to his brethren; but they covered their father's nakedness.[36]

The theme of Ham's laughter was subsequently adapted by early Christian writers, notably Origen, Ambrose, and Sulpicius Severus (ca. 360–420),[37] and was featured in medieval legend.[38] The leaders of the Reformation made ridicule an emblem of Ham's transgression, and the motif was transmitted by nineteenth-century commentator Adam Clarke, who declared that "Ham, and very probably his son Canaan, had treated their father on this occasion with contempt or reprehensible levity."[39]

It is remarkable the number of serious exegetes—Jews, Christians, and Muslims alike—who have conveyed this extratextual theme.[40] Perhaps something in the textual logic of Genesis 9 steers readers to conclude that Ham "told his brothers" of Noah's condition in a jocose or raucous fashion. Yet despite the motif's longevity and range, American affirmations of Ham's laughter occupy a distinctive place in the history of interpretation. First, unlike previous interpreters, proslavery Bible readers adamantly denied that Noah was deserving of abuse. Second, and more important, outside nineteenth-century America mockery was never viewed as a sufficient condition for Noah's curse. In fact, it was routinely supplemented—and eclipsed—by discussion of iniquities presumably more deserving of perpetual servitude.[41]

Condemnatory references to laughter abound in American proslavery literature. For instance, Leander Ker described Ham's crime as "insulting and mocking,"[42] and the author of *The Governing Race* declared that Ham "mocked at his father." But the extent to which derisive laughter became a stock theme in antebellum renderings of Ham's transgression is best gauged from popular versions of the curse. In discussing a bill before Congress in 1860, Jefferson Davis invoked Genesis 9 by alleging that when "the low and vulgar son of Noah, who laughed at his father's exposure, sunk by debasing himself and his lineage by a connection with an inferior race of men, he doomed his descendants to perpetual slavery." Further evidence of the theme's prominence in popular renditions of the curse is found among its victims. In the 1930s, former slave Gus "Jabbo" Rogers related this account of the biblical tale for a WPA interviewer:

> God gave it [religion] to Adam and took it away from Adam and gave it to Noah, and you know, Miss, Noah had three sons, and when Noah got drunk on wine, one of his sons laughed at him, and the other two took a sheet and walked backwards and threw it over Noah. Noah told the one who laughed, "Your children will be hewers of wood and drawers of water for the other two children, and they will be known by their hair and their skin being dark." So, Miss, there we are, and that is the way God meant us to be. We have always had to follow the white folks and do what we saw them do, and that's all there is to it. You just can't get away from what the Lord said.[43]

In these popular summaries of the biblical story, we perceive the deep concerns for order that underlie laughter-readings of Ham's disgrace. For Rogers the ex-slave, Ham's disorderly conduct is tied thematically to his descendants' punishment, which requires that Negro order be reestablished through emulation of whites. Similarly, in Davis's mind, Ham's laughter manifests a disorder that is constitutive of the African character:

> In this District of Columbia you have but to go to the jail and find there,
> by those who fill it, the result of relieving the negro from that control which
> keeps him in his own healthy and useful condition. It is idle to assume that
> it is the want of education: it is the natural inferiority of the race; and the
> same proof exists wherever that race has been left the master of itself—
> sinking into barbarism or into the commission of crime, as it happens to be
> isolated or in contact with those upon whom it could prey for subsistence.[44]

These words indicate how the assumption that Ham must have mocked his father was dependent on the broader themes of order and disorder, including the "barbarism" and "crime," which, in Davis's view, demanded social control of an inferior race.

The prominence of the laughter theme in proslavery commentary on Genesis 9 raises some intriguing questions. First, in that Ham's laughter lacked any support in the biblical text (and not a single American advocate of the curse claimed otherwise), we must ask why it was so widely affirmed in antebellum readings of Genesis 9. Habit is not a sufficient explanation for this phenomenon, not in a culture that, at least in principle, held that truth was revealed in the letter of scripture. Rather, Ham's mockery of Noah must have communicated something indispensable to proslavery commentary on Genesis 9. Second, how did Ham's laughter become a sufficient condition for the curse? Under what conditions does laughter—even explosive, mocking laughter—come to be regarded as behavior worthy of a perpetual malediction?

Both questions are illuminated by research into the dread of slave insurrection that periodically seized the Old South. According to historians, Southern fears of slave rebellion were notably disproportionate to the threat; insurrection was an "abstract, awesome danger from within" that led whites to imagine an overturned social order.[45] As early as 1822, "A South Carolinian" defended the peculiar institution by offering a careful review of slave rebellions throughout the South. He wrote that "we regard our negroes as the 'Jacobins' of the country, against whom we should always be upon our guard."[46] Over the next four decades, as slavery came under assault and abolitionist literature infiltrated the South, the fear of slave insurrection intensified until, in the wake of John Brown's 1859 raid, the region was gripped by "the most intense terror of slave insurrection [it] ever experienced."[47]

Historians also tell us that Southern whites interpreted changes in black demeanor as harbingers of slave rebellion. When blacks "smile[d] deferentially and laugh[ed] softly," the world was deemed orderly and safe. But when accustomed deference gave way to "unaccustomed disobedience and impudence," white insecurities were amplified. "A glum stare, a brusque reply to a question, a reluctant move," were all taken as clues that rebellion was at hand.[48] Thus, as a "prelude to insurgency," slave insolence was an emotional trigger for white fears of insurrection, the gravest threat to order in the American slavocracy. The prominence of laughter in proslavery readings of Genesis 9 suggests that in the slaveholding imagination Ham's mockery functioned much like slave "impudence"—as a symbol of unruliness in the black character. Just as whites interpreted slave flippancy as a token of impending social chaos, they read Genesis 9 as an episode of black impertinence. Especially when juxtaposed with the quiet and respectful behavior of Shem and Japheth, Ham's jocose demeanor became an emblem of the disorder for which the Negro was notorious in the Anglo-Saxon mind.[49]

Ham and Black Ungovernability

Many antebellum whites reckoned that because Africans were incapable of self-rule, servitude was essential to their survival in America.[50] Reflecting this view of black ungovernability, an anonymous proslavery author presented an imaginary conversation between the first descendants of Ham and Japheth in North America. The Hamite acknowledges that "we never have been governed aright . . . [and] cannot govern ourselves." He then pleads for the white man's help: "Take us then and mould us to your will. Think for us: guide us; teach us our duty to the God whom we have forgotten and who has made you what you are. Take care of us and our little ones."[51] The conviction among antebellum whites that blacks were virtually ungovernable is significant for our purposes inasmuch as it elucidates proslavery readings of Genesis 9 that are otherwise difficult to classify.

For instance, in a tract published in 1823, Frederick Dalcho condemned Ham's "abominable wickedness," while designating Hamites as "peculiarly wicked, and obnoxious to the wrath of God." In neither case did Dalcho describe this purported villainy, but evidence for inferring his view of Ham's disgrace can be gleaned from his discussion of a recent slave insurrection. Dalcho asks why "the late conspiracy" involved no Negroes belonging to the Protestant Episcopal Church. Is it, he wonders, because

> in the sober, rational, sublime and evangelical worship of the Protestant Episcopal Church, there is nothing to inflame the passions of the ignorant enthusiast; nothing left to the crude, undigested ideas of illiterate black class-leaders? Is it because the coloured leaders in that Church, were not permitted to expound the Scriptures, or to exhort, in words of their own; to use extemporary prayer, and to utter at such times, whatever nonsense and profanity might happen to come into their minds? Is it because the order and language of the worship of that Church, being precomposed and arranged, cannot be perverted or abused to party purposes? . . . Here was nothing to mislead the weak, excite the passions of the wicked, or impose upon the credulous. The exercises were rational and pious and the audience decorous. . . . [52]

Conversely, Dalcho observes, the recent rebellion "had its origin and seat, chiefly in the *African Church*, which was entirely composed of negroes, under preachers of their own colour." His conclusion is that "much animal excitement" is to be found in such churches but little real devotion.[53] Thus, we can infer that the "abominable wickedness" Dalcho attaches to Ham and his putative descendants is intimately related to animal excitement and crude passions—that is, disorder.

Dalcho further illumines the ties between slavery and order when he censures Northerners who presume to instruct slaves without appreciating the South's "times and laws." Drawing on personal experience, Dalcho emphasizes the difficulty of discerning "the real character of Negroes." "I am likewise aware," he continues, "of the measure of prudence which is necessary to improve their moral and spiritual condition, without deranging the existing order of society."[54] Concern for the slaves' well-being, in other words, must not threaten the maintenance of societal order, and Northerners must not ignore the "chain which binds together the various orders of *our* community, which must not be broken."[55]

Louisianan Samuel Cartwright is another proslavery apologist whose concern for order is reflected in his reading of Genesis 9. In his 1843 treatise on Noah's curse, Cartwright fails to specify Ham's sin, but he does identify the absence of order as one of its consequences. In Cartwright's view, "the Ethiopian" suffers not so much a deficiency of intellect as a lack of "balance between his animality and intellectuality." Black animality, according to Cartwright,

> rules the intellect and chains the mind to slavery—slavery to himself, slavery to his appetites, and a radical savage in his habits, wherever he is left to himself. His mind being thus depressed by the excessive development of the nerves of organic life, nothing but arbitrary power, prescribing and enforcing temperance in all things, can restrain the excesses of his animal nature and restore reason to her throne. Certain it is that nothing but compuson [*sic*] has ever made him lead a life of industry, temperance and order; and nothing but compulsion has ever converted him into a civilized being. When the compulsive hand of arbitrary power is withdrawn, he invariably relapses into barbarism; proving that when he has his personal liberty, he is not a free agent to choose the good and avoid the evil—whereas, under that government which God ordained for him, the excesses of his animality are kept in restraint and his free agency is restored.[56]

In Cartwright's view, blacks live in figurative slavery to their impulses and appetites; therefore, literal slavery is necessary to prescribe and enforce temperance among them, to restrain them, and to restore them to reason and order. Because Cartwright regards Ham as the eponymous ancestor of Africans, he leads readers to infer that blacks inherited their condition from him.

A postbellum Bible reader who interprets Genesis 9 through the prism of Negro ungovernability is J. W. Sandell, a Confederate veteran who was

extolling the virtues of the Old South as late as 1907.[57] Sandell traces directly
to the curse the Negro's purported lack of fitness for government: "Noah
prophesied the future of his three sons, including all the races in regard to
government through all time. Japheth was the first born: his father said, 'God
shall enlarge Japheth and he shall dwell in the tents of Shem; and Canaan
shall be his servant.' "[58] Sandell avers that "the spirit of this prophecy has been
manifested in the United States": "There are races of men who are not fit for
self-government—all may serve, but all cannot govern. The negroes as a race
are not capable of appreciating such a government as the Constitution of the
United States provides for, and as rulers they should not be in the house of
the Lord or government of these States."[59]

For Sandell, "the curse upon Canaan has never been absolved and nothing
the race achieved in the early ages of the human family can justify the claim
of the negro to equality with the white man in the government of the world.
The race is prophetically condemned to an inferior relation to that of Shem
and Japheth."[60] In fact, "a people descended from such maledictions as were
put upon Canaan" ought to be content to remain under the protection of a
government that offers it liberty. Sandell's interpretation of Genesis 9 allies
him with antebellum advocates of the curse. Like them, he regards the disorder punished and prophesied by Noah as a perennial gauge of Hamite character and destiny.

Ham, Disorder, and Amalgamation

Another species of disorder present in antebellum readings of Genesis 9 has
been associated with Ham and his offspring since the start of the common
era. Early Christian Gnostics taught that intermarriage between beings of different orders had been the source of antediluvian corruption.[61] This kinship
between miscegenation and divine punishment—dormant for most of interpretive history—was reestablished in 1852 when Louisianan John Fletcher invoked "race mixing" as an explanation for Noah's curse.[62]

Confident that "God never sanctions a curse without an adequate cause;
a cause under the approbation of his law, sufficient to produce the effect the
curse announces," Fletcher contended that Ham's real transgression had to be
located prior to his conflict with Noah. "The ill-manners of Ham no doubt
accelerated the time of the announcement of the curse," according to Fletcher,
but were not its sole cause.[63] That act alone "could not produce so vital, so
interminable a change in the moral and physical condition of his offspring."
In Fletcher's mind, "adequate cause for the immediate degradation of an unborn race" could be only Ham's marriage with the cursed race of Cain (a
union that transmitted to Ham's descendants the black skin Cain received
following his act of fratricide).[64] Noah's "prophecy," then, was properly speaking an announcement. Even without the curse, however, the consequences of

Ham's iniquity would have manifested themselves soon enough. "Suppose, even at this day," Fletcher reasoned, "a descendant of Japheth should choose to amalgamate with the Negro, could not his father readily foretell the future destiny of the offspring,—their standing among the rest of his family?"[65]

For Fletcher, Ham's sin was the one that nineteenth-century white Americans regarded as the quintessential violation of order. Because this fear of race mixing existed in symbiosis with popular conceptions of African sexuality, perhaps Fletcher should be considered a rare example of an antebellum author who indulged in sexualizing the character of Ham. But there are good reasons to understand Fletcher's reading of Genesis 9 as concerned primarily with order rather than sex. First, Fletcher virtually ignores Ham's indignity against Noah, while devoting most of a seventy-page chapter to his prior marriage to a Cainite woman. Second, for Fletcher intermarriage is not a fruit of carelessness, lust, or submission to bestial passion but a deliberate attempt to subvert the order of creation. Thus, whether or not it involves sexual sin, intermarriage bespeaks rebellion and leads to chaos. As Fletcher writes, [man] "was placed under the government of laws adapted to his condition. But a want of conformity to any item of such law necessarily disorganized and deranged some portion of his original condition."[66]

That white concerns with racial amalgamation were rooted in fears of social chaos is suggested by the work of unrepentant Southerners writing in the aftermath of the Civil War. For dystopic predictions regarding the effects of black emancipation, "Ariel's" *The Negro: What is His Ethnological Status?* (1867) is unsurpassed. As this disillusioned Confederate interpreted the unfolding of American history through the lens of scriptural apocalypse, he likened the United States to the biblical societies that became subject to divine wrath. Like them, postbellum America was guilty of racial amalgamation, the only sin for which there is no atonement: "This crime *can not* be expiated—it never has been expiated on earth—and from its nature never can be, and, consequently, *never was forgiven by God, and never will be.*"[67] Like the generation of the Deluge, the conspirators at Babel, the inhabitants of Sodom and Gommorah, and the Canaanites, race-mixing Americans can expect quick and bitter judgment. For "Ariel," the choices are clear:

> The people of the United States have now thrust upon them, the question of negro equality, social, political and religious. How will they decide it? If they decide it one way, then they will make the *sixth* [actually, the fifth, unless "Ariel" regards the recent war as an episode of divine chastisement] cause of invoking God's wrath once again on the earth. They will begin to discover this approaching wrath: (1) By God bringing confusion. (2) By his breaking the government into pieces, or fragments, in which the negro will go and settle with those that favor this equality. (3) In God pouring out the fire of his wrath, on this portion of them; but in what way, or in what form, none can tell until it comes, only that in severity it will equal in intensity and torture, the destruction of fire burning them up. (4) The states or people

that favor this equality and amalgamation of the white and black races, *God will exterminate.*[68]

Will Americans repeat the fatal error committed by their biblical forebears? "Ariel" fears the worst: "Will *you* place yourselves . . . against God? All analogy says *you will!*" If antebellum proslavery literature connected the Negro with disorder and rebellion and the prospect of widespread manumission led Southerners to predict rebellion, race war, and economic disaster, the Emancipation Proclamation and radical reconstruction invested these fears with an apocalyptic spirit.

Disorder and Ham's Name

The obsession with Negro rebellion that made laughter a compelling theme among proslavery advocates of the curse also gave rise to a variety of depictions of Ham that accentuated his disorderly character. Some slavery apologists even "discovered" disorder in Ham's name.[69] Typical is Josiah Priest, who wrote that Ham's cognomen is so apropos of his personality that his parents "could not well have named that child any thing else but *Ham*, and keep within the bounds of the dialect of their language." The name was prophetic of his character and fortune, as well as those of his entire race, for Ham "not only signified black in its literal sense, but pointed out the very disposition of his mind":

> The word doubtless, has more meanings than we are now acquainted with, two of which, however, besides the first, we find are *heat* or *violence* of temper, exceedingly prone to acts of ferocity and cruelty, involving murder, war, butcheries and even *cannibalism*, including beastly lusts and lasciviousness in its *worst* feature, going beyond the force of these passions, as possessed in common by the other races of men. Second, the word signifies deceit, dishonesty, treachery, low mindedness, and malice.[70]

"What a group of horrors are here," Priest concludes, "all agreeing in a most surprising manner with the color of Ham's skin."[71] Note how many of the horrors Priest lists as cognates of "Ham"—violence, ferocity, cruelty, and lasciviousness, for example—reflect white fears of black disorder.

The Symbiosis of Honor and Order

What is the connection between the honor- and order-bound readings of Genesis 9 surveyed in this and the previous chapter? Although these themes have been treated independently, this should not obscure the fact that they informed and reinforced one another in the antebellum biblical imagination.[72]

In James Sloan's interpretation of Noah's curse, for example, honor and order operate in tandem.[73] According to Sloan, Ham's fault was his failure to observe God's command to honor parents. Very simply, "Ham deserved death for his unfilial and impious conduct." But there is more: Because Ham sought to involve his brothers in his unseemly enjoyment, despite their refusal to participate in the "improper and sinful sport of their brother," his conduct is both dishonorable and disorderly. Sloan writes that as punishment for his transgression "the Great Lawgiver ... set *a mark of degradation* on him ... that all coming generations might know and respect the laws of God."[74] Thus, in Sloan's mind, the concern for honor in Noah's family is inseparable from the desire that future generations preserve order by acting in accordance with divine law. Similarly, Leander Ker's honor reading of Ham's offense (in which he condemns the "conduct of Ham in exposing his father's shame") also resonates with disorder: Ham's is "the first deliberate and wilful offence [which] as in the case of Adam, according to the moral government of God, must be punished with the utmost rigor of law."[75] Finally, the author of *African Servitude,* in the midst of a thoroughgoing honor reading of Genesis 9, establishes this connection between dishonor and disorder: "In refusing to honor his parent, he refused to honor all governors, natural civil, ecclesiastical, human, and divine."[76]

Once again, the profound link between honor and order in the proslavery worldview is illumined by Southern historians. Exploring the meaning slave rebellions took on for Southern men of honor, Kenneth Greenberg observes that Nat Turner and John Brown could not be perceived as honorable men, despite their principled and sacrificial actions. Rather than one who preferred an honorable death over life in bondage, Turner was portrayed as a trickster and manipulator, an ignorant, superstitious, and cunning man.[77] Similarly, Bertram Wyatt-Brown writes that the antebellum code of honor "not only affected the way southern whites thought of themselves and others, but also influenced how they viewed hierarchy, government, and rebelliousness. The concept of honor was designed to give structure to life and meaning to valor, hierarchy, and family protection."[78]

Conclusion

The Civil War only strengthened resolve among Southern advocates of Noah's curse. As late as 1864, the General Assembly of the Presbyterian Church in the Confederate States of America defiantly proclaimed that "the long continued agitations of our adversaries have wrought within us a deeper conviction of the divine appointment of domestic servitude, and have led to a clearer comprehension of the duties we owe to the African race. We hesitate not to affirm that it is the peculiar mission of the Southern Church to conserve the institution of slavery, and to make it a blessing both to master and slave."[79]

But with Union victory came social and political realities that necessitated psychological adjustment among conquered Southerners. Noah's curse had been severely discredited by abolitionist exegesis, by the rise of scientific racism, and by Confederate defeat. The curse had functioned as a rationale for black slavery, and now slavery had disappeared, most likely forever. As Southerners no longer required biblical sanction for their peculiar institution, references to Genesis 9 abruptly disappeared from their writings.[80] If the curse was invoked in postbellum discussions of segregation, miscegenation, and voting rights, allusions were brief and vague. Precisely because Genesis 9:20–27 was considered so germane to the question of American slavery, it did not seem applicable to race relations in a free society. Thus, confident references to Genesis 9 so common in the antebellum period became conspicuously absent, as proponents of white superiority looked elsewhere to support their case.

But if the American attachment to Noah's curse was invisible in the century following the Civil War, it was not dead. When legal segregation came under concerted attack in the 1950s, the first impulse of many white Christians was to revive the curse to serve as a biblical defense of racial separation. Perhaps the linchpin in the biblical defense of slavery could be refashioned, segregationists wagered, for battle with the forces of integration. The most robust effort to apply Noah's curse to American segregation appeared in 1959 in Humphrey K. Ezell's *The Christian Problem of Racial Segregation*.[81] Claiming to engage in "a careful study of the Bible passages that relate to this subject," Ezell offered a gloss on the curse specifically adapted to the needs of the Christian segregationist. In a chapter titled "The Old Testament Teaches Racial Segregation," Ezell quoted Genesis 9:20–27 in its entirety, calling it "an important passage on racial segregation."[82]

The key in applying this passage to the situation at hand was Ezell's contention that "in this account God has segregated the races. Shem and Japheth are to dwell in tents together; but a curse is placed upon Ham and his descendants, and they are to be servants to Shem and Japheth."[83] Essential to Ezell's rehabilitation of Genesis 9 for segregationist use was his assertion that the white race in America is comprised of the descendants of Japheth and Shem, whereas the Negro is descended from Ham. To what he regards as this clear teaching (!) of Genesis 9, Ezell added that "the descendants of both Shem and Japheth have made far greater contributions to the advancement of the human race" than have Ham's. Further, the fact that human beings are "of one blood" (cf. Acts 17:26) does not remove "the curse of racial segregation and servitude" that has resulted from "Ham's sin." Finding no indication in either testament that the sentence of servitude upon Ham's descendants had been abrogated, Ezell likened the normative relationship between white and black to that of master and hired servant.

Although Ezell does not characterize Ham's fault, his description of the inevitable results of integration and racial mixing resonates with antebellum themes in the interpretation of Noah's curse, particularly order and disorder. Ezell calls attention to the so-called psychological characteristics of Negroes, which he argues include high emotionality and "childish gaiety"; he laments the "discord and strife," "confusion," "disciplinary problems," "mob rule," and "lawlessness" that integration promises to visit upon American society; he argues that as a principle of creation, segregation is necessary to maintain "growth and prosperity," "domestic tranquility," and "the general welfare and health of our people"; he contends that racial separation enables whites to demonstrate the "efficiency" that is their trademark; and he warns that removing traditional barriers to racial interaction will cause "the downfall of our nation," just as surely as Solomon's alliances with foreign women "laid the foundation for the downfall of the nation of Israel."

Because he was virtually alone in looking to Noah's curse as a primary rationale for maintaining American apartheid, Ezell's argument for "Bible segregation" is atypical. However, as his version of the curse traffics in the same concerns for societal order that inspired segregationists to introduce Nimrod and his tower to American racial discourse, Ezell's reading of Genesis 9 provides a natural segue to our discussion of the curse's transformation in post-bellum America.

6

Grandson of Disorder

Nimrod Comes to America

Now the whole earth had one language and the same
words. And as they migrated from the east, they came
upon a plain in the land of Shinar and settled there. And
they said to one another, "Come, let us make bricks, and
burn them thoroughly." And they had brick for stone, and
bitumen for mortar. Then they said, "Come, let us build
ourselves a city, and a tower with its top in the heavens,
and let us make a name for ourselves; otherwise we shall
be scattered abroad upon the face of the whole earth."
The LORD came down to see the city and the tower, which
mortals had built. And the LORD said, "Look, they are one
people, and they have all one language; and this is only
the beginning of what they will do; nothing that they propose to do will now be impossible for them. Come, let us
go down, and confuse their language there, so that they
will not understand one another's speech." So the LORD
scattered them abroad from there over the face of all the
earth, and they left off building the city. Therefore it was
called Babel, because there the LORD confused the language of all the earth; and from there the LORD scattered
them abroad over the face of all the earth.

Genesis 11:1–9

AS WE SAW in the previous chapter, slavery apologists developed explanations
of Ham's transgression that implicated African Americans in a primordial

violation of order. The present chapter explores how similar concerns are reflected in the portrait of Nimrod sketched by American Bible readers during the nineteenth and twentieth centuries. Americans embellished Nimrod's legend in distinctive ways, including a darkening of his portrait. Analyzing American versions of Nimrod's unauthorized biography will reveal how Bible readers have appropriated the leitmotifs of rebellion and disorder forged in antebellum readings of Noah's curse.

Ham and Nimrod

One of the strange ironies associated with Nimrod's legend is that it originated in a portion of scripture notably lacking in anti-African sentiment. Because the Table of Nations in Genesis 10 follows immediately upon Noah's curse, we might expect anti-Hamite prejudice to be inscribed there. However, as Gene Rice notes, "not only are such feelings absent, but all peoples are consciously and deliberately related to each other as brothers. No one, not even Israel, is elevated above anyone else and no disparaging remark is made about any people, not even the enemies of Israel."[1] Yet, while the Table of Nations may evoke images of equality and coexistence, its canonical proximity to Genesis 9:20–27 has encouraged Bible readers to make fast distinctions between Noah's descendants. If a brief and undisparaging allusion to Nimrod as a "mighty hunter before the Lord" gave rise to the profoundly vilifying interpretive tradition reviewed in chapter 3, this was due in part to the fact that Nimrod was only one generation removed from Ham.

In the history of interpretation, Ham shadowed, but never eclipsed, Nimrod. The two figures remained remarkably distinct in European readings of Genesis, and occasionally Nimrod's qualities were reflected onto Ham. But in the American biblical imagination, Nimrod has never escaped the contours of the Hamite character imagined in proslavery readings of Genesis 9. This fact has determined two aspects of Nimrod's American portrait: his depiction as a black man and as an archrebel. Nimrod's racial identity was based in the assumption that Ham was the progenitor of the African race and in influential texts—most notably Priest's *Slavery* and Hislop's *The Two Babylons*—that consciously racialized his grandson. Perceptions of Nimrod's rebellious character were rooted in the history of interpretation[2] and in order readings of Genesis 9. A brief history of Hamite disorder was sketched by Josiah Priest in 1843: "After Ham makes a mockery of him whom he ought to have respected . . . he leaves his father and his godly brothers and sets up a new kingdom for himself on the earth. Finally his oldest son presents him with a grandson, Nimrod, who, after setting up his power through tyranny, afflicts the godly descendants of Noah in various ways, establishes a kingdom for himself, and assumes sole sovereignty over it."[3] Priest moves from Ham's laughter to Nimrod's tyranny in just two sentences. While most American

Bible readers did not make the transition so swiftly, their portraits of Nimrod were profoundly influenced by the proslavery tradition of Hamite disorder. As this chapter reveals, postbellum Americans refused to relinquish Genesis 9–11 as a resource for comprehending their nation's history and destiny. Although the credibility of Noah's curse had been radically diminished, they preserved the Bible's relevance for American race relations by displacing Ham with Nimrod, who became the true patriarch of rebellion, the genuine personification of Hamite disorder.

Antebellum Period

The most important biographers of Nimrod in antebellum America were Josiah Priest and Jerome Holgate. Priest's *Slavery as It Relates to the Negro or African Race,* well known for its discussion of Ham and his curse, also included an influential treatment of Nimrod.[4] Priest averred that the Tower of Babel "was intended, under the administration of the ferocious Nimrod, as the nucleus of a kingdom of Idolatry"[5] and declared that Hamites alone were responsible for constructing the tower. None of the other "people of the house of Noah" were involved, nor were they affected by the resulting confusion of languages. Priest inferred these things from the biblical statement that Babel was the beginning of Nimrod's kingdom and "the natural antipathy of the children of Shem toward the blacks."

Priest ascribed responsibility for this enmity to Nimrod himself: The Hamites "rebelled against the religion of Noah and Shem, and the other patriarchs, under the rule of the terrible Nimrod . . . the black king of Babel . . . the first sovereign and tyrant of the age, as well as the abettor of idolatry."[6] Furthermore, it is from "the great rebel against God and his religion" that Africans inherit their "marked opposition to the religion of Noah, more than . . . the opposition of all the other nations of the earth put together."[7] According to Priest, Nimrod's spiritual rebellion was designed to "produce and consolidate a power, by which to protect his race against the threatened servitude of Noah . . . as well as to establish a contrary system of religion, which would subserve the same end."[8] As charges of rebellion and idolatry naturally invite association with the father of rebellion and idolatry, Priest likened Nimrod to "Satan among the fallen angels."

In Priest's conception of the Hamite character, idolatry is symptomatic of a lack of self-restraint. Whereas the white man views liberty as a path to moral and physical improvement, to "government of the passions" and a "well ordered society"; for the Negro—slave or free—"the idea of liberty is but the idea of a holyday, in which they are to be let loose from all restraint without control; they are to play, work or sleep, as may suit their inclination, following out to the utmost, the perfect indulgence of indolence, stupidity, and the animal passions."[9] Nimrod is the very embodiment of these qualities, as an illustration in Priest's book attests: Dressed in an animal skin, Nimrod wields a club against wild beasts. Priest embellishes this portrait of Nimrod's physical potency by drawing on the history of biblical interpretation, as well as secular mythology: "As to Nimrod, the hero of Babel, being the great type of all the Herculeses of the ancient nations, there can be no doubt; for the legends of every country who have claimed him to be a god, represent him as always being armed with a *club* of enormous size, with which he slew the monsters of the earth—dreadful serpents, wild beasts, &c."[10]

Anticipating the use to which Nimrod's legend would be put later in American history,[11] Priest notes that "a grand law of God in nature" is the adaptation of men or animals to their proper location. He maintains that the providence which led "blacks" to settle in the south, "whites" in the north, and "reds" in between "was in exact conformity with their several physical characters and constitutions, as well as a remarkable adaptation to their respective complexions. . . . If there was not a Divine hand in all this, why did . . . each division of the three sources of mankind studiously [keep] themselves apart in a great measure, and doubtless, far more so in the first ages?"[12] Here we have an American expression of the traditional notion that God directed the sons of Noah to prearranged spots on the globe and that Nimrod and the Hamites resisted this dispersion by squatting in territory reserved for Semites.

Priest's Nimrod is a fascinating admixture of biblical and mythological attributes, including brute strength, idolatrous rebellion, and Mephistophelean ingenuity. Yet Priest never loses sight of the genealogical link between Nimrod and his grandfather, the putative recipient of Noah's curse. To highlight the connection, Priest depicts Ham and Nimrod as contemporaries. According to Priest, it was Ham who left Noah's tents near Ararat and migrated toward the plain of Shinar, where Nimrod founded his empire, and it was "Ham and all the race" who participated in building the tower. Clearly, Priest's interest in Nimrod's legend is a function of its usefulness in depicting Ham's descendants as a beastly, uncivilized lot, suited for slavery. But Nimrod confronts him with the same paradox that had faced earlier Bible readers: How can a man as ferocious, mighty, and clever as Nimrod—a "gigantic and fierce" leader who becomes an object of popular veneration[13]—represent a race destined for servitude? Priest's answer seems to be that Nimrod's physical prowess represents another compelling reason to enslave American Negroes. In Priest's picture of Nimrod, we encounter the ambivalence of proslavery thought toward the African American, whose docility was celebrated precisely because he possessed inchoate power and a proclivity for resisting authority.

A different sort of portrayal of Nimrod is found in Jerome B. Holgate's 1860 novel, *Noachidae: or, Noah, and His Descendants*. This 350-page work was a fictionalized retelling of Genesis 6–11 (that is, accounts of the Flood and its immediate aftermath).[14] Although Ham's infidelity and disobedience are a major theme, the novel's real villain is Orion[15] (Nimrod), to whom an entire chapter is devoted. Orion is introduced as

a son of Cush, a gigantic youth, who was at least a head taller than his
brethren of the same age. He was not only taller and larger, but proportion-
ately stouter. He had the skin of a lion, which he had killed with his own
hands, fastened around his loins, and his head was covered with eagle's feath-
ers, and those of other birds, which he had killed. His bow was equal to his
fathers [sic] in size and force. To the families of Shem and Japhet he was an
object of considerable curiosity, and at first was quite a hero among them,
but his disposition was morose and overbearing. He was hardly known to
laugh, and if much pleased, or excited any way, would usually give vent to
his emotions, by a guttural ejaculation much like a whoop, or *ugh*, forced
up unwillingly, while his large dark eyes would blaze up and send out ser-
pentine gleams of light.... He was fond of hunting, rambling for days
among the woods and hills, crouching among the rocks and shooting at the
wild beasts as they passed.[16]

This description includes many references to the history of interpretation,
particularly Nimrod's prodigious size and strength, his success as a hunter,
his aggressive and unrefined character and his lack of intelligence. Adept at
fighting hordes of wild animals with a javelin and bow, Holgate's Orion is
quite similar to—and may have been influenced by—the Nimrod of Josiah
Priest.[17]

Not surprisingly, Holgate assumes Orion to have been the architect of the
infamous Tower of Babel. After departing Ararat, the Hamites experience mis-
adventure and famine until Nimrod convinces them to set out in pursuit of
Eden. In search of the garden, they arrive on the Plain of Shinar, where they
encounter Semites from the family of Asshur, to whom Noah has assigned
this region. Asshur asks Nimrod how "it could ever become necessary for one
branch of our father Noah's family to employ force to compel another branch
of it to obey his decrees."[18] But Nimrod will not acknowledge Noah's role as
God's vice-regent in the postdiluvian world; he rationalizes that defying his
great-grandfather is quite different from disobeying God.

The Semites know they are the land's rightful heirs, yet they cannot resist
the mighty Orion's appeal. The young men gather around him and exclaim,
"We will do as you say!" as Orion looks "on the excited crowd, with an
emotion visible in his countenance, and a smoky, smiling gleam of the eye."[19]
He encourages the sons of Shem to join the Hamites in constructing a city
and "a big tower, that will be above the waters." Young men from the families
of Lud and Arphaxad gather round him, forming "a kind of armed force, that
live[s], not so much by agricultural pursuits as by a shepherd's life, and by
hunting."[20] Others, coming near to catch a glimpse of the tower, are "be-
witched" by Nimrod and join the building campaign.

Even before completing the square structure that will measure eight hundred feet on each side, Orion is using it as an altar to the sun. Hearing of
this, Noah opines that "the foolish Hamites, rebelling against the Almighty in
one case, do not receive his spirit, and, being open to the attacks of Satan,

they are liable to be seduced away into some act of disobedience, as our poor mother Eve was."[21] In one scene, Orion ascends the tower with a sacrificial horse; Noah arrives to denounce this idolatry and to note that "Satan is making a speculation out of your conceit, my son." The tower's demise is realized when it is enveloped in a "column of phosphorescent light" and its upper portion tumbles to the ground "shaking the earth for miles around."[22] Although the rumor circulates that "the Almighty has killed Nimrod," hunters visiting the site a few days later discover a man crawling out of a hole in the ruins. The book concludes with the ominous words, "it was Nimrod."

If Holgate's Ham is a relatively benign character, his Nimrod is incorrigibly wicked. He and his work are described again and again as "wicked," and he embodies the perpetuation of antediluvian corruption in the post-Flood world. He is a gigantic and brutal man who boasts, "See how potent I am!" before performing feats of strength. He has a penchant for violence, as well as "a strong relish for the juice of the grape." He is the mastermind behind the ill-fated Tower of Babel and a blatant idolater. Noah calls Nimrod a "Titan—earth-born, carnal, without the spirit of the Almighty," his open revolt against God making him "conspicuously Titan." Nimrod represents a different brand of humanity than the "heaven-born,—spiritual men" who constitute the rest of Noah's family.[23] In Holgate's Dantean depiction, Nimrod is a "giant" not only in stature but also in his spiritless carnality. To complete this demonic portrait, Nimrod's mother confides to her son that she has always believed he was "the promised seed."

Significantly, Nimrod exemplifies Hamite evil not through sexuality, dishonor, violence, or idolatry, but through rebellion and disorder. He recognizes his obligation to leave the territory occupied by the descendants of Shem, but Noah's curse leads him to devise a rebellious plan. If we scatter and divide as our father Noah commands, Orion warns, we will become servants just as he predicted. Instead, he says, "we must make ourselves strong by union, and who'll make servants of us then? . . . This country given to Shem, eh? . . . Who told our father Noah to give it to him? We should have been consulted,—we are an item! Ugh! . . . let us build a city, and tower that will reach unto heaven, and keep together, and make ourselves strong; then who will make slaves of us?"[24] Throughout the novel, the narrator condemns this Hamite contempt for the divinely appointed ordering of the world. For instance, as construction begins on the tower, a Semite woman appears to convince Nimrod that the dispersion of Noah's sons must be strictly enforced:

> The Almighty knows best what is for our interest. Our father Noah says, his children must be distributed over the earth, so as to prevent their interfering with one another. It might answer very well for a little while, but in time, if they are not widely separated, it will bring trouble. There will be no end of it, he says, when they once begin; so you are setting yourself directly against his decrees, and he may drown you all with another flood. . . . [25]

Because he personifies resistance to this dispersion of the "races," Nimrod is a primordial threat to the world's order. Thus, *Noachidae* is primary concerned not with the curse on Ham's descendants but with the need for human dispersion and the Hamites' propensity for rebellion.

Occasional references to Nimrod in the writings of proslavery intellectuals confirm that his role as exemplar of Hamite disorder was well established during the antebellum period. In 1823, Frederick Dalcho asserted that "the sons of Canaan usurped Palestine, as well as the sons of Cush, under Nimrod, the land of Shinar, or Babel."[26] Two decades later, Thomas Smyth, Presbyterian divine of South Carolina, used Nimrod's behavior to illustrate the effects of the curse. In a vigorous defense of the biblical view of creation, Smyth averred that "the 10th and 11th chapters of Genesis are unquestionably the best ethnographical document on the face of the earth." According to Smyth, this document teaches that the descendants of Ham "refused to abide by the allotment of God, and under the arch-rebel Nimrod, drove out Asshur and his sons, who had been located in the plains of Shinar (Chap x. 11)."[27] In reiterating this ancient dimension of the Nimrod legend, Smyth and Dalcho confirm that among antebellum proslavery intellectuals Cush's son was viewed as an exemplar of Hamite rebellion.[28]

Nimrod was also featured in the works of abolitionist writers who relied on Ham's grandson to advance the case for anti-slavery.[29] For example, Joseph P. Thompson wrote in 1856 that since "NIMROD [was] . . . the founder of that Assyrian empire which for ages ruled all western Asia, . . . the growth of all this grandeur and power . . . surely does not verify the curse of perpetual bondage *said* to have been pronounced upon the posterity of Ham."[30] Another opponent of slavery who employed Nimrod to cast doubt on Ham's curse was William Henry Brisbane. In 1847, Brisbane asked his readers to recall that Noah's malediction did not fall upon all of Ham's posterity. In fact, "the very first man mentioned as a *mighty one* in the earth was Nimrod, a descendant from Ham. In the same lineal descent from Ham was Asshur, who built Nineveh. The posterity of Abraham who descended from Shem were carried captive into Assyria of which Nineveh was the capital."[31]

Nimrod was put to quite another use by black abolitionist James W. C. Pennington, who invoked Ham's grandson to explain the historic degradation of the African people. Although Pennington contended that blacks were descendants of Cush and Mizraim, he felt obliged to explain why Africans had strayed so far from the pure religion of Noah. The culprit, according to Pennington, was "the doctrine invented by Nimrod, [which] began to prevail immediately after his death, as he was worshipped by his posterity. He is the Belus or Baal of sacred history. This doctrine was adopted by the Ethiopians of the second generation, and became firmly incorporated into their theology, their government, and their literature."[32] Pennington found the legend of Nimrod useful for explaining the immorality, heathenism, idolatry, and ancestor worship current in Africa during his own day. Thompson and Brisbane utilized Nimrod as a foil to Ham's curse. But each inadvertently transmitted Nimrod's legend, including aspects that could be put to racist use.

Postbellum Period

The first postbellum author to give Nimrod prominence in a published discussion of racial matters was Buckner H. Payne, who wrote under the pen name Ariel a forty-eight-page pamphlet titled *The Negro: What Is His Ethnological Status?* (1867) that confirms Eugene Genovese's observation that following the Civil War Southerners were increasingly receptive to "scientific" arguments for black inferiority. "Ariel" contends that his opinions are guided solely by the Bible, history, and the "logic of facts." Yet he dissents dramatically from prewar tradition by defending "the maligned and slandered Ham" and insisting that the Negro is a pre-Adamite beast of the field who was preserved on the ark. According to "Ariel," Negroes entered the ark with the other creatures, probably by sevens.

While his desire to dehumanize blacks forces him to relinquish Noah's curse, "Ariel" ingeniously preserves the stigma of Nimrod and his tower. He replaces the genetic link between the Adamite Ham and the beastly Negro with an associative link between Nimrod and his followers, whom he characterizes as "mostly negroes." How do we know that "the great multitude that assembled on the Plain of Shinar," a multitude "assembled by his arbitrary power, and other inducements," were primarily blacks? The "facts" are stated in Genesis 10: Nimrod "*must* have resorted to [negroes] to get the multitude that he assembled on the Plain of Shinar; for the Bible plainly tells us where the other descendants of Noah's children went, including those of Nimrod's immediate relations; and from the Bible account where they did go to, it is evident that they did not go with Nimrod to Shinar."[33] "Ariel" finds further support for his theory in the observation that the Negro, "when unrestrained, never inhabits mountainous districts or countries; and therefore we readily find him in the level Plain of Shinar."[34]

Despite his commitment to an "ethnological" theory of black identity, "Ariel's" picture of Nimrod is profoundly reliant on the history of biblical interpretation.[35] Nimrod is portrayed as a tyrant, "the first on earth who began to monopolize power and play the despot," a hunter of men as well as wild animals. "Ariel" even connects Nimrod with the biblical Flood narrative, combining the ancient view that the Tower of Babel was a scheme to protect the builders from another deluge with the notion—popularized in the 1850s by John Fletcher—that the Flood represented God's reaction to the sin of race mixing.[36] Combining these disparate strands of tradition, "Ariel" reasons that if Nimrod expected a flood he must have intended to perpetuate the same sin for which the first deluge was unleashed—amalgamation between Adamites and soulless beasts. Clearly, "Nimrod was not entirely cured, by the flood, of this antediluvian love for and miscegenation with negroes."[37] Otherwise, why build such a tower? "Ariel" also retrieves the tradition that the tower builders resisted the postdiluvian dispersion, though he adapts it to his theory of black origins. Because the "Babel-builders knew they were but beasts . . . [and that] it was the very *nature* of beasts to be scattered over the earth," they sought a name for themselves by constructing the tower. The conspirators also proposed to build a city where their power could be concentrated, making it impossible for Noah's descendants to subdue the earth. It was precisely "to prevent this concentration of power and numbers, that God confounded their language, broke them into bands, overthrew their tower, stopped the building of their city, and scattered or dispersed them over the earth."[38]

Despite his ambitious attempt to refashion white racism in "scientific" terms, "Ariel" remained dependent on the legend of Nimrod and its association with Hamite disorder. On one hand, Nimrod subdues Negroes "for the purposes of rebellion against God," and his identity as a "*mighty* hunter . . . *against* the Lord" is intimately related to this fact. On the other hand, Nimrod's tyranny becomes a racial crime in itself: "*Kingly power* had its origin in love for and association with the negro. Beware!" Thus, the ancient conception of Nimrod as the primordial human rebel and the modern view of Nimrod as a shameless miscegenist are carefully combined in "Ariel's" portrait of the grandson of disorder.

Writing forty years after "Ariel," the Mississippi cleric and Confederate war veteran J. W. Sandell reflects a similar shift from Genesis 9:20–27 to Genesis 10–11 as the epicenter of American racial readings of Genesis. In *The United States in Scripture,* Sandell reiterates the efficacy of Noah's curse, though four decades after the Emancipation Proclamation he is obliged to view it in terms of ungovernability rather than servitude. Sandell interprets the curse to mean that the Negro race was "prophetically condemned to an inferior relation to that of Shem and Japheth, was not fit for self-government and should not rule in either church or state."[39] In much the same way as "Ariel," Sandell exploits Nimrod's legend, although he focuses on its potential as a biblical rationale for racial segregation. "It is an outrage upon nature," Sandell writes, "to undertake to force the extremes of the races to equality with each other." This was demonstrated in the sinful attempt to construct the Tower of Babel, which symbolizes "the desire to be great and to have a name as one great nation." Because "the ambition for a great central government with one fallible human creature as supreme ruler is not at all pleasing to the Supreme Ruler of the universe, . . . God has divided the races of men and they are scattered over the face of the earth."[40] For Sandell, the tower symbolizes what die-hard Confederates regarded as the chief threat to human freedom—a centralized and self-aggrandizing federal government. Sandell compared such governments to Babel (Genesis 11) and Babylon (Revelation) alike.

American society underwent momentous changes between 1843 (when Priest presented his portrait of Nimrod), 1867 (when "Ariel" completed his own portrayal), and 1907 (when Sandell rendered his). Curiously, though, while these authors differed fundamentally on the origin and ethnological status of blacks, they agreed that the Tower of Babel was the product of a Negro-led or executed rebellion that was a threat to human survival in the past and a warning to Americans in the present. This consensus anticipated the pivotal role Nimrod and his tower would play in white perceptions of the African American during the twentieth century.

Twentieth Century

As we have seen, despite the diminished potency of Noah's curse that naturally accompanied slavery's demise, in the second half of the nineteenth century Genesis 10 and 11 figured prominently in American discussions of black inferiority and the necessity of racial segregation. In the first half of the twentieth century, when segregation and racial hierarchy were largely uncontested, arguments claiming biblical sanction for black subjugation were less likely to find their way into print. During this period, the legend of Nimrod and his tower was kept alive in popular biblical commentaries and preaching aids. While ignoring the question of Nimrod's racial identity, these works reiterated aspects of the interpretive tradition that were foundational to American versions of his legend:

- The postdiluvian chapters of the primeval history (Genesis 9–11) set out the principles upon which our world is founded.
- God willed that after the Flood Noah's descendants should disperse and repopulate the world.
- Those who resisted this dispersion were very likely led by Nimrod, whose name means "let us rebel."[41]
- The emblems of this postdiluvian defiance were the Hamite usurpation of Semitic land and the building of the Tower of Babel.[42]
- Nimrod, like Ham and Canaan, forsook the religion of Noah and encouraged idolatry.
- Nimrod was a hunter of men, "a cruel oppressor and bloody warrior," who renewed the practice of war.
- Nimrod was the first tyrant and the first to found and rule a world empire.[43]
- God thwarted the rebellion at Babel and dispersed the builders according to the original divine scheme.

Some biblical expositors found in Nimrod's legend an edifying message in the otherwise tedious genealogical tables of Genesis 10. Joseph Exell, for example, presented the mighty hunter as a model for "gospel archery." Imagining the hero with "broad shoulders and shaggy apparel and sun-browned face, and arm bunched with muscle," Exell asked, "if it is such a grand thing and such a brave thing to clear wild beasts out of a country," is it not a better thing "to hunt down and destroy those great evils of society that are stalking the land with the fierce eye and bloody paw, and sharp tusk and quick spring."[44] Arthur Pink fashioned Nimrod as a forerunner of "the last great World-Ruler" who precedes Christ's Second Coming. Among seven parallels between Nimrod and the coming Antichrist, Pink noted their names (cf. "The Rebel" and "The Lawless One"), their rebellions (both head great confederacies in open revolt against God), their identities as "king," their occupations as "hunters of men," and their inordinate desire for fame.[45] In his description of this "complete typical picture" of Antichrist, Pink merged the interpretive tradition and modern premillennial eschatology:

> In Nimrod and his schemes we see Satan's initial attempt to raise up a universal ruler of men. In his inordinate desire for fame, in the mighty power which he wielded, in his ruthless and brutal methods—suggested by the word "hunter"; in his blatant defiance of the Creator (seen in his utter disregard for His command to replenish the earth) by determining to prevent his subjects from being scattered abroad; in his founding of the kingdom of Babylon—the Gate of god—thus arrogating to himself Divine honors;.... and finally, in the fact that the destruction of his kingdom is described in the words, "Let us *go down* and there confound their language" (11:7—foreshadowing so marvelously the *descent of Christ* from Heaven ...).[46]

Other Christian authors writing in the first half of the twentieth century, equally uninterested in racializing the biblical patriarchs, applied the legend of Nimrod to contemporary world politics. In *God and the Nations* (1947), Harry Lacey advanced the familiar argument that following the Deluge God moved each race "to its own appointed region with its particular character and climate."[47] God prepared each land, Lacey argued, "with a view toward separating the sons of Adam," that each nation might live out its national experience before God. Lacey identified a clear lesson for postwar America in God's decision to divide the human race "rather than communising it."[48] It may appear desirable, Lacey wrote, to "unite mankind in federation, working as one to accomplish human ambitions." But Lacey contended that such "arranged federations" would lead not to true human fellowship, but to "uniformity or monotonous sameness."[49] Attempts to abolish national or racial distinctions would not prevent wars, Lacey warned. In fact, that current attempts to unify humankind are but the forerunners of greater and more ambitious schemes is clearly revealed in the word of God. Although these attempts may gain some measure of success, they "will be as anti-God in [their] object and prove as disastrous in [their] end as original Babel was."[50] For Lacey, Genesis 10–11 validated the separate existence of nations while cautioning against schemes of international confederation. In a shrinking postwar world defined by the cold war, the tower became the "symbol of human unity so signally confounded by Divine intervention."[51]

Defending Segregation

Racial readings of Genesis 9–11 reemerged with a vergeance during the segregation debates of the 1950s and 1960s. Not surprisingly, the story of Noah and his sons played a symbolic role in these debates. For instance, in his contribution to a 534-hour Senate filibuster against the 1964 Civil Rights Act, Senator Robert Byrd of West Virginia read the Authorized Version of Genesis 9:18–27 into the Congressional Record, remarking that "Noah apparently saw fit to discriminate against Ham's descendants in that he placed a curse upon Canaan."[52] Ingeniously, Byrd applied Noah's curse to the impending Civil Rights legislation by recasting it as a biblical rationale for "discrimination."

Further indications of the curse's popularity during the civil rights era can be gleaned from the writings of moderate Christians who assailed the biblical and theological bases of segregation.[53] Indeed, religious integrationists writing during the second half of the 1950s identified Genesis 9:20–27 as a fundamental underpinning of segregationist sentiment. According to T. B. Maston, who in *The Bible and Race* devoted an entire chapter to Noah's curse, proponents interpreted the curse to mean "that the Negro, as a descendant of Ham, is destined by God to fill permanently a subservient place in society, that he should never be considered an equal by the white man. On the basis of the curse, some even contend that the Negro is innately inferior and that he can never lift himself or be lifted to the intellectual, cultural, or even moral level of other races."[54] Progressive authors such as Maston, embarrassed by the curse's enduring popularity in the churches, took up the abolitionists' mantle in an effort to loosen the curse's grip on the Christian mind.[55] Yet they virtually ignored Nimrod and his tower as sources for a religious defense of racial separation.[56] To the extent that they were unaware of the potent connection between Ham, Nimrod, and Babel, their assault on "Bible segregation" was misplaced, for thoughtful Christians in search of a biblical rationale for separation concluded that, like Nimrod's kingdom, they should begin at Babel.

Published justifications of segregation that relied on racial readings of Nimrod and his tower began to appear in the immediate aftermath of the 1954 Supreme Court decision in *Brown v. Board of Education.* Among the first to enter the fray was Rev. T. G. Gillespie, a Southern Presbyterian who was President of Bellhaven College in Jackson, Mississippi. In a celebrated address entitled "A Christian View of Segregation," Gillespie explored the biblical foundations for racial separation.[57] Gillespie emphasized an argument popularized in nineteenth-century American racial discourse: Following the Deluge, Noah's three sons "became the progenitors of three distinct racial groups, which were to repeople and overspread the earth." According to Gillespie, the descendants of Shem occupied most of Asia, the progeny of Japheth traveled west toward Europe, and the children of Ham moved southward in the direction of the tropics and the continent of Africa. This biblical record of human dispersion, which Gillespie maintained had not been successfully disputed by anthropologists or ethnologists, implied "that an all-wise Providence has 'determined the times before appointed, and the bounds of their habitation' [Acts 17:26]." This same Providence was "responsible for the distinct racial characteristics which seem to have become fixed in prehistoric times, and which are chiefly responsible for the segregation of racial groups across the centuries and in our time."[58]

According to Gillespie, the confusion of tongues at Babel and the consequent scattering of peoples was "an act of special Divine Providence to frustrate the mistaken efforts of godless men to assure the permanent integration of the peoples of the earth." Incidentally, he argued, the development of different languages also became an effective means of preserving the separate existence of racial groups. Interpretations of this and other biblical texts (he treats twelve, four of them from Genesis) comprise the heart of Gillespie's argument that racial segregation is fully compatible with Christianity. Although Gillespie does not name Nimrod, his argument is based on precisely the same fears—black rebellion and disorder—that white Bible readers saw personified in the figures of Ham and his grandson.[59]

In 1956, Kenneth R. Kinney presented a similar argument for segregation in *The Baptist Bulletin*.[60] Titled "The Segregation Issue," Kinney's article proclaimed his "firm conviction that *God* ordained, for the period of man's life on earth, the segregation (which term is the equivalent of the familiar Biblical term 'separation') of the three lines which descended from the sons of Noah— that is, the Japhetic, the Shemitic and the Hamitic."[61] Leaning on these biblical precedents, Kinney counseled his readers to "face the fact that God drew the lines of segregation (or separation) according to His purpose." Kinney emphasized, however, the profound historical reality that one of these three segregated groups—the Hamitic—possessed "a spirit of rebellion." According to Kinney, this spirit was manifest in Hamite occupation of the Semites' inheritance in the land of Shinar. "The judgment of Babel," then, came as a result of resistance to God's decree that Noah's descendants separate and disperse according to plan. Each group would be under the blessing of God as long as it observed "the bounds of their habitation." That the Hamites did not and have not done so may well account for their inferior position in society, Kinney opined. However,

> the correction of their condition is not to be found in falling in with the spirit of Hamitic rebellion, but for them to return to the proper observation of God's order; thus to develop their own culture. Thus, we believe, to return to the principle of *separate* but *equal* cultures. . . . [I]t would seem that as it was the Hamitic family of old which rebelled against God's "order," so their descendants are doing today, aided and abetted by spurious liberals whose

bleeding hearts are likely more concerned about *votes* than about the people involved.[62]

"What this orderly line of segregation would have meant to the world," Kinney laments, "was never to be seen because of the disorderly conduct of the Hamitic family." Segregation is Kinney's prescription for ensuring order in the future. In fact, because God intended that the three original groups should maintain familial and national identity, the descendants of these groups are scripturally bound to do the same. Furthermore, intermarriage between "Japhetic (European), Shemitic (Oriental) and Hamitic (African) groups" ought to be forbidden. Like Gillespie, Kinney does not mention Nimrod by name. But he does refer parenthetically to Genesis 10:6–9 and 11:1–9, the very passages earlier Bible readers had used to link Nimrod with the rebellion at Babel. These authors demonstrate that in the wake of the momentous Supreme Court decision that struck down "separate but equal" public schools, the rhetoric of rebellion and disorder that figured so prominently in nineteenth-century racial readings of Genesis 9–11 reanimated conservative religious discourse.

Dake's Annotated Reference Bible, first published in 1963 by Georgian Finis Jennings Dake, includes a long annotation on Nimrod and his tower. It begins with the observation that Nimrod's name is derived from the Hebrew "*marad,* to rebel, or 'we will rebel.' It points to some violent and open rebellion against God. . . . His rebellion is associated with the beginning of his kingdom and suggests that his hunting and mighty deeds were related primarily to hunting men by tyranny and force." In his "despotic rule over men," Nimrod became a great leader, taught men to centralize, and defied God to send another flood. Nimrod "established the first kingdom and the first great universal false religion opposing God. . . . That is why God, when He came down to see Babel, took action to counteract the rebellion of Nimrod (11:1–9)." Here we see the beginning of empires among men, writes Dake, "the achievements of lawless tyrants who taught men to revolt against divine laws and duly constituted authority."[63] Dake discusses the tower in a short article entitled "Separation in Scripture":

> God made "all nations of men" from "one blood"; [Acts 17:27] also speaks of "the bounds of their habitation." In spite of a common ancestry, from Adam first and later Noah, it was God's will for man to scatter over the earth, to "be fruitful and multiply" (Gen. 1:28; 8:17; 9:1). Man's failure to obey caused God to confuse his language (Gen. 11:1–9) and to physically separate the nations by dividing the earth into continents (Gen. 10:25). Both physically and spiritually, separation has been a consistent theme for God's people.[64]

In presenting racial segregation as God's will and Nimrod as a rebellious Negro in the line of Ham,[65] *Dake's Annotated Reference Bible* combines the elements of Nimrod's legend that were embraced by white Christians who resisted the civil rights movement.

By the mid-1960s, the legal status of segregation had been settled in America's courts and political chambers. But segregation's staunchest proponents continued to fight, insisting that integration was the leading edge of a social revolution bent on "overthrowing God's established order."[66] As conservative Christians reacted to what they regarded as perilous change, they pressed Nimrod's legend into service. One example is Corey Daniel of Dallas, a Baptist preacher who utilized the legend to depict integration as part of a demonic social scheme. More explicitly than Gillespie or Kinney, Daniel combined race and disorder in his portrait of Nimrod, "the Negro leader of the Babel-builders (Gen 10:6–10), whose name means 'Rebel.' "[67]

Evidence of a divine blueprint for separation Daniel located in the creation story,[68] as well as in the tripartite division of humankind after the Flood:

> Just as the good Lord assigned three different habitations—air, sea and land—to the fowls, the fish and the animals, so He assigned three parts of the earth (proportionate with their future numbers) to the three sons of Noah and their families. That is why we are told that "When the most High gave the nations (or races) their inheritance, when he separated the children of men, HE SET THE BOUNDS OF THE PEOPLE according (in proportion) to the number of children of Israel" (Deut. 32:3 A.S.V.).[69]

According to Daniel, this segregationist pattern is inscribed in the books of nature and scripture alike. Just as the Bible "repeatedly forbids the co-mingling of the children of Shem, Ham and Japheth, so Mother Nature with her huge barriers of oceans, deserts and gigantic mountain ranges clearly confirms the same lesson."[70]

The Tower of Babel was built in open defiance of God's plan of separation.[71] Daniel's description of the tower centers on Nimrod ("Let us Rebel"), a powerful leader who commanded the tower builders. In terms reminiscent of the interpretive tradition, Daniel casts Nimrod as "a twofold rebel, a double-dyed anarchist," who resisted both God's plan of salvation and God's scheme of racial segregation. All this may be inferred, Daniel believes, from the reasons given for building the tower: "FIRST, TO 'MAKE US A NAME.' Nimrod ignored the 'name Above Every Name,' the Lord Jesus Christ. . . . SECONDLY, 'LEST WE BE SCATTERED ABROAD UPON THE FACE OF THE WHOLE EARTH.' That was just exactly what the Lord had told them to do many years before then—to scatter and separate from one another racially. When they persistently refused to do so GOD HIMSELF scattered them."[72] According to Daniel, God confounded the speech of the tower builders in an effort to resegregate the "three races" and to remove all temptation toward reunion.

A novel contribution to the legend of Nimrod and his tower is Daniel's discussion of Habakkuk 3:6–7:

> He stopped and shook the earth;
> he looked and made the nations tremble.

The eternal mountains were shattered;
along his ancient pathways
the everlasting hills sank low.
I saw the tents of Cushan under affliction;
the tent-curtains of the land of Midian trembled.

According to Daniel, this passage refers to God's condemnation of the Babel builders; its theme "is God's wrath at the integration of the Babel-builders and His forcible separation of the 'nations,' the three major races, at the Tower of Babel. Then it was that 'the tents of Cushan' (the descendants of Cush, the father of Nimrod) were in affliction."[73] Daniel regards this as "God's poetic way of saying that all nature united to express its approval of His three-fold division of the human family." He adds that Ham's grandson "was so obviously the mouthpiece of the Devil that I might have done better if I had entitled this section [of the sermon] 'Satan the Original Integrationist.' "

Like many Southern conservatives, Daniel associated the campaign for civil rights with socialism, internationalism, and revolutionary dictatorship. In fact, the alliance between integration and the loss of individual freedom is exceedingly close in Daniel's mind.[74] Using epithets such as "those first unholy one worlders" and "the United Nations' modern tower of Babel," Daniel applies Genesis 11 to popular anxieties about America's role in a changing world. In another reference to Habbakuk 3, he claims that "the tents of Cushan" are "the headquarters of the rebellious opposition [to God's will] which was determined to keep all the people of the world integrated when God wanted them segregated (Gen. 10:32 to 11:1–9). . . . In 'driving asunder' that first unholy bunch of One-Worlders, God has given us a fairly good idea of what He thinks about the present-day bunch and of what he plans eventually to do with them."[75] In the United Nations, Daniel perceives "an amazing parallel" to the tower. Like the Babel-builders, the UN seeks to integrate races and governments, "lest [they] be scattered abroad upon the face of the whole earth." Again like the architects of that ancient UN, the modern internationalists "are ignoring, when they are not actively blaspheming, the Lord Jesus Christ and His glorious gospel blood redemption."[76] Thus, in Daniel's view, Nimrod is the patriarch of all schemes to consolidate in rebellion against God.

In *Place of Race* (1965), C. E. McLain connected the Tower of Babel with the "sons of God" of Genesis 6:1. McLain reasoned that because "Babel" means "gateway to the gods," the tower builders of chapter 11 must be identical with the *Nephilim* mentioned in chapter 6. Drawing on the interpretive tradition, McLain combined the image of a giant Nimrod with the assumption that the "sons of God" (= *Nephilim*) were prodigious beings as well.[77] Babylon's founder was Nimrod, whom scripture refers to as "a mighty hunter before the Lord" because he was a "hunter of men to the subversion of the soul." Nimrod's name offers insight into his character. In fact, the Bible's description of Ham's grandson comprises a "portrait of the world's first human dictator. The Scriptures as well as the facts of history reveal that Nimrod did the most complete job of brainwashing that the world has ever known."[78] In a chapter titled "Straight Ahead Lies Babel," McLain identifies Karl Marx and Charles Darwin as modern counterparts to the Nimrod of old, and he opines that we are still living in "the days of Noah," whose signs include "twentieth-century Babel (one-worldism)."

In McLain and Daniel, we encounter versions of Nimrod's biography that address both the specific challenge of government-mandated integration and the intellectual and political forces dreaded by conservatives in post-1960s America. Viewed as the original project of human consolidation, Nimrod's tower is an emblem of modern social ills, including intermarriage, internationalism, socialism, communism, evolution, and church unification.[79] Uniting these threats and connecting them with Genesis 9–11 is the theme of "rebellion," a term that becomes synonymous with Nimrod's name and character.

Conclusion

Our explorations in this chapter indicate that the traditions linking Nimrod and the Tower of Babel have attracted white American Bible readers in four distinct cultural milieux. Nimrod's legend was first embraced by nineteenth-century proslavery intellectuals, some of whom saw in the archetypal warrior an embodiment of black disorder, others a vision of primal rebellion useful in condemning federal "tyranny." In both cases, the significance of Nimrod and his tower were determined by proslavery readings of Genesis 9, the rebellion of Ham's grandson reflecting white fears of slave insurrection. During the first half of the twentieth century, the legend of a deracialized Nimrod was transmitted in popular Bible commentaries and devotional aids. Then, in the wake of *Brown v. Board of Education*, a Negro Nimrod reemerged in the writings of white segregationists, who portrayed him as the personification of rebellion against legitimate order and his tower as a symbol of integrationist schemes. Finally, since the mid-1960s, the tradition of Nimrod's tower has been favored by conservative, separatist Christians who are instinctively fearful of ecumenical and international movements. This is illuminating evidence of the process by which Bible readers have seized upon Ham's mysterious grandson to interpret their experiences and project their fears. In the portrait of Nimrod that emerges in American readings of Genesis between the antebellum period and the end of the twentieth century, his character and career are transparent expressions of American cultural concerns.

III

NOAH'S CAMERA

7

Noah's Sons in New Orleans

Genesis 9–11 and Benjamin Morgan Palmer

If we ascend the stream of history to its source, we shall discover God dividing the earth between the sons of Noah, "every one after his tongue, after their families, in their nations"; and with such remarkable precision that to this day we can trace "the bounds of their habitations," even as they were originally appointed. Indeed, the outspreading landscape of all history is embraced within the camera of Noah's brief prophecy; showing how from the beginning God not only distributed them upon the face of the earth, but impressed upon each branch the type of character fitting it for its mission.

Benjamin M. Palmer, 1863

BENJAMIN M. PALMER was the "founding father" of the Southern Presbyterian church, one of New Orleans's most esteemed citizens during the second half of the nineteenth century, and among the great pulpit orators of his generation.[1] He is credited by friend and foe alike with tipping the scales in favor of secession in Louisiana and with boosting the Confederacy's moral legitimacy in the Old Southwest. As one recent study has concluded, "no Southern clergyman outdid Palmer . . . in bellicosity from the pulpit in the early months of 1861 and throughout the next four years."[2]

These facts are acknowledged by all who assess Palmer's career; yet scholars have failed to gauge the centrality of Genesis 9–11 in the thought of this Southern clergy intellectual. It is well documented that Palmer was an influential and unrepentant advocate of slavery prior to 1861. What is overlooked is that he regarded Noah's curse as a rationale not only for slavery in general but also for the enslavement of Africans in particular. Eugene D. Genovese has argued that the basic Southern religious argument for slavery had little to do with race and that many antebellum divines regarded the Noahic curse as "feeble."[3] Neither was true of Palmer, in whose mind Noah's curse had everything to do with "race" and with the racial hierarchy that fueled American destiny. Scholars have also failed to note the abiding significance of Genesis 9–11 for Palmer's understanding of church and society following the Civil War. Although "scientific" racism did exercise an influence upon his reading of the Bible, Palmer turned again and again to Genesis 9–11 when called upon to apply the biblical witness to crucial societal issues during and after Reconstruction. Genovese has written that following the demise of slavery Southern divines opposed integration "with arguments grounded in politics rather than Scripture."[4] Again, this generalization does not apply to Palmer, who failed to embrace secular arguments to sustain his social and political views. In fact, Palmer may be unique insofar as his attention to Genesis 9–11 and its implications for race relations intensified during and after the Civil War.

Thus, assessment of Palmer's use of Genesis 9–11 between 1855 and 1901 elucidates our study of Noah's curse in several important ways. First, because Palmer survived the Civil War to become a religious leader of great stature, he allows us to glimpse some of the continuities in the American biblical imagination. Second, Palmer's writings provide a unique opportunity to observe the unfolding of religious racism within a single mind. The evolution of his racial discourse is particularly helpful in clarifying the transition between Ham and Nimrod in the application of scripture to American race relations. As we have seen, for those who sought in Genesis a blueprint for the organization of American society, the Civil War marked a shift in focus from Noah's curse to Nimrod's tower. This is confirmed in Palmer's case, with the center of gravity in his interpretation of Genesis moving from curse to dispersion sometime in 1863.

Third, careful analysis of Palmer's writings enables us to identify some of the intellectual currents that have buttressed antiblack biblical interpretation in American history. For Palmer, these were the Schlegelian concepts of historic and unhistoric nations, the notion that societies are organic entities invested with divine trusts, "scientific" speculation concerning racial difference, and white common sense. As Mark Noll has noted, the spirit of biblical interpretation that dominated nineteenth-century America was "a hermeneutic compounded of reformed theological instincts and commonsense literalism."[5] However, among advocates of slavery, common sense often was replaced by racist instincts or intuitions. "On slavery, exegetes stood for a commonsense reading of the Bible. On race, exegetes forsook the Bible and relied on common sense."[6] This "intuitive racism" is particularly clear in Palmer's case, as he used history and science to confirm a racial hierarchy that is foreign to scripture. The various ingredients in Palmer's racial discourse—a romantic philosophy of history, a view of Providence in which God guides the character and history of nations, scientific racism, and white common sense—were combined in various measures depending on the time, place, and audience Palmer was addressing. Yet the fact that he did not alter his basic hermeneutical recipe after the 1850s is testimony to the remarkable flexibility of Genesis 9–11 as a source of American racism.

Finally, Palmer's career is instructive because students of postbellum America have concluded that the twenty-five-year period between the end of the war and the full implementation of legal segregation around 1890 represented a unique window of opportunity for the creation of an integrated South.[7] Because Palmer was "at the summit of his powers and productivity" during this period, he might have made a mighty contribution toward the goal of a truly new South, had he been compelled to do so. However, between 1865 and 1890 Palmer devoted tremendous energy and moral capital to ensuring that God's economy of racial separation and Anglo-Saxon domination were reflected in church and society alike.

The preeminent role Genesis 9–11 played in Palmer's worldview is suggested by the image he was fond of applying to Noah's pronouncement in Genesis 9:25–27. Palmer claimed that "the outspreading landscape of all history is embraced within the camera of Noah's brief prophecy." As we shall see, *Noah's camera* was the lens through which Palmer consistently viewed American history during the second half of the nineteenth century. As such, it is also a lens for clarifying the effects of biblical faith in American history. This chapter surveys Palmer's evolving interpretation of Genesis 9–11 between 1855 and 1902 and explores how he applied these chapters to emerging episodes in American racial history, particularly when they could no longer be applied to the defense of slavery.

Palmer's Life and Times

As pastor of First Presbyterian Church in New Orleans from 1856 until his death in 1902, Benjamin M. Palmer was New Orleans's preeminent clergyman. He was a moving force in the Southern Presbyterian church from its inception in 1861, was elected to chairs at leading academic institutions, and was called to moderate several of his denomination's general assemblies. In addition, Palmer was a founding editor of both *Southern Presbyterian Review* and *Southwestern Presbyterian*. Due largely to his skill as a pulpit orator, Palmer's First Presbyterian Church of New Orleans was the largest in the Synod of Mississippi and the fourth largest in the denomination. And his vociferous advocacy of the Confederacy's cause gained him the reputation of being one of the South's staunchest patriots.

When he mounted the First Church pulpit in New Orleans's Lafayette Square, Palmer's congregation of two hundred swelled to as many as a thousand. From that spot, Palmer delivered a series of influential homilies, including the "Thanksgiving Sermon" of November 1860, the "National Responsibility before God" sermon of June 1861, and the "Century Sermon" of January 1901. Each of these addresses has been anthologized by scholars of American religious history and celebrated by advocates of Palmer's legacy.[8]

Exiled from New Orleans when Federal forces occupied the Crescent City in 1862, Palmer traversed the South, rallying Confederate troops and stoking the passions of a dispirited populace. Palmer ministered to Confederate soldiers behind the battle lines and addressed Albert Sidney Johnson's army as they prepared for the Battle of Shiloh. In 1863, when Palmer's church appointed him to serve as a commissioner to the Army of Tennessee, he "preach[ed] in all the brigades and most of the regiments of this army corps until the army fell back to Chattanooga."[9] Otherwise, Palmer spent the war years in Columbia, South Carolina, whose destruction by Sherman's army he witnessed in February 1865. Following the war, Palmer returned to New Orleans, steadfastly assuring its citizens that the South's cause had been God's own.

Genesis and America's Historic Mission

Soon after his arrival in New Orleans in 1856, Palmer made a series of proclamations regarding slavery and the relationship of the "races." These addresses are significant because they indicate the centrality of the Bible's primeval history (Genesis 1–11) for Palmer's understanding of God's relationship to humanity.

In "The Import of Hebrew History," an essay that appeared in *Southern Presbyterian Review* in 1856, Palmer introduced what would become distinctive elements in his perception of the providential ordering of societies.[10] According to Palmer, Hebrew history reveals the formation of a people apart from others and thus confirms the normative role of disunity in human communities. Palmer wrote that "to prevent admixture of races, these are separated by the occupancy of distinct territory, by opposition of manners, employment and religion, and still more by the power of caste which, as now in India, clearly defined and rendered impassable the boundaries of social life."[11] Later in this essay, Palmer commented on an aspect of history that "possesses great attractions for the philosophic historian," and affords "further illustration of the design of this whole economy": "It is a striking proof of the divine wisdom," Palmer noted, "that society is broken up into these small and independent communities, where the human will is first subdued, and obedience to authority enforced, under the mild despotism of the family. Hence, in the original formation of society, the Patriarchal rule must be held as preceding every other . . ."[12] Here Palmer adumbrates the "law of separation," which he regarded as a fundamental principle in God's administration of the world following the Flood.

In 1858, when Palmer was invited to speak at La Grange Synodical College in Tennessee,[13] he set out to delineate the American people's providential role in world history in an address titled "Our Historic Mission." In this allocution Palmer referred explicitly to Genesis 9–11. He did so by commending the notion of "a lively French writer"—the Swiss "historical geographer" F. de Rougemont—"that each of the three divisions into which the human family was separated after the Flood, has been occupied with a distinct mission throughout the entire tract of their history." According to Palmer's reading of Rougemont,

> the race of Shem was providentially selected as the channel for transmitting religion and worship; . . . Japhet and his race . . . seem designated to be the organ of human civilization, in cultivating the intellectual powers. . . . The Japhetic whites, spreading over the diversified continent of Europe, through a protracted discipline develope [sic] the higher powers of the soul in politics, jurisprudence, science and art: while the Asiatic Japhetites dispersed over a more monotonous continent, embark in those pursuits of industry fitted to the lower capacities of our nature. The descendants of Ham, on the contrary, in whom the sensual and corporeal appetites predominate, are driven like an infected race beyond the deserts of Sahara, where under a glowing sky nature harmonizes with their brutal and savage disposition.[14]

In the published version of "Our Historic Mission," Palmer acknowledged another intellectual debt—to German philosopher Friedrich von Schlegel and his idea that *historic* peoples are the principal actors in the drama of world history. Following Schlegel, Palmer remarked that "every truly historic people is marked by its own characteristic traits; and will contribute its quota to complete the civilization which is the joint product and property of them all."[15]

Significantly, Palmer rejected Schlegel's opinion that America is a "dependency, the mere continuation of old Europe on the other side of the Atlantic."[16] While acknowledging that the American "race" is a "confluence of all the tribes and tongues of Europe," Palmer maintained that this people bears traits that are "national and distinctive."[17] Furthermore, he insisted that the Creator has assigned the American people a unique historic mission and that "never, since the institution of civil magistracy in the death-penalty commanded to Noah [that is, since the Flood] has a nation existed upon the face of the globe under conditions so favorable for working out the problems of the historic calculus and giving its grand equation to the world."[18] Among these are the "economic" problem, the essence of which is determination of the proper relationship between capital and labor. Palmer contends that "there is no people beneath the arch of heaven under conditions so favorable to grapple with [this problem's] difficulties and to master its dangers." This is because "in the patriarchal form in which [slavery] exits amongst us, it does reconcile, so far as it goes, this mighty conflict between capital and labor."[19]

In "Our Historic Mission"—and in many of the sermons and addresses that would follow—Palmer cultivated a perspective on the history of nations that was simultaneously philosophical, biblical, and thoroughly American.[20] As he forged a philosophy of history in which America held pride of place, Schlegel's conviction that only a few of the world's nations are "historic" proved particularly useful.[21] Assigning America its proper place in the stream of history, Palmer would argue that Americans are indeed a historic people; that the limits of their cultural achievements are as yet unknown; that they have been entrusted with a special mission, the fulfillment of which represents their contribution to the organic body of human civilization; and that part of this mission is to preserve human servitude in its biblical form. In the conclusion to "Our Historic Mission," Palmer expressed these sentiments this way:

> Let us say, with all the distinctness and emphasis with which words of destiny are ever uttered, that we will conserve this institution of domestic servitude, not only from the pressure of necessity and from the instinct of interest— not only from a feeling of trusteeship over the race thus providentially committed to us—not even at last from a general conviction of the righteousness of our course—but also from a special sense of duty to mankind.[22]

Following the outbreak of war, Palmer would reaffirm this defense of the South's peculiar institution. But increasingly after 1860, he would attempt to justify the South's cause with reference to passages in Genesis 9–11.

Genesis, Secession, and War

Palmer's first address to gain wide acclaim was the "Thanksgiving Sermon" he delivered in New Orleans on November 29, 1860. By this time, Palmer had earned a considerable reputation among the citizens of New Orleans, both for his pulpit skills and for his brave pastoral service during the Yellow Fever epidemic of 1858.[23] Yet his two-hour Thanksgiving oration "catapulted Palmer into South-wide fame overnight."[24] According to H. Shelton Smith, "the New Orleans *Daily Delta,* a zealous advocate of secession, published the entire discourse three times within a period of four days, and many other papers throughout the South published all or large portions of it. It was distributed by the thousands in pamphlet form. As a generator of disunion sentiment, it excelled every other pulpit deliverance of southern clergy."[25] Mitchell Snay observes that Palmer's "Thanksgiving Sermon" is "perhaps the best text" for understanding the secessionist argument in its original form, for "it illustrates as well as any other text the religious understanding of the sectional conflict."[26] By late December, news of Palmer's rhetorical coup had reached Princeton, New Jersey.[27] In mid-January, a Boston newspaper featured a front-page review of the published version.[28]

On November 29, a thousand people packed the First Presbyterian Church auditorium to hear the forty-two-year-old divine address the looming national crisis, and they were not disappointed. Palmer began by noting that it was not his habit to meddle in politics, but "at a juncture so solemn as the present, with the destiny of a great people waiting upon the decision of an hour, it is not lawful to be still." Palmer's response to destiny's call was a forceful expression of the view he had advanced in 1858—that the historic mission of Southern whites consisted of a "providential trust . . . to conserve and to perpetuate the institution of slavery as now existing . . . a trust to preserve and transmit our existing system of domestic servitude, with the right, unchallenged by man, to go and root itself wherever Providence and nature may carry it."[29] Palmer in fact reaffirmed many of the arguments he had advanced during the 1850s: that "a nation often has a character as well defined and intense as that of an individual," that it is based in "the original traits which distinguish its stock from which it springs," and that this character alone "makes any people truly historic, competent to work out its specific mission, and to become a factor in the world's progress." He added that because a people's particular trust becomes their pledge of divine protection, the South would relinquish its peculiar institution at the cost of its very survival. Interestingly, while Palmer referred to Genesis several times in this sermon, he did not invoke Noah's curse as a rationale for human servitude.[30]

It is not surprising that in 1860 Palmer publicly welcomed military conflict and did his best to sanctify it in the minds of Southerners. Yet during the first year of the war, Palmer's proclamations reflected an increasingly refined apology for civil strife as part of the divine will, indeed, as integral to the South's exercise of its providential trust. In a special Sabbath sermon delivered to the Crescent Rifles in May 1861, Palmer emphasized that "in the comprehensive government of Jehovah nations have their assigned mission, which they must execute through the conflicts which Providence may ordain for them."[31] That same month, addressing members of the Washington Artillery from the steps of City Hall before more than five thousand onlookers, Palmer affirmed that "history reads to us of wars which have been baptized as holy; but she enters upon her records none that is holier than this in which you have embarked."[32] Nor was Palmer's fervor diminished by the failure of the South's holy warriors to score a quick victory. "What nation," Palmer asked at the end of 1862, "save Judah alone, ever had such trusts committed to its hands?"[33] In Palmer's view, resistance and conflict only confirmed the Confederacy's role in the divine plan and served to remind Southerners that the preservation of slavery was a divine trust. For a while at least, this bellicose perception of history allowed Palmer to maintain the rectitude of the South's cause through the reversals of war. Even in 1863, Palmer could respond to the Confederacy's declining military fortunes by citing the necessity of "duty in the face of trial."

According to Wayne C. Eubank, "no other southern sermon on slavery and secession received greater acclaim or wider attention"[34] than Palmer's

"Thanksgiving Sermon" of 1860. Not far behind, however, was the homily "National Responsibility before God," delivered June 13, 1861, two months after the commencement of hostilities. This sermon is often cited for the dramatic parallel Palmer draws between seceding Southerners and the children of Israel fleeing oppression in Egypt.[35] But it also contains the first explicit invocation of Ham's curse in Palmer's published writings. Although Palmer had previously indicated the influence of Genesis 9 on his thinking, it was not until the war was under way that he held up Noah's curse as a prophetic blueprint for the destinies of the "white," "black," and "red" peoples.

In "National Responsibility before God," Palmer relied on Noah's curse to explain the historical position of the African, to confirm the dependency of the American Negro, and to provide a theological justification for slavery. He established the importance of Genesis 9 by noting that "if we ascend the stream of history to its source, we find in Noah's prophetic utterances to his three sons, the fortunes of mankind presented in perfect outline."[36] The benediction given to Shem, Palmer writes, marks him for a "destiny predominantly religious," and the divine trust of the Hebrew Semites until the time of Christ was to "testify for the unity of God against the idolatry of mankind." Turning to the descendants of Noah's son Japheth, Palmer contends that the "enlargement" promised him in Noah's blessing can be seen in "the hardy and aggressive families of this stock [that] have spread over the larger portion of the earth's surface, fulfilling their mission as the organ of human civilization." According to Palmer, the task of civilizing the world, assigned first to Greeks and Romans and later to the various nations of Europe, has been realized through Japhetic achievements in the scientific, artistic, and public realms. Finally, Palmer delineates the fortunes of Ham as indicated in Noah's prophecy:

> Upon Ham was pronounced the doom of perpetual servitude—proclaimed with double emphasis, as it is twice repeated that he shall be the servant of Japheth and the servant of Shem. Accordingly, history records not a single example of any member of this group lifting itself, by any process of self-development, above the savage condition. From first to last their mental and moral characteristics, together with the guidance of Providence, have marked them for servitude; while their comparative advance in civilization and their participation in the blessings of salvation, have ever been suspended upon this decreed connexion with Japhet and with Shem.[37]

Palmer concludes that "these facts are beyond impeachment; and nothing can be more instructive than to see the outspreading landscape of all history embraced thus within the camera of Noah's brief prophecy."[38]

Significantly, Palmer observes that Noah's oracle reveals "the hand of God upon nations—not only 'appointing the bounds of their habitations,' but impressing upon each the type of character that fits it for its mission." Thus, by the middle of 1861, Palmer was linking Noah's prophecy with physical separation (God's appointment of the bounds of human habitation). Most antebellum proslavery intellectuals did not strike this theme, and the post-bellum thinkers who associated the curse with separation tended, as Palmer eventually did, to invoke Nimrod and his tower in the process. But in his earliest direct reference to Genesis 9, Palmer perceived in Noah's utterance not only a description of the distinct roles Providence had prepared for human beings but also a decree for their physical separation. This is a reflection of the consistency with which Palmer invoked Genesis 9–11 before and after the Civil War.

After the capture of New Orleans by Federal forces in 1862, Palmer was exiled from his pulpit. The wartime orations he delivered to Confederate troops have been lost to posterity, and his sermons in Columbia and elsewhere are attested only in the diaries of those who heard them.[39] But during 1863, the pivotal year of the war, Palmer was invited to address legislative bodies in Georgia and South Carolina on official holidays of "fasting, humiliation and prayer." The texts of Palmer's comments before the Legislature of Georgia (March 27) and the General Assembly of South Carolina (December 10) have been preserved, and both addresses bear on our topic.[40]

In his "Georgia Fast Day Sermon," Palmer sought to establish the relevance of Genesis 9–11 for clarifying the South's noble path. He averred that in their political isolation Southerners were called to defend God's "government of the universe" revealed so clearly following the flood.[41] And what does the biblical record of postdiluvian history reveal about God's design for human societies? First, Palmer affirmed

> that in the organic law under which human governments were constituted by God, not *consolidation* but *separation* is recognized as the regulative and determining principle. If we ascend the stream of history to its source, we shall discover God dividing the earth between the sons of Noah, "every one after his tongue, after their families, in their nations" [Gen. 10:5, 20, 31]; and with such remarkable precision that to this day we can trace "the bounds of their habitations," even as they were originally appointed. Indeed, the out-spreading landscape of all history is embraced within the camera of Noah's brief prophecy; showing how from the beginning God not only distributed them upon the face of the earth, but impressed upon each branch the type of character fitting it for its mission.[42]

Thus, the American schism is only "a new application of the law by which God has ever governed the world; that of breaking in two a nation which has grown too strong for its virtue, in order to its preservation and continuance." Next, Palmer briefly delineated the character of each of Noah's sons, refining the lines he sketched in the late 1850s: "Shem as the conservator of religious truth; Japhet, as the organ of human civilization; and Ham as the drudge, upon whom rested the doom of perpetual servitude." Significantly, Palmer's prewar description of Ham's descendants as possessing a "brutal and savage disposition" was revised to fit the contours of Noah's curse. Finally, Palmer introduced a novel element into his reading of Genesis:

> Let it be observed, moreover, that the first public and recorded crime of Postdiluvian history was the attempt to thwart God's revealed purpose of separation, and to construct upon the plains of Shinar a consolidated Empire whose colossal magnitude should overshadow the Earth. "Go to," said they, "let us build us a city, and a tower whose top may reach unto heaven; and let us make us a name, lest we be scattered abroad upon the face of the whole Earth." The insane enterprise was only checked by the immediate intervention of Jehovah, breaking the unity of human speech, and thus separating the conspirators by the most impassable of all barriers.[43]

In the very midst of civil war, Palmer employed the Babel episode to place the American conflict in biblical perspective: While the South was faithfully conserving the societal structures initiated through Noah the planter patriarch, an urbanized, industrialized Northern empire was replicating the primordial rebellion at Babel. Thus, the war between the states was cast as a conflict of biblical scale, with the opposing sides representing the forces of righteousness and rebellion that have been at odds since the beginning of time.

His "Georgia Fast Day Sermon" indicates that by early 1863 Palmer had found in Genesis 9 more than a divine sanction for Hamite servitude. The question of slavery aside, Palmer viewed Noah as a "second Adam" who foresaw the character and destiny of his descendants and against whose authority humanity would fatefully rebel. In Palmer's mind, Noah's prophecy continued to signify the righteousness of slavery, but with increasing relevance it illumined the "regulative and determining principle" of separation that was the logos of God's re-creation after the Deluge—a structure implemented in the division of the world among Noah's sons and reiterated in God's dispersion of the conspirators at Babel. As we shall see, the conclusions Palmer wished to draw from the providential ordering of human society in the days of Noah would shift over time. But in this address to Georgia legislators, he utilized Genesis 9–11 to argue that whoever might regard Southerners as "rebels" ought to "ascend to that fundamental law, by which in the first organization of society God constituted civil government." They will be forced to conclude, Palmer argued, that "this law of separation is that 'law of nature and of nature's God which entitles us to assume a separate and equal station among the powers of the earth.' "[44] In other words, the right of Southern states to secede from the Union was rooted in neither political documents nor intellectual presuppositions, but in the original pattern of separation determined by the Creator and revealed in scripture.[45]

At the end of 1863, Palmer addressed the general assembly of his home state of South Carolina. His tone was chastened and subdued, unmistakably reflecting the course of the war since the previous summer. Palmer's text, Psalm 60:1–4, is a lament that resonates with the spirit of the time: "O! God, thou hast cast us off; thou hast scattered us; thou has been displeased: O! turn thyself to us again. Thou hast made the earth to tremble; thou hast broken it: heal the breaches thereof, for it shaketh. Thou hast showed thy people hard things; thou has made us to drink the wine of astonishment; thou has given a banner to them that feared thee, that it may be displayed because of the truth."[46] While echoing the Confederacy's dubious future, Palmer's "South Carolina Fast Day Sermon" again elaborated the pattern of divinely willed separation so wonderfully revealed in Genesis. Palmer celebrated "the perfect isolation in which the Southern Confederacy [was] now battling for those rights which are so dear to the human heart"[47] and evinced puzzlement at the opponents of slavery who "have presumptuously pronounced against the Divine administration from the beginning of time."[48] With irony, Palmer noted that "whilst slavery has existed in every variety of form through the whole tract of human history, it has been reserved to our times to beat up a crusade against it under precisely that patriarchal form in which it is sanctioned in the word of God, and in which it has never been found since the overthrow of the Hebrew empire, until now."[49] Palmer also revisited the theme of divine trust that had figured so prominently in his writings leading up to the war. He claimed that "in the comprehensive scheme of Divine providence, all such [historic] nations have an assigned work, and are preserved in being till that work is done."[50] Palmer then reminded his audience that because the South's commission "binds her to duty in the face of trial," she must not "shrink from the discipline to which all nations are subjected in working out their allotted destiny."[51]

Palmer alluded to the racial question by offering the hope that the war would "teach mankind that the allotment of God, in the original distribution of destinies to the sons of Noah, must continue,"[52] and by referring to the Hamites' "native condition of fetishism and barbarism." Even when in contact with superior races, Palmer asserted, blacks "have never been stimulated to become a self-supporting people, under well regulated institutions and laws"; invariably, they lapse into "their original state of degradation and imbecility." Despite his emphasis on the innate inferiority of African Americans, Palmer did not insist on their perpetual bondage. He did reiterate, however, that the evidence of prophecy and history points in this direction: "All the attributes of the negro character, and . . . the whole history of God's dealings towards him, and . . . all the light shed upon his destiny from the sacred Scriptures" lead to the conclusion that the Negro's "true normal position" is as a servant of servants. This reference to Genesis 9 indicates that, at least through 1863, Noah's curse and its satellite texts remained the foundation for Palmer's theological superstructure of race, history, and destiny.

Genesis and Societal Segregation

When hostilities ceased in 1865, Palmer made his way again to New Orleans and resumed pastoral duties among a defeated and frightened populace.

Though some greeted his return with surprise, Palmer's wartime efforts on behalf of the Confederacy led the city to warmly embrace him.[53] During Reconstruction, Palmer's stature as a Southern patriot and paragon of clerical virtue grew as he became a leader in commemorating the South's Lost Cause. One of Palmer's chief concerns during this period was the education of Southern whites. In April 1870, under pressure from the Reconstruction legislature, the New Orleans Board of Education admitted black pupils to white public schools. The city's Presbyterians responded swiftly, and First Church led the way. One of Palmer's parishioners oversaw the development of a system of white parochial schools, with the suggestion to do so probably coming from Palmer himself.[54] Between 1870 and 1877 (when the public schools were once again racially segregated), eight institutions enrolling eight hundred students were operated by the Presbyterian churches of New Orleans. Palmer's congregation housed the Sylvester Larned Institute for girls.[55]

Also illustrative of his convictions regarding race were Palmer's public statements during this period. In a much celebrated eulogy for Robert E. Lee delivered in 1870, Palmer asked how it was that the leaders of both the first and second American revolutions hailed from Virginia. In answer, he asserted that "unquestionably . . . there is in this problem the element of race; for he is blind to all the truths of history, to all the revelations of the past, who does not recognize a select race as we recognize a select individual of a race, to make all history."[56] Significantly, the term *race* has replaced *nation* in Palmer's description of how history is made. Would Palmer now rely on secular language to describe the South's future, or would he continue to invoke the "law of separation" laid out in Genesis 9–11? For an answer to this question, we turn to "The Present Crisis and Its Issue," a speech Palmer delivered at Washington and Lee College in June 1872.[57]

Addressing the student body at this "center for Lost Cause orations," Palmer announced that he was "making a pilgrimage to [his] country's shrine."[58] In this hallowed space, Palmer offered a meditation on the tragedy of the South's recent past and its uncertain future. The future would have to be segregated, Palmer observed, because the problem of race is paramount "in adjusting the relations between two distinct peoples that must occupy the same soil." To support this argument, Palmer revisited the philosophy of history he had elaborated in the 1850s, though he referred to historic "peoples" and "races" rather than "nations." He boasted that when speaking to representatives of the black race, he preaches that "if you are to be a historic people, you must work out your own destiny upon your own foundation. . . . If you have no power of development from within, you lack the first quality of a historic race, and must, sooner or later, go to the wall."[59] Although each race seeks "the opportunity . . . to work out its mission," society must be governed by strict segregation. In fact, "the true policy of both races is, that they shall stand apart in their own social grade, in their own schools, in their own ecclesiastical organizations, under their own teachers and guides."

Palmer's hope that the details of social segregation would be worked out "under the direction of a wise Providence which still holds the destines of the two together" should not obscure the preponderance of secular terminology in this address. "As I can understand the teachings of history," Palmer says, "there is one underlying principle which must control the question. It is indispensable that the purity of race shall be preserved on either side; for it is the condition of life to the one, as much as to the other."[60] Phrases such as "the teachings of history" and "the purity of race" evince a turn toward secular phraseology. Nevertheless, Palmer emphasizes that the new South must be modeled on the biblical pattern revealed in Genesis.

> The argument for this I base upon the declared policy of the Divine Administration from the days of Noah until now. The sacred writings clearly teach that, to prevent the amazing wickedness which brought upon the earth the purgation of the Deluge, God saw fit to break the human family into sections. He separated them by destroying the unity of speech; then by the actual dispersion, appointing the bounds of their habitation, to which they were conducted by the mysterious guidance of his will.[61]

In the wake of defeat and Reconstruction, Palmer explicitly racializes the divine command for dispersion. The "one underlying principle" inferred from Genesis 9–11 is no longer separation per se but "racial purity." Also significant is that, following the transition evident in his addresses of 1863, Palmer identifies the paragon for divine action in Genesis 11 (where God "destroy[s] the unity of speech") rather than Genesis 10 (where "God divid[es] the earth between the sons of Noah, 'every one after his tongue, after their families, in their nations' "). God now disperses the human family not to ensure societal order in a world where each nation possesses a unique character and mission, but as a hedge against humanity's sinful tendencies. Finally, the narrative voice in which Palmer relates the message of Genesis 9–11 assumes a new tone. When Palmer elucidated the postdiluvian divine economy in the spring of 1863, God had "divided" the earth with remarkable precision, "appointed" the bounds of human habitation, and "distributed" the nations according to his will. In 1872, the same process is described in judgmental and even apocalyptic terms: God "breaks" the human family into sections, "destroys" the unity of speech, "disperses" and "separates" people.[62] Just as Palmer's claim to find a rationale for "racial purity" in Genesis 9–11 reflected the fear of amalgamation that seized white Southerners after the Civil War, the stark and punitive tone in which he describes God's organization of human society echoes the Southern mind-set during the "dark days" of Reconstruction.

In keeping with this more pessimistic view of the human condition are Palmer's comments on Genesis 11 at Washington and Lee. Palmer avers that "the first pronounced insurrection against [God's] supremacy, was the attempt by Nimrod to oppose and defeat this policy [of divine separation]; and the successive efforts of all the great kingdoms to achieve universal conquest have been but the continuation of that primary rebellion—always attended by the same overwhelming failure that marked the first."[63] Palmer had referred to the Babel episode nine years earlier, but his emphasis then was on "the immediate intervention of Jehovah, breaking the unity of human speech, and thus separating the conspirators by the most impassable of all barriers." In 1872, the "conspirators" at Babel are replaced by Nimrod the primordial tyrant, who personifies the intent of "great kingdoms to achieve universal conquest."[64] Undoubtedly, Palmer has in mind the U.S. government in its recent "war of aggression" against the Southern states. In Palmer's thinly veiled critique of the federal government, Northerners are the true "rebels," and their recent conquest the latest chapter in an anarchist tradition of "primary rebellion."

Palmer's published comments during Reconstruction indicate that he was assimilating secular racial rhetoric while remaining steadfast in his conviction that Genesis 9–11 contained both a blueprint for the ideal postdiluvian society and a record of the forces that threaten it. In "The Present Crisis and Its Issue," Palmer cleverly applied this section of the Bible to the societal issues at hand in 1872, merging Nimrod's "rebellion" with the desire to forcibly convene distinct races:

> There is no escape from the corresponding testimony, biblical and historical, that the human family, originally one, has been divided into certain large groups, for the purpose of being kept historically distinct. And all attempts, in every age of the world, and from whatever motives, whether of ambitious dominion or of an infidel humanitarianism, to force these together, are identical in aim and parallel in guilt with the usurpation and insurrection of the first Nimrod.[65]

In 1872, Southerners would have heard this reading of history in light of Genesis as an allusion to the racial policies of Reconstruction, which were nothing if not an attempt to "force . . . together" distinct groups by a mixture of "ambitious dominion" and "infidel humanitarianism."

Genesis and Ecclesiastical Separation

Following the death of James Henley Thornwell in 1862, Palmer became the undisputed intellectual and emotional leader of the Presbyterian Church in the Confederate States of America (after 1865, the Presbyterian Church in the United States). Following the war, Palmer was repeatedly elected to chair or moderate bodies charged with establishing the church's racial policy. In this way, Palmer was able to make the church a mouthpiece for his own reading of scripture.

For instance, Palmer was the animating force behind an overture submitted to the PCUS General Assembly in 1874.[66] The overture noted that since the end of the war Southern Presbyterians had "been steadily moving" toward a separate Negro church, a pattern preferred by the blacks themselves. Furthermore, the exodus of African Americans from the white churches had been prompted by "the most controlling sentiment known to the human heart— *the instinct of race.*" This separatist solution to racial diversity in the church would "quietly" shelve "all those thorny questions which arise from the commingling of two dissimilar races, and which no amount of diplomatic skill can harmoniously adjust."[67] The overture, which in tenor and diction alike resounds with Palmer's voice, was adopted by the 1874 assembly.

The debate over "organic union" with Northern Presbyterians provides another example of the way Palmer's outlook came to dominate the church's stance on racial issues. Two decades after Appomatox, there was considerable support in the Southern church for reunion of the Presbyterian bodies that had split in 1861. However, at the 1887 PCUS General Assembly, Palmer reminded the advocates of consolidation that "the race problem" constituted "an insuperable barrier" to reunification with Northern Presbyterians. Predictably, Palmer invoked Genesis 9–11:

> It cannot be denied that God has divided the human race into several distinct groups, for the sake of keeping them apart. When the promise was given to Noah that the world should not be again destroyed with a flood, it became necessary to restrain the wickedness of man that it should not rise to the same height as in the ante-diluvian period. Hence the unity of human speech was broken, and "so the Lord scattered them abroad from thence upon the face of all the earth" [Gen. 11:9].[68]

Facing a rising tide of proreunion sentiment, Palmer stood fast on the scriptural ground he had occupied since the 1850s. He alleged that the postdiluvian dispensation in human history is regulated by a divine law of separation designed to forestall human wickedness. But he supplemented this familiar argument of separation as divine will with the rhetoric of physical distinction as empirical fact:

> Now co-ordinate with this "confusion of tongues," we find these groups distinguished by certain physical characteristics—and that, too, as far back as history carries us. We are not warranted in affirming that this differentiation through color and otherwise was accomplished at the same time, and as part of the same process, with the "confusion of tongues;" but since the distinction exists from a period in the past of which history takes no note, and since science fails to trace the natural causes by which it could be produced, the inference is justified which regards it as fixed by the hand of Jehovah himself.[69]

Palmer is very careful here. Addressing his church's largest governing body, he must maintain the appearance of orthodoxy and eschew suspicions that he is relying on secular arguments. Nevertheless, it is clear that nineteenth-century American racial discourse has become a hermeneutical key for Palmer's reading of the Bible. What he calls the "stubborn facts lying on the face of history" are actually the views prevailing among the racial theorists of his day. Palmer is aware that current knowledge of human origins does not allow him to confidently racialize the Babel episode, but because science has not established the how or when of human difference, he does not hesitate to depict racial diversity as a providential intervention of God.

The conclusion to Palmer's 1887 address reflects this careful merging of biblical and scientific arguments. Invoking both the rebellion at Babel and white concerns for "purity of blood," Palmer maintains that "all the attempts to restore the original unity of the race by the amalgamation of these severed parts have been providentially and signally rebuked."[70]

Genesis and the Lost Cause

After the Civil War, New Orleans became a center for activities of the Lost Cause. When the Southern Historical Society formally organized in the Crescent City in 1869 and named Palmer its first president, he effectively became high priest in the new religion.[71] In return for his devotion to the cause, Palmer received the undying admiration of Confederate veterans. According to a testimonial signed by soldiers who had known him, Palmer was an "Exemplar for Southern Youth and Manhood" who, like Lee himself, knew no grander word than "Duty." He bears to us, the testimonial continued, "and to the Historic Cause, in which we were gloriously associated with him, a unique and inseparable relation." Palmer's sacerdotal role was to preserve "the Ark, containing our sacred canons of Justice, Liberty and Truth." His tragic death in 1902 removed from the South "the greatest recent Exponent of our Case, and among the greatest ever connected with it."[72]

Palmer earned such veneration in recognition of his eloquent advocacy of the cause. Particularly after 1880, Palmer was called on to speak at public gatherings that were civic rather than ecclesiastical in nature. In these addresses, several of which were published in the *Southern Historical Society Papers*, the official Lost Cause journal, Palmer reassured his auditors that despite the results and opinions stemming from the "late revolution," the tribunal of history would vindicate the South, the honor of its soldiers, and the character of its people. In these secular sermons, Palmer did not refer explicitly to Genesis 9–11. However, by revisiting the notions of historic people and divine trust, he reasserted the tripartite division of humankind under Noah that formed the basis of his biblical worldview.

At a New Orleans fundraiser for the Southern Historical Society in 1882, Palmer concluded a raft of speakers that featured Jefferson Davis. The sixty-four-year-old divine introduced his comments by asking a packed opera house whether the society and its work were necessary. Palmer answered this rhetorical question by observing that "the history of every historic people should be fully written," especially in that "but a very small portion of the earth's surface and few of its nations are historic." Instead of citing the South's credentials as historic, Palmer proceeded to systematically disqualify the non-European nations from historic nation status. "You may, for example, throw all Africa overboard, except its Mediterranean coast and a small portion that lies upon the delta of the Nile. In like manner, nearly the whole of the massive and monotonous continent of Asia may be discounted."[73] Palmer reassured his audience that in contrast to the unhistoric peoples that clutter the pages of world history, "we who have dwelt on this continent for the last 300 or 400 years are the descendants of nations that are historic." Thus, although he did not cite the Bible, Palmer's reading of world history adhered to the pattern he saw set down in Genesis 9–11: Japheth (Europe/America) is ever destined to dominate Ham (Africa) and Shem (Asia).

In addressing a group of Confederate veterans in 1890, Palmer assessed world history by revisiting the notion that God invests nations with unique trusts.[74] According to Palmer, every organized society possesses such a trust, for which it is held responsible before God. However, not all societies become stewards of the divine gift by making history:

> Why, there is China, with her four hundred millions of people—nearly one-half the population of the globe—yet without adding a fraction to the general history of the world. There is Africa, stretching its length between the Tropics and beyond them, occupied for thousands of years by naked savages engaged in internecine and tribal wars; yet, so far as the broad record of mankind is concerned, the Dark Continent might just as well have been sunk in the depths of the two oceans which wash its borders—utterly dead, without a history.[75]

And because the American continent had been dominated by Shem's posterity until the arrival of the Japhetic European, "so far as history is involved it might as well have emerged only three hundred years ago from the waters of the sea to become the home of a ripe civilization of its immortal records."[76] Again, Palmer neither refers to scripture nor invokes the division of humankind under Noah, yet his interpretation of history is rooted ultimately in his reading of Genesis 9–11. Maintaining the hierarchy of Noah's sons with the language of divine trust and historic mission, Palmer reaffirms the unfavored status of Shem (China) and Ham (Africa).

In the face of postwar challenges—the emancipation of millions of freed slaves, the forced integration of Southern society and institutions, the push for closer relations with Northern Presbyterians, and the need to sustain the South's Lost Cause—Palmer relied on the same biblical texts he had utilized in the antebellum era to justify racial inequality, slavery, secession, and war. In the postbellum era, Palmer's thinking reflected American intellectual currents regarding race and race mixing more clearly than Romanticism and Southern nationalism, yet the biblical principle that guided his reading of ancient and contemporary history was the same: Following the Flood, God ordained the separate existence of nations, established a law of separation that human beings would violate at their peril, invested nations with specific trusts, and determined through prophecy that Asia and Africa would be eclipsed by the "enlargement" of Europe and America.

Genesis and the American Century

Just over a year before his death, his health failing at the age of eighty-three, Palmer preached one of his most celebrated homilies. The "Century Sermon," delivered on New Year's Day of 1901, was a civic event in the Crescent City. The lead headline in the January 2 *Daily Picayune* announced:

THE CENTURY SERMON
PREACHED BY DR. PALMER
At the Request of Prominent Citizens, Irre-
spective of Creed
A Magnificent Audience Gathering at First
Presbyterian Church
To Hear the Patriarchal Man of God Trace the
Divine Purpose
Through Different Civilizations and Epochs, Until
the New Era's Dawn Brings Nearer
Peace and Good Will on Earth

According to press reports, the throng of two thousand souls that crowded First Church to hear Palmer's ninety-minute oration included "Methodists, Baptists, Episcopalians, Jews, German Protestants, Lutherans, merchants, scholars, professional men, representatives of the great business and railroad interests, shipping people, strangers in the city, young men and women, old men and women, some of them as old as the venerable pastor himself, and little children."[77] But as the "Century Sermon" addressed God's design in "the new era's dawn," it sounded the very themes Palmer had elaborated through-out the second half of the nineteenth century. Specifically, the sermon sought "to trace the hand of God in history, the part that the historical peoples have severally played, in the great drama, according to the Divine economy,"[78] discussed the God-given mission of the American people, and employed the postdiluvian narratives of Genesis. Given "how little use [Palmer] made of old speeches, notwithstanding the pressure of years and the burdens of his office,"[79] his reliance on these themes in 1901 is further evidence of their centrality in his thought.

The "Century Sermon" contains two extended references to Genesis 9–11. In the first, Palmer asserts that "the history of this world is an organic whole, and all of its parts are connected together by a holy and divine purpose." In amplifying this statement, he observes that

almost before the waters of the deluge had subsided from the face of the
earth, you have the tripartite division of the human race, all of it yet to be
born, signalized in the destinies assigned to the three sons of Noah. "Cursed
be Canaan, a servant of servants shall he be unto his brethren." "God shall
enlarge Japheth, and he shall dwell in the tents of Shem." "Blessed be the
Lord God of Shem." Servitude to the first, enlargement to the second, and
a sort of priestly function assigned to the third, fulfilled in the fact that his
seed were first put in possession of the oracles of God through which the
whole human race is finally to be blessed.[80]

Remarkably, this passage includes the only quotation of Genesis 9:25–27 in all
of Palmer's published writings. Clearly, the "new era's dawn" had not diminished Palmer's confidence in the relevance of Noah's curse. Furthermore, Palmer assumes that his auditors will grasp the prophecy's import: "I need not
pause upon this remarkably prophetic outline of all human history, for there
is not an intelligent hearer in this audience that does not know how punctually
each one [of these destinies] has been fulfilled in the whole history of mankind."[81]

But in his invocation of Noah's curse for a new era, Palmer expresses
more interest in Shem and Japheth than in Canaan or Ham. As Thomas
Peterson has noted, Shem became a major actor in the sacred drama of Ham's
myth as American Bible readers wished to relate the "growth of the American
nation in terms of manifest destiny by explaining that the red man's demise
was part of the divine will."[82] This is precisely Palmer's goal when he announces that "we who are gathered here in this assemblage on this first day
of the century, are dwelling to-day in the tents of Shem." This clause served
to link Palmer's auditors with Noah's son Japheth, while identifying the American continent with the "tents of Shem." After directing his hearers to Genesis
10's Table of Nations (and its presumed confirmation in Acts 17),[83] Palmer
returns to develop this link between Noah's prophecy and America's conquest
by the Anglo-Saxon. In relating the fate of America's "wild native Indians,"
Palmer briefly summarizes Native American history:

During all the past, as far back as any knowledge of time goes, this vast
continent was inhabited by tribes of wild native Indians. Nothing was heard
in all those vast primeval forests, in conjunction with the roar of the wild
beasts, save the savage war cries of these naked and painted Indian tribes,
engaged in their internecine wars. What do we see to-day? The Indian prac-
tically extinct; the vast forests through which he pursued his game leveled to
the earth, and the fertile bosom of the soil receiving culture and yielding its
fruit a thousand-fold to the industry of man. Instead of the war-whoop of
the Indian, we hear the chimes of Sabbath bells, and songs of praise issuing
from myriads of Christian homes to the glory of that God "who hath prepared his throne in the heavens, and whose kingdom ruleth over all."[84]

So that his congregation will perceive the hand of Providence in this momentous departure of a people from the stage of history, Palmer reminds

them that "the God who reigns in the heavens is the God of supreme justice, and that he has judgments for all that neglect or reject him." The preacher finds an apt analogy in scripture:

> It was in the way of a judgment, strictly retributive in character, that [God] swept the old Canaanites into the pathless deserts surrounding their land, in order to find room for his chosen people; and when the Indians had, for countless centuries, neglected the soil, had no worship to offer to the true God, with scarcely any serious occupation but murderous inter-tribal wars, the time came at length when, as I view it, in the just judgment of a righteous and holy God, although it may have been worked out through the simple avarice and voracity of the race that subdued them, the Indian has been swept from the earth, and a great Christian nation, over 75,000,000 strong, rises up on this . . . [day].[85]

Palmer was certainly not the first to assert that Native Americans' displacement by Europeans was an act of Providence.[86] Nevertheless, it is fascinating to observe him applying a text that was pivotal in American debates regarding the destinies of Africans and Europeans to illumine the fate of the American Indian. As a Christian rhetorician, Palmer's goal was to demonstrate that the "practical extinction" of Native Americans under the pressure of an expanding white civilization was in conformity with the divine plan revealed in scripture. To do so, he incorporated this historical development in the "outspreading landscape of Noah's brief prophecy." Relying on the popular belief that Anglo-Saxons were descendants of Japheth, Palmer suggested that Noah's plea that God "make space for [or enlarge] Japheth and let him live in the tents of Shem" (Gen. 9:27) was a prophetic reference to the displacement of the red man by the white in North America.

But even if Palmer has correctly interpreted this mysterious prediction, Noah's curse could not be applied to the situation of Native Americans without allusion to the divinely approved destruction of an indigenous people. Faced with the challenge of justifying the utter elimination of those who once dwelt in Shem's tents, how would Palmer proceed? Through the history of Christian interpretation, two traditions—one historical and the other spiritual—had developed with respect to Noah's prayer for the enlargement of Japheth in the tents of Shem.[87] Neither, however, was serviceable for applying this text to the experience of Anglo-Saxons in America. So Palmer wove a novel reading of Genesis 9:27 from two disparate strands of tradition: the belief that Native Americans were Semites mysteriously separated from their "red" brothers in Asia (perhaps they were even the "lost tribes" of Israel) and the alternate and conflicting "Canaanite ideology," which cast Native Americans as a savage and idolatrous race, interlopers in the American promised land.[88] To advocate a literal application of Genesis 9:27 to Native Americans' disappearance from history, Palmer was compelled to employ both traditions, conflicting though they were. The European descendants of Japheth, he claimed, were now dwelling in the "tents" of red Semites, from which they had been expelled during the previous century. But the Indians' metaphorical identity as "Canaanites" justified their extinction as well.

Of course, within the logic of Noah's prophecy, it was not possible to view Native Americans as Semites *and* Canaanites. After all, Canaan was a son of Ham, not Shem. Portraying American Indians as Hamites (through Canaan) might make them fit for servitude but not for extermination. Then again, to call Native Americans descendants of Shem was to link them with an original recipient of Noah's blessing and an ancestor of Christ. Indeed, as Semites, Indians were cousins of the chosen people for whom Christians generally—and Palmer in particular—had great respect. But the pressure of Palmer's need to view the European conquest of North America in light of Noah's curse blurred this familial distinction. To accept the textual desideratum that predicted Japheth would dwell in Shem's "tents," Palmer had to affirm the identity of Native Americans as descendants of Shem, but to establish a biblical rationale for their extermination, Palmer had to call upon the more popular designation of Native Americans as "Canaanites," whose removal could be compared to that of the savage idolaters ousted from their habitations by the Israelites. Thus, Palmer fed heterogeneous interpretive strands into the mythical loom of Noah's prophecy and fashioned a seamless reading of Genesis that justified the history of American conquest in North America as the fulfillment of a divine mission. That doing so was difficult rhetorical work confirms the strength of Palmer's devotion to the scriptural texts that formed the basis for his vision of God's activity in history.

In Palmer's evolving understanding of Genesis 9–11 as a blueprint of God's design for America, we glimpse an unrepentant advocate of Noah's curse eager to apply the myth to successive episodes in the struggle between whites and people of color—first to justify the enslavement of blacks; then to discover divine sanction for the law of separation as it applied to political secession, civic segregation, and ecclesiastical separation; and finally as a warrant for the "practical extinction" of Native Americans. Palmer's use of these biblical narratives over a period of fifty years elucidates both their role in American racial discourse and their remarkable flexibility in the hands of someone in search of a transcendent warrant for racial hierarchy.

8

Honor, Order, and Mastery in Palmer's Biblical Imagination

> I am willing, at the call of my honor and my liberty to die
> a freeman. I'll never, no never, live a slave; and the alter-
> native now presented by our enemies is secession or slav-
> ery. Let it be liberty or death.
>
> Benjamin M. Palmer, 1860

AS WE HAVE SEEN, throughout his long and distinguished public career, Benjamin M. Palmer utilized Genesis 9–11 to explicate God's ways with humankind, interpret American history, and proclaim the gospel of Southern— and, later, Anglo-Saxon—election. And yet, despite his reliance on Noah's prophecy as an intellectual touchstone, Palmer never gave the slightest indication of how he understood the transgression that had occasioned it. Chapter 4 noted that antebellum proslavery readings of the curse fall into three general categories: those that cite the story, those that paraphrase or recount it but fail to characterize Ham's offense, and those that retell the story while describing or intimating the nature of Ham's misdeed. Without question, Palmer's references to Genesis 9 fall into the first category; despite referring to Noah's prophecy in addresses and published writings across his career, he never even alluded to Noah's drunkenness or Ham's response. Thus, if we are to sustain the thesis that proslavery readings of Genesis 9 were influenced by white concerns for honor and order, the case of Benjamin M. Palmer poses a challenge. This chapter presents evidence that, like his fellow proslavery intellectuals, Palmer instinctively understood Genesis 9 in terms of honor and order.

Honor

Honor in Palmer's Vindication
of Slavery and Secession

Palmer's rhetoric provides one index of honor's pivotal role in his weltanschauung. Very simply, honor is a dominant motif in his best known sermons and addresses. For instance, in the "Thanksgiving Sermon" of 1860, Palmer proclaimed that he was "willing, at the call of my honor and my liberty to die a freeman. I'll never, no never, live a slave; and the alternative now presented by our enemies is secession or slavery. Let it be liberty or death." This homiletic paean to Southern honor did not go uncompensated. The New Orleans *Daily Delta* applauded the "manly and patriotic position taken by Dr. Palmer" and editorialized that Palmer "acted the part of a Christian gentleman and scholar, of a Southern patriot, of a frank, earnest, brave and high-souled man."[1]

To illustrate how "traditional sensibilities about manhood and glory" supplemented biblical themes in the Southern case for secession, Bertram Wyatt-Brown explores the language of Palmer's "Thanksgiving Sermon." It is prime evidence, he observes, that in the Southern discourse of secession "honor to God and honor to self were closely bound together. As a result, it was possible for church-goers to reconcile the traditional ethic and evangelical belief."[2] When Palmer adopted the secessionist cause, he made "rhetorical use of southern adherence to the ancient ethic."[3] Wyatt-Brown quotes from the "Thanksgiving Sermon" to illustrate Palmer's conviction that in response to Northern fanaticism in electing a sectional candidate, Southerners were obligated "to uphold and perpetuate what they cannot resign without dishonor and palpable ruin." Wyatt-Brown credits Palmer with providing

> the basis for the dramatic turn that soon overwhelmed the Whiggish clergy, even outside the lower South. He challenged Unionists like [Robert J.] Breckenridge of Kentucky, who contended that the federal executive was not the servant of the sovereign states but their master. "Had the Constitution been regarded as a compact whose bonds were mutual honor and good faith," Palmer concluded, "the apprehension of a rupture would have been the surest guaranty of its observance." The northerners' "numerical majority" encouraged their aggression and imperialist ambitions, whereas a loose bond of states would have upheld "every consideration of honor and interest." Such sentiments as these led the clergy of the lower South into the secessionist ranks as their states left the Union in the early months of 1861.[4]

Given Palmer's avid support for secession, it is not surprising that the first clerical authority to propose disunion in 1860 was *Southern Presbyterian*, the journal Palmer had cofounded in Columbia, South Carolina, before departing for New Orleans.[5]

Palmer's celebration of honor—" 'the lingua franca' of Southern section-alism"[6] —was not limited to his "Thanksgiving Sermon." In "National Responsibility before God" (June 1861), the preacher proclaimed that "liberty is better than gold, and honor more precious than fortune."[7] And a few months earlier, in a review of works by Robert J. Breckenridge, professor at Danville Theological Seminary, Palmer linked honor and slavery in an attack on abolitionism: "In the great impending crisis, the South would be recreant to every obligation of duty and to every principle of honor, and to every instinct of interest if she did not effectively contradict and rebuke the insufferable arrogance of those who assume into their hands the prerogatives of Divine legislation."[8] Thus, during the secession crisis, when Noah's prophecy provided a biblical foundation for his defense of slavery, Palmer revealed his profound attachment to Southern honor.

Palmer's rhetoric of honor during this period cannot be appreciated apart from the images being broadcast by his clerical opponents. In ecclesiastical debates regarding the moral status of Southern secession, there were strenuous attempts to cast the South's position as one of disloyalty, treachery, and rebellion. Palmer himself, in fact, was described with these very epithets.[9] Thus, Palmer's embrace of honor was no doubt a response to the shameful stigma his opponents were attaching to slavery, secession, and the "men of God" who defended them. Particularly opprobrious in Palmer's mind was the charge of "rebellion." The controversy came to a head among Old School Presbyterians when the notorious "Spring Resolutions" were adopted by that church's general assembly in May 1861. The resolutions declared it the church's duty "to promote and perpetuate, so far as in them lay, the integrity of the United States, and to strengthen, uphold, and encourage the Federal Government in the exercise of its functions under the Constitution."[10] Southerners and their sympathizers opposed the Spring Resolutions, ostensibly because they placed the church in a position that was subordinate to the state. On an emotional level, however, the resolutions rankled because they made allegiance to the United States a condition of church membership and equated the sectional impulse with disloyalty. For his part, Palmer relentlessly countered the allegation of Southern rebellion by claiming that the South's course was the honorable path of "revolution."

The depth of Palmer's convictions regarding honor and secession may be gauged from his published response to the work of Robert J. Breckenridge. In early 1861, Breckenridge published two works accusing the South of indefensible rebellion. In a passionate article, "A Vindication of Secession and the South," Palmer offered his rejoinder.[11] According to Palmer, the "great revolution" (not rebellion!) under way in the South had been made necessary by an overwhelming and hopeless despotism. Because Breckenridge assumes "this is a consolidated nation," Palmer wrote, he is forced to denounce secession "as sedition, anarchy and rebellion, which must be crushed by the central authority."[12] No greater insult could one Southerner pronounce upon

another: "Anarchy, disloyalty, revolt, revolution, rebellion, fanaticism, sedition, for the alphabet of an almost exhaustless invective, which, by endless
transposition and iteration, make up a description so hideous that its very
deformity should prove it a caricature."[13] For his part, Palmer detects not a
hint of anarchy in the Southern cause; the right of secession antedates American history, for it is a "prerogative of sovereignty" that was exercised "not
against law, but in accordance with a law which was deemed by the parties
both fundamental and organic." Breckenridge "affirms secession to be rebellion, which must be suppressed at every hazard: we, that it is an inherent
right of sovereignty."[14]

Not surprisingly, biblical images are scattered throughout this "review."
Palmer alleges that Breckenridge is kept from acknowledging the law of separation by "his idolatry of the empire—that great image of Nebuchadnezzar,
set up on the plain of Dura."[15] Further on, Palmer writes that the division of
America was inevitable, "simply because, from the beginning, two nations
have with us been in the womb—and the birth, however long delayed, must
come at length."[16] For Palmer, the fundamental fallacy pervading Breckenridge's argument is his "misconception that [the union] is a consolidated
popular Government, instead of being a Congress of Republics."[17] The term
consolidated, of course, anticipates the language Palmer would use in 1863 and
after to describe the "primary rebellion" of Nimrod.

After the war commenced, Palmer continued to dispute the charge that
Southerners were engaged in rebellion. Preaching at a funeral service for General Maxcy Gregg in late 1862, he attempted to set the record straight: "Should
every thing be lost, and the base foot of an insolent invader tread upon our
high and beautiful places," Palmer preached, "we will rally around the tombs
of our dead, and fight the last battle of freedom over their honored dust."
Never, he continued, shall our country's foe "be suffered to erase our inscrip-
tions of love upon their tombs, and write the word 'rebel' upon their sacred
dust. Beside this bier we take the irrevocable oath to die upon his grave, ere
it shall be thus desecrated."[18] In February 1863, while in exile in South Carolina, Palmer managed to publish a pamphlet titled "Oath of Allegiance," in
which he defended the citizens of Louisiana who were refusing to comply with
General Benjamin Butler's infamous Order No. 28 requiring an oath of loyalty
to the Federal government.

Palmer's tract is primarily concerned with the stigma of dishonor and
rebellion that some attached to Southerners' refusal to recognize the Union.
He accuses the Federals of attempting to disgrace a people it cannot conquer.
He expresses deep sympathy for those who have been subjected to the "disaster of a dishonored name," as well as burning anger toward their captors.
He refutes the Northern view that "the South has embarked in a wicked
rebellion, upon crushing which, the very life of the nation depends." The truth
is that "a monstrous despotism has grown up" that "brands with the infamy
of rebellion" the bravery of a great people. In "Oath of Allegiance," Palmer

turns the tables on those who view Southern resistance as disloyalty by referring to Louisianans who have acquiesced in Butler's oath as "traitors to the
South." He urges these recreants to recover their manhood: "There is no alternative but that of a dishonored name, cleaving to you and to your children
as long as history shall last."[19]

As we have seen, when sentiment for reunification with Northern Presbyterians gained momentum in the 1880s, Palmer led the Southern church's
opposition. Significantly, the biblical basis for Palmer's resistance was a paraphrase of Genesis 9–11: "It cannot be denied that God has divided the human
race into several distinct groups, for the sake of keeping them apart," he
maintained. "When the promise was given to Noah that the world should not
be again destroyed with a flood, it became necessary to restrain the wickedness
of man that it should not rise to the same height as in the ante-diluvian
period. Hence the unity of human speech was broken, and 'so the Lord scattered them abroad from thence upon the face of all the earth.'" Yet there is
evidence that Palmer's opposition to reunion was based in wounded honor
as much as in theological conviction.

In 1870, when the establishment of official "correspondence" between the
two ecclesiastical bodies was proposed, Palmer emphasized the lingering
wound of dishonor inflicted upon Southerners in 1861. In the "Pastoral Letter
of 1870" authored by Palmer for the church's general assembly, a condition
of correspondence with Northern Presbyterians was "the unequivocal retrac-
tion of the imputations against ourselves, industriously circulated throughout
Christendom." This requirement was "compelled by a proper sense of self-
respect, and a due regard to the honour of our own Church."[20] Specifically,
former statements accusing the Southern church of "heresy and blasphemy"
had to be canceled, because "any form of intercourse, while they remain upon
record, would be a tacit acquiescence in the same, and a submission to the
dishonour which has been cast upon the name of our people and or our
Church."[21] One who witnessed Palmer's comments on this issue before the
Louisville Assembly called it "the most pathetic, soul-stirring utterance to
which I ever listened."[22]

During the Civil War, Northern Presbyterians charged that the country's
peace had been destroyed by "treason, rebellion, anarchy, fraud, and violence"
contrary to all religion and morality.[23] For years afterward, they accused
Southern Presbyterians of "wicked rebellion" and called them to repent. Thus,
it is not at all surprising that whenever Palmer discussed slavery, secession,
war, or defeat, he witnessed to his conviction that Southerners had acted
honorably, while their opponents were guilty of impugning Southern honor.

Honor in Palmer's Character

The centrality of honor is evident not only in Palmer's rhetoric but also in
his life and legend. To many who knew him, Palmer personified the code he
so frequently invoked. Proof was offered in stories of a dramatic incident

occurring during Palmer's second year at Amherst College. According to the account recorded by Thomas Carey Johnson, Palmer belonged to an Amherst literary society,

> the members of which were bound by a solemn pledge not to disclose what occurred at its meetings. One of the exercises consisted of the reading by the secretary of anonymous papers which had been deposited in a box at the door. A paper was read at one of the meetings which contained caustic but humorous criticisms of the professors. A divinity student betrayed his fellow-members by informing the Faculty. At the next meeting of the society, an order was read forbidding the exercise, whereupon Palmer, then about 16 years of age, moved that the paper conveying the order be tabled indefinitely, alleging that the Faculty could not know of the exercises except through the treachery of one of the students, and that it was unworthy of the dignity of the professors to accept perjured testimony as evidence. The president was afraid to put the motion to vote, but two members held him in the chair while the question was put and carried.[24]

The Amherst faculty sought to uncover the offender's identity by requiring society members to swear their innocence. When Palmer was summoned, "he informed that body that he was in honor bound to take no part in disclosing what went on in a society the members of which were pledged to secrecy." Threatened with expulsion, Palmer responded: "Well, sirs. I will take expulsion at your hands rather than trample upon my sense of honor."[25] According to a version of the story recorded after Palmer's death, the treacherous "divinity student" was future abolitionist Henry Ward Beecher, who "true to the instincts of his nature . . . betrayed his fellow members by informing the faculty."[26] The narrator contrasts the two men's behavior, noting that the story exemplifies "the lack of moral principle so noticeable in [Beecher's] whole career." Over time this dramatic tale became emblematic of Southern honor and Northern treachery among the caretakers of Palmer's legacy.

Before Palmer could return from Massachusetts to South Carolina, his honor was assaulted by Northern perfidy once again. As Palmer sojourned in New York City before sailing for home, he entered a secondhand bookstore and attempted to make a purchase with a fifty-dollar note. When a clerk left the store in search of change, Palmer patiently awaited his return until it became apparent he had been robbed. "In grim desperation he resolved to stay in that store as long as it should be possible that he might confront the scoundrel upon his return. After six weary hours had passed the man cautiously ventured back to the neighborhood. . . . While the knave was trying to discover whether the coast was clear of the purchaser, that severely tried young man caught sight of him, dashed upon him, when for very shame the shabby fellow gave up the money."[27] According to Palmer's biographer, this episode exerted a lasting influence on the young man.

The place of honor in Palmer's adult identity is indicated in his private correspondence with Princeton divine Charles Hodge. In 1860, Palmer was unanimously elected by the General Assembly of the Presbyterian Church

(Old School) to occupy a professorial chair at Princeton Seminary. Although the invitation to join the faculty of his church's flagship institution was a great tribute, Palmer was compelled to turn it down. In a letter to Hodge, he explained that the decision was based upon neither sectional feelings nor family obligations. Rather, it was honor that held him in New Orleans:

> In the first place then, I am restrained by a sentiment of honor from accepting the post to which the Assembly has invited me. The sole office upon which, four years ago, the Synod of South Carolina consented to sunder my connexion with the Columbia Seminary, was, that I did not feel called to a scholastic life. . . . The acceptance therefore of a position at Princeton would not only expose me to the charge of inconsistency and fickleness, but might be construed as a breach of faith towards my brethren in Carolina. This may seem to some the mere prudishness of honor; but the sentiment sticks to me and rules out every solicitation to embark in academic labour.[28]

In public and in private, Palmer defended himself, his church, and his country by claiming that all were guided by the instinct honor. In this sense, he reflects the values of the antebellum evangelical preachers recently examined by Christine Leigh Heyrman. Aspiring to be treated as gentlemen, these men accepted "the most basic assumption of the code of honor . . . the axiom that the measure of a man is his reputation—the public judgment of his outward performance, particularly his behavior in the company of other masters."[29] According to Heyrman, these clergymen accommodated themselves to the culture of honor by creating "idealized masculine selves." Like Baptists and Methodists who were "primed by decades of proving themselves men of honor in recognizably southern ways," Palmer, too, "rose readily to defend slavery in the 1830s, secession in the 1850s, and the holy cause of upholding both with force of arms in 1861."[30]

Order

Order in Palmer's Defense of Slavery

The association between Palmer's advocacy of slavery and his concern for order is evident primarily in his insistence that slavery as it existed in the South was "domestic" and "patriarchal." Slavery was domestic inasmuch as the slaveholder was required to protect as well as extract labor from servants in his extended family. It was patriarchal because it was modeled on the ideal family structure revealed in the early chapters of Genesis and celebrated in the South. At the beginning of history, Palmer and other Southerners believed, God had enumerated the normative structure of society by simultaneously instituting family and church. As Palmer wrote in 1872, the close tie between these institutions was iterated at three crucial junctures in biblical history: in the first family, where Adam served as priest; in the family of Noah, where, after the Flood the patriarch "offered sacrifices for his combined household"; and in the first century, when the church took its final form and "was again founded in the house."[31]

Related to the conviction that slavery was essential to domestic order was Palmer's perception of slaves as children. In his "Thanksgiving Sermon," Palmer averred that "my servant, whether born in my house or bought with my money, stands to me in the relation of a child. Though providentially owing me service, which, providentially, I am bound to exact, he is, nevertheless, my brother and my friend, and I am to him a guardian and a father." This relationship, Palmer maintained, "binds upon us the providential duty of preserving the relation that we may save him from a doom worse than death."[32] As disorderly and ungovernable children, blacks benefitted from slavery as much as whites. In fact, according to Palmer, the Southern Negro owed his very existence to this providential institution; if returned to Africa blacks would lapse into "primitive barbarism," and if liberated in America they would be overtaken by "rapid extermination before they had time to waste away through listlessness, filth and vice."[33]

Significantly, the nexus between order and servitude persisted in Palmer's mind long after slavery itself had disappeared. In a popular work titled *The Family, in Its Civil and Churchly Aspects* (1876), Palmer addressed the "authority of masters" and the "subjection of servants." While not wishing to "perplex [his] discussion by so much as touching the vexed question of slavery," Palmer supposed that "in some one of its many forms, servitude is a permanent relation, in all the conditions of human society."[34] The vital connection between family, order, and servitude Palmer expressed in a number of ways. First, he insisted that the family serves "as the primary state instituted for the purpose of establishing order. It is the first government under which will is placed, that it may be broken in and taught obedience." With family, Palmer continued, "vanishes the last hope of order, government and law in society at large."[35] Further, Palmer alleged that servitude protects society from the antagonism of the classes and is necessary because servants are naturally prone to a spirit of anarchy and insubordination. The theology of family articulated by Palmer in the 1870s testified to his enduring belief that servitude was as essential to human order as family or church.

Order in Palmer's Vindication of Secession

In a passage rife with the language of "yoke," "vassalage," and "oppression," Palmer declared in his "Thanksgiving Sermon" that "no despotism is more absolute than that of an unprincipled democracy, and no tyranny more galling than that exercised through constitutional formulas."[36] In "National Responsibility before God," he charged that the true rebels were Northerners who rejected both the Constitution and "organic law." Characterizing the Federal government as a "tyranny" behind the president and "a despotism under

which we cannot consent to live," Palmer upheld the Confederacy as the last
hope of self-government on the continent. He declared that "the spirit of
insubordination is . . . the highest treason" and blamed the dissolution of the
American nation on leaders who were "tinctured with the free-thinking and
infidel spirit" that animated the French Revolution. In decrying the "despotism of the mob," Palmer condemned those who had "sinned in a grievous
want of reverence for the authority and majesty of law."[37]

Later in 1861, Palmer had a guiding hand in the pastoral letter composed
by founding members of the Presbyterian Church in the Confederate States.
This document, titled "To All the Churches of Jesus Christ throughout the
Earth . . . ," contended that the Southern church possessed a right of existence
that corresponded to that of a distinct Southern nation. In exercising these
rights, both had embarked on natural and orderly paths. Separate existence,
the letter stressed, did not spell disorder in the ecclesiastical realm. "We should
be sorry to be regarded by our brethren in any part of the world as guilty of
schism. . . . Our aim has been to promote the unity of the Spirit in the bonds
of peace." It became necessary to pursue the path of disunion, the letter
continued, when the church adopted a political theory that "made secession
a crime, the seceding States rebellious and the citizens who obeyed them
traitors." Under these conditions, Southern Presbyterians were forced to go
their own way precisely to maintain order and avoid "a mournful spectacle
of strife and debate."[38]

As we have seen, beginning in 1863 Palmer invoked Nimrod and his tower
to argue that Northerners were engaged in sinful rebellion. According to Palmer, the political consolidation sought by advocates of the Union was a clear
violation of divine law that reiterated Nimrod's rebellion on the Plain of
Shinar. In other words, at the very time Palmer was affirming Noah's curse
as a rationale for slavery, he was accusing the North of rebellion and defending
Southerners as apostles of order.

Disorder and Abolition

The link in Palmer's mind between slavery and order is also evident in his
relentless diatribes on the immorality of abolitionism. For Palmer, antislavery
was synonymous with infidelity, rebellion, and chaos. Relying on well-
established proslavery conventions, Palmer incessantly conjoined abolitionism
and the dissolution of society. For example, his sermons were punctuated with
frightening references to the slave insurrection in Santo Domingo (Haiti). If
the South misses its sublime moment and does not save itself, Palmer predicted in 1860, "within five and twenty years the history of St. Domingo will
be the record of Louisiana."[39] This was a classic trope of proslavery orators,
one repeated many times following the late-eighteenth-century Haitian up-
rising.[40]

Another proslavery rhetorical strategy was to associate the assault on slavery with apocalypse. Palmer adopted this tactic in his "Thanksgiving Sermon," proclaiming that "we have fallen upon times when there are 'signs in the sun, and in the moon, and in the stars; upon the earth distress of nations, with perplexities; the sea and the waves roaring; men's hearts failing them for fear and for looking after those whinings which are coming' in the near yet gloomy future."[41] Similarly, in "National Responsibility before God" Palmer thanked his Maker for the storm of war, for "it has come in time to redeem us from ruin. Though the heavens be overcast, and lurid lightnings gleam from the bosom of each dark cloud, the moral atmosphere will be purged—and from our heroism shall spring sons and daughters capable of immortal destinies."[42] Another proslavery expedient was the charge that abolition was, without remainder, moral rebellion and infidelity. We encounter this allegation throughout Palmer's writings of the 1850s and 1860s, but particularly in his crisis sermons of 1860 and 1861.

When Palmer characterized abolitionism as infidelity, he was articulating beliefs that were simultaneously personal, regional, and denominational. As Thomas Peterson has pointed out, slavery dampened the religious enthusiasm associated with the Second Great Awakening and caused Southerners to associate revivals in other parts of the country with sects, utopian communities, and the "isms" that threatened societal stability.[43] Fears that revivalism threatened the slavocracy were confirmed when Northern revivalists joined the antislavery campaign. Among Presbyterians, the 1837 split between "Old School" and "New School" reflected concerns over revivalism and antislavery. Thus, as an Old School Presbyterian and a Southerner, Palmer naturally associated abolition with religious enthusiasm and "fanaticism." His conviction that antislavery sentiment could be traced to the European Enlightenment led him to identify this fanaticism with infidelity; and his assumption that slavery safeguarded the social order caused him to connect both with rebellion.

Following fellow South Carolinian John C. Calhoun, Palmer maintained that the spurious Enlightenment doctrine of human equality had created anarchy in Europe and threatened to do the same in America. Calhoun taught that because humanity's "individual affections" tend toward anarchy, they must be checked by government.[44] Similarly, in his "Thanksgiving Sermon" Palmer described abolitionism as a "reckless radicalism which seeks for the subversion of all that is ancient and stable, and a furious fanaticism which drives on its ill-considered conclusions with utter disregard of the evil it engenders."[45] Later in the same address, Palmer invoked the specter of the French Revolution and its spirit of "discord and schism":

> The abolition spirit is undeniably atheistic. The demon which erected its throne up on the guillotine in the days of Robespierre and Marat, which abolished the Sabbath and worshipped reason in the person of a harlot, yet survives to work other horrors, of which those of the French Revolution are but the type. . . . From a thousand Jacobin clubs here, as in France, the decree

has gone forth which strikes at God by striking at all subordination and law.[46]

In forgetting that Providence must govern human beings, abolitionists disregarded "the delicate mechanism of Providence, which moves on, wheels within wheels, with pivots and balances and springs, which the great Designer alone can control." They war against "constitutions and laws and compacts, against Sabbaths and sanctuaries, against the family, the State, and the Church." In other words, they wreak chaos and disorder.

In "National Responsibility before God," Palmer struck a similarly dramatic chord. "Like the attraction of gravitation in physics, law binds together all the spheres of human duty and holds them fast to the throne of God. In all the concentric circles of society, obedience is man's first obligation.... The spirit of insubordination is therefore the highest treason, for it breaks the tie which binds the universe of moral beings together."[47] In the same sermon, Palmer extended his critique of abolitionism to the American Constitution, whose authors, he claimed, were "tinctured with the free-thinking and infidel spirit which swept like a pestilence over Europe in the seventeenth and eighteenth centuries, and which brought forth at last its bitter fruit in the horrors of the French Revolution."[48]

Of course, abolitionists responded to the charge of infidelity with equal vehemence. In The "Infidelity" of Abolitionism (1860), William Lloyd Garrison wrote:

> If therefore, [the American Anti-slavery Society] be an infidel Society, it is so only in the sense in which Jesus was a blasphemer, and the Apostles were pestilent and seditious fellows, seeking to turn the world upside down. It is infidel to Satan, the enslaver; it is loyal to Christ, the redeemer. It is infidel to a Gospel which makes man the property of man; it is bound up with the Gospel which requires us to love our neighbors as ourselves, and to call no man master.... It is infidel to the Bible as a pro-slavery interpreted volume; it is faithful to it as construed on the side of justice and humanity.[49]

Garrison's response indicates how fundamental the charge of infidelity was to the religious proslavery argument.

Order and American Racism

Even as Palmer began to assimilate "scientific" concepts after the Civil War, his racial rhetoric trafficked in themes of order and disorder. For instance, when he turned to the question of African destiny in his 1863 address before the South Carolina Assembly, Palmer emphasized "facts" he believed had been "grievously overlooked by [slavery's] fanatical assailants."[50] Among these were that "the negro race ... has never in any period of history been able to lift itself above its native condition of fetishism and barbarism ... except as it has indirectly contributed by servile labor to human progress"; "that the highest type of character, ever developed among [Negroes], has been in the condition of servitude"; and "that, in the fairest portions of the earth, after the advantage of a long discipline to systematic toil, emancipation has converted them instantly from productive laborers into the most indolent and squalid wretches to be found upon the globe."[51] In other words, slavery was necessary to protect the free Anglo-Saxon, the African slave, and the earth itself from the results of Hamite disorder and ineptitude. It was difficult for Palmer to envision any alternative to black thralldom: "My individual belief," he offered, "is, that servitude, in some one of its forms, is the allotted destiny of this race and that the form most beneficial to the negro himself is precisely that which obtains with us.[52]

In 1887, in his campaign to block the reunion of Northern and Southern Presbyterians, Palmer invoked disorder in terms that resonate with modern racial stereotypes. He stressed that "upon no point are the Southern people more sensitive, to no danger are they more alive, than this of the amalgamation of the two races thrown so closely together and threatening the deterioration of both."[53] Presbyterians in the North may be untroubled by the Negro problem, Palmer wrote, because "the infusion of two or three drops of ink into a tumbler of water will not discolor it." Perhaps there is little danger that the Northern church will be ruled by a Negro majority, "fastening their crude superstitions and fantastic usages upon those so far superior to them in intelligence and virtue." But, Palmer warned, the situation is much different in the South, where "Negro churches could be multiplied of infinitesimal proportions, packing our courts with Presbyters of that race to whom the entire Church would be in hopeless subjection." Palmer then referred obliquely to the social peril implied in the prospect of ecclesiastical reunion:

> How can the two races be brought together in nearly equal numbers in those confidential and sacred relations which belong to the ministry of the Word, without entailing that personal intimacy between ministers and people which must end in the general amalgamation of discordant races? We simply hint at evils which we do not desire to discuss in detail: the mere suggestion of them will put the readers of this paper upon their own line of reflection, filling out the argument to its due proportion.[54]

For Palmer, the specter of racial amalgamation eclipsed even the benefit of white control over black churches.

Genesis 9–11, Mastery, and Victimhood

Christine Heyrman's analysis of evangelical Southern clergymen illumines the way these antebellum preachers embraced the cultural ideal of mastery. Heyrman does not relate the aspiration for mastery to the Southern clergy's fondness for Noah's curse, but the connection is compelling. Whether they iden-

tified with Noah the patriarch or Japheth the eponymous white man, Southern
divines read Genesis 9 in a fashion that could only buoy their self-perception
as masters. Noah's divine authority, the language of "enlargement" applied to
the first European, and the perennial servitude predicted for Ham no doubt
combined to bolster the ambition of Southern clergy to be counted among
their society's masters. Likewise, the historical events that spelled an end to
Southern white ascendancy provide a background for clarifying the transition
from Ham to Nimrod in the white biblical imagination.

Remarkably, Nimrod emerged in Palmer's racial discourse precisely at the
moment he began to express sentiments of victimhood. From the 1850s
through the early years of the war, Palmer referred often to Ham (and Noah's
other sons) but made no mention of Nimrod. Conversely, from 1863 through
the 1880s, Nimrod and his tower were staples in Palmer's rhetoric, as Ham
became virtually absent. In other words, Ham remained an integral part of
Palmer's worldview as long as he sought to validate the claim that Southern
whites had both a right and responsibility to master the "sons of Ham." Even
after their region was invaded by Federal troops, Southerners retained confidence in the righteousness of the Confederacy and the inevitability of its
victory. But this confidence, which sustained Southerners' self-perception as
masters rather than victims of history, waned with pivotal defeats at Gettysburg and Vicksburg.

It was precisely at this time—late 1863—that Palmer came to rely on
Genesis 10 and 11 to defend the South's cause. As he began to portray himself
and his countrymen as victims of occupation, usurpation, tyranny, and cruelty, Palmer invoked the menacing image of Nimrod. Palmer's first public
reference to Ham's grandson appeared in his "South Carolina Fast Day Sermon" (December 1863), whose tone unmistakably echoed the Confederacy's
martial setbacks of that year. When Palmer proclaimed that "the first pronounced insurrection against [God's] supremacy, was the attempt by Nimrod
to oppose and defeat this policy [of divine separation]; and the successive
efforts of all the great kingdoms to achieve universal conquest have been but
the continuation of that primary rebellion—always attended by the same
overwhelming failure that marked the first," he was portraying the Union as
an empire bent on conquest and the South as its pitiable victim.[55]

Nimrod figured prominently once again in "The Present Crisis and Its
Issue" (1872), when Palmer offered a theological rationale for racial separation.
In this address, Palmer located the fountainhead of segregation in "the immediate intervention of Jehovah, breaking the unity of human speech, and
thus separating the conspirators by the most impassable of all barriers," and
its necessity in the "usurpation and insurrection of the first Nimrod," which
was emblematic of the desire of "great kingdoms to achieve universal conquest." Nimrod materialized yet again in 1887 in Palmer's response to the
campaign for reunification with Northern Presbyterians. Compelled to thwart
his church's attempts at ecclesiastical unification, Palmer appealed to the Babel
episode to certify that separation was God's will for human societies.

In other words, on the occasions when Palmer applied Nimrod and his legend to American history he also intimated the South's victim status. When Palmer and other Southerners were confident in their role as masters, Noah's prophecy seemed to indicate why and how. When they began to regard themselves as history's righteous victims, the legend of Nimrod and his tower elucidated the reasons for this condition. In Palmer's maturing interpretation of Genesis 9–11, we glimpse some of the emotional dynamics that accompanied the transition from Ham to Nimrod in Southern racial discourse following the Civil War.

Palmer as Patriarch and Dishonorable Son

Benjamin Palmer, we have argued, was drawn to Noah's prophecy by the same forces that attracted other antebellum Southerners—honor, order, and mastery. But if we examine his biography, it is possible to discern an ever deeper connection between Palmer and the biblical passage that gripped him. Biographers have described Benjamin's relationship with his father as a happy one characterized by mutual admiration. A letter penned on the occasion of his father's birthday contains evidence of Benjamin's esteem: "What a clear, bright day has your life been on earth . . . It has been a long life, undimmed by a single reproach—as it seems to us, not obscured by a single mistake. . . ."[56] Yet there are also indications that father and son experienced serious conflicts.

One occasion for conflict was the crisis precipitated by Benjamin's abrupt departure from Amherst in 1834. When Palmer arrived home unannounced following his expulsion, Edward Palmer's reaction led Benjamin's mother "to act as mediator in order to avoid a permanent break between father and son."[57] Another episode in Palmer's childhood must have generated unresolved feelings in the young boy. In 1821, when Benjamin was only three, Edward Palmer left home and family to enroll at Andover Seminary in Massachusetts. We can imagine the young Benjamin's sense of abandonment during his father's two-year absence; we know that Edward's departure was dramatic and memorable. Biographers record that as the elder Palmer departed from South Carolina, he raised Benjamin in his arms and announced: "My poor little Benny, I suppose I shall never see you again in this world. You will hardly live to pass your fifth year."[58] Such a remarkable prophecy could only intensify the young Palmer's sense of desertion. Indeed, to the three-year-old Benjamin, his father's farewell must have seemed a parental curse. In that the dispiriting prediction had the authority of the family's patriarch, it might as well have come from the mouth of God.

Genesis 9 is inscribed with ambiguity as to whether Noah's curse is aimed at his son Ham or grandson Canaan. And so it was in the Palmer family. If Benjamin defiantly resisted his father's prediction of an early death by living into his eighties, his own son could not escape the patriarchal curse. Several

decades later Palmer's own son Benjamin would succumb to a slow and ag-
onizing demise before reaching the age of two. Given his conflicted relationship to paternity, it is not surprising that Palmer lived for more than forty
years with the image of Benjamin Blakely languishing like a "breathing skel-
eton" upon his mother's lap.

9

Beyond Slavery, Beyond Race

Noah's Camera in the Twentieth Century

> God has separated people for His own purpose. He has
> erected barriers between the nations, not only land and
> sea barriers, but also ethnic, cultural, and language barri-
> ers. God has made people different one from another and
> intends those differences to remain.
>
> Letter to James Landrith from
Bob Jones University, 1998

THROUGHOUT THE SOUTH, buildings, streets, parks, schools, and orphanages bear Benjamin Palmer's name, but it is doubtful that anyone associates these monuments with his legacy of religious racism. Palmer's influence was certainly evident in clerical resistance to integration during the 1950s. When Southern Presbyterians such as Thomas Gillespie declared that segregation represented the providential pattern for human relations, they were asserting an updated version of Palmer's hermeneutic of separation.[1] Today, however, the caretakers of Palmer's legacy do not advance biblical warrants for racial discrimination. Palmer is honored as an apostle of evangelical Christianity, his sermons are posted on the World Wide Web, an edition of his biography published in 1906 remains in print, a recent book celebrates him as a paragon of Christian preaching,[2] and a prominent Southern institution of higher learning honors him as "the father of [the] institution."[3] But he is no longer associated with the biblical justifications for white supremacy on which he labored for decades.

Yet given the longevity and flexibility of the American interpretive traditions surrounding Genesis 9–11, it would be naive to conclude that they do not survive in some form. In fact, just as postbellum Bible readers transformed Noah's curse by applying it to racial segregation, more recently Noah's prophecy has been salvaged by Christians seeking to rehabilitate Genesis 9–11 for a postracist age. In doing so, they have sustained the legacy of Benjamin Palmer in the largest sense, by asserting the relevance of Noah's curse and its satellite passages to life in contemporary America.

Beyond Slavery

Palmer symbolized his enduring conviction that God's intentions for the human family were revealed in Genesis 9:25–27 by invoking the image of "Noah's camera."[4] Palmer was able to salvage Noah's camera despite Confederate defeat and slave emancipation because he had avoided defining just what Ham's curse entailed. He spoke of servitude in relation to Genesis 9 but not slavery as such. For Palmer, Noah's prophecy was a poetic description of the way God would "divide the earth between the sons of Noah." The great message of the curse was not thralldom per se but the destinies of Japheth, Shem, and Ham, who were assumed to correspond with the red, black, and white "races" identified by nineteenth-century common sense. When the prophecy's connection with chattel slavery fell away after the Civil War, its racial dimension survived. In fact, Palmer affirmed this dimension of Noah's camera until the end of his life.

What distinguishes Palmer among former slavery apologists—his stubborn refusal to relinquish the curse's relevance to American race relations—is something he shares with American Bible readers more generally. To wit, Palmer represents the American penchant for reading Genesis 9–11 as a manifesto of racial destiny quite apart from the question of slavery. Another nineteenth-century American author whose work is indicative of this popular fascination with Noah's family is Jerome Holgate. In 1860, this New Yorker wrote *Noachidae: or, Noah, and his Descendants,* a fictional re-creation of the stories and genealogies contained in Genesis 9–11—from Noah's disembarkation to God's judgment on the Tower of Babel. Assuming the historicity of this material, Holgate sought to communicate its message for the modern American reader.[5]

As it ultimately was for Palmer, for Holgate Genesis 9–11 was about the distinctive and indelible characters inherited by modern racial groups from their eponymous ancestors. In *Noachidae,* Ham is an infidel who doubts God and has little respect for creation. His diminutive faith is rooted in a small mind. As Japhet remarks: "Ham believes what he knows; and knowing very little, has very little faith. . . ."[6] Holgate sets the stage for Noah's malediction this way: "Ham started for his encampment, and passing his father's tent, stopped, looked in for a moment, and then turning back, went up to his brothers, saying something, while a lurid smile played upon his visage. Shem and Japhet, with looks of indignation, turning round, went up to their father's tent, and taking down a woolen mantle, hanging there, spread it out behind them, going backward, and disappeared, for a moment, within the tent."[7] When Noah awakes the following morning, he examines the wine he had imbibed the night before and complains that "it had a most extraordinary effect upon me; I think something unusual must have got in it . . . I was very thirsty, and drank immoderately of it."[8] As the family gathers for morning worship, Noah turns "slowly and with dignity toward Ham," saying, "disrespect to parents is disrespect to the Almighty. . . . The Almighty has given you also, in connection with your brethren, this beautiful earth. Should you not be thankful for it?"[9] When the young Canaan replies that "we did not ask the Almighty to give it to us," a shudder runs through the families of Shem and Japhet. Calling them "ungrateful children," Noah announces that Ham and his descendants

> will enjoy the poorest portion of the earth. I see it; I see trouble. You will seek to rule, but you will be slaves; for the Almighty humbles the proud. Beware! Ambition, covetousness will be the ruin of your race, and of every race . . . that gives way to them. . . . [I]n Canaan will your own passions and disobedience meet their speediest recompense. Foolish children . . . to rebel against the Almighty—against your own father that has in his hands all goodness. Shem . . . the Almighty will bless you. But these blessings will be more spiritual than physical, at first, and Canaan shall be your servant. . . . Japhet, in physical good you will be blest. The largest portion of the earth will be yours, and Shem shall administer to your spiritual comfort. Expanding, you shall expand and Canaan shall be subordinate to you. . . . My children . . . the Almighty rules.[10]

Although Holgate does not present Noah's sons as progenitors of separate "races" in the modern sense,[11] he makes it clear that Ham and his descendants have been assigned to dwell in Africa. Yet more essential than racial identities are the distinctive characters of Noah's sons. Following a tradition embraced by Palmer and other nineteenth-century writers, Holgate connects the post-diluvian dispersion with the sons' unique roles in civilization building: Semites have received spiritual blessings and responsibilities through which they are to "administer to [the] spiritual comfort" of others; Japhethites have been blessed physically, intellectually, and geographically. Hamites, meanwhile, are incorrigibly proud, ambitious, covetous, passionate, disobedient, and rebellious. These traits are so fundamental to Holgate's conception of Noah's sons that they appear throughout his narrative. For instance, while Noah conducts a religious ceremony,

> Shem and Elisheba [his wife] were the most devotional; Asia appeared more so than Japhet, yet his air and manner was that of profound reverence and respect, yet there was a certain wandering of the eye and vacant expression of the countenance that indicated not quite so much devotion as was exhibited by his younger brother; still this might have been the result of temperament and an active imagination. But Ham's demeanor was different. He was restless and uneasy in his manner, and the expression of his countenance indicated a distaste for the whole ceremony.[12]

Holgate's Ham is neither the irredeemably evil figure previous interpreters had made him nor the quintessential Negro he became for proslavery apologists. Rather, he is a living canvass whose personal traits become a portrait of the nations that will spring from him.

Testifying to the depth at which Genesis 9 informed the popular imagination in the nineteenth century are African American divines who read Noah's prophecy as predicting a unique historical role for the children of Ham. Among these men was Edward Wilmot Blyden (1832–1912), who in 1862 proclaimed that

> Africa will furnish a development of civilization which the world has never yet witnessed. Its great peculiarity will be its moral element. The Gospel is to achieve some of its most beautiful triumphs in that land. "God shall enlarge Japheth, and he shall dwell in the tents of Shem," was the blessing upon the European and Asiatic races. Wonderfully have these predictions been fulfilled. . . . The promise to Ethiopia, or Ham, like that to Shem, is of a spiritual kind. It refers not to physical strength, not to large and extensive domains, not to foreign conquests, not to wide-spread dominions, but to the possession of spiritual qualities, to the elevation of the soul heavenward, to spiritual aspirations and divine communications. "Ethiopia shall stretch forth her hands unto God" [Ps. 68:31]. Blessed, glorious promise! Our trust is not to be in chariots or horses, not in our own skill or power, but our help is to be in the name of the Lord.[13]

Blyden declared that because God had so faithfully fulfilled Noah's prediction of enlargement to Japheth, the realization of the later promise to Ham (in Psalm 68) was inevitable as well.[14]

In 1884, Bishop James Theodore Holly evolved a similar theological interpretation of Genesis 9 in which he posited separate ages of humanity corresponding to Noah's three sons. In "The Divine Plan of Human Redemption, In Its Ethnological Development," Holly used Genesis 9–11 to forge a dispensational schema in which the children of Ham complete the work of salvation previously assigned to Shem and Japheth:

> In the development of the Divine Plan of Human Redemption the Semitic race had the formulating, the committing to writing and the primal guardianship of the Holy Scriptures during the Hebrew dispensation. The Japhetic race had the task committed to them of translating, publishing and promulgating broadcast the same Holy Scriptures. . . . But neither the one nor the other of those two races have entered into or carried out the spirit of those Scriptures. This crowning work of the will of God is reserved for the millennial phase of Christianity, when Ethiopia shall stretch out her hands directly unto God. . . . [Both Semitic and Japhetic races] alike await the forthcoming ministry of the Hamitic race to reduce to practical ACTION that spoken word, that written thought.[15]

The extent to which this tripartite historical schema structured Holly's theological vision is evident in a prayer he offered at London's Westminster Abbey in 1878:

O Jesus, Son of the living God; who when thou was spurned and rejected and delivered into the hands of sinful men, by the Jews, of the race of Shem; and, who, when thou wast mocked and cruelly ill treated by Pontius Pilate and the Roman soldiers of the race of Japheth; had'st thy ponderous cross borne to the summit of Golgotha on the stalwart shoulders of Simon of Cyrene, of the race of Ham; remember this poor, forlorn, and despised race when thou art come into thy Kingdom. And give me, not a place at thy right, nor at thy left, but as a door keeper, that I may see the redeemed of my race sweeping into the New Jerusalem, with the children of Abraham, Isaac, and Jacob. Amen.[16]

Holly's son Alonzo Potter Burgess Holly extended this tradition of interpretation into the twentieth century when he wrote that God placed the sons of Japheth in a superior position not to enslave or despise blacks but to exercise "the stewardship of training and developing the Children of Ham for their prophetic mission on Earth, according to the Divine Plan for the Redemption of Africa."[17]

In these black revisions of Noah's curse, Ham's future glory is perceived as an extension of Shem's trust involving "spiritual aspirations and divine communications" or as a new ministry that will "reduce to practical action" what Semites and Japhethites have only recorded and reflected upon. Yet the formal similarities with white readings of Genesis 9 during the same era are profound. In the vein of Palmer and Holgate, Noah's words are invested with prophetic status, are a preview of human interrelationships in future ages, and confirm that each of his descendants has been endowed with a unique mission.

Beyond Race

In the nineteenth century, Noah's prophecy was believed to specify any number of past and future racial hierarchies.[18] After 1900, however, race receded into the background of mainstream American commentary on Genesis 9–11. During the first half of the twentieth century, a few religious publications applied "the curse of Canaan" to race relations,[19] but these were rare before the mid-1950s, when it began to be invoked in connection with the nascent struggle for black civil rights. More common were treatments of Genesis 9 that assiduously avoided questions of slavery and race while seeking to inspire devotion for the Old Testament.[20]

Quite common in these Christian commentaries and preaching aids is the designation of Genesis 9:20–27 as "Noah's Fall." A link with the original Fall (Genesis 2–3) is often established via references to Noah as the second Adam.[21] Noah's drunkenness is occasionally construed as "the believer's fall," since it communicates a universal moral lesson regarding the susceptibility of the righteous to sin—even when they are advanced in age, have not sinned previously, or have earned the appellation "God's saint."[22] The evils of drink are commonly recited, as is the axiom that "the sins of intemperance and impurity are twin sisters."[23] Yet despite their refusal to overlook Noah's culpability before God, pious commentators in the first half of the twentieth century regarded the patriarch's drunkenness as an occasion for revealing "the hearts of his sons"[24] and the character of their descendants. In this way, Noah's prophecy became an inspired "sketch of the future history of the world" that delineated the character of "the founders of the three great branches of the human family." In these six or seven sentences, "we have an epitome of the world's history."

As Arthur Pink put it in 1950, Noah's prophecy is "a remarkable unfolding of the future destinies of the new humanity":

> Noah's prediction contains an outline sketch of the history of the nations of the world. The great races of the earth are here seen in their embryonic condition: they are traced to their common source, through Shem, Ham and Japheth, back to Noah. The nature of the stream is determined by the character of the fountain—a bitter fountain cannot send forth sweet waters. . . . A history that *started* with Ham's shameful impropriety can have only one course and end.[25]

For the discerning reader, Noah's "remarkable prophecy" is not a reflection of the patriarch's ire at his son or grandson, nor is it a "hasty ejaculation" provoked by humiliation or temporary resentment. Rather, it is a revelatory statement whose divine provenance is wonderfully confirmed in its historical fulfillment: "Being so accurate a delineation of the future of the three branches of the human family as we shall find this word to be, it approves itself to the thinking man as a truly prophetic utterance." For, "who but He who knows the end from the beginning could have outlined the whole course of the three great divisions of the postdiluvian race so tersely and so accurately!"[26] Of course, the conviction that Noahs words contain a capsule of subsequent history must influence interpretation of the narrative that precedes the prophecy. Although Shem and Japheth alike are praised for their behavior, Shem's blessing is realized in the spiritual and Japheth's in the material realm—perhaps in Europe's cultural achievements and colonial empires. Unless, that is, Anglo-Saxons are viewed as the "true Israel," in which case Shem's blessing becomes the earthly kingdom traditionally associated with Japhet.[27]

These pious Christian commentators who celebrate Noah's prophecy as a God's-eye view of human history are careful to neither support nor condemn slavery. The curse on Ham is treated with spiritual bromides ("sin always reduces a sinner to slavery"),[28] historicized with the argument that Noah's prediction of enslavement was fulfilled in biblical history, or passed over with the observation that the curse was realized in modern racial slavery.[29] Rare indeed is the affirmation that Noah's malediction "still rests upon the race."[30] Thus, despite a studied lack of interest in the history of interpretation and a refusal to discuss the morality of slavery, American devotional commentaries from the first half of the twentieth century extend the tradition of viewing Noah's prophecy as a unique statement on the origin, character, and destiny of postdiluvian humanity.[31]

Noah's Camera Revisited

In the post–civil rights era, writers in the religious mainstream have even more conscientiously distanced themselves from racist readings of the curse. Yet rather than ignoring Genesis 9's antiblack legacy, they have contended that Noah's malediction applies only to one branch of the Hamite family, that it expired centuries ago, that cursed Canaanites have no connection with Africa, or that, emerging from a drunken stupor, Noah was in no condition to speak for God.[32] Yet these same authors defend Genesis 9–11's historical reliability and theological salience and, in the process, reveal how steeped they are in the interpretive tradition. On one hand, they reiterate crucial elements of interpretive history, claiming, for instance, that Canaan may have encouraged his grandfather to become intoxicated or to commit some unnatural sexual act; that Ham's behavior was "dastardly," that he symbolically castrated his father, or that he is the progenitor of paganism; that the ministry of Shem and Japheth is "the ministry of the family to itself in the midst of shame—a ministry of protection, a surrounding sense of comfort and restored dignity"; that Noah was "completely conscious and capable of sober reflection"; or that his malediction was "spoken by the Spirit of God."[33] On the other hand, they reflect the American compulsion to view Genesis 9–11 as a telescopic image of subsequent history.

A fine example is Arthur C. Custance's *Noah's Three Sons* (1975). Custance revises traditional interpretations of Noah's curse by citing examples of Hamites' "inventive genius" (an attribute ascribed to all the "colored races"). Nevertheless, he reaffirms the curse and makes Hamites responsible for erecting the Tower of Babel. Custance perceives in the "threefold framework" of Genesis 9:24–27 a revelation of distinct characters among the major divisions of humankind. He calls the tenth chapter of Genesis

> a completely authentic statement of how the present world population originated and spread after the Flood in the three families headed respectively by Shem, Ham and Japheth. I further propose that a kind of division of responsibilities to care for the specific needs of man at three fundamental levels (the spiritual, the physical, and the intellectual) was divinely appointed to each of these three branches of Noah's family. History subsequently bears out this thesis in a remarkable way. . . . Rightly understood, the thesis is a key that proves to be an exciting tool of research into the spiritual, the technological, and the intellectual history of mankind since the Flood.[34]

Another recapitulation of Noah's prophecy as a biblical camera for beholding human history appeared in the evangelical weekly *Christianity Today* in 1973.[35] Titled "The Curse of Ham—Capsule of Ancient History," this article evinced popular Christianity's enduring fascination with Noah's prophecy. After quoting Genesis 9:25–27, author Robert Brow opined "that the curse of Ham cannot be applied to black people is easily shown from the text itself. [But] what is usually missed is the astonishing unfolding of world history that the words of this oracle refer to."[36] Brow then embarked on a complex defense of the historicity of Genesis 10's "outline of racial origins." The "tremendous significance" of Noah's curse, according to Brow, is elucidated in light of the Table of Nations's window on human beginnings. Noah's prophecy predicts three historical phenomena that would disastrously affect the Canaanite nations: the enslavement of Canaanites by brother Hamites (Egypt), by the Shemites (Israel), and by Japhethites (Greece under Alexander). Brow argued that Noah's "capsule prophecy" is too important for "crankish misuse by racists" because it demonstrates so effectively that "God is in control of the empires of men." Other Christian authors writing at about this time affirmed Brow's contention that Noah uttered a "sane, sensible prophecy of what the Lord intended to do in each life," leaving us in Genesis a preview of the relative destinies of Noah's descendants.[37]

In 1980, Allen P. Ross offered a more scholarly treatment of Noah's prophecy, but one resonating with similar themes. Ross denied that "the bizarre little story" from which the "curse of Canaan" is derived has any relevance for American race relations, yet he noted that "Ham's impropriety toward his father prompted an oracle with far-reaching implications."[38] Ross perceived in Noah's prophecy the "vast movements of ancient peoples." And like Brow, who saw in Noah's curse "the unfolding of world history," Ross updated the tradition of viewing Genesis 9:25–27 as a resume of virtues and vices among "the families of the world." The purpose of this section of Genesis was to portray "the characteristics of the three branches of the human race in relation to blessing and cursing. In pronouncing the oracle, Noah discerned the traits of his sons and, in a moment of insight, determined that the attributes of their descendants were embodied in their personalities."[39]

These American Christian authors share telling assumptions with regard to the meaning of Genesis 9 in post–civil rights America. While refusing to exploit Noah's prophecy as a rationale for the subordination of African Americans, they invest his words with remarkable prophetic efficacy. In doing so, they demonstrate anew the American biblical imagination's affinity for Noah's curse, quite apart from its value in undergirding specific racial hierarchies.

Back to Babel

The legend of Nimrod and his tower is another atavism that continues to thrive in post–civil rights America. For conservative and moderate Christians who are loathe to seek an explanation of life's beginnings in science, the biblical tale of differentiation and dispersion contained in Genesis 11 seems to offer a compelling myth of origins. Even today, many Christians cite the Tower of Babel story as an explanation of human diversity.[40] This account of racial and ethnic origins appears to be suasive because it takes seriously human differences while safeguarding the historicity of Genesis, and thus the biblical version of creation.

A scholarly effort to harmonize the tower with scientific and historical perspectives on human beginnings was offered in 1973 by Thomas Figart. In *A Biblical Perspective on the Race Problem* (1973), Figart warned Bible-believing Christians that because God is "no respecter of persons," racism is a grievous sin. But Figart was aware that people of faith are often exposed to biological and anthropological theories that threaten to undermine their confidence in scripture. In such a perilous intellectual environment, Figart argued, Genesis 11 offers a reasonable account of human diversity that relies neither on the theory of evolution nor the vast epochs of time it implies. His desire to historicize Genesis and harmonize it with scientific evidence led Figart to speculate that

> at the time of the dispersion of Babel four things, as recorded in the Genesis account, are said to have occurred. The inhabitants were scattered throughout the world "in their lands." Immediately people were thrust into new environments, which also involved new occupations and diets. All this in turn had a lasting effect on stature and resulted in some measurable changes in facial features. Second, they were scattered "after their tongues," causing new thought patterns, writing and speaking habits, and effectively isolating each from their neighboring clan. Third, they were grouped "after their families." Beginning with relatively small groups of several hundreds, perhaps, the gene pools were somewhat limited. The resultant variations through manifestation of recessive genes could well have been the major factor in racial change. Finally, they are said to have been divided "in their nations," a possible reference to development in size from the original "family" units, or a reference to cultural patterns which tended to stabilize the national entities with their peculiar physical characteristics.[41]

Figart concluded that "anthropologically, it is not unreasonable to support the Biblical account of the beginning of the races from 6000 B.C. as a result of the dispersion at the tower of Babel."[42]

In *Noah's Three Sons* (1975), Arthur Custance combined a historicized tower with the tradition that it was constructed by rebellious Hamites. Custance wrote that "the family of Ham, who had become politically dominant, initiated a movement to prevent further dispersal by proposing the building of a monument as a visible rallying point on the flat plain, thus bringing upon themselves a judgment which led to an enforced and rapid scattering throughout the earth."[43] The tradition of Hamite rebellion is also reflected in a discussion of Genesis 9 that appeared in *Commentary* in 1992. Ham, according to author Leon Kass, was a would-be tyrant who delighted "in rebelling against or exposing preexisting law and authority." It is thus fitting that "one of his descendants, Nimrod (whose name connotes rebelliousness) will conquer an empire and will seek to make himself the all-powerful and self-sufficing lord of the earth."[44] Adding tyranny to this portrait of Hamite rebellion, Kass likened Nimrod to Sophocles' Oedipus.

In 1990, fantasy author James Morrow paid tribute to Nimrod's legend in a short story, "Bible Stories for Adults, No. 20: The Tower."[45] This tale of hubris and retribution is set in New York in the 1980s and narrated by God. Concerned with the activities of real estate magnate Daniel Nimrod, God rents the penthouse of Nimrod Tower in upper Manhattan to keep an eye on him. After an interview with Nimrod in which his plans for projects such as Nimrod Gorge and Nimrod Mountain are confirmed, God decides once again to intervene:

> Don't ask Me why I found the Shinarites' Tower so threatening. I simply did. "And now nothing will be restrained from them, which they have imagined to do," I prophesied. My famous curse followed forthwith. "Let Us go down, and there confound their language, that they may not understand one another's speech."
>
> But that didn't stop them, did it? They still did whatever they liked.
>
> This time around, I got it right.[46]

"This time" the punishment is not confusion but perfect understanding. All the people say just what they mean, and in the absence of subtlety, dissimulation, and verbal subterfuge, chaos reigns: "Half the planet is now a graduate seminar, the other half a battleground. . . . Plagued by a single tongue, people can no longer give each other the benefit of semantic doubt. To their utter bewilderment and total horror, they know that nothing is being lost in translation."[47] The fact that Morrow's story is uproariously funny obscures just how much he draws on the interpretive tradition regarding Nimrod and the tower. From the multiethnic security force that guards Nimrod Tower and the "tiers of polyglot shops" housed there, to Nimrod's ambition and "overbearing vanity," to God's description of the tower as "vulgar and arrogant," to the story's final image of Nimrod stealing a "fiberglass hunting bow and a quiver of arrows" from a New Jersey sporting goods store and setting out to bag a deer, Morrow's tale is a veritable primer in Nimrod's legend.

"Black" biblical studies have also contributed to the survival of Nimrod's legend in contemporary America. Although *The Original African Heritage Study Bible* (1993) downplays the "curse of Canaan" and its putative application to persons of color, an annotation titled "The Sons of Ham and the Birth of Nimrod" transmits many aspects of Nimrod's unauthorized biography:

> Within the Hamitic lineage, the son of Cush, Nimrod, was known to be an eminent African hunter and architect. Nimrod, grandson of Ham and the mighty hunter before God, was the first man to try to build his way to

heaven (Gen. 11:1–9). Nimrod managed to draw and begin work on a gigantic tower that would allow him and his fellow servants to see heaven as well as earth. This tower was built in a city called Babel, in the beginning of his empire. Nimrod is rightfully considered to be the great innovator and builder of such ancient Babylonian cities.[48]

Like nineteenth-century abolitionists, the editors perceive in the prominence of Ham's grandson a case against the curse. However, they appear oblivious to the link between Nimrod's tower and antiblack interpretive traditions.

Yet another contemporary source for Nimrod's legend is Alexander Hislop's *Two Babylons,* the magnum opus of nineteenth-century Nimrodiana, which was republished twice in the United States during the second half of the 1990s.[49] If we consider the recirculation of such classic texts, together with the vestiges of the interpretive tradition that are transmitted in everything from fantasy literature to "Afro-centric" study Bibles, we are forced to conclude that as long as Genesis is read, the legends of Ham and Nimrod are likely to persist.

Genesis and Genocide

In the twenty-first century, such legends appear quaint and harmless. They may be reflected in popular adaptations of the Bible, in conservative politics, or in the discrimination practiced by fringe institutions like Bob Jones University. But most Americans do not perceive them as threats to their peace and security. In an age of mass murder, however, we must remain sensitive to the genocidal potential of biblical texts.

Historically speaking, Genesis 9:20–27 and its satellite passages have exercised an ambiguous effect on the destiny of Africans. While Noah's curse provided an ideological basis for racial slavery in Europe and the Americas, it also affirmed blacks' humanity when "scientific" rationales for their extermination were being broadcast. Indeed, when explaining why genocide did not befall African Americans in the years immediately following the Civil War, we must not overlook widespread belief in the historicity of Genesis and the biblical assumption that blacks were human beings descended from Noah and Adam. This does not mean, however, that the ideology of Noah's curse is without genocidal potential or that under certain conditions it could not transmogrify into a rationale for Africans' "removal."

As applied by white theorists beginning in the middle of the nineteenth century, this quasi-biblical ideology designated certain Africans—those purportedly descended from a fair-skinned "Mediterranean race" and thus bearing European civilization—as "Hamites." Scientific racists in South Africa utilized the Hamitic hypothesis to distinguish "Negroes" from "Bantus," whom they believed possessed "Hamitic" blood. But the genocidal potential in the hypothesis was revealed not in southern Africa but in the Great Lakes Region.

William F. S. Miles helpfully summarizes the ideological background to the Rwandan massacres of 1994:

> Colonial-era race classifications, based on the so-called Hamitic myth, prop-
> agated the belief that Tutsis were an intellectually superior, non-indigenous,
> Caucasoid (but not Caucasian) people who bettered their Bantu (including
> Hutu) neighbors. Hamites were understood to be Semitic, not Negroid, orig-
> inating in Egypt and the Upper Nile, introducing higher order institutions
> and thought process to an intellectually inferior African interior.[50]

Rwanda's German and later Belgian colonizers became convinced that "the tribal configuration they oversaw conformed neatly to the Hamitic Hypothesis: Tutsis, a monarchical, pastoralist, and dignified people, were Hamites; aceph-alous, farming Hutus were Bantus."[51]

Reflecting on the influence of the Hamite hypothesis in the Rwandan catastrophe, Miles observes that "racist-driven genocides are compulsively steeped in ancient mythic notions of bloodlines and national origin."[52] In the case of the Hamitic Hypothesis, the integration of nineteenth-century rational racism and biblical terminology was pioneered by John Hanning Speke, a British explorer who set out to discover the source of the Nile and published a journal of his expedition in 1863. Like other nineteenth-century westerners, Speke saw Africans as descendants of "our poor elder brother Ham [who] was cursed by his father, and condemned to be the slave of both Shem and Japheth." But Speke made an original contribution to white perceptions of Africa with a theory of ethnology "founded on the traditions of the several nations, as checked by my own observation of what I saw when passing through them." Speke surmised, based on their distinctive physical appear-ance, that the Wahuma (Tutsis) were descendants of "the semi-Shem-Hamitic [people] of Ethiopia," cattle-herding "Asiatic" invaders who eventually moved south, losing their original language and religion and becoming darkened through intermarriage. Speke presented his theory before a Tutsi king:

> taking a Bible to explain all I fancied I knew about the origin and present con-
> dition of the Wahuma branch of the Ethiopians, beginning with Adam, to
> show how it was the king had heard by tradition that at one time the people of
> his race were half white and half black. Then, proceeding with the Flood, I
> pointed out that the Europeans remained white, retaining Japhet's blood; while
> the Arabs are tawny, after Shem, and the Africans black, after Ham. And, fi-
> nally, to show the greatness of the tribe, I read the 14th chapter of 2d Chronicles,
> in which it is written how Zerah, the Ethiopian, with a host of a thousand, met
> the Jew Asa with a large army, in the valley of Zephathah, near Mareshah; add-
> ing to it that again, at a much later date, we find the Ethiopians battling with
> the Arabs in the Somali country, and with the Arabs and Portuguese at Omwita
> (Mombas)—in all of which places they have taken possession of certain tracts
> of land, and left their sons to people it."[53]

For obvious reasons, Speke's Hamitic Hypothesis was warmly received by Tutsi leaders. More importantly, it was embraced by western intellectuals who needed to explain how "civilization" came to Africa, by missionary educators as a way of undergirding colonial theories of Tutsi superiority, and by Hutu revolutionaries who sought to cast Tutsis as non-indegenous invaders from the north. Indeed, although it conforms neither to biblical logic nor traditional interpretation, the Rwandan version of the Hamitic Hypothesis preserves an important strand of the interpretive tradition: In both colonial and revolutionary versions of the hypothesis, "Hamite" Tutsis are perceived as "invaders" who serveral centuries ago usurped control of the land from its indigenous inhabitants. During the Rwandan genocide, in fact, Hutu Power extremists bragged of sending Tutsis "back down the Nile."

Saul Debow observes that the Hamitic Hypothesis has endured largely owing to its capacity to adapt to changing ideological demands.[54] As we have seen, the very same could be said of the biblical curse tradition in America. Recall that in his "Century Sermon" Benjamin Palmer utilized Noah's prophecy as an ex post facto rationale for his government's removal of Native Americans "from the earth." Faced with the challenge of justifying the elimination of those who once dwelt in "Shem's tents," Palmer wove a novel reading of Genesis 9:27 from disparate and conflicting strands of interpretive tradition. According to strict biblical logic, it was not possible to portray Native Americans as Semites *and* Canaanites, as dwellers in Shem's tents *and* idolatrous interlopers in the promised land. But Palmer's rhetorical skill, his conviction that "Noah's camera" enabled one to envision the movements of history through the eyes of God, and his auditors' confidence that he could be trusted to interpret the Word for their time combined to obscure these logical inconsistencies.

The result was a genocidal reading of Noah's curse in the American tradition. It is terribly fitting that this justification for Native American extermination was delivered as the twentieth century dawned, for it greeted an era that would see the phenomenon of genocide become an all-too-familiar dimension of human experience. Palmer did not live to witness the horrors the new century would reveal or the role religion would play in abetting them. But he was most likely the country's first public figure to crown the annihilation of a people with a biblical blessing.

Significantly, this was not the first or only time Palmer hinted at the genocidal dimension in white readings of Noah's curse. Since at least 1860, Palmer's defense of slavery was tied to predictions of African American extinction. In his notorious "Thanksgiving Sermon," Palmer averred that outside the institution of slavery the black race would experience "rapid extermination before they had time to waste away through listlessness, filth and vice."[55] In 1863, Palmer characterized the North's assault upon his region as a "double crime which involves the extermination both of the white and of the black race now upon the soil."[56] If "defeat means extermination" for the South, experience teaches that "except in the condition of servitude, an inferior race cannot be intermingled with a superior, without annihilation."[57] Palmer was confident that although "the descendants of Ham have thriven under the

South's patriarchal system," the North's philanthropy would mean their "absolute destruction." "If the fate of the red man be not theirs," he contended, the "triple scourge of indolence, disease and vice shall sweep them from the earth."[58] Given the way he would later use Genesis 9 to legitimate "the fate of the red man," such predictions are sobering indeed.

Even after the crisis of war had passed, the language of genocide was perceptible in Palmer's racial rhetoric. In "The Present Crisis and its Issue" (1872), Palmer boasted of giving blacks this candid warning: "If you are to be a historic people, you must work out your own destiny upon your own foundation. . . . If you have no power of development from within, you lack the first quality of a historic race, and must, sooner or later, go to the wall." During the 1880s and 1890s, Palmer evinced an equally cavalier disposition before the appearance and disappearance of nations. In 1882, he observed that although "the history of every historic people should be fully written . . . only a small portion of the earth's surface and few of its nations are historic. You may, for example, throw all Africa overboard, except its Mediterranean coast and a small portion that lies upon the delta of the Nile. In like manner, nearly the whole of the massive and monotonous continent of Asia may be discounted."[59] Speaking to a group of Confederate veterans in 1890, he sounded similar themes, arguing that China's 400 million people have not added "a fraction to the general history of the world." Furthermore, "so far as the broad record of mankind is concerned, the Dark Continent might just as well have been sunk in the depths of the two oceans which wash its borders—utterly dead, without a history."[60]

What the development of Palmer's racial rhetoric during the second half of the nineteenth century reveals is not, as Eugene Genovese suggests, the eclipse of the Bible by science. Rather, it is the influence of scientific racism in exacerbating the genocidal potential in readings of Genesis by representatives of a dominant white culture. When the curse became irrelevant to the labor question, Palmer read Noah's prophecy as a blueprint for the natural hierarchy of human groups. But the influence of scientific racism on this white Bible reader led him to value the Hamitic Negro even less than Southern slaveholders had done. By 1890, Palmer described Ham as simply unfit for history, even a history of servitude in which he was exposed to the blessings of civilization. He no longer spoke of preservation through servitude, but of "discounting," "throwing overboard," and "resigning to the watery depths."

Happily, the American legacy of Noah's curse has not been genocidal. Yet the United States has been hospitable ground for the same conjunction of religious and scientific racism that has abetted genocide in both Europe and Africa. Given the enduring American fascination with Noah's curse, its potential for justifying a genocidal assault on a minority population should never be discounted.

IV

REDEEMING THE CURSE

10

Challenging the Curse

Readings and Counterreadings

> Closely as [slaveholders] cling to it, "cursed be Canaan" is
> a poor drug to stupify a throbbing conscience—a mock-
> ing lullaby, vainly wooing slumber to unquiet tossings,
> and crying "Peace, be still," where God wakes war and
> breaks his thunders.
>
> Theodore Dwight Weld, 1838

THIS CHAPTER explores counterreadings of Genesis 9 developed by Bible
readers. Over the centuries, rabbis and church fathers, abolitionists, African
Americans, historical critics of the Bible, and authors of fiction and poetry
have challenged the curse by clarifying Genesis 9's historical context, by denying its putative racial dimensions, by employing logic and the rules of biblical exegesis, and by undermining textual assumptions through creative rereading. Because the longevity of the orthodox interpretive paradigm has been
crucial in sustaining traditional readings of Noah's curse, we revisit the history
of interpretation with particular focus on subversive counterreadings.

Long before modern writers attacked Noah's curse in an effort to sever
the nerve that animated the Christian defense of slavery, early Bible readers
resisted the textual logic of Genesis 9:20–27 and the momentum of the interpretive tradition. This practice of resistance reaches back to the rabbis, who
on occasion strenuously contested the antiseptic view of Noah canonized in
Genesis—for instance, in the claim that "it was by the grace of God, not on
account of his merits, that Noah found shelter in the ark before the overwhelming force of the waters."[1] Another example of the rabbinic tendency to

temper Noah's reputation for righteousness is this gloss on his drunkenness: "Noah lost his epithet 'the pious' when he began to occupy himself with the growing of the vine. He became a 'man of the ground,' and this first attempt to produce wine at the same time produced the first to drink to excess, the first to utter curses upon his associates, and the first to introduce slavery." It all came about, according to rabbinic legend, when "Noah found the vine which Adam had taken with him from Paradise, when he was driven forth." He tasted Adam's grapes and planted the vine; on the very same day the vine bore fruit, Noah made wine and was dishonored.[2] Although rabbinic commentary on the tale of Noah's drunkenness conforms to the orthodox interpretive paradigm by vilifying Ham and honoring Noah, it also warns of the woeful effects of alcohol—and, by extension, agriculture itself—on the conduct of the righteous.[3]

In contrast to the rabbis, the church fathers tended to downplay or excuse Noah's drunkenness.[4] If the standard view of Noah as a type of Christ was to be upheld, insobriety had to be viewed as something that happened *to* him. As Augustine wrote: " 'And he was drunken,' that is, He suffered."[5] Medieval Christian representations of Genesis featured a more didactic take on Noah's intoxication, as visual artists utilized Noah's "sin" as an object lesson for the pious.[6] No doubt the best known artistic interpretation of Noah's intemperance is Michelangelo's *Drunkenness of Noah,* in which "the old Titan is down and his sons stand before him shocked into laughter or into shame."[7] Christian skepticism regarding Noah's celebrated righteousness probably peaked in the work of Guillaume Du Bartas. The same sixteenth-century French author who so imaginatively denigrated Ham also cast Noah in an unflattering light. In Du Bartas's version of the patriarch's crapulous behavior, Noah wants "to overcome the sadness that cruelly afflicted his trembling old age." He becomes drunk and, "thinking he can drown his gnawing boredom in such sweet poison, drowns his reason." Noah's "wandering speech . . . becomes confused, unhealthy, stuttering, truncated. He feels his inebriated chest wracked by winds and his whole shaken pavilion turns unsteadily." No longer able to stand, Noah is "a dirty pig of a man [who] drops his snoring carcass shamelessly in the middle of the lodging. Forgetting himself, and drowned, he fails to cover the members that Caesar [insisted must be] covered even when dying."[8] After he is dishonored by Ham, "the ol' boy wakes up, recognizes his error, and ashamed, marvels at the wine's potency, and piqued by a strong concern from his prophetic gut, speaks thus to his sons: 'Cursed be you, Ham, and cursed as well be your little darling Canaan; may pearly Dawn, pure Evening, and gleaming Noon forever see your neck charged with a heavy yoke; may God sustain Shem, and may his grace soon spread the teeming race of Japheth.' "[9]

Around the same time, Noah's reputation for probity was challenged by no less a Bible exegete than John Calvin. Rejecting traditional justifications for Noah's lapsed sobriety, Calvin regarded the story as "a lesson of temperance for all ages." Because Moses does not indicate that Noah's drunkenness occurred the first time he tasted wine, Calvin concluded that the story teaches "what a filthy and detestable crime drunkenness is. The holy patriarch, though he had hitherto been a rare example of frugality and temperance, losing all self-possession, did, in a base and shameful manner, prostate himself naked on the ground, so as to become a laughing-stock to all. Therefore, with what care ought we to cultivate sobriety, lest anything like this, or even worse, should happen to us?"[10] The weightiness of Noah's sin is reflected in God's decision to brand him "with an eternal mark of disgrace."[11] Calvin's reading of the episode did not lead him to eschew an otherwise orthodox reading of Genesis 9,[12] but his stubborn refusal to excuse Noah's behavior extended a significant countertrajectory in the history of interpretation.

Seventeenth-century commentators influenced by the Reformation followed Calvin's lead in elaborating readings of Genesis 9 that foregrounded Noah's infraction. Like Calvin, these exegetes assessed the patriarch's inebriation as a regretful failure that constituted a valuable lesson in temperance. In 1637, Gervase Babington fully acknowledged Noah's "foule fall" and warned readers to "marke the filthinesse of drunkennesse, [how] it maketh him lie *uncovered in his Tent,* undecently, unseemely, nay beastly, and rather like a beast than a man."[13] Babington emphasized that the patriarch's shame should fill readers with humility: After all, he warned, "*wine . . . spared not his first inventor, therefore beware.*"[14] Andrew Willet adopted a similar view: "For Noah was so oppressed and intoxicate, that he forgat himselfe, as a man for the time not regarding comeliness: for he lay uncovered . . . by his own negligence and ouersight, and that in the middle of the tent, as it were in the floore and pavement. . . ."[15] According to Willet, Noah's intemperance should not be assigned to ignorance or inadvertence unless we are also willing to excuse Lot and Judas. Nevertheless, the story edifies; "by such examples we should rather take heede: for if the strong may be thus ouertaken, how much more circumspect ought the weaker sort to be."[16] In his famous Bible commentary, Matthew Henry conceded that while "it was said of Noah that he was *perfect in his generations . . .* [his fall] shows that it is meant of sincerity, not a sinless perfection. . . ." Henry went on to remark that although Noah shamed himself as had Adam, at least the first man "sought concealment; Noah is so destitute of thought and reason that he seeks no covering. This was the fruit of the vine that Noah did not think of."[17] Thomas Newton adopted a similar view of Noah's intoxication, observing that although "it is an excellent character that is given of Noah . . . the best of men are not without their infirmities." Newton concluded that as a faithful historian, Moses was compelled to record "the failings and imperfections of the most venerable patriarchs."[18]

The view that Noah's fall may be of benefit to the religious reader was underlined by biblical commentators into the twentieth century. For instance, Marcus Dods's treatment of "Noah's Fall" in 1901 noted that "the righteous and rescued Noah lying drunk on his tent-floor is a sorrowful spectacle. God had given him the earth, and this was the use he made of the gift; melancholy presage of the fashion of his posterity. . . . In that heavy helpless figure, fallen insensible in his tent, is as significant a warning as in the Flood."[19] Dods remarked that Noah is not the only man who has "walked uprightly and kept his garment unspotted from the world so long as the eye of man was on him, but who has lain uncovered on his own tent-floor."[20]

Modern Counterreadings

In the modern era, "secular" writers have proffered more radical challenges to the interpretive tradition. For instance, in "Of the Blackness of Negroes," Sir Thomas Browne (1605–1682) emphasized the difficulty of tracing the lines of human descent and observed that blackness is not shunned by all. He wrote that "whereas men affirm this color was a Curse, I cannot make out the propriety of that name, it neither seeming so to them, nor reasonably unto us; for they take so much content therein, that they esteem deformity by other colours, describing the Devil, and terrible objects, white."[21] Subsequent remonstrances against the curse were anticipated by Henry St. John (Lord Viscount) Bolingbroke (1678–1751). In his "Letters on the Study and Use of History," Bolingbroke cited Noah's prophecy as a notorious example of the historical unreliability of scripture. Bolingbroke noted that the terms of Noah's "prophecy" were not clear and complained that "the curse pronounced in it contradicts all our notions of order and of justice. One is tempted to think, that the patriarch was still drunk; and that no man in his senses could hold such language, or pass such a sentence."[22] Bolingbroke protested that "Ham alone offended; Canaan was innocent" and observed that those "who would make the son an accomplice with his father, affirm not only without, but against, the express authority of the text."[23] Bolingbroke evaluated traditional attempts to defend the integrity of the text:

> Will it be said—it has been said—that where we read Canaan we are to understand Ham, whose brethren Sem and Japhet were? At this rate, we shall never know what we read: as these critics never care what they say. Will it be said—this has been said too—that Ham was punished in his posterity, when Canaan was cursed, and his descendants were exterminated? But who does not see that the curse, and the punishment, in this case, fell on Canaan and his posterity, exclusively of the rest of the posterity of Ham; and were therefore the curse and punishment of the son, not of the father, properly?[24]

Although such textual queries challenged the application of Noah's curse to African slavery, they were not motivated by a desire for social reform. Rather, Bolingbroke's commitment to the burgeoning science of history led him to seize on inconsistencies in the biblical text to demonstrate the impossibility of deriving from it "any thing like universal chronology and history."[25]

Abolitionist Counterreadings

The goal was quite different among abolitionist writers, who defied the curse as a method of striking at the heart of the proslavery argument. From colonial times, it was widely recognized that the Bible was a crux for the justification of forced servitude, and as early as the 1670s American opponents of slavery published attacks on "the assumption that Negro slavery was a fulfillment of the curse of Canaan."[26]

In an early abolitionist tract, *The Selling of Joseph: A Memorial* (1700), Samuel Sewall anticipated a number of objections to his assertion that slavery amounted to a "barbarous Usage of our Friends and Kinsfolk in Africa." The first of these was that *"these Blackamores are of the Posterity of* Cham, *and therefore are under the Curse of Slavery. Gen. 9. 25, 26, 27."*[27] Sewall responded to the putative connection of slaves with Noah's son Ham in a fashion that would characterize many subsequent abolitionist assaults on the curse. First, he noted that "to be an Executioner of the Vindictive Wrath of God" is not an office that should be wished for. How do we know, for instance, that the commission to do so is not long out of date? Sewall warned that "many have found it to their Cost, that a Prophetical Denunciation of Judgment against a Person or People, would not warrant them to inflict that evil. If it would, *Hazael* might justify himself in all he did against his Master, and the Israelites, from 2 Kings 8.10, 12."[28] Second, Sewall observed that deriving a curse on Ham from Genesis 9 violated the natural meaning of the text. It is possible, he suggested, "that by cursory reading, this Text may have been mistaken. For *Canaan* is the Person Cursed three times over, without the mentioning of *Cham*. Good Expositors suppose the Curse entailed on him, and that this Prophesie was accomplished in the Extirpation of the *Canaanites,* and in the Servitude of the *Gibeonites. Vide Pareum."*[29] Finally, Sewall asserted that black Africans could not be the descendants of the cursed Canaanites, in that "the Blackamores are not descended of Canaan, but of Cush." Citing Psalm 68:31, Sewall declared that "Princes shall come out of *Egypt* [Mizraim]. *Ethiopia* [Cush] shall soon stretch out her hands unto God. Under which names, all *Africa* may be comprehended; and their Promised Conversion ought to be prayed for."[30]

Sewall's ambition of denying the purported relevance of Noah's curse would be reflected in American abolitionist literature for the next century and a half. As the antislavery campaign heated up after 1830, proslavery apologists tightened their embrace of Genesis 9. By 1838, abolitionist Theodore Weld could remark that Noah's malediction was "the *vade mecum* of slaveholders, and they never venture abroad without it. It is a pocket-piece for sudden occasion—a keepsake to dote over—a charm to spell-bind opposition, and a magnet to attract 'whatsover worketh abomination, or maketh a lie.' "[31] Of course, attention to Noah's curse reflected not only its prominence in the rhetoric of slavery's defenders but also the conviction of many abolitionists that redemption from the sin of slavery lay in careful attention to biblical revelation. Caroline L. Shanks has observed that "all Christians both north and south agreed that the Scriptures were consistent with themselves and formed a 'perfect rule of duty'; the conflict came over the formation of this 'perfect rule.' "[32]

In their efforts to demonstrate that proslavery exegesis of Genesis 9 was in error, antebellum abolitionists employed a variety of tactics. Among their technical points were that the Hebrew and Greek terms translated "servant" in English Bibles were not synonymous with "slave"[33] and that the ancient practice of slavery was not analogous with that of modern America. Abolitionists also insisted that a literal, commonsense reading of Genesis 9 yielded a curse on Canaan rather than on Ham. Along with the observation that Noah's prophecy names Canaan, they stressed that according to Genesis 10 Canaan could not be regarded as the ancestor of Africans.[34] Although most opponents of slavery considered the biblical genealogy to be a reliable account of human origins, some questioned whether blacks were Hamites at all.[35]

Another abolitionist strategy called attention to the dubious circumstances attending Noah's "prophecy." Advocates of the curse alleged that Noah spoke for God when he announced that Ham or Canaan would serve his brothers.[36] But abolitionists sought to drive a wedge between God and Noah by contending that while the patriarch's indignation at his son may have been justified, his malediction carried no particular authority.[37] In 1847, William Henry Brisbane flatly denied that Noah spoke "by the inspiration of the Holy Ghost" and asked: "Is there any thing about [the curse] that implies that Noah spake as moved by the Spirit of God? Is it any thing more than an historical fact in the life of Noah?"[38] Many abolitionists endeavored to deflate Noah's curse by downgrading it from "prophecy" to "prediction."[39] In the 1830s, John Rankin declared that "predications are not given in Scripture as rules of moral action. It was predicated, and even decreed, that Jesus Christ should be crucified, and yet his crucifiers were full as guilty as they would have been if no such predication and decree had ever existed."[40] During the 1840s and 1850s, various versions of this argument became mainstays in the abolitionist assault on Noah's curse.[41]

Abolitionists battled the curse on historical grounds as well, marshaling data calculated to refute the efficacy of Noah's words. Faced with the contention of proslavery apologists that the remarkable fulfillment of Noah's "prophecy" constituted proof of its divine sanction, abolitionists countered in one of two ways. Some argued that the curse had been fulfilled in the Israelite conquest of Canaan or some other episode in ancient history; others that Noah's vision of Canaan serving Shem and Japheth had never been fulfilled and never would. As Brisbane observed, "the very first man mentioned as a *mighty one* in the earth was Nimrod, a descendant from Ham. In the same lineal descent from Ham was Asshur, who built Ninevah." Meanwhile, he noted, Shem's posterity were carried captive into Assyria, were servants to the Babylonians, and to Ham's posterity in Egypt.[42]

When other expedients were exhausted, abolitionists challenged the curse by vilifying its advocates on the proslavery side. John Rankin opined that because "the whole argument for slavery drawn from Noah's curse, is without foundation," it must be the product "of avaricious derangement."[43] Similarly, J. L. Stone charged that the notion that Noah's words justified the enslavement of Africans "is founded upon a demonstrable mistake—and a mistake so palpable, that it is a subject of great wonder how the prevalent belief in the existence of such a prophecy ever came to be general, and how it has managed to survive to this day."[44] Stone found it "difficult to decide whether the monstrous or the ludicrous predominates, when we hear a pious defender of Slavery solemnly justifying the buying and selling of human beings, and the breeding of them like hogs for the market, by quoting the curse of Noah and calling it a prophecy."[45] Mixing disdain with sarcasm, he continued:

> Four thousand years ago, Noah awoke from his drunken sleep (I use the epithet of the Record itself "he drank the wine and was drunken") and angry that his younger son had looked upon his nakedness, he uttered the half-dozen words above quoted. To-day, in a new world, unknown when the words were uttered, the men who "use up" an estimated number of "niggers" during each "season" in raising sugar and cotton, on the Mississippi and Red Rivers, quote these half-dozen words uttered 4000 years ago by the patriarch in his anger against his son, as a proof that their practices are well pleasing in the sight of God. And plenty of "reverend gentlemen" are to be found, who gravely endorse the soundness of the reasoning, and "heartily shake hands" upon it, with the "southern gentlemen" who take a pious delight in resting their beloved institution upon a Scriptural basis.[46]

In a similar vein, George B. Cheever railed against the curse as a "ludicrous and wicked refuge of oppression" that constituted "the wildest, vastest, most sweeping and diabolical forgery ever conceived or committed." It was "a more frantic forgery than madness itself, unless it had the method of the deepest depravity, could have ever dreamed."[47] Cheever demanded to know of the curse's American advocates:

> Where is the sentence [of Scripture] in which God ever appointed you, the Anglo-Saxon race [over another people], you, the mixture of all races under heaven, you, who can not tell whether the blood of Sem, Ham, or Japhet mingles in your veins, you, the assertors of a right to traffic in human flesh, you, worse Jews, by this very claim, more degraded, more debased in your moral principles, than the lowest tribe of Jews who were swept for their sins from the promised land. . . . You might as well go to Russia, and take the subjects of the Czar. You might as well go to England, and take your cousins of the sea-girt isle, the descendants of your own great-grandfathers.[48]

For all their vitriol and social radicalism, American abolitionists did not contribute a great deal to the history of biblical interpretation. While aggressively attacking the biblical rationale for slavery, they failed to read against the textual grain in which Noah's curse was inscribed. In fact, like their pro-slavery opponents, they instinctively read Genesis 9 according to the orthodox interpretive paradigm; that is, abolitionist authors rarely disputed Noah's righteousness, the fact that Ham or Canaan had sinned against the patriarch, or that one or both deserved judgment.[49] The influential Elihu Coleman could affirm that "there was unclean beasts went into the ark as well as clean, and that it was the will or permission of God, that there should be a Ham, as well as a Shem and Japhet: by which we may see that God suffers wicked men to live as well as righteous."[50] Similarly, antebellum abolitionists energetically maintained that Canaan rather than Ham was the object of Noah's malediction, and many were content to deflect the curse upon the "Canaanites," whom they regarded as its proper object.[51]

Even African American abolitionist James W. C. Pennington was willing to sacrifice Canaan to rescue Ham. The gist of Pennington's assault on the curse was the claim that American blacks "are not the descendants of Canaan ... [but] the sons of Cush and Misraim amalgamated." Pennington reasoned that because Africans are not Canaanites, those wishing to hold slaves "must discharge the Africans, compensate them for false enslavement, and go get the Canaanites." But this clever (and certainly facetious) conclusion left the impression that the curse rested perennially on the posterity of Canaan.[52] Although most antislavery authors recognized that casting aspersions upon Ham was counterproductive, they failed to subvert the dynamics of blame and punishment in Genesis 9.[53] Perhaps this inability to escape the confines of orthodox interpretation explains why, as the rhetorical war over African servitude raged during the second third of the nineteenth century, abolitionists increasingly pitched the battle on extrabiblical grounds.[54]

Biblical Criticism: Reading behind the Text

In the 1870s, Bible readers began to utilize the tools of historical-critical analysis to examine the textual basis for the assumption that Ham's descendants bore a perennial curse. Since that time, historical critics have explored Genesis 9's prehistory, illumined its setting in the life of ancient Israel, and implicitly challenged its role in sustaining the myth of Noah's curse. Following Julius Wellhausen, critics have tended to categorize the story of Noah and his sons as an ethnological tradition emerging from antagonism between Israel and "Canaan" and reflecting either Israel's conquest of the promised land ("Canaan will serve Shem") or its own experience of subjugation ("Japheth will dwell in Shem's tents").[55] Given the ongoing role of Noah's curse in public discourse, scholarly analysis of the text has proceeded apace.

Attention to the story's redactional history has been fueled by a textual conundrum that puzzled the earliest interpreters: If Ham is the guilty party, why does the curse fall on Canaan? The explanation advanced by Wellhausen in 1876 and reaffirmed by subsequent commentators is that this textual inconsistency is the result of a redactor's careless work in forging two originally separate traditions. Recently, Randall Bailey has suggested that the text's current form is not haphazard: In the Priestly school's final editing of the Pentateuch, he argues, an old curse against Cannaan was recast within the story of Ham's performance of a suspicious sexual act. Bailey identifies a twofold polemical purpose in this redaction: (1) to keep Israel from adopting sexual practices linked with Egypt and Canaan (cf. Lev. 18:3: "You shall not do as they do in the land of Egypt, where you lived, and you shall not do as they do in the land of Canaan, to which I am bringing you") and (2) to demean the putative ancestor of Africans as a foil to the Israelite custom of regarding Africa as a standard of valuation.[56]

Offering an alternative version of the story's editorial history, Gene Rice contends that the tensions in Genesis 9 are resolved when we discern two parallel but divergent traditions concerning the makeup of Noah's family. One of these is universal in scope and presents Noah's sons as Shem, Ham, and Japheth, while a more limited and parochial tradition identifies Noah's offspring as Shem, Japheth, and Canaan. According to Rice, "the text in its present form represents an effort to minimize the discrepancy between these two traditions by equating Ham in the one with Canaan in the other."[57] This solution implies that Ham's association with Noah's curse is the artificial creation of an editor who inserted "Ham the father of" in v. 22 to harmonize disparate strands of tradition. But this explanation raises another question: When and why were these traditions joined? Although a number of early biblical critics (including Hermann Gunkel) dated Genesis 9:20–27 to the second millennium B.C.E., other scholars have placed it in the period of Israelite conquest under Joshua or in the early monarchy. Rice, for instance, sets the passage in the first seven and a half years of David's reign, interpreting the reference to Japheth dwelling "in the tents of Shem" in v. 27 as an echo of David's special relationship with the Philistines. According to this view, the text refers to Israel's original conquest of Canaan: "Was this conquest simply a naked act of aggression without any moral justification? And what should Israel's attitude be toward the Philistines (Japheth) who were also bent on conquering the Canaanites? Genesis 9: 20–27 justifies Israel's right to displace the Canaanites in their native land on the grounds that there was a basic moral flaw, a perverse sexuality in the character of the Canaanites."[58]

Alternatively, Gunther Wittenberg contends that the Pentateuchal redactor was motivated by the need to justify Canaanite forced labor under Solomon. Although in its earliest form Noah's curse had nothing to do with genealogy, Israelite resentment toward the exploitative Canaanite city-state—and the Table of Nations's association of Ham's descendants with urban-centered kingdoms—led to the linking of Ham and Canaan.[59] According to Umberto Cassuto, the apparent confusion of culprits in Genesis 9 springs from the conviction that "the sons of Ham . . . acted in sexual matters in accordance with customs that the Israelite conscience regarded as utterly abominable."[60] Cassuto declares that Ham represents the Canaanite people who were known to Israel. Rather than signaling a redaction, the phrase "Ham the father of Canaan" expresses that Ham's affinity with the children of Canaan is manifest in his immoral act. Thus, "the Canaanites were to suffer the curse and the bondage not because of the sins of Ham, but because they themselves acted like Ham, because of their own transgressions, which resembled those attributed to Ham in this allegory."[61] With regard to the text's original setting, Cassuto opines that Noah's reference to Canaan serving Shem applies to the situation related in Genesis 14:4, where it is said that the children of Canaan are serving Chedorlaomer, king of Elam (a son of Shem).

Cassuto goes on to suggest that Genesis 9 may have originally "had a coarser and uglier character," reflecting the Canaanite legend of a god who castrates his father.[62] Robert Graves and Raphael Patai explore the influence of non-Israelite traditions by comparing Genesis 9:20–27 with a Greek myth in which five brothers—Coeus, Crius, Hyperion, Iapetus, and Cronus—conspire against their father, Uranus, and Cronus successfully castrates him. In a similar Hittite myth, the authors observe, Anu's genitals are bitten off by his rebel son Kumarbi (who laughs at his triumph, as Ham is said to have done), after which he is cursed by Anu. Albert I. Baumgarten offers another suggestion regarding the story's mythological background. He argues that to distinguish the Flood story from the Mesopotamian and Phoenician sagas that influenced them, the author(s) of Genesis consciously humanized Noah. According to this view, Genesis 9:20–27 was preserved not only to vilify Hamites and Canaanites but also to differentiate Noah from the divinized flood survivors of other Near Eastern tales.[63] Since in this literary context the theme of castrating a father appears exclusively in divine myths, Baumgartner concludes it is unlikely the biblical authors "would have utilized a motif with such clear divine associations in a story told to stress the humanity of the flood survivor."[64]

A few modern scholars have utilized the tools of biblical criticism in an effort to uncover the original crime underlying the biblical text. Frederick W. Bassett, for instance, contends on the basis of Leviticus 18 and 20 that the Hebrew phrase "to see the nakedness of one's father" denotes intercourse with one's father's wife. He surmises that because the text's redactor missed this idiomatic meaning he made sense of the story by adding a reference to Shem and Japheth covering their father's nakedness in the literal sense. Bassett's proposal not only accounts for the severity with which Ham's offense is punished but also explains why Canaan, if he is the fruit of an incestuous relationship, must bear Noah's curse. Anthony Phillips disagrees, maintaining that references in the Hebrew Bible to uncovering "the nakedness of the father" should be interpreted literally. In his reading, Ham's transgression was an actual seduction of Noah, "an act so abhorrent that the author is unwilling to spell it out."[65] Randall Bailey, meanwhile, concludes from internal textual evidence that "it must have been only voyeurism on Ham's part."[66]

The application of historical-critical analysis to Genesis 9:20–27 indicates both the promise and limitations of biblical criticism. On one hand, modern scholars have plausibly reconstructed Genesis 9's prehistory, illuminated its setting in life, and identified its purposes as a polemical text. On the other hand, they have done little to challenge the notion, implicit in the text and inscribed in the history of interpretation, that Ham and Canaan are villainous characters. In 1949, for instance, C. F. Keil and Franz Delitzsch averred that "in the sin of Ham, there lies the great stain of the whole Hamitic race, whose chief characteristic is sexual sin."[67] In the 1960s, Umberto Cassuto opined that "the primary sin of Ham was his transgression against sexual morality, the disrespect shown to his father being only an aggravation of the wrong."[68] At about the same time, Robert Graves and Raphael Patai, while judging that Ham should not be blamed for beholding his father's nakedness, found quite plausible the rabbinic legend in which Canaan castrates his grandfather. Their conclusion that "the sinner was little Canaan, not Ham" effectively historicized this "Hebrew myth."[69] In 1991, Gunther Wittenberg wrote that "Canaan and Ham are symbols, just as Babel is a symbol, of man's deep-seated urge to dominate and enslave others. As such they are cursed and stand under God's judgement, even today."[70] In some cases, biblical critics have given renewed credence to accusations launched earlier in the history of interpretation, as in Frederick Bassett's revival of the view that Ham committed incest with his mother.

Biblical critics often express great confidence in the capacity of historical-critical analysis to elucidate texts with a pernicious history of interpretation, and nowhere is this confidence more apparent than in the case of Noah's curse. If the story's precise meaning has not been rendered by scholarly analysis, it is simply a matter of time until a consensus is reached. Once the text receives "proper clarification" as a product of disparate pentateuchal sources,[71] the antiblack mythology to which it has given rise is fated to disappear like morning mist in the midday sunshine. Recent studies such as Steven L. McKenzie's *All God's People* and Cain Hope Felder's *Troubling Biblical Waters* apply historical criticism to problematic texts with such confidence. If Bible readers can be educated to observe the hermeneutic controls established by scholars, these authors believe, the racist interpretive traditions associated with texts like Genesis 9 can be neutralized.

Because the tradition of Noah's curse is rooted in a biblical narrative, biblical criticism seems a natural method for extirpating it. But we should not assume the adequacy of historical-critical analysis for challenging the curse's role in American racial discourse. If the history of interpretation reveals anything, it is that the myth of Ham's curse is not reducible to the story on which it is based, for it emerges in the interplay of Bible readers, textual cues, interpretive traditions, and contemporary social realities. As Thomas Peterson has observed, "mythological propositions . . . do not yield to scientific and historical analysis because their basis in reality includes a subjective and emotional involvement with the world."[72]

Reading with Desire

Even if we consider the biblical text per se (as opposed to the mythology it has spawned), Genesis 9:20–27 has proved quite resistant to the "clarifications" of historical criticism. After all, showing how a text may have come to be is not tantamount to explaining what it means. Aware of biblical scholarship's failure in this regard, a new generation of critics has sought to comprehend Genesis 9 not as a careless merging of Pentateuchal traditions but as the source of profound psychological insights regarding the nature of human desire. Given the sexual overtones in Genesis 9:20–27, it is not surprising that these authors have developed counterreadings of Noah's curse that exploit the story's libidinous tensions.

Howard Eilberg-Schwartz portrays the "myth" in Genesis 9:20–27 as a second creation story whose purpose is to condemn the desire between fathers and sons. Drawing on contemporary art and film studies, Eilberg-Schwartz identifies a bond in the ancient Israelite imagination between desire and the male gaze. Ham's homoerotic gaze challenges the heterosexual norm established at creation, and thus he is cast as a villain in Genesis 9:20–27. According to Eilberg-Schwartz, this story is more than a projection of Canaanite sexual deviance into primordial time; it is an expression of the male Israelite's discomfort with a masculine deity. Because they were to imagine themselves as both lovers and children of God, Israelite men experienced profound ambivalence around notions of divine corporeality and sexuality. As Ham is condemned for seeing too much of his father, his story establishes boundaries in the Israelite relationship with Yahweh: "An Israelite male who gazed at God was like Ham, who looked at his naked father. Israelite men were expected to be Semites, virtuous sons of Shem who avert their gaze from their father in heaven."[73]

H. Hirsch Cohen is another interpreter who foregrounds desire in the story of Noah and his sons. In *The Drunkenness of Noah,* Cohen combines linguistic analysis and psychoanalytic theory in an attempt to uncover the events behind this enigmatic tale. Like many readers before him, Cohen is keen to explain how the presumably righteous Noah came to be drunk and naked in his tent. An important clue, he believes, is the symbolic meaning of wine in ancient cultures. Cohen explores Israelite and other traditions to elucidate a complex relationship between alcohol, fire, and sexuality. Drawing on this connection, he surmises that Noah's drunkenness is indicative not of a deficiency in character but of a good-faith attempt to replenish the earth following the Flood. Indeed, Noah's "determination to maintain his procreative ability at full strength resulted in drinking himself into a state of helpless intoxication." How ironic, Cohen notes, that in acceding to the divine command to renew the earth's population, Noah suffered the opprobrium of drunkenness. In Cohen's view, he "deserves not censure but acclaim for having played so well the role of God's devoted servant."[74] As for the behavior of Ham or Canaan, Cohen finds plausible the rabbinic conjecture that Noah was castrated by his son or grandson while he "lay uncovered in his tent."

More noteworthy for Cohen than any sexual assault, however, is Ham's voyeurism, which reveals a plot to usurp Noah's sexual potency by "identification." Cohen speculates that Noah became intoxicated as a prelude to sexual congress and that Ham "must have been present throughout the act [of intercourse]—until Noah fell asleep—peering from his hiding place to assimilate thereby his father's strength in his gloating stare."[75] Ham regarded his father's potency as the key to gaining preeminence among his brothers, a standing that would guarantee him "the mantle of leadership on Noah's death." Cohen suggests that the "garment" with which the brothers covered Noah's nakedness was provided by Ham, who produced it as "proof" that he had witnessed Noah in the sex act: "Ham must have skirted the sleeping, naked Noah, picked up his father's garment that had been cast aside, and stepped outside to show 'the garment' to his brothers."[76] Accordingly, the brothers' backward approach betokens not respect for the fallen patriarch but a desire to avoid gazing on him in his weakened state. Cohen interprets Noah's curse as a deathbed bequest occasioned by Ham's theft of his potency. The curse was directed at Canaan, Cohen explains, so that Ham could not transmit the "potency of leadership" to his own son and his progeny: "Far from acting out of vengeance, Noah seemingly degraded the future generations of Canaan to frustrate Ham's design of transferring his newly acquired special strength and power to Canaan and his progeny."[77]

By far the most creative discourse on desire in Genesis 9 is Arthur Frederick Ide's *Noah and the Ark*.[78] Ide combines historical, linguistic, and psychoanalytic arguments to recast Genesis 9:20–27 as a tale of sexual liberation. Ide does not limit himself to what can be gleaned or inferred from the biblical text; rather, he consults a variety of ancient documents, including apocryphal and pseudepigraphic texts such as the Ethiopian *Book of Enoch*, *The Generations of Noah*, and the *Book of the Generations of Adam*. Ide presumes these sources to be crucial for reconstructing the story of Noah behind the biblical text.

Setting the background for the events narrated in Genesis 9, Ide alleges that a group of divine beings ("the yahwehs") sent the archangel Uriel to advise Noah that they are disturbed by the casual nature of human sexuality and the absence of rule and order. The gods forewarn that "unless random, casual sexuality was restrained and sex occurred without emotion or pleasure, the gods were determined to destroy the world and everyone and everything in it."[79] Later, in an effort to control Israelite sexual behavior, the story of

Noah's drunkenness was censored by the "priests of Shiloh." The sexual nature of the tale, Ide writes misleadingly, "has either been overlooked or deliberately ignored." Ide labors to restore the story's sexual motifs with quasi-pornographic descriptions of Noah and his sons.[80]

In Ide's description of the Flood's aftermath, Noah drinks to forget the desolation and the loss of mortal life. He drinks also "to shield himself from his own lust and carnal desire for a sexual experience future generations would be taught to hold in disgust."[81] Predictably, Noah becomes intoxicated: "Tipsy, Noah stripped off his clothing. The fermentation within the bowels of his cup made his own bowels hot. Returning to his primal state in a fabric womb . . . Noah declared his freedom from the aprons first fashioned by Adam. He spun, danced, and made joyful noise in celebration of his gods. . . ."[82] At this juncture, Ide contends, Canaan perpetrated a practical joke by entering his grandfather's tent, looping a cord around his genitals and unmanning him. Finding his father's emasculation humorous, Ham reported it to his brothers. Unlike the rabbis on whom he is dependent, however, Ide reserves a significant role for Ham. Rather than finding his father drunk, Ham actually drinks with him, obliges Noah's "longing to be sodomized" (this is Ide's interpretation of the phrase "seeing his father's nakedness"), reaches orgasm, and departs the tent, leaving Noah "sexually anxious and distraught, with but one goal: to also reach orgasm and spend his sperm."[83]

According to Ide, this was not sexual assault. Noah did nothing to stop the liaison and made no protestation until his other sons learned what had happened. Noah's self-preserving malediction was provoked not by Ham's sodomy but by Canaan's castration. Thus, in Ide's thorough sexualizing of the biblical story, Ham emerges not as a villain but as a hero of sexual liberation: "Ham wasn't ashamed of either his father's nakedness nor his own sexuality. Shame, identical to that exhibited and expressed by Adam, was the deficiency of Shem, Japheth and Noah for they would not permit themselves to accept the reality that occurred or the truth that all sexual expressions are equal with no particular sexual play less than any other."[84] The brothers' "embarrassment that a natural biological action and normal psychological curiosity took place condemns them, not the participants." Their proximity to Noah's tent indicates their "covert desire to have been part of the family orgy." In any case, because they did nothing to prevent or denounce the act, Shem and Japheth must be regarded as coconspirators.

Ide's interpretation of Genesis 9 is difficult to categorize. On one hand, his reading of the story fits squarely within an interpretive history that imagines the transgression of Ham-Canaan in sexual terms. On the other hand, Ide is part of a modern tradition of counterreading that attempts to subvert the story's dynamics of blame. Ham becomes the tale's hero and Noah is cast as its villain: His prediluvian chastity is construed not as personal righteousness but sexual confusion, he is accused of engaging in "rank sexual escapades" after the Deluge, and he is regarded as a willing accomplice in genocide. According to Ide, "those who/which were to be saved had to be humble and 'crouch down' before Noah. The proud were to be cast aside in a manner identical to the whimsical lottery of the doctor of death, Josef Mengele,. . . ."[85] Nevertheless, Ide's manifesto of homosexual freedom does not subvert the story's system of blame. It merely shifts moral condemnation onto Noah, Shem, Japheth, and any who would use religious warrants to control sexual behavior.[86]

Even more recently, Regina M. Schwartz has analyzed Genesis 9:20–27 in terms of desire for the father and fear of displacement. In *The Curse of Cain*, Schwartz attempts to explain "what is going on in the allusive story of Noah's curse."[87] In doing so, she relies primarily on the Freudian concept of paternal identification, noting that "Freud reinscribes the Bible in a secular key for our time."[88] Schwartz observes that commentators have not been able to rid suggestions of homosexual incest from the story of Noah and his sons, yet she contends that the real fear addressed in Genesis 9:20–27 is displacement of a father by his son. The fear of displacement inscribed in the text is what Schwartz calls the "Noah complex," in which "love/hate for the father with whom the son identifies issues in intolerable guilt for that incestuous desire, a guilt projected onto an omnipotent monotheistic deity who punishes, maintaining his preserve at the price of his sons' dissension, turning the brother into the reviled Other."[89] In the case of Noah and Ham, the incestuous wish for the parent issues in a curse, which by setting brothers against one another offsets "the danger that, bonding together, they will threaten the father, like Freud's primal horde."[90]

According to Schwartz, Ham's need to identify with Noah is easily confused with a desire to displace him and thus must be figured as a challenge to his authority—as naked aggression. Meanwhile, his desire produces emotional ambivalence in Ham, "prompting both love for the object of identification and fury toward it because the identification is never wholly successful."[91] Finally, as in the other primeval narratives of Genesis, Noah's sons are destined to live in conflict, because their cooperation only confirms the parent's fear of being supplanted. Schwartz perceives the "Noah complex" at work throughout the Hebrew Bible, pervaded as it is by the concern that if men love each other, they will overthrow their fathers. "And so the biblical norm of paternal dominance deliberately promotes rivalry, not love, among brothers."[92] Schwartz's reading of Genesis 9 is perhaps the most insightful by a contemporary Bible scholar. It is distinguished particularly by her attention to sibling rivalry, a theme that, as will be argued in the next chapter, is indispensable for comprehending the story's dynamics of desire.[93]

Literary Counterreadings

Given the role played by Noah's curse in modern racial discourse, it is not surprising that allusions to the curse pervade American literature. Authors who refer to Genesis 9 in their works of fiction include Hugh Henry Brackenridge in the eighteenth century, Mark Twain and Charles W. Chesnutt in the nineteenth, and James Baldwin in the twentieth. While never offering full-blown counterreadings of the biblical story, these authors attempt to subvert Noah's curse by employing irony or ridicule.

No doubt influenced by the abolitionist writers of his day, Brackenridge wrote in *Modern Chivalry* (1792–1805) of the imagined origins of black slavery:

> Some supposed, that it was the curse pronounced upon Canaan, the son of Noah, for looking at his father's nakedness. They got rid by this means of the difficulty of the flood; but by Moses' own account, the Canaanites were the descendents of Canaan; and we do not hear of them being Negroes; which, had it been the case, we cannot doubt would have been laid hold of by the Israelites as a circumstance to justify their extirpating, or making slaves of them. . . . [94]

Twain included an ironic allusion to the curse in *Pudd'nhead Wilson* and in *Letters from the Earth* claimed that the microbes Ham carried onto the ark were discharged in Africa, where they became responsible for the "sleeping sickness" that "has for its victims a race of ignorant and unoffending blacks whom God placed in a remote wilderness. . . ."[95] In Chesnutt's story "The Fall of Adam" (1886), 'Lijah Gadson asks his pastor Brother Gainey for help in comprehending the origins of color difference. In delineating his confusion, Gadson offers this sardonic gloss on the curse:

> I ben 'flectin' dat subjic' over a long time, and axin' 'bout it; but nobody doan' seem to know nuffin' surtin' 'bout it. Some says it's de cuss o'Caanyun but I never could'n' understan' bout dis here cuss o'Caanyun. I can['t] see how de Lawd could turn anybody black jes' by cussin' 'im; 'case 'fo I j'ined de church—dat was 'fo de wah—I use' ter cuss de overseah on ole marse's plantation awful bad—when he was'n' da—an' all de darkies on the plantation use'ter cus 'im, an' it didn' make de leas' changes in 'is complexion.[96]

Concluding that "de subjec' is too deep fur readin'," pastor Gainey seeks an answer in prayer. He soon falls into a trance and is transported by angels to the Garden of Eden. There it is revealed to him that in Adam's futile attempt to escape God after eating the apple, the first man attempted to jump over the sun, but "de fiah wus so hot, it scawched 'im black as a crisp, an' culed up his ha'r so he nevuh couldn'n't git it straight agin." Thus, according to the explanation rendered by Pastor Gainey the following Sunday, Adam's children before the Fall were white, those born after the Fall were black. In *Go Tell It on the Mountain*, Baldwin's first novel, the narrator invokes the episode in Genesis 9 to characterize the protagonist's relationship with his father: "Yes, he had sinned: one morning, along, in the dirty bathroom, in the square, dirt-gray cupboard room that was filled with the stink of his father. Sometimes, leaning over the cracked, "tattle-tale gray" bathtub, he scrubbed his father's back; and looked, as the accursed son of Noah had looked, on his father's hideous nakedness."[97]

The first full-blown retelling of Ham's legend in American literature is Zora Neale Hurston's one-act play *The First One,* published in 1922.[98] Hurston's drama plays on renderings of Noah's curse that are foundational to American racist readings of Genesis. In fact, her Ham is something of a Sambo figure who laughs and dances with a bird perched on one shoulder. In contrast to his hardworking and earnest brothers, Ham does "naught but tend the flock and sing." At the same time, Hurston's play is subversive of the interpretive tradition; despite his happy-go-lucky independence, Ham is clearly Noah's favorite. To the brothers' dismay, Ham receives his father's vineyards. "Jehovah knows Noah loves Ham more than all," declares Ham's wife, Eve. Noah is also portrayed nontraditionally: While "Mrs. Ham" gazes in horror at the dead who float in the receding waters of the Deluge, Noah seeks the "juice of the grape to make us forget." "Drink wine, forget water—it means death, *death!*" he cries.

Hurston's presentation of the fateful encounter between Noah and Ham is simultaneously traditional and subversive. When Noah collapses inside his tent and dreams that he is "sinking down in the WATER!" his favorite son decides to join him in drunken slumber. Very soon, though, Ham "is heard laughing raucously" and emerges to announce that Noah has "stripped himself, showing all his wrinkles." Hearing the news, "Mrs. Shem" perceives an opportunity for her husband to displace the favored son. "Rise up," she counsels Shem, "and become owner of Noah's vineyards as well as his flocks." Although his birthright is at stake, Shem is slow to understand. His wife explains: "Did he not go into the tent and come away laughing at thy father's nakedness? Oh (she beats her breast) that I should live to see a father so mocked and shamed by his son to whom he has given all his vineyards! (She seizes a large skin from the ground.) Take this and cover him and tell him of the wickedness of thy brother."

Sensing the opportunity, "Mrs. Japheth" implores her husband to help cover Noah as well. When the dutiful sons have followed their wives' advice, Mrs. Shem counsels them to wake Noah in order to receive credit for their good deed. With the wives weeping ostentatiously in the background, Shem informs the patriarch that he "has been scoffed, and [his] nakedness made a thing of shame. . . ." Then, before he can ascertain the culprit's identity, Noah announces that "he shall be accursed. His skin shall be black!" Over Eve's protestations, he continues: "He shall serve his brothers and they shall rule over him. . . ." When the curse has been uttered, Mrs. Noah denounces her husband: "Thou art no lord of the Earth, but a drunkard. Thou has cursed my son." Even "Mrs. Shem" is stunned. "It is enough," she says, "that he should lose his vineyards." The scene concludes with Noah, Shem, Japheth, and Ham's wife, Eve, lamenting the curse and condemning the drunken state in which it was uttered. Entreated by his family to "unsay it all," Noah pleads for Jehovah to "record not my curses on my beloved Ham." Even "Mrs. Shem" is uncharacteristically repentant, asking that Ham's "punishment be mine." When the inexorable curse takes effect, everyone but his wife shrinks in horror from Ham's blackness. The play concludes with Ham and Eve setting off "where the sun shines forever, to the end of the Earth. . . ." As they depart, Ham announces a countercurse, as it were: "Oh, remain with your flocks and fields and vineyards, to covet, to sweat, to die and know no peace. I go to the sun."

Hurston's play is unique among modern literary glosses on Genesis 9, the only drama since the Renaissance based on the theme of "Noah's nakedness" and the closest thing in twentieth-century literature to a full-blown reinterpretation of the curse. *The First One* is also richly allusive, featuring references to traditional readings of Genesis 9, to Greek mythology, and to other biblical stories—including David's self-incrimination before the prophet Nathan and Jesus' passion. Along with the name of his wife, Ham's departure for the sun indicates his heroic and even messianic stature: Like Christ himself, Ham is a second Adam betrayed by the greed of his brothers and sisters. In the next chapter, we will further develop this portrait of the Ham-Christ.

African-American Counterreadings

As abolitionists, biblical critics, and authors of drama and fiction, African Americans have been zealous opponents of Noah's curse. Having considered literary figures such as Zora Neale Hurston and James Baldwin,[99] we should also note antebellum black intellectuals like David Walker and Frederick Douglass, both of whom vigorously assaulted the curse and its role in upholding slavery. In 1829, Walker denied that any curse on blacks—whether applied to the seed of Cain or Canaan—could be derived from scripture and charged that whites "act more like the seed of Cain, by murdering" than do blacks. In 1845, Douglass observed that miscegenation between masters and slaves gave the lie to any concept of a "race of Ham." "If the lineal descendants of Ham are alone to be scripturally enslaved," Douglass reasoned, "it is certain that slavery at the south must soon become unscriptural; for thousands are ushered into the world, annually, who, like myself, owe their existence to white fathers, and those fathers most frequently their own masters."[100]

A careful African American refutation of the curse appeared in 1862, when Alexander Crummel published "The Negro Race Not Under a Curse: An Examination of Genesis ix.25." In his article, Crummell advanced standard objections to Noah's curse—that it had been pronounced upon Canaan rather than Ham, that neither Ham nor three of his four sons were affected, that the Negro race did not descend from Canaan, and that slavery, as a general evil pertaining to the entire human family, did "not imply mental degradation or intellectual ineptitude."[101] James W. C. Pennington, a Congregational minister and former slave, employed Genesis 9 and 10 to argue that blacks were descended from Ham through an amalgamation of Cush and Mizraim and thus bore no relation to Canaan or his curse.[102]

Perhaps more significant than these African American intellectuals are the generations of black preachers who have inventively reinterpreted or relativized Noah's curse as they searched the scriptures to discover God's way with the African. Some preachers have contended that the curse was wiped out when the Old Testament was superseded by the New; others have utilized Genesis 10 to link African Americans with the early Egyptians or—through Nimrod—to the ancient Babylonians, a strategy that has led some blacks to boast of their identity as children of Ham.[103] Following Edward Wilmot Blyden and Bishop James Theodore Holly (both discussed in the previous chapter), many black preachers have embraced the Hamitic origins of the Negro while recasting Genesis 9 in light of "the rising glory of the sons of Ham," the imminent liberation of Africans, or the evangelization of Africa by former slaves.[104] Probably the most exhaustive study of "the Hamitic race" by a black preacher was published in 1937 by Alonzo Potter Burgess Holly, son of James Theodore. In *God and the Negro,* the younger Holly declared that "God Almighty has shown, throughout the Bible Record, a peculiar interest in His people of Hamitic Descent." Holly affirmed the Canaanite ancestry of the Negro and a curse of limited duration but insisted that a perennial malediction would "run counter to the plan of redemption."[105]

More recently, black scholars including Latta Thomas, Charles B. Copher, Cain Hope Felder, Katie Geneva Cannon, and Randall Bailey have submitted Genesis 9:20–27 to careful critical and ethical analyses.[106] In the process, they have illumined the legendary and etiological aspects of the story, the historical and literary contexts in which it developed, the cultural forces that sustain the curse, and the forms of modern eisegesis that racialize it.[107] Felder defends the moral integrity of scripture, insisting that there is no Bible narrative whose original intent was "to negate the full humanity of black people or view blacks in an unfavorable way."[108] The development of Ham's curse he regards as a chief example of *sacralization,* or "the transposing of an ideological concept into a tenet of religious faith." However, while acknowledging that ambiguities in the passage have yielded "a fantastic variety of suggestions about the incident," Felder is confident that "the crime" in question is Ham's seeing the nakedness of his drunken father without immediately covering him. "In error, Ham leaves his father uncovered (according to Hebrew tradition, an act of great shamelessness and parental disrespect) while he goes to report on Noah's condition to Shem and Japheth."[109] Felder criticizes scholars who conclude that Noah's curse is probably historical, yet by historicizing Ham's transgression he leaves undisturbed the dynamics of blame in Genesis 9:20–27. Felder's work represents both the possibilities and pitfalls of biblical criticism in challenging the curse.

African American readings of Genesis 9 are not uniformly subversive of the curse. For instance, according to the recently published *Black Bible Chronicles:*

Noah had three boys named Shem, Ham and Japheth. The nations of the earth came from Noah's three boys. Noah became a farmer and planted a vineyard and made wine. One day he drank too much and lay 'round his tent without a stitch on. Ham the father of Canaan, saw his father without any clothes on and went and told his other brothers. Now Shem and Japheth got a robe and walked backwards into the tent so that they wouldn't see their daddy naked and covered him up. Noah was really mad after he sobered up and found out what had happened, so he laid a heavy trip on Ham and cursed his further generation. "I swear," said Noah, "that the future generations of Ham shall be slaves and lowest of slaves, at that." And to the future generation of Shem and Japheth he said, "May the almighty bless both Shem and Japheth and be righteous by them. And may Ham's kids be Shem's slaves and let Japheth share in his riches."[110]

Black Bible Chronicles translates Genesis 9 into the "language of the streets" but does nothing to challenge the legacy of Noah's curse. In fact, because Canaan is not mentioned in this retelling, the burden of Noah's oracle falls directly upon Ham.

Overall, black approaches to Noah's curse reflect the same methodological and interpretive differences common throughout the world of biblical scholarship. For instance, some scholars now embrace a so-called New Hamite hypothesis, according to which the Hamites of the Bible are viewed as "white."[111] Others resist the effective banishment of blacks from the Bible that is implied by the hypothesis,[112] and some popular Afrocentrist readings of Genesis assume Noah and his sons alike were black.[113]

Noah's Forbidden Fruit

During the last quarter of the twentieth century, a number of talented authors recast Genesis 9:20–27 with particular attention to Noah's drunkenness and its repercussions in his family.[114] One of these is Frederick Buechner, who relates the encounter between Ham and Noah this way:

Ham was the youngest of Noah's three sons and by tradition the progenitor of the black race.

After the Flood was over and the family had settled down into the wine business, Noah did a little too much sampling one hot afternoon and passed out buck naked in his tent. Ham happened to stick his head in at just the wrong moment and then, instead of keeping his mouth shut, went out and treated his brothers to a lurid account of what he'd seen.

When Noah sobered up and found out about it, he blew his top. Among some other unpleasant things he had to say was a curse to the effect that from that day forward Ham was to be his brothers' slave.[115]

A more irreverent retelling of the story appears in Julian Barnes's novel *A History of the World in 10½ Chapters* (1989), in which the events in Noah's life following the Flood are related by a woodworm who stows away on the ark. The narrator anticipates the incredulity of readers who are familiar with the biblical portrait of Noah. "There were times when Noah and his sons got quite hysterical. That doesn't tally with your account of things? You've always been led to believe that Noah was sage, righteous and God-fearing, and I've already described him as a hysterical rogue with a drink problem?"

Take the story of Noah's nakedness—you remember? It happened after the landing. Noah, not surprisingly, was even more pleased with himself than before—he'd saved the human race, he'd insured the success of his dynasty, he'd been given a formal covenant by God—and he decided to take things easy in the last three hundred and fifty years of his life. He founded a village (which you call Arghuri) on the lower slopes of the mountain, and spent his days dreaming up new decorations and honours for himself: Holy Knight of the Tempest, Grand Commander of the Squalls and so on. Your sacred text informs you that on his estate he planted a vineyard. Ha! Even the least subtle mind can decode that particular euphemism: he was drunk all the time. One night, after a particularly hard session, he'd just finished undressing when he collapsed on the bedroom floor—not an unusual occurrence. Ham and his brothers happened to be passing his "tent" (they still used the old sentimental desert word to describe their palaces) and called in to check that their alcoholic father hadn't done himself any harm. Ham went into the bedroom and . . . well, a naked man of six hundred and fifty-odd years lying in a drunken stupor is not a pretty sight. Ham did the decent, the filial thing: he got his brothers to cover their father up. As a sign of respect—though even at that time the custom was passing out of use—Shem and the one beginning with J entered their father's chamber backwards, and managed to get him into bed without letting their gaze fall on those organs of generation which mysteriously incite your species to shame. A pious and honourable deed all round, you might think. And how did Noah react when he awoke with one of those knifing new-wine hangovers? He cursed the son who had found him and decreed that all Ham's children should become servants to the family of the two brothers who had entered his room arse-first. Where is the sense in that? I can guess your explanation: his sense of judgment was affected by drink, and we should offer pity not censure. Well, maybe. But I would just mention this: *we* knew him on the Ark.[116]

A less humorous reflection on the episode is offered by poet and biblical scholar Alicia Suskin Ostriker, who counts Noah as one of "my fathers, whom I intend to pursue. . . . Needing to remember that I am my fathers, just as much as my mothers."[117] Ostriker refocuses the story of Noah and his sons by combining the perspective of Ham with her own experience as the child of an alcoholic father:

I thought the vineyard idea was a good one, the old man had to be kept busy somehow. Then he started drinking. Steadily. After all we had been through. The pity of it. And he would lie in his tent uncovered, naked and sweating. Father, how could I turn my back? I wanted to cover your pathetic flabby body.

I told my brothers: our father is lying naked in the tent dead drunk. They said no. That doesn't happen in families like ours. Only gentiles are alcoholics. Shut up, they said, and quickly turned their backs. Then our father woke up and began screaming, cursing me.

You'll be black, he screamed. The sweat stood out on his forehead. You'll never get anywhere. Your children will be slaves and servants. He retched and flung himself backward shivering. That ought to teach you respect, he screamed.[118]

These and other[119] glosses on Genesis 9 that highlight the systemic effects of intoxication reflect contemporary concerns about alcohol abuse. Often drawing on personal experiences, these authors clarify the ambiguous legacy of Noah's wine. On one hand, fermented grapes cover his "painful memories of destruction and desolation."[120] On the other hand, Noah's wine becomes a toxin that poisons him temporarily, and his family for generations.

Significantly, these contemporary authors are extending an interpretive tradition that is centuries old. No doubt aware of the ambiguity with which fermented drink is presented in the Hebrew canon,[121] curious rabbis and pious Protestants refused to ignore the significance of Noah's wine for interpreting Genesis 9:20–27. The forbidden fruit's effects were foregrounded in much early Jewish commentary. According to one tradition,

> Noah's assistant in the work of cultivating the vine was Satan . . . [who] conveyed to Noah what the qualities of wine are: before man drinks of it, he is innocent as a lamb; if he drinks of it moderately, he feels as strong as a lion; if he drinks more of it than he can bear, he resembles the pig; and if he drinks to the point of intoxication, then he behaves like a monkey, he dances around, sings, talks obscenely, and knows not what he is doing.[122]

Another set of rabbinic comments on the passage relates Noah's drunkenness to Israel's national misfortunes:

> A. "And he lay uncovered in his tent" (Gen. 9:21):
>
> B. R. Judah bar Simon, R. Hanan in the name of R. Samuel b. R. Isaac: "What is written is not 'lay uncovered' but 'uncovered himself,' and [since the consonants of the word for 'uncover' can yield the meaning, 'exile,' we may read the passage to indicate that it was that sort of drunkenness that] brought about both for himself and generations to come the penalty of exile."
>
> C. "The ten tribes were exiled only on account of wine, in line with this verse: 'woe to those who get up early in the morning to follow strong drink' (Is. 5:11)."
>
> D. "The tribes of Judah and Benjamin went into exile only on account of wine, in line with this verse: 'But these also erred through wine' (Is. 28: 7)."[123]

These rabbinic glosses offer timeless insights into alcohol's bewildering effects on human beings. The first suggests that while a little wine has an exhilarating effect on the body ("he feels strong as a lion"), too much debases the mind ("he behaves like a monkey"). The second indicates the poison's long-term effects on human communities.

Among Christian writers who have perceived in Genesis 9 an object lesson in the mysterious dangers of drink are seventeenth-century interpreter Abraham Rosse, who urges readers to consider the relation between "the sinne of Adam, and this of Noah":

> *Adam* the father of the first world sinned shortly after his creation, and *Noah* the father of the second world, sinnes shortly after his preservation: secondly, *Adam* transgressed by eating the fruite of the forbidden tree, and *Noah* transgresseth by drinking the fruite of the vine tree: thirdly, the sequel of *Adams* sinne was nakednesse, and the sequel of *Noahs* sinne is the same: fourthly, *Adam* was ashamed, and the shame of *Noah* is delivered: fifthly, *Adams* nakednes was covered with skinnes, and *Noahs* nakedness is covered with a garment: sixthly, a curse upon *Adams* posteritie, is the effect of *Adams* eating, and a curse upon Canaan, *Noahs* posteritie, is the effect of *Noahs* drinking.[124]

These counterreadings of Genesis 9—from the rabbis to Buechner, Barnes, and Ostriker—elucidate Noah's *phamakon*, the classical term for a substance that is both remedy and poison.[125] In doing so, they illustrate alcohol's dual function as an antidote to fatigue and memory with potentially toxic effects on mind and body. If we are more sensitive than our predecessors to alcohol's human cost, it is probably in our understanding of the *pharmakon*'s corporate reach. We know that when it is chronically abused alcohol's impact is rarely limited to a single individual, or even a single generation. But contemporary authors who identify in Genesis 9 the dynamics of a family under wine's curse reveal more than our society's ambivalence toward fermented drink. Their graphic and pathetic images of Noah's drunkenness raise a basic interpretive question: Why has the tradition portrayed Noah so consistently as the story's victim?

Part of the answer may lie in the observation that the families of those who have carelessly imbibed the *pharmakon* are often divided by their reactions to the imbiber. Those who remain oblivious to the problem preserve a semblance of peace in the family. But the cost of this false security is the exclusion or vilification of those who cannot ignore the disease. When a family member dares to reveal the naked truth about the remedy that has become a poison, fear of family instability leads to a closing of ranks behind the abuser. Thus, the one who would speak for the victims is victimized. If this brave soul cannot rescue the family from the *pharmakon*'s grip, the poison slowly works its way into the deep structures of family life, where it can remain for generations after the original abuser has died.

Perhaps this scenario applies to the second first family after the Flood. Noah the husbandman discovers a remedy for his sweat and fatigue, but his excess turns the antidote into a poison and he falls victim to the *pharmakon*.

Moreover, the son who would intervene and point out the father's defeat is met by his brothers' denial and his father's rage. His reward for naming the *pharmakon* in a moment of crisis is a curse on himself and his descendants. If textual dynamics and the history of interpretation have obscured the impact of Noah's wine on his family, then understanding the text will require attention to the *pharmakon*.

The various challenges to Noah's curse reviewed in this chapter testify to Bible readers' creativity, their careful attention to textual seams and gaps, and their willingness to accent previously silenced voices. In different ways, these strategies for counterreading hint that the story might be redeemed through subversive reinterpretation. In the next chapter, we will follow some of these leads as we strain to hear the victim's voice in the story of Noah and his sons.

11

Redeeming the Curse

Ham as Victim

This crime of Ham was the first transgression recorded after the flood, and probably the first committed; and you
must remember, in the next place, that Noah now was to
the world what Adam was, when created—the official
head—the Viceregent of Heaven—and, therefore, the first
deliberate and wilful offence, as in the case of Adam, according to the moral government of God, must be punished with the utmost rigor of law.

Leander Ker,
Slavery Consistent with Christianity

BECAUSE IT HAS reflected and transmitted antiblack sentiment for nearly
two millennia, Noah's curse requires a cure. The virulent ideology to which
Genesis 9 plays host has been eradicated by neither slave emancipation nor
the application of historical criticism. Rather, in the wake of such attacks, the
curse has undergone dangerous mutations, drawn strength from proximate
passages in Genesis 10 and 11, and survived in the minds and hearts of Bible
readers.

Because a majority of Americans now share the vision of an integrated
society that energized the Civil Rights movement, it is tempting to regard
Noah's curse as discredited and irrelevant. Yet the stereotypes and myths that
once animated racial readings of Genesis continue to operate in the American
imagination. The early chapters of Genesis are invoked in political debates
concerning antimiscegenation laws and in religious affirmations of capital

punishment. Radio and television airwaves carry references to the curse tradition, from the rantings of Christian fundamentalists to slick Hollywood miniseries. *The Dake Annotated Reference Bible* (currently in its twenty-seventh printing) affirms Genesis 9's racial implications, though in a less explicit form than previously. *The Black Bible Chronicles,* inexplicably it would seem, updates the curse for a generation of hip Bible readers. Biblical commentaries interrogate history and tradition but continue to find fault with Ham. And even liberationist readings of Genesis 9 affirm the curse for their own purposes.

For all these reasons, the curse should not be regarded as an ideological relic as long as people read the Bible and seek justifications for group hegemony. Noah's curse may be dormant, but it is not dead; it may be in remission, but it is still in need of a remedy. Where are we to find such a cure, a method of interpreting the story of Noah and his sons that precludes the denigration of "Hamites," "Canaanites," or the groups with whom readers wish to associate them? Critics of biblically sanctioned white hegemony have long sought a cure for the curse in the application of "scientific" remedies, including logic, biblical scholarship, and moral suasion. American abolitionists employed all of these strategies, and when the curse was revivified during the 1950s and 1960s to oppose government-sponsored integration, antisegregationists found themselves administering the same treatments pioneered a century earlier. With the help of these prospective antidotes, the curse was displaced (by the insistence that it befell Canaan rather than his father or brothers) softened (with the claim that Noah's oracle was predictive rather than prophetic), or deracialized (its link with the putative ancestor of African Americans challenged). But these strategies did not cure the curse, for they left intact a textual logic of blame and punishment and did nothing to challenge the assumption that Genesis 9–11 reflects a divine compulsion for differentiation.

A more radical cure for the curse and its troublesome legacy has been sought by those who discredit the biblical version of human origins. But this counteragent carries undesirable side effects, most notably loss of the emphasis on human unity that is assumed throughout the Bible. It is beneficial to remember that in American intellectual history Genesis 9–11 has functioned not only as a ground for racism but also as a vantage point for perceiving human beings as the descendants of common parents, created in the divine image, and worthy of redemption. For instance, in response to the polygenetic theory advanced by the American School of Ethnology in the 1840s, advocates of slavery invoked Genesis as incontrovertible proof of blacks' humanity. But when the biblical defense of slavery was discredited after the Civil War, scientific racism and its secular theory of human origins received an unexpected boon. Their need to justify black servitude obviated, some Christians abandoned the traditional assumption that Africans were Hamites for the scientifically fashionable hypothesis that blacks were actually pre-adamite humans or soulless beasts.[1]

Thus, Genesis 9–11's American legacy is ambiguous: Despite these chapters' role in justifying slavery and segregation and vilifying the purported ancestors of blacks, their canonical context has helped establish the full humanity of America's putative Hamites when it was called into question by "science."[2] The biblical version of creation may lack scientific credibility, but as a theological account of human origins it possesses distinct advantages over secular renderings.[3] Because the biblical myth of creation and its aftermath offers a transcendent basis for the conviction that human beings are equally valuable as bearers of God's image and objects of God's love, strategies for curing the curse that undermine confidence in the revelatory potential of the Bible are purchased at an ideological price.[4] But the conviction that scripture witnesses to a redeeming God obligates us to resist the curse by reading for redemption. Doing so is difficult work, for Genesis 9 establishes patterns of condemnation that readers, even scholarly readers, have found extraordinarily difficult to contravene. But this does not relieve us of the obligation to keep trying.

This chapter offers an interpretive strategy for countering Noah's curse and its interpretive field in Genesis 9–11 by exploiting textual clues that point toward the curse's redemption. Two assumptions guide this experimental effort at redeeming the curse. First, the oppressive potential of Genesis 9:20–27 can be neutralized only when the biblical version of the curse has been revised and reimagined, the textual dynamics of blame subverted. Second, this can be accomplished only when the story is read in the context of the biblical canon and its message of redemption. The tentative interpretive scheme developed here draws on a variety of historical, literary, and imaginative resources, some of them discussed in earlier chapters. As we have seen, over the centuries a series of bold interpreters have consciously subverted the identities of victim and victimizer that the biblical narrative assigns to Noah and Ham, respectively. Although these subversive retellings of the scriptural story have contested Noah's status as a paragon of righteousness, only very recently—for instance, in the works of Zora Neale Hurston, Arthur Frederick Ide, Julian Barnes, and Alicia Suskin Ostriker—have they imagined Ham as an innocent victim of familial violence. As we strain to perceive more clearly the echoes of Ham's voice in Genesis 9, we will be aided by this tradition of counterreading.

Canonical Clues for a Cure

Hebrew Bible

To subvert the curse while retaining the theological advantages of the biblical doctrine of creation, Genesis 9:20–27 must be viewed in light of the canonical context in which the story functions. A consideration of Genesis 9's setting in the Hebrew canon reveals, first of all, unmistakable linguistic and thematic connections with the story of Eden (Genesis 1–3). These parallels are neatly summarized by *The New Interpreter's Bible*:

> Noah, a new Adam, takes up the creational task once again in "planting" and tilling the "ground"; his skill leads to a taming of what the ground produces and hence ameliorates the curse (3:17; 5:29). Yet, Noah as the new Adam (and one child) also fails as miserably as the old Adam. Similar themes appear in both stories: nakedness after eating fruit, and intrafamilial conflict, including human subservience and its affect [*sic*]. The curse on the serpent and the ground parallels the curse on Canaan, both of which affect life negatively. Yet, the act of Shem and Japheth in covering the naked one mirrors earlier action of the deity (3:21).[5]

Other allusions to the garden appear in 9:1 and 9:7, which repeat the divine command to "Be fruitful and multiply, and fill the earth."

As these Edenic references indicate, 9:20–27 recalls the imprecation of Genesis 2. In fact, tracing the curse's career in the Bible's primeval history reveals a fatal bond between pre- and post-Flood humanity. The LORD curses the serpent, but the curse migrates—first to the ground, then from the blood-soaked earth to Cain. The announcement of Noah's birth (5:29) promises relief from the soil's execration, a promise fulfilled when God announces that the newly "cleansed" earth will not be cursed again. But the postdiluvian dispensation begins inauspiciously, with the curse entering the world of the second Adam as quickly as that of the first. Ironically, it is Noah himself who reintroduces the curse, transmitting it to his son and grandson in chapter 9. Based on the preceding eight chapters of Genesis, we should expect the LORD to be intimately involved in the judgment visited upon Ham-Canaan. Previous transgressions—the Fall of the first couple, Abel's murder, and the general wickedness of humankind—have precipitated specific expressions of divine displeasure, including expulsion from the garden, Cain's terrible stigma, and a catastrophic purging of the earth. But in chapter 9, for the first time in biblical history, God remains curiously silent in the midst of human "sin." Noah breaks this silence with the only words he will speak in scripture.

Links between 9:20–27 and the rest of the primeval history are also evident in the tale of Cain and Abel in Genesis 4. Like chapter 4, chapter 9 features brothers, transgression, and stigmatization. But the tale of Noah and his sons does not conform to the general pattern of Genesis "brother stories": [6] The younger brother is a shepherd who is favored by one or both parents and by God, the older brother is displaced, the younger brother endures an ordeal, and there is some sort of reconciliation or reintegration of the two.[7] Curiously, none of these elements is present in Genesis 9: There are no shepherds, only vintners; Ham is called the "youngest son" (9:24), but the birth order in Noah's family is far from clear, and the text provides no evidence that Ham is favored by his father or "chosen" by God. Ham can be said to endure an ordeal, but the story offers no reconciliation. Nor is the displaced sibling enfolded in God's care or "won back" for the larger story, a pattern evident in other Genesis sibling stories. Finally, there is no inversion of primogeniture; in fact, this is one of the few stories in Genesis where the youngest son fares worse than the oldest.[8]

Analysis of Genesis 9's canonical setting requires consideration of its place within the Flood narrative (Genesis 6–9). The thematic symmetry in this narrative is delineated by Terry Prewitt: "The two chapter parts of Genesis 6 are neatly mirrored in Genesis 9. First, God blesses Noah and makes his covenant with all future generations. Second, Noah's son Ham disgraces his father by seeing his nakedness, resulting in the curse of Canaan. The 'nakedness' of Noah is indicative of a sexual crime by Ham, a disgrace comparable to the 'divine beings' or 'sons of God' taking the daughters of men as wives."[9] In both chapters 6 and 9, in other words, the leading themes are transgression, covenant, and sacrifice. Before the Deluge, God is concerned with the world's "violence," decides to "make an end of all flesh," and selects Noah to preserve a remnant of living things. After the Flood, the divine relationship with Noah and animal sacrifice are formalized. God announces a covenant with the survivors of the Deluge, including the animals, "as many as came out of the ark" (9:10).

Never again, God proclaims, shall all flesh be cut off or the earth destroyed by flood. The sign of this apparently unconditional arrangement (it applies to "all future generations," according to v. 12) is God's "bow in the clouds" (9:13). God tells Noah, "This is the sign of the covenant that I have established between me and all flesh that is on the earth" (9:17). Previously, the LORD declared that the survivors "shall not eat flesh with its life, that is, its blood" (Gen. 9:4); God will "require a reckoning" (9:5) for the lifeblood of animals and humans alike. Nevertheless, Noah's postdiluvian sacrifice introduces a threat to nonhuman beings: "The fear and dread of you shall rest on every animal of the earth, and on every bird of the air, on everything that creeps on the ground, and on all the fish of the sea; into your hand they are delivered. Every moving thing that lives shall be food for you; and just as I gave you the green plants, I give you everything" (9:2–3). According to the biblical narrative, then, the LORD declares upon receiving Noah's sacrifice that the continuity of human history, and consequently the natural world, will not again be broken. With Noah's offering of clean animals and birds, the cycle of human wickedness that led to the Deluge has been shattered. It will be recalled that in Genesis 6 "violence" is given as the chief cause for the flood.[10]

This brief review of Genesis 9:20–27's canonical context raises several intriguing questions. First, in that the passage recalls in many ways the tale of Cain and Abel, are we to conclude that the forces responsible for the demise of antediluvian civilization are similar to those at work after the Flood? Second, are the theological motifs that dominate the flood narrative—particularly the interplay of human violence and animal sacrifice—useful for understanding the story of Noah and his sons as well? And third, given God's unusual

silence in the story, why have Bible readers assumed that Noah's malediction
has divine sanction?

This last question is the easiest to address since the history of interpretation would suggest that a variety of textual forces have conspired to nudge
readers toward the conclusion that Noah speaks for God: This episode follows
a description of the covenantal relationship God has forged with Noah, "a
righteous man, blameless in his generation" (Gen. 6:9); the story's narrator
privileges Noah with the gift of speech that in Genesis is often a divine prerogative; and the poetic typography afforded these words in most translations
lends them the patina of authority, for it echoes divine imprecations elsewhere
in the primeval history while anticipating the prophetic tradition in which the
word of the LORD is often revealed in verse. Furthermore, Bible readers may
encounter this story already convinced, based on prominent brother stories
in Genesis and elsewhere, that God shares Noah's concern with the relative
ranking of sons.

These tacit links between Noah's oracle and the divine voice have led
generations of readers to conclude that Noah's curse is also God's curse, thus
reinforcing the orthodox interpretive paradigm in which Ham is victimizer
and Noah victim. However, the biblical text offers no explicit support for the
assumption that Noah acts as God's agent. Exploiting the gap between the
human and divine wills that is opened by the story's canonical context (and
by counterreading) creates space for considering whether Noah's malediction
reliably reflects the character of God. For those who regard the Bible as scripture, this means asking if the curse conforms to the will of the One to whom
the text bears witness. If we can resist the textual and interpretive forces that
lead us to associate Noah with God, it may be possible to perceive Ham's role
as victim, and this perception may illumine a canonical link between Ham
and Jesus the victim. Once this link has been imagined, further parallels between these biblical sons emerge—from their rejection by family members to
their problematic relationship with their father's "houses" (the Jerusalem Temple and Noah's tent). But how do we pursue this canonical hunch that Ham
is a victim, that Noah—and perhaps Shem and Japheth—have victimized
him? This is where the mimetic theory of René Girard proves extraordinarily
useful.

The Promise of Girard

Any successful strategy for redeeming Noah's curse must attend to its historical, literary, and psychological elements, must have a track record of fruitful
application to religious texts, and must be concerned with the mythical origins
of violence (for what is the curse if not a narrative justification for organized
violence?). Given these requirements, the work of literary critic René Girard
is quite promising. In a series of seminal writings over several decades, the

French American theorist has elucidated the nature of myth, the historical events that generate it, and the primordial violence it shrouds. To "expose to the light of reason the role played by violence in human society,"[11] Girard has developed a powerful critical theory based on what he calls "mimetic rivalry." Although he has not written explicitly on Genesis 9:20–27,[12] Girard and scholars influenced by him have demonstrated the relevance of mimetic theory to biblical texts, their prehistory, and their reception.[13] Girard's work is particularly applicable to stories that are concerned with the origins of human society, for he contends that the nascence of civilization can be located in original events of sacrifice that are barely repressed in myth and literature.

Girard has devoted special attention to analyzing "persecution texts," which he defines as "accounts of real violence, often collective, told from the perspective of the persecutors, and therefore influenced by characteristic distortions . . . [which] must be identified and corrected in order to reveal the arbitrary nature of the violence that the persecution text presents as justified."[14] In *The Scapegoat,* Girard explores the classic literary stereotypes of persecution, which include representation of a crisis that is precipitated by the breakdown of social differentiation, "accusations made against victims onto whom the alleged crimes undermining law and order are transferred," and "signs" of the victim.[15] The overall impression given by persecution texts, Girard writes, is a loss of social order "evidenced by the disappearance of the rules and 'differences' that define cultural divisions."[16] According to this description, Genesis 9:20–27 would seem to be a typical persecution text: It features a crisis allegedly precipitated by a breakdown in order, it makes accusations against a character who is charged with eliminating crucial differences, and it marks him with "preferential signs of victimage," including reprehensible behavior and association with a known outsider (cf. Ham's identification in 9:22 as "the father of Canaan").

Girard notes that persecution texts attribute to their victims "deformities that would reinforce the polarization against the victim, were they real."[17] Among the accusations that are particularly characteristic of collective persecution are violent crimes against untouchables: "a king, a father, the symbol of divine authority . . . then there are sexual crimes: rape, incest, bestiality. The most frequently invoked [accusations] transgress the taboos that are considered the strictest in the society in question."[18] In overturning a society's distinctions, the wrongdoer "must either attack the community directly, by striking at its heart or head, or else they must begin the destruction of difference within their own sphere by committing contagious crimes such as parricide and incest."[19] In the history of biblical interpretation, Ham has been impeached on all of these counts, with each accusation stemming from the story's claim that Ham has blurred crucial distinctions or overturned order in his family. Inspired by Girard's phenomenological description of the persecution text and its apparent relevance to Noah's curse, let us engage in a more thorough Girardian analysis of Genesis 9:20–27.

Mimetic Desire, Scapegoating, and Sacrifice

One of Girard's original insights concerns the way classic texts reveal "the imitative nature of desire," often observable in what he calls the discord between doubles. Girard is particularly alert to the rivalry that develops when two persons desire a similar object. As Leo Kuper writes, "men come to desire precisely the same things, and they engage in conflict not because they are different but because they are essentially the same."[20] From his earliest work, Girard has sought to clarify mimetic desire's triangular structure. The angles of the mimetic triangle are the self, the other as "mediator" or "model," and "the object that the self or subject desires because he or she knows, imagines, or suspects the mediator desires it."[21] Conflict arises when the mediator can no longer fulfill the role of model without also becoming an obstacle. "Like the relentless sentry of the Kafka fable, the model shows his disciple the gate of paradise and forbids him to enter with one and the same gesture."[22]

If unrelieved, rivalry between the self and other leads to a mimetic crisis in which "there will be an inexorable movement toward finding a scapegoat."[23] As hominids experienced in the process of becoming human and many societies have discovered since, "convergence upon a victim brings them unanimity and thus relief from violence."[24] The scapegoat effect, according to Girard, is "that strange process through which two or more people are reconciled at the expense of a third party who appears guilty or responsible for whatever ails, disturbs, or frightens the scapegoaters. They feel relieved of their tensions and they coalesce into a more harmonious group. They now have a single purpose, which is to prevent the scapegoat from harming them, by expelling and destroying him."[25] The scapegoating mechanism, which "curtails reciprocal violence and imposes structure on the community,"[26] is the empirical or historical referent that generates myth, and myth's function is to obscure this fact.

Another central concern for Girard is the role of sacrifice in the founding of human societies. Girard defines sacrifice (much like scapegoating) as violence that is limited for the sake of maintaining order. As "a collective action of the entire community, which purifies itself of its own disorder through the unanimous immolation of a victim,"[27] sacrifice mediates the reordering of a community in crisis. As Girard observes in *Violence and the Sacred*, scapegoating and sacrifice are linked by substitution.[28] The nexus in Girard's thought between mimetic desire, scapegoating, sacrifice, and myth suggests rich possibilities for a Girardian reading of Genesis 9:20–27. But how does the claim that unrestrained mimetic rivalry brings societies to the brink of violence illumine the tale of Noah and his sons? To clarify the mimetic crisis that may have taken place in Noah's family, let us highlight some specific aspects of the biblical story: Noah's role as God's vice-regent, Ham's failure to display proper regard for his father, and the curious relationship of Shem and Japheth.

Noah's identity as a virtuous man beloved by God is so underscored by the text and its canonical setting that Bible readers through the centuries have ascribed to Noah a semidivine stature. Even modern biblical scholars confirm Noah's exalted status by comparing him with the heroes of other ancient flood stories (e.g., *The Gilgamesh Epic's* Utnapishtim) or the gods credited with the discovery of viticulture and wine (e.g., Osiris in Egypt and Dionysus in Greece). In text and imagination, then, Noah is an untouchable whose humiliation creates a serious exigency for the postdiluvian community. The biblical narrator communicates the severity of the situation by intimating that a sexual assault has been perpetrated on God's righteous one, by attaching stereotypes of persecution to the alleged perpetrator, and by relating the story in terms of striking reversal: It is precisely while Noah is "in his tent" (a place generally associated with security) that the crisis occurs.[29] These are all indications of a significant crisis in Noah's family. But what is the nature of the crisis?

Girard argues that because human beings do not know what to desire, they emulate each other's desires. "The model is likely to be mimetically affected by the desire of his imitator. He becomes the imitator of his own imitator, just as the latter becomes the model of his own model."[30] Mimesis leads to rivalry, rivalry to scapegoating, victimization, and violence. Modern attempts to clarify Genesis 9:20–27 by analyzing traces of desire in the text have assumed that the passions animating this tale are libidinous. Subversive though these counterreadings seek to be, they inevitably reinscribe the orthodox interpretive paradigm in which Noah is a righteous victim and Ham a vilified villain.[31] If we are to detect the sort of desire Girard claims operates in many classic texts, we must read for traces of mimetic rivalry. And the clearest signal of rivalry is the doubling behavior of Shem and Japheth.

The brothers take a garment, lay it across their shoulders, walk backward in tandem until they reach Noah's tent, and together cover him. In depicting this scene, visual artists have assigned the lead to one of the brothers.[32] But the biblical narrator gives us a striking image of physical and emotional proximity. As Umberto Cassuto notes, this description "assumes an almost poetic form": "The clause *and walked backward* is paralleled by the clause *their faces were turned away;* the words *and they did not see their father's nakedness* correspond to the hemistich *and covered their father's nakedness.* The expression *their father's nakedness,* which occurs here twice, echoes the words *his father's nakedness* in v. 22; this threefold use of the phrase serves to emphasize it."[33] In other words, the brothers' act is narrated with a parallelism and symmetry that reflect the unanimity of the act itself. In their movements and the language employed to describe it, Shem and Japheth merge into a single character.

The relationship of Shem and Japheth has not caught the attention of many Bible readers. A rabbinic gloss on the story declares that both brothers deserved credit for covering their father, but, as it was Shem's idea, he earned "the greater meed of praise." Conversely, an illustration in the fifteenth-century Cologne Bible depicts Japheth as the leader in this act of filial piety.[34] John Calvin interprets Noah's prophecy as a prediction that there would "be temporary dissension between Shem and Japheth."[35] Although such comments on the brothers' relationship are rare, they remind us how very odd is the scriptural image of two adult brothers thinking and acting as one. Are these men extraordinarily comfortable in each other's presence, unusually well-coordinated, virtual twins in the spitting image of their righteous father? From a Girardian perspective, the doubling behavior of Shem and Japheth indicates that they may be archrivals whose mimetic desire has made them mirror images of one another.[36] In motion toward the object of their common longing, they are frozen in mimetic rivalry.

But what is the object of the brothers' rivalrous desire? Typically, the sibling stories in Genesis are fueled by the quest for a father's blessing, and this is very likely the case in our story. Because Noah's family members are the only survivors of the Flood, the aged patriarch's benediction means rulership of the earth for its recipient. Presumably, Noah's blessing will fall on only one of his sons. As Regina Schwartz observes, there is a principle of scarcity at work in monotheistic narratives in which humans seek God's approval, a principle which dictates that everything—"land, prosperity, power, favor, even identity itself"—must be competed for. In Schwartz's words, "scarcity imposes sibling rivalry: a shortage of parental blessings and love yields fatal competition for them. Scarcity imposes parental hostility: it presumes that in order to imitate the father successfully, he must be replaced, not joined. Scarcity imposes hierarchy: the short supply of prestige or power or whatever must issue in an allocation of those resources, and some will invariably get more than others."[37]

Who will be the beneficiary of scarcity in Noah's family? Normally, the paternal blessing would fall on the eldest. But perhaps the enormous trauma through which the family had passed led the brothers to wonder if the "old ways" of primogeniture would be retained in the new world.[38] Moreover, the birth order of Noah's sons is not clear in the biblical text, so perhaps linguistic confusion indicates familial confusion as well.[39] Assuming, as most commentators have, that Shem is the firstborn, the dynamics of mimetic desire in Noah's family would evolve this way: The expectation that Noah will favor the eldest makes Shem a model for Japheth, who simultaneously becomes Shem's imitator and obstacle. Likewise, Shem's uncertainty regarding Noah's blessing—no doubt intensified by his brother's name, derived from the Hebrew *yapht*, to "extend" or "enlarge"—makes Japheth Shem's model and obstacle.

In the closed system of Noah's family, the brothers' common desire for their father's blessing locks them in a mimetic dance Girard calls "internal mediation," connoting that the physical and emotional distance between the antagonists is minimal. The brothers' proximity catalyzes their desire until it has shifted from jealousy to intense antipathy. After all, "only someone who prevents us from satisfying a desire which he himself has inspired in us is truly an object of hatred."[40] Such a relationship is captured in one of Girard's descriptions of mimetic rivalry: "The antagonists are caught in an escalation of frustration. In their dual role of obstacle and model, they both become more and more fascinated by each other. Beyond a certain level of intensity they are totally absorbed and the disputed object becomes secondary, even irrelevant."[41] This mutual fascination, according to Girard, can reach the level of a "hypnotic trance." Mimetic antagonism is ultimately unitive, in that it provides an object the antagonists can share. But the quiescent conflict it implies is full of peril for the community.

Considered mimetically, the biblical image of Shem and Japheth walking in tandem to cover their father is emblematic of their intense rivalry. While being careful to keep his brother in sight, each strains to earn the all-important blessing. This rivalry, while apparently benign, actually threatens to destroy Noah's family, which has become synonymous with the human family. According to mimetic theory, the conflict can be relieved and the danger eschewed only if a scapegoat is found. But by necessity in this lonely postdiluvian world, the scapegoat must come from Noah's family. Thus, the community can be spared an eruption of murderous violence only if one of its own members is destroyed through the scapegoating mechanism. This is precisely the solution revealed in Noah's pronouncement, in which Shem and Japheth are blessed while the family's shame is projected upon Ham or Canaan.

Shem is given priority over his brother ("Japheth will dwell in the tents of Shem"), but Japheth, too, is blessed and vested with authority over Ham and Canaan. This is the family's solution to the crisis precipitated by unrelieved mimetic rivalry. The object of the brothers' desire—their father's blessing—is shared in exchange for their complicity in scapegoating a third party. The collusion is evident in the very structure of Noah's oracle, as the malediction is reiterated in connection with each brother. Averting the crisis requires not only the identification of a scapegoat but also a repudiation of the rivalry that made the scapegoating necessary. This is provided in Noah's declaration "May God make space for Japheth, and let him live in the tents of Shem" (v. 27), which indicates that the brothers will coexist in peace and proximity.[42]

The mimetic crisis in Noah's family is arrested when Ham-Canaan is accused of excessive desire. In fact, The brothers' simultaneous covering of their father symbolizes the family's unanimity in projecting upon Ham the desire for Noah that is the essence of their own rivalry. The story's displacement of desire upon Ham brings a resolution to the crisis, rescuing the community from the violent result of rivalry that visited the first Adam's family when Cain murdered Abel. Noah's righteousness is preserved inasmuch as his own failures are obscured by Ham's dishonor, and the brothers' dangerous desire is projected upon the scapegoat.

Through the collective violence of scapegoating, then, disorder is trans-ferred from the community to the victim. But there is a problem: Although Ham's choice as scapegoat may be obvious from our perspective, mimetic theory dictates that his selection appear to be "by chance."[43] Because Ham is the only surviving male of his generation not caught in mimetic struggle, he is hardly an arbitrary choice. However, the biblical text reveals slippage in the scapegoat's identity. Although it is Ham who is accused of unleashing destruc-tive desire, it is Canaan who becomes the object of Noah's curse. This dis-crepancy, which has troubled Bible readers for generations, is evidence that the text's authors have taken pains to transform Ham from an arbitrary victim to a dangerous criminal. Ham is the "obvious" scapegoat only because readers are given a sign of his victimage ("Ham the father of Canaan").

According to this analysis, Genesis 9 contains what Girard calls an "ex-emplary scapegoat myth." Such myths begin with disorder or undifferentia-tion,[44] themes that are often expressed in a quarrel between relatives, pref-erably twin brothers. Then a third individual stands convicted of some fault: "It may be a heinous crime . . . or an accidental faux-pas; but it has brought the state of chaos from which the community suffers." Once the scapegoat is identified with the help of "preferential signs of victimage," he or she is "killed, expelled, or otherwise eliminated," either by the entire community or by a single individual. Finally, "peace returns, order is (re)generated."[45] But can Ham be a sacrificial victim if he is not annihilated?

Bearing on this question is the classical Greek concept of *pharmakos,* a person "maintained by the city at its own expense and slaughtered at the appointed festivals as well as at a moment of civic disaster."[46] Walter Burkert notes that in classical drama the *pharmakos* is not always destroyed. In *Oe-dipus the King,* for instance, "Oedipus, assuming the role of the pharmakos, is not killed violently but voluntarily led away." Burkert notes that "even when there is annihilation in the scapegoat complex, it is characteristically left to 'the others,' to hostile forces be they demons or real enemies. The basic action seems to be abandonment."[47] Burkert has described, it would seem, precisely the way Ham functions as a sacrificial victim in Genesis 9: Although he is not killed, Ham is marginalized and abandoned. He becomes a perpetual human sacrifice, surviving as a target for whatever postdiluvian corruption must be accounted for. Abandoned to dishonor but never consumed, Ham is available for literary lynching whenever needed.

The Flood and Sacrifice

Like the rest of the primeval history of Genesis, the Flood narrative is believed to have undergone final redaction by the Priestly school. It should not surprise us, then, that the language used in Genesis 9 to denote Ham's transgression resonates with the sexual prohibitions of the Holiness Code in Leviticus 18 and 20.[48] This intertextuality suggests not only an active Priestly editorial hand but also Genesis 9's affinity with sacrifice and ritual. Because Girard has consistently argued that the origins of sacrifice as sacred violence are to be found in the scapegoating effect, it is necessary to revisit the canonical context of Genesis 9:20–27, particularly its proximity to a description of animal sacrifice.[49]

According to Genesis 8:19–21, after "every animal . . . went out of the ark by families . . . Noah built an altar to the LORD, and took of every clean animal and of every clean bird, and offered burnt offerings on the altar." When God found pleasing the odor of Noah's sacrifice, "the LORD said in his heart, 'I will never again curse the ground because of humankind, for the inclination of the human heart is evil from youth; nor will I ever again destroy every living creature as I have done.' " Significantly, this slaughtering of clean animals follows immediately the announcement of a prohibition against shedding human blood. Noah and his sons are instructed not to "eat flesh with its life, that is, its blood" (Gen. 9:4) because God will "require a reckoning" for the lifeblood of animals and human beings alike, "each one for the blood of another, I will require a reckoning for human life" (Gen. 9:5). Verse 6 expresses this restriction poetically: "Whoever sheds the blood of a human, / by a human shall that person's blood be shed; / for in his own image / God made humankind." This juxtaposition of opposites—slaughter of the animals that had sojourned in the ark alongside a strict interdiction against shedding human blood—clarifies Noah's sacrifice as a method of limiting violence in the postdiluvian community, a way of stemming the flood of violence that precipitated the Deluge.

Girard observes that in stories of sacrifice "it is the god who supposedly demands the victims; he alone, in principle, who savors the smoke from the altars and requisitions the slaughtered flesh. It is to appease his anger that the killing goes on, that the victims multiply."[50] Genesis 8 implies that the LORD desires Noah's sacrifice ("the LORD smelled the pleasing odor"). But a Girardian reading of this sacrificial episode must inquire whether "the sacrifice serves to protect the entire community from its *own* violence."[51] A key to comprehending sacrifice's relation to violence in the human community is found in Girard's observation that "all victims, even the animal ones, bear a certain resemblance to the object they replace."[52] Are there such resemblances in Genesis 9? The animals are "clean" and thus differentiated from their peers; like Noah and his family, they have been rescued from the Flood; like the rivalrous brothers, they come in pairs. Then are these animals who resemble their caretakers on the ark substitutes for some member of Noah's family?

Violence, Girard points out, is much like a flood: Left unappeased, it accumulates and overflows its confines, inundating its surroundings. The role of sacrifice is to "redirect violence into its 'proper' channels." If Noah initiates the slaughter of animals immediately after the LORD's flood has subsided, then we are left to ask what sort of crisis emerged on the high seas that threatened a flood of violence in the surviving community. The legend of the mysterious fourth son of Noah—the mythical Jonathan—offers one provocative answer to this question. Perhaps this legend, according to which the youngest of Noah's sons is lost in the Flood, contains a trace of historical and religious truth. Did Jonathan become a sacrificial victim while the human remnant languished on the ark, unsure of how to appease the angry God who was purging the earth? If Jonathan became a victim of the very violence that precipitated the Flood, this might explain why animal sacrifice was resorted to immediately after the ark reached dry ground. Why else slaughter rescued animals upon arrival in the new world, unless a sacrificial crisis had developed in transit?

In this case, substitutionary sacrifice would have become the literal foundation of the postdiluvian human community. This would explain why, when a crisis erupted again in the episode of Noah's drunkenness—when Ham caught a glimpse of "things hidden from the foundation of the world," that is, Noah's own role in the violence that threatened human survival—it was not possible to repeat the originary violence. One fourth of Noah's potential descendants had been lost with Jonathan; should another fourth part be sacrificed with Ham? To end the cycle, an alternative form of substitution was required.

The Innocent Victim

Another Girardian insight embraced by many biblical critics is the revelatory function of the Bible in illuminating the dynamics of mimetic conflict, victimage, and sacrifice. According to Girard, the Bible portrays the fate of the innocent victim in a way that elucidates the violent origins of human civilization. Controversially, Girard regards the New Testament accounts of Jesus' passion as the paragon of revelation, in that they describe God's innocent victim suffering to end the cycle of scapegoating and violence.[53] In Girard's view, although the Hebrew Bible provides glimpses of the redemptive process narrated in the Gospels (particularly in the Prophets' concern for victims), it is of secondary importance for breaking the pattern of violence on which human societies are founded.[54] In this sense, Girard is open to the charge that he reinscribes traditional forms of Christian supersessionism vis-à-vis Judaism. At his best, however, Girard regards concern for the victim as a general characteristic of biblical revelation. He affirms that the Bible contains "revelation of victimage and its refusal" and possesses "a counter-mythical thrust in the treatment of victimage."[55] This thrust is present, Girard writes, in countless texts that "espouse the perspective of the victim rather than the mythical perspective of the persecutors."[56] Girard notes the Bible's tendency to "side with the victims" and cites Hebrew Bible texts as evidence, including the stories of Cain and Abel and Joseph and his brothers (along with Job, Psalms, and the suffering servant passages in Isaiah).[57]

On its surface, Genesis 9:20–27 does not appear to be one of these texts that espouses the perspective of the victim. If Israel is a "community that bears the memory of its own marginal, often victimized situation through the centuries,"[58] this memory has been thoroughly repressed in Genesis 9. Yet Girard emphasizes that traces of the scapegoating mechanism are often elusive, because "the mythic systems of representation obliterate the scapegoating on which they are founded, and they remain dependent on this obliteration."[59] In addition, episodes of mimetic violence and their subsequent reconciliation are recollected from the perspective of their beneficiaries. The community could not be at peace "if it doubted the victim's enormous capacity for evil. . . . The victim cannot be perceived as innocent and impotent; he (or she, as the case may be) must be perceived . . . as a creature truly responsible for all the disorders and ailments of the community."[60] From this perspective, Genesis 9's history of interpretation—from church fathers through American segregationists—can be viewed as an extension of the original impulse to vilify an innocent victim as "subversive of the communal order and as a threat to the well-being of the society."[61]

As we have seen, the great majority of tellings and retellings of this tale follow the logic of the text and the momentum of interpretive history in treating it as an account of Noah's victimization by his son Ham. How do we resist these forces and recover the voice of the true victim? Within the field of the orthodox interpretive paradigm, the victim's voice has been silenced by an overwhelming emphasis on his penchant for disorder. Even opponents of the curse, while questioning Noah's righteousness and acquitting his son of any crime, have rarely attended to Ham's voice. Meanwhile, advocates of the curse have usurped Ham's speech in order to argue that he is content with or complicitous in his own thralldom.[62] Redemption of the curse, then, will require us to listen for the voice of Ham, the scapegoat who falls victim to his brothers' mimetic rivalry. The imaginative retelling of the family's history that follows takes the perspective of its silent victim.

Noah's Dream

In the beginning, there was no victim, because there was no crime. But I was chosen to be a victim, so a crime had to be invented. That was the real crime. Let me tell you how it happened.

After God flooded the world, things settled down for those of us who survived. On the ark we had done a lot of arguing. In fact, the one thing we agreed on was that we couldn't wait to get off the boat and find some personal space. But when the waters subsided we faced an eerily silent, unfamiliar world. The animals must have been as frightened as we were, because they stayed pretty close as well.

Soon, life took on a routine. Dad started to tend grapes and learned to ferment them. He got into the habit of treating himself to the fruit of his labor at day's end. Nothing wrong with that, we all agreed. He'd been a good father, raised us right, got us through that extended family cruise without us drowning or suffocating in the stench of animal shit. Who were we to begrudge him this one little vice?

I only worried about him when he started having nightmares. How do I know about his dreams? I could hear him talk in his sleep. My tent was next to his and I was a light sleeper. My two older brothers shared a tent on the other side of the old man. But I doubt if they ever heard dad carrying on. They slept like babies, exhausted from their attempts to win his approval. I laughed it off at the time, not knowing how their sibling rivalry would affect me.

Anyway, from what I overheard at night, dad's dreams were mostly about the flood, in which, as you know, all our friends and neighbors drowned. He knew the Lord approved of that carnage, but he came to have reservations. Dad developed what you call survivor guilt, and it seemed to get the best of him when he went to bed drunk.

One night after we retired to our tents I was lying awake thinking about the day I would leave home. Eventually, dad started moaning in the usual way. But then I heard what sounded like an argument. I wondered who he could be talking to, so I poked my head out of the tent and into the night air. There I saw dad sprawled out on the ground, naked as a jay bird. He was chattering away in his sleep, and I wondered how I could cover him without waking him up.

From what I could glean, dad's dream took him back on the ark. He was discussing with God what sacrifice he would offer when we got through the flood. Dad's part of the conversation went something like this: "I thought you wanted them? No? Are you sure? Well, you certainly deserve them; see how young and strong they are, how virile, how righteous, how much like their father. I'll still have the youngest one; he's my favorite anyway. Clean animals are nice, sure, but after all you've done for us, you really deserve better. No? Well, how about just one of them."

None of this made any sense to me then. But looking back, I realize that dad was fed up with the way Shem and Japheth incessantly competed for his blessing. It got to where one didn't trust the other out of his sight, lest they pull ahead in the quest for Noah's favor. If one helped him harvest grapes, the other had to be there, too. If one got up early to go hunting, the other one was off behind him before his sandals were on. To be honest, when they left home together I half expected one of them to return with the guilty look Cain wore after taking care of Abel. Anyway, back to the story.

Dad's "conversation" became so animated that even Shem and Japheth woke up. Each assumed dad was in trouble and neither wanted the other to get credit for coming to his assistance. So side by side they stumbled toward us. Immediately, it occurred to me that I couldn't let them get near enough to hear dad talk about them this way. So I told them to find something we could use to cover the old man. One found a blanket, and the other grabbed it in an effort to secure part of the credit.

While they silently struggled for sole possession, I was thinking about what to do next. Just then, dad woke up and found me standing there staring dumbly at him. He opened his bloodshot eyes, looked up, and mumbled,

"You can't have that one." Then he grabbed his head, moaned, and went back to sleep. When the dynamic duo arrived with the blanket, I said, "I'll make sure each of you gets credited for that act of filial piety." Then we all went back to our tents. How was I to know that my days at home had already come to an end?

The next morning at the crack of dawn I awoke to the sound of dad preaching—the sort of thing he had done before the flood to warn our neighbors. When I realized he had decided to get on with the much-awaited paternal blessing, I laid there and thought to myself: "Finally, things will settle down around here." First he blessed Shem, the oldest—no surprise there—but then he blessed Japheth, too. "Hmm, that's clever," I thought. He threw in permission for Japheth to live in Shem's tents—just so they could keep an eye on each other, no doubt. That's when it got weird. Noah said something about how I was going to serve both of them. I laid there in stunned disbelief. What did I have to do with any of this?

Best I can figure, dad awoke in his birthday suit and through the fog of his hangover pieced together memories of the night before. He must have wondered how much of his little discussion with the Lord I had overheard. If I did know his secret, he wanted to make sure I wouldn't use it against him. So he went on the offensive. He claimed that I had dishonored him by laughing at his nakedness and telling my brothers about it. Of course, I did tell them, but only to keep them from hearing dad's ramblings about giving them back to the Lord! Exactly what he was accusing me of was unclear, but as time went on the story got more outlandish. The fact that dad had passed out naked that evening must have been a stimulant to my brothers' imaginations.

The story was full of inconsistencies, of course—they couldn't even decide whether it was me or Canaan who had threatened Noah's five-hundred-year-old manhood. But that didn't deter them. Shem and Japheth seemed happy to have the blessing matter settled so they could spend their energy on something more constructive—like ganging up on me. With all of them making sick accusations, and everyone starting to treat me like I was their slave or something, I decided to leave. I've never been home since, though I hear they tell some strange stories about me.

Noah's Curse and Revelation

When we follow this or some other path toward a clarification of Ham's identity as scapegoat, we gain a new perspective on Genesis 9:20–27's revelatory potential. If "the revelation of God is the disclosure of . . . the standpoint of the victim, who is always either innocent or arbitrarily chosen,"[63] then the story of Noah and his sons may be regarded as an adumbration of the willing victimhood of God's Christ. If the church fathers thought that Noah represented the suffering Christ and Ham those who mocked him, we now see Ham as the true type of Christ, the innocent victim who put an end to scapegoating by refusing to retaliate.[64]

The type is not the reality, of course: Ham is made a victim by the collusion of family members, and Jesus chooses victimhood to expose the violent foundations of his culture. Nevertheless, though Ham is not "the scapegoat for all" (as Girard claims for Jesus), his victimhood can be good news for a culture affected by racism and the biblical myths that sustain it. Nor is the Hamitic Christ without precedent. During the first few decades of the twentieth century, when lynching was a way of life in the United States, the African American was routinely depicted as a Christ figure subjected to persecution and crucifixion. In works of fiction—including W. E. B. Dubois's "Jesus Christ in Texas" and Countee Cullen's "The Black Christ"—and in paintings, sketches, and cartoons, black suffering was viewed through the prism of the crucified Jesus.[65] A Girardian reading of Genesis 9 enables us to do the same.

If we recast the story of Noah and his sons so that Ham's identity as victim is highlighted, how do we avoid making victimizers of the story's other characters? Helpful in this regard is the classical Jewish concept of Noahides.[66] The designation was developed by Jewish readers of the Hebrew Bible to refer generically to non-Jews. According to the logic of Genesis, however, all human beings are Noahides. Before we are Hamites, Semites, or Japhethites; Caucasians, Hispanics, or Asians; Jews, Christians, or Muslims; we are "sons of Noah." If we are all "sons of Noah," Genesis 9:20–27 suggests that we are all victims, all victimizers, all at the center of our own myths, all in need of rescue and redemption, all loved and favored by God, all revealed in our depravity by God's truth. Seen in this light, the designation "Noah's curse" not only displaces the stigma of guilt from Ham the innocent victim but also implies that the curse and the responsibility for redeeming it belong to all.

Of course, as this study has emphasized, Noah's curse is inscribed in a section of scripture that can function perniciously even without explicit reference to Genesis 9:20–27. Do our efforts to redeem the curse diminish the racist potential in the texts to which the curse has been linked?[67] If the story of Noah and his sons tells us more about Noah, Shem, and Japheth than about Ham, more about the origins of segregation and oppression in the scapegoating mechanism than about the derivation or subsequent history of human beings, then the postdiluvian history as a whole can be read anew, no longer chronicling God's plan for differentiation and physical separation, but desire's role in compromising the unity of creation. Regarding the theological message of Genesis 1–11, we arrive at the conclusion reached by Desmond Tutu, who speaks with authority for millions of victims of racist readings of Genesis. From the first chapters of the Bible, writes Tutu, "one learns that unity and wholeness were God's will for the creation. But this primal unity was disrupted by sin. The Genesis stories culminate in the shattering story of the Tower of Babel where human community and fellowship become impossible." This is the ultimate consequence, Tutu writes, "of sin, separation, alienation, apartness."[68] Tutu calls it "a perverse exegesis" that would see in the Tower of Babel "a justification for racial separation, a divine sanction for the diversity of nations." For this would be to confuse the divine intention for humankind with the divine punishment for sin. And that, Tutu declares, would be a fundamental misreading of the Bible.

12

Conclusion

Racism, Religion, and Responsible Scholarship

WHAT SHALL WE conclude from this study of American racism and its biblical dimensions? Several intellectual pitfalls must be avoided. One of these—the assumption that religious belief is not relevant for comprehending contemporary social problems—has caused scholars to overlook the evidence linking religion and racism. Since the 1950s, analysis of prejudice has been the province of the social sciences, and because social-scientists are wont to view religion as an epiphenomenal projection of more essential needs and desires, the social-scientific approach has failed to gauge the religious aspects of racial prejudice.

An instructive example of this failure is Elisabeth Young-Bruehl's *The Anatomy of Prejudices.* In this six-hundred-page-plus tome, Young-Bruehl proffers a neo-Freudian analysis of prejudice as a function of repressed desires. In her view, racism is a form of hysterical prejudice "that represents or symbolizes genital power or prowess and sexual desires by bodily features like skin color, thick hair, muscularity, or big breasts; it equates strength, size and darkness with primitivity, archaic and unrestrained sexual activity forbidden in civilization."[1] Apart from being virtually unfalsifiable (the repressed desires that purportedly underlie racism are not directly observable), Young-Bruel's definition excludes attention to the beliefs and traditions transmitted by religious communities. Thus, like social scientists in general, she cannot explain why scripture has so often been a touchstone for racist thinking and behavior, or why American readings of key biblical texts—texts that openly invite the sort of sexual projections she describes—are often conspicuously void of sexual content.

Those who succeed in keeping the religious dimensions of racism in view are vulnerable to other hazards. One is the scholarly axiom that religious traditions in general—and Christianity in particular—are intrinsically exclu-sivist.[2] Scholars who embrace this dictum assume that an inclusive and tol-erant society requires that the influence of religious ideas and institutions be limited. Such unexamined prejudices may be de rigueur in sectors of the academy, but they cannot survive critical examination.

Another trap looms for those who are determined to redeem religion by identifying the roots of theologically sanctioned racism. The quest for the fountainhead of religious racism has given rise to a spirited scholarly debate over whether Judaism, Christianity, or Islam is finally responsible for linking Noah's curse to skin color and thus providing the religious ideology under-girding modern racial slavery. This book includes much evidence that could be used to incriminate Jews and Christians alike; although Islamic readings of the curse have not been surveyed, it is also possible to connect Ham, black Africa, and slavery in the writings of Muslim exegetes beginning in the late medieval period.[3] But quests for the historical moment in which the purity of scripture was tainted by racist exegesis obscures the racist potency in mod-ern Bible readers and in the Bible itself.

A balanced scholarly method for studying the complex interconnections between religion and race must avoid these pitfalls on the road to understand-ing—based in unfounded assumptions that religion is irrelevant for compre-hending or alleviating social problems, that religion necessarily breeds racism, or that sacred texts provide no foothold for racist thinking. This book has sought to navigate a path between these hazards. In any case, it provides voluminous evidence that, whatever else may be said about the history and dynamics of American racism, its stubborn links with religion in general and scriptural traditions in particular should not be underestimated or approached simplistically. Given the apparent permanence of racism in the United States, the American revival of religion and spirituality, and the unlikely survival of biblical images in an otherwise secularized culture, it would be naive indeed to assume that the American mind has become resistant to racist readings of the Bible with the advent of a new millennium. If cultural expressions of these readings are subtler than in the past, the task of the scholar becomes that much more challenging—not to mention crucial.

Notes

Preface

1. The Palmer Memorial Tablet was unveiled on the occasion of the college's jubilee and inaugural celebration (November 26–28, 1925), during which dedicatory exercises for the new administration building were held in the newly completed Palmer Hall. An address by a member of the board of directors on "Benjamin Morgan Palmer, Father of Southwestern" followed. See W. Raymond Cooper, *Southwestern at Memphis 1848–1948* (Richmond, Va.: John Knox Press, 1949).

2. Letter of Benjamin M. Palmer to Rev. Dr. C. C. Hersman, dated May 27, 1889, in Burrow Library Archive, Rhodes College. I am indebted to Heather Lea Woods, who transcribed this letter.

3. Thomas Carey Johnson, *The Life and Letters of Benjamin Morgan Palmer* (1906; reprint, Edinburgh and Carlisle, Pa.: Banner of Truth Trust, 1987), 620.

4. Richard T. Hughes and C. Leonard Allen, *Illusions of Innocence: Protestant Primitivism in America, 1630–1875* (Chicago: University of Chicago Press, 1988).

5. Thomas V. Peterson, *Ham and Japheth in America: The Mythic World of Whites in the Antebellum South* (Metuchen, N.J.: American Theological Library Association, 1978).

6. Ibid., 110.

7. John F. A. Sawyer, *The Fifth Gospel: Isaiah in the History of Christianity* (New York: Cambridge University Press, 1996).

8. According to Sawyer, among the established scholarly approaches to the Bible that take seriously interpretive traditions are *Rezeptiongeschichte* (reception history), *Wirkungsgeschichte* (history of a text's effects), and reader-response criticism.

9. Sawyer, *The Fifth Gospel*, 13.

Chapter 1

1. Philip Martin, "Interracial Marriage Ban," *Morning Edition,* April 15, 1999.
2. The report included a spokesman for the Southern Baptist Convention who pointed out that the denomination had eschewed racism in its well-known 1995 statement on slavery and stated that "to wrap our prejudice in the Scripture is a sinful thing to do."
3. The letter is posted at http://www.multiracial.com (July 1999).
4. Ibid.
5. Benjamin Braude, letter to the author, January 24, 2001. See also Benjamin Braude, "The Sons of Noah and the Construction of Ethnic and Geographical Identities in the Medieval and Early Modern Periods," *William and Mary Quarterly* 54, no. 1 (1997): 120ff.
6. In W. E. B. Dubois's story "The Second Coming," "white," "black," and "yellow" bishops descend on Valdosta, Georgia, to greet the birth of the black Christ. In *Darkwater: Voices from within the Veil* (New York: Harcourt, Brace and Howe, 1920), 105–8.
7. I am indebted to Benjamin Braude for this observation.
8. According to the time line developed by Bishop James Ussher (1581–1656) and still widely accepted among fundamentalist Christians, Noah entered the ark in 2348 B.C.E. and died in 2006 B.C.E. Ussher dated the Tower of Babel episode at 2233 B.C.E. See Ferdinand Ruprecht, *Bible History References: Explanatory Notes on the "Advanced Bible History,"* vol. 1, *Old Testament Stories* (St. Louis: Concordia, 1947), 448.
9. Braude, "The Sons of Noah," 111, 112, 114. Braude concludes that "the racial identities [Noah's] sons have borne have been remarkably unstable. Shem, Ham and Japhet have been ever-changing projections of the likes and dislikes, hatreds and loves, prejudices and fears, needs and rationales through which society continually constructs and reconstructs its selves and its opposites" (142).
10. Harry Lacey, *God and the Nations* (New York: Loizeaux Brothers, 1947), 23. See also p. 24: "God thus apportioned the inheritance of the nations: He moved the Japhetic group of families to the northern parts of the earth, the group of families springing from Ham to the southern continents, the Semitic peoples to the central belt; and later Israel received the crown of the lands in the center of all when God had developed that nation from Abraham." In the twentieth century, Genesis 10 has been regarded as the key for understanding the origins of both nations (as in the preceding title) and races. See A. H. Sayce, *The Races of the Old Testament* (London: Religious Tract Society, 1925).
11. Nimrod's association with the Tower has meant that his geographical assignment among Bible readers has been fairly stable relative to the other descendants of Noah mentioned in Genesis 10. The link between Nimrod and Babel has been encouraged by interpreters who note that "Nimrud" was an ancient city in Mesopotamia.
12. Benjamin Braude characterizes the evidence from these texts this way: "The language is allusive and unclear. Clear references to black skin or negroid features are absent. The statements may be metaphorical and not physical" (letter to the author, January 24, 2001).

13. Origen, "Genesis Homily XVI," in *Homilies on Genesis and Exodus,* trans. Ronald E. Heine (Washington: Catholic University of America Press, 1982), 215.

14. Augustine writes: "It is with justice, we believe, that the condition of slavery is the result of sin. And this is why we do not find the word 'slave' in any part of Scripture until righteous Noah branded the sin of his son with this name. It is a name, therefore, introduced by sin and not by nature." *City of God,* 19:15, in Philip Schaff, ed., *A Select Library of the Nicene and Post-Nicene Fathers of the Christian Church,* vol. 2, *St. Augustine's City of God and Christian Doctrine* (Grand Rapids, Mich.: Eerdmans, 1955). Augustine interprets the curse of slavery thus: The good make skillful use of the wicked for their own training in endurance or for their own development in wisdom. Augustine's view was adopted by Pope Gelasius I, John Chrysostom, and others and was resurrected among American Catholic slavery advocates in the nineteenth century. See *Letters of the Late Bishop England to The Hon. John Forsyth, on the Subject of Domestic Slavery: To Which are Prefixed Copies, in Latin and English, of the Pope's Apostolic Letter, Concerning the Atlantic Slave Trade, With Some Introductory Remarks, Etc.* (New York: Negro Universities Press, 1969), 23–24.

15. Jean Devisse, *The Image of the Black in Western Art,* vol. 2, part 1, trans. William Granger Ryan (Cambridge: Harvard University Press, 1979), 18.

16. Werner Sollors, *Neither Black nor White yet Both: Thematic Explorations of Interracial Literature* (New York: Oxford University Press, 1997), 87. The text of Ephrem cited by Sollors may be pseudepigraphical.

17. See, e.g., David H. Aaron, "Early Rabbinic Exegesis on Noah's Son Ham and the So-Called 'Hamitic Myth,' " *Journal of the American Academy of Religion* 63, no. 4 (1995): 721–59; Steven L. McKenzie, "Response: The Curse of Ham and David H. Aaron," *Journal of the American Academy of Religion* 65, no. 1 (1997): 183–86; Paul Freedman, *Images of the Medieval Peasant* (Stanford, Calif.: Stanford University Press, 1999); Ephraim Isaac, "Genesis, Judaism, and the 'Sons of Ham,' " in *Slaves and Slavery in Muslim Africa,* ed. John Ralph Willis (London: F. Cass, 1985) 1:75–91, and "Ham" in *The Anchor Bible Dictionary,* ed. David Noel Freedman (New York: Doubleday, 1992); David M. Goldenberg, "The Curse of Ham: A Case of Rabbinic Racism?" in Jack Salzman and Cornel West, eds., *Struggles in the Promised Land: Toward a History of Black-Jewish Relations in the United States* (New York: Oxford University Press, 1997), 21–52; and Charles B. Copher, "Blacks and Jews in Historical Interaction: The Biblical/African Experience," *Journal of the Interdenominational Theological Center* 3 (1975): 9–16.

18. See Devisse, *Image of the Black,* 143. Devisse writes that the genealogy of Christ from the Cathedral of St. Patroklus, Soest (ca. 1230) portrays the family of Cush as blacks, "recognizable by their profile and the conventional details of the hair, and like the text, locates them in Ethiopia, 'which today is called Africa.' "

19. Braude, "The Sons of Noah," 132.

20. See William McKee Evans, "From the Land of Canaan to the Land of Guinea: The Strange Odyssey of the 'Sons of Ham,' " *American Historical Review* 85, no. 1 (1980): 26: "More than ten centuries separate the appearance of the story of Ham in the book of Genesis from the elaboration and explanation of the tale that occurs in rabbinic literature. During these centuries the face of servitude had darkened in the Near East."

21. This story will be clarified in Benjamin Braude's forthcoming book, *Sex, Slavery, and Racism: The Secret History of Noah and His Sons.*

22. Some scholars date the emergence of racial interpretations of Genesis 9:20–27 in Europe to the sixteenth or early seventeenth centuries. See, e.g, Winthrop Jordan, *White over Black: American Attitudes toward the Negro, 1550–1812* (Chapel Hill: University of North Carolina Press, 1968). Gene Rice locates the curse's European origins in the publication of J. L. Hannemann's *Curiosum scrutinum nigridinis filiorum Cahm* ("Curious Inquiry into the Blackness of the Children of Ham"), published in 1677. See "The Curse That Never Was (Genesis 9:18–27)," *Journal of Religious Thought* 29, no. 1 (1972): 27 n. 117. More controversially, Ivan Hannaford traces the origins of the racial idea in Western thought to the twelfth-century Jewish philosopher Moses Maimonides. See *Race: The History of an Idea in the West* (Baltimore: Johns Hopkins University Press, 1996), 112.

23. See Louis Ruchames, ed., *Racial Thought in America,* vol. 1, *From the Puritans to Abraham Lincoln* (Boston: University of Massachusetts Press, 1969), 47–58.

24. Ibid., 53.

25. William Summer Jenkins, cited in Randy J. Sparks, "Mississippi's Apostle of Slavery: James Smylie and the Biblical Defense of Slavery," *Journal of Mississippi History* 51 (1989): 100 n. 26.

26. Among scholars of the curse, Thomas Peterson comes closest to illuminating these themes in *Ham and Japeth in America: The Mythic World of Whites in the Antebellum South* (Metuchen, N.J.: American Theological Library Association, 1978). He notes that those who invoked Noah's curse "all agreed that Ham had dishonored his father," but he concludes that Ham's real offense was "an attack against the authority of the family and thereby against God's chosen institution for governing the human race" (49). He also analyzes the "oppositions" in the antebellum myth of Ham, which include "Ham act[ing] like a foolish child (laughing, and joking about his father)" and "Ham act[ing] like a villain (the heinous sexual crime)" (117–121). But Peterson does not tie what he calls the "dominant political, social and religious ideas of the Old South" to the conceptions of Ham's transgression that prevailed among Southern Bible readers.

27. See, e.g., Malcolm Ritter, "In South, Insulting a White Guy Can Get You a Black Eye," *Salt Lake Tribune,* 15 July 1996; and Cynthia Tucker, "Road Rage, Southern Style," *Memphis Commercial Appeal,* 29 November 1999.

28. Mark Twain, *Life on the Mississippi by Mark Twain. Illustrated by Thomas Hart Benton. With an Introduction by Edward Wagenknecht, and a Number of Previously Suppressed Passages, Now Printed for the First Time, and Edited with a Note by Willis Wager* (New York: Heritage Press, 1959), 272. See also Clement Eaton, *The Growth of Southern Civilization, 1790–1860* (New York: Harper Brothers, 1961), 318–20.

29. Edward Wagenknecht, "Introduction," in ibid., xiii.

30. In *The Mind of the Old South* (Baton Rouge: Louisiana State University Press, 1964), Clement Eaton confirmed and expanded Osterweis's argument. Eaton's emphasis on Southern honor is significantly greater in this and other works subsequent to his *A History of the Old South* (New York: Macmillan, 1949).

31. Orlando Patterson, *Slavery and Social Death: A Comparative Study* (Cambridge: Harvard University Press, 1982), 95. According to Patterson, Franklin argued that "the institution of slavery had a profound effect on Southern character" (66) and began to draw a connection between the martial spirit and slavery, in which honor, too, is implicated.

32. Clement Eaton, "The Role of Honor in Southern Society," *Southern Humanities Review* 10 (1976, supplement): 47–58; Bertram Wyatt-Brown, *Southern Honor: Ethics and Behavior in the Old South* (New York: Oxford University Press, 1982), and *Honor and Violence in the Old South* (New York: Oxford University Press, 1986); and Patterson, *Slavery and Social Death.*

   See also Kenneth S. Greenberg, *Honor and Slavery: Lies, Duels, Noses, Masks, Dressing as a Woman, Gifts, Strangers, Humanitarianism, Death, Slave Rebellions, the Proslavery Argument, Baseball, Hunting, and Gambling in the Old South* (Princeton, N.J.: Princeton University Press, 1996); Steven M. Stowe, *Intimacy and Power in the Old South: Ritual in the Lives of the Planters* (Baltimore: Johns Hopkins University Press, 1987); John Hope Franklin, *The Militant South: 1800–1861* (Cambridge: Harvard University Press, 1956); Ted Ownby, *Subduing Satan: Religion, Recreation and Manhood in the Rural South, 1865–1920* (Chapel Hill: University of North Carolina Press, 1990); Christine Leigh Heyrman, *Southern Cross: The Beginnings of the Bible Belt* (Chapel Hill and London: University of North Carolina Press, 1997); and Michael P. Johnston, "Planters and Patriarchy: Charleston, 1800–1860," *Journal of Southern History* 46, no. 1 (1980): 45–72.

33. Wyatt-Brown, *Honor and Violence in the Old South,* ix, 17.

34. John W. Blassingame, *The Slave Community: Plantation Life in the Antebellum South* (New York: Oxford University Press, 1972). William McKee Evans ("From the Land of Canaan to the Land of Guinea," 22) suggests the psychological appeal of the Sambo stereotype by observing that it was shared by ancient Roman, Greek, and Hebrew masters.

35. Blassingame, *The Slave Community,* 134. See also Patterson, *Slavery and Social Death,* 79. Patterson regards the antebellum Sambo stereotype ("the typical plantation slave, [who] was docile but irresponsible, loyal but lazy, humble but chronically given to lying and stealing; his behavior was full of infantile silliness and his talk inflated with childish exaggeration"—Stanley Elkins) as "simply an elaboration of the notion that the slave is quintessentially a person without honor" (*Slavery and Social Death,* 96).

36. Theodore Dwight Weld, *The Bible against Slavery: An Inquiry into the Patriarchal and Mosaic Systems on the Subject of Human Rights* (New York: American Anti-Slavery Society, 1838).

37. Mark A. Noll, "The Bible and Slavery," in *Religion and the American Civil War,* ed. Randall M. Miller, Harry S. Stout, and Charles Reagan Wilson (New York: Oxford University Press, 1998), 62. Noll continues: "Occasional theologians like Philip Schaff or Rabbi Raphal might be willing to speculate on the relevance of the passage to the modern situation of American slaves. But most elite theologians had long since dismissed that kind of application in favor of a reading that saw the prophecy fulfilled when the children of Israel conquered the Promised Land."

38. Eugene D. Genovese, *A Consuming Fire: The Fall of the Confederacy in the Mind of the White Christian South,* Mercer University Lamar Memorial Lectures 41 (Athens and London: University of Georgia Press, 1998), 81. In addition to John Henley Thornwell and Robert L. Dabney, Presbyterians J. B. Adger and George Howe were reluctant to apply the curse to racial slavery.

39. Eugene D. Genovese, letter to the author, 29 May 1998.

40. In the passage quoted, Weld continues: "But closely as they cling to it, 'cursed by Canaan' is a poor drug to stupify a throbbing conscience—a mocking lullaby,

vainly wooing slumber to unquiet tossings, and crying 'Peace, be still,' where God wakes war and breaks his thunders."

41. Thomas V. Peterson, *Ham and Japheth in America: The Mythic World of Whites in the Antebellum South* (Metuchen, N.J.: American Theological Library Association, 1978), 117.

42. Ibid., 48. According to Peterson, the story of Ham's curse was thought to account for the supposed inferiority of blacks emphasized by scientific racists during the nineteenth century, while also explaining the black color of Ham's descendants (*Ham and Japheth*, 70). Peterson writes that "there is no question that Ham was popularly identified as the progenitor of the black race, especially among those people who accepted the Bible as the literal word of God that to some degree prophesied future events," and claims to have discovered only one antebellum Southern clergyman who unequivocally rejected Ham as the progenitor of the black race (102).

43. W. E. B. Dubois, " 'The Servant in the House,' " in *Darkwater*, 113.

44. Noll, "The Bible and Slavery," 66. Noll is undoubtedly correct that racist assumptions about Africans functioned as a "hidden hand" in the process of proslavery biblical exegesis. But this hidden hand was less intrusive in the case of Genesis 9, because the text itself was assumed to elucidate the destinies of humankind's three great races.

45. Among the antebellum proslavery writers who believed that Genesis 9 was concerned as much with racial differentiation as with slavery were Josiah Priest, who exercised a tremendous influence in the South, T. R. R. Cobb, and J. R. Graves. On Cobb, see Eugene D. Genovese, *"Slavery Ordained of God": The Southern Slaveholders' View of Biblical History and Modern Politics*, Twenty-fourth Annual Fortenbaugh Memorial Lecture (Gettysburg, Pa.: Gettysburg College, 1985), 12ff. On Graves, see Harold S. Smith, "J. R. Graves," in *Baptist Theologians*, ed. Timothy George and David S. Dockery (Nashville: Broadman Press, 1990), 234–36.

46. Genovese writes that "not until after the fall of the Confederacy did a racial-imperialist ideology emerge in full force, as the South adapted to the values and policies of a triumphant Yankeedom. Indeed, in essential respects, the Southern embrace of imperialism represented a substitute for—and a betrayal of—the ideals and visions of the proslavery worldview, although it was tailor-made for a New South bent on continuing the racial subordination of blacks" (*A Consuming Fire*, 92).

47. Though Methodists and Baptists were numerically dominant among Southern Protestants, Presbyterians and Episcopalians exercised an inordinate influence on Southern culture. Presbyterians in particular controlled many educational institutions in the Old South, including ostensibly public universities.

48. James Oscar Farmer Jr., *The Metaphysical Confederacy: James Henley Thornwell and the Synthesis of Southern Values* (Macon, Ga.: Mercer University Press, 1986), 117, 263.

49. Mitchell Snay, *Gospel of Disunion: Religion and Separatism in the Antebellum South* (Cambridge: Cambridge University Press, 1993).

50. Ibid. Generally, Snay observes, those who exploited the Old Testament in arguing for Southern secession viewed contemporary conflicts in the light of Israel's history under prophets, judges, and kings. The division of the Israelite kingdom following the death of Solomon was the passage most often cited among Southern preachers as a biblical precedent for disunion. According to Snay, Israel's "national division

along sectional lines of North and South understandably captured the imagination of Southern Protestants" (192). However, while seemingly apropos of the South's political situation, Jereboam's rebellion (1 Kings 12) was limited in applicability by its "historical" nature.

Particularly in the Presbyterian context, the appeal to the primeval history of Genesis was fortuitous. As James Oscar Farmer has shown, it was precisely as the Civil War loomed that the standard Presbyterian view of the relationship of church and state moved away from theocracy—with ancient Israelite society as paradigm—toward the doctrine of "the spirituality of the church." This meant that appeals to texts from the history of Israelite theocracy would gradually lose their authority among Southern Presbyterians. See Farmer, *Metaphysical Confederacy*, 256ff.

51. Genovese, *A Consuming Fire*, 160 n. 7.
52. When Palmer wrote that "the outspreading landscape of all history is embraced within the camera of Noah's brief prophecy," it is not clear what sort of instrument he imagined. Since the first successful photographic process had been made public in 1839, it is possible that Palmer had in mind a primitive version of the modern camera. Yet the image works better if we view "Noah's camera" as a telescopic lens capable of capturing small or distant objects and making them discernible to the human eye. According to this understanding, the person who peered through Noah's "camera" was privileged to a perspective on human history very close to God's own.
53. On pre-Adamism, see Michael Barkun, *Religion and the Racist Right: The Origins of the Christian Identity Movement* (Chapel Hill: University of North Carolina Press, 1997), 150–56.
54. Ibid., 150.
55. Ibid., 161–62. This is also true of the earlier two-seedline view associated with Daniel Parker and William Branham, who viewed Ham, along with Cain, Ahab, and Judas Iscariot as representatives of the seed of Satan.
56. The former view is articulated in H. Ben-Judah, *When? A Prophetical Novel of the Very Near Future* (Vancouver, B.C.: British Israel Association of Greater Vancouver, 1944). The latter is fostered by the Aryan Nations and Church of Jesus Christ Christian in Hayden Lake, Idaho. See Barkun, *Religion and the Racist Right*, 177, 131.
57. In the nineteenth century, Joseph Smith published the view that Cain entered into a secret covenant with the Devil, and Dominick M'Causland portrayed Cain as a "strong-minded resolute man, endowed with capacity and attainments superior to those of his new associates," over whom he quickly gained ascendancy. In the early twentieth century, Ellen Bristowe argued that Cain became the "leader, teacher and absolute lord and master of an inferior race," and Frederick Haberman associated him with the production of physical giants. More recently, Identity writers have imagined Cain as the founder of the first "Super World government," the leader of a satanic rebellion against God, the originator of idolatry, and the first to institute cannibalism. See Barkun, *Religion and the Racist Right*, 154–55, 166–67.
58. As Barkun (ibid., 193) makes clear, the group known as the Covenant, Sword and the Arm of the Lord represents an important exception to this observation.
59. James L. Kugel, *The Bible as It Was* (Cambridge: Harvard University Press, 1997), 108.
60. See Barkun, *Religion and the Racist Right*, 142.

61. Interview with Thom Robb in the documentary film *Blood in the Face,* by Anne Bohlen, Kevin Rafferty, and James Ridgeway (Right Thinking Productions, 1986).

62. See *Human Relations and the South African Scene in the Light of Scripture* (Cape Town: Dutch Reformed Church Publishers, 1976), 19: "There is no Scriptural basis for relating the subordinate position of some present day peoples to the curse on Canaan. . . . It simply is not true that Ham and all his descendants were for ever cursed: in the first place, the curse was specifically limited to Canaan and therefore does not apply to the other sons of Ham."

63. Cited in Willem Vorster, "The Bible and Aparteid 1," in John W. DeGruchy and Charles Villa-Vicencio, *Apartheid Is a Heresy* (Grand Rapids, Mich.: Eerdmans, 1983), 102. The NGK report was the final product of a commission constituted by the General Synod in 1970.

64. *Human Relations and the South African Scene,* 14.

65. Ibid., 15–16.

66. Ibid., 18.

67. Recognizing the role of Babel in the religious defense of apartheid, opponents have focused on passages such as Zeph. 3:9, 11, and Isa. 66:9–11, texts in which the Lord promises that when the process of salvation is fulfilled, the curse of Babel will be reversed. See Douglas Bax, "The Bible and Apartheid 2," in *Apartheid Is a Heresy,* 124. In addition, the story of Pentecost can be read as a reversal of Babel, in contrast to the Afrikaner interpretation that sees it as a reaffirmation of Babel's message. Biblical critic Gunther Wittenberg provides another gloss on Genesis 11, based on his socioeconomic analysis of Genesis 9 and 10: "In the present South African system the true children of Ham are not the blacks. They are much more like the 'apiru, the "Hebrews" of the ancient Near East. The true children of Ham are the whites who have attempted to erect a new Tower of Babel in their 'system' of exploitation and oppression." Gunther Wittenberg, "Let Canaan Be His Slave" (Genesis 9:26). Is Ham Also Cursed?" *Journal of Theology for Southern Africa* 74 (1991): 55.

Chapter 2

1. According to an early Aramaic version of the Hebrew Bible, "Noah learned by revelation in a dream what had been done to him by his son. . . ." See Jack P. Lewis, *A Study of the Interpretation of Noah and the Flood in Jewish and Christian Literature* (Leiden: E. J. Brill, 1968), 98.

2. See Louis Ginzberg, *The Legends of the Jews,* vol. 1, *Bible Times and Characters from the Creation to Jacob,* trans. Henrietta Szold (Philadelphia: Jewish Publication Society of America, 1968), 145: "When [Noah] was taken from the hand of the midwife, he opened his mouth and praised the Lord of righteousness. His father Lamech . . . said . . . 'I have begotten a strange son . . . [who] resembles the children of the angels of heaven, and his nature is different, and he is not like us, and his eyes are as the rays of the sun, and his countenance is glorious.' " Within the biblical canon, Noah is often alluded to as an outstanding example of righteousness. See, e.g., Ezek. 14:14.

3. Ibid., 169.

4. "As Ham was made to suffer requital for his irreverence, so Shem and Japheth

received a reward for the filial, deferential way in which they . . . covered the na-kedness of their father. Though Shem and Japheth both showed themselves to be dutiful and deferential, yet it was Shem who deserved the larger meed of praise. He was the first to set about covering his father." See Ginzberg, *Legends of the Bible* (Philadelphia: Jewish Publication Society of America, 1956), 81. One rabbinic text suggests Shem and Japheth covered their father with their prayer cloaks. See Lewis, *A Study of the Interpretation of Noah and the Flood*, 153.

5. Robert Graves and Raphael Patai, *Hebrew Myths: The Book of Genesis* (New York: Greenwich House, 1983), 121.

6. Ginzberg, *Legends of the Bible*, 80; Graves and Patai, *Hebrew Myths*, 121

7. Ginzberg, *Legends of the Bible*, 79. The reference here is to the *Babylonian Talmud, Tractate Sanhedrin*. The charge that Ham could not remain continent on the ark appears in Islamic sources as well.

8. See Jacob Neusner, ed., *Genesis Rabbah: The Judaic Commentary to the Book of Genesis, A New American Translation*, vol. 2 (Atlanta: Scholars Press, 1985), 33.

9. Werner Sollors finds this tradition in *Sachsenspiegel* (ca. 1200). See *Neither Black nor White yet Both: Thematic Explorations of Interracial Literature* (New York: Oxford University Press, 1997).

10. Neusner, *Genesis Rabbah*, 33.

11. Ginzberg, *Legends of the Bible*, 80. Not surprisingly, passages such as these have led scholars to view rabbinic reflections on Genesis 9 as the ultimate source for identification of Ham's descendants with black Africa. But although such readings represent a clear precedent for modern racializing interpretations of the passage, care is required in interpreting them. See especially David H. Aaron, "Early Rabbinic Exegesis on Noah's Son Ham and the So-Called 'Hamitic' Myth,'" *Journal of the American Academy of Religion* 63, no. (1995): 721–59, for a discussion of this and other rabbinic passages dealing with Ham and their usefulness for understanding European views of Africans.

12. Stephen Gero, "The Legend of the Fourth Son of Noah," *Harvard Theological Review* 73 (1980): 322.

13. Cited in James L. Kugel, *The Bible as It Was* (Cambridge: Harvard University Press, 1997), 115. As Kugel notes, the image of Noah the preacher was adopted by a variety of Jewish and Christian authors.

14. Lewis, *A Study of the Interpretation of Noah and the Flood*, 31.

15. Ibid., 40.

16. Ibid., 56, 57, 72, 73. Kugel, *The Bible as It Was*, 116.

17. In Ivan Hannaford, *Race: The History of an Idea in the West* (Baltimore: Johns Hopkins University Press, 1996), 91.

18. Ibid., 94–95. Berossus was rediscovered when an anthology of his "missing volumes" was published in 1498 by Annius of Viterbo.

19. Cited in Sollors, *Neither Black nor White*, 87.

20. "The Divine Institutes" ch. xiv, in *The Ante-Nicene Fathers*, vol. 7 (New York: Charles Scribner's Sons, 1926), 63. Clement wrote that Noah, "being found faithful, preached regeneration to the world through his ministry"; thus he was preserved so that he "might anew repair the world." See "Recognitions of Clement," Book I, ch. xxx, in *The Ante-Nicene Fathers*, vol. 7, 137; and "The First Epistle of Clement," ch. viii in *The Ante-Nicene Fathers*, vol, 1, 7. See also Irenaeus, "Against Heresies," in Cyril Richardson, ed. and trans. *Early Christian Fathers*, vol. 1 (Phil-

adelphia: Westminster, 1953), 368. As Jack Lewis points out, Marcion's vilification of Noah and denial of his salvation are unique in the classical Christian tradition (*A Study of the Interpretation of Noah and the Flood*, 110).

21. Justin Martyr, "Dialogue with Trypho," ch. cxxxvii, in *The Ante-Nicene Fathers*, vol. 1, 268.

22. See Origen, "Genesis Homily II," in *Homilies on Genesis and Exodus*, trans. Ronald E. Heine (Washington: Catholic University of America Press, 1982), 72–88. Origen's second homily on Genesis is an extended exposition on the story of Noah's ark and its spiritual significance. Origen perceived Noah as a type of Christ and the biblical description of the ark as an extended Christian allegory.

23. In the Reformation era, this symbolic view of the ark reappeared in "The Second Helvetic Confession" (1566): "For as there was no salvation outside Noah's ark when the world perished in the flood; so we believe that there is no certain salvation outside Christ, who offers himself to be enjoyed by the elect in the Church. . . ." See *The Constitution of the Presbyterian Church (U.S.A), Part I: The Book of Confessions* (Louisville, Ky.: Office of the General Assembly, 1996), 90.

24. Dom Cameron Allen, *The Legend of Noah: Renaissance Rationalism in Art, Science and Letters* (Urbana: University of Illinois Press, 1963), 155–56.

25. See, e.g., Cyprian of Carthage, *On Christian Doctrine*. Jerome noted that as Noah planted a vineyard, Christ planted the church and suffered, and identified Ham's attitude toward his father with the Jews' attitude toward the cross. According to Augustine, that Noah's nakedness occurred in his house typified the treatment Jesus received from his own nation. That the two sons went backward symbolized the turning back on the sins of the Jews, which one does when reverencing the passion. See Lewis, *A Study of the Interpretation of Noah and the Flood*, 177–78. These fathers contributed to a long Christian tradition—extending at least through the fifteenth century—that linked Ham and unbelieving Jews.

26. Augustine, "City of God," XVI: 2, in Philip Schaff, ed., *A Select Library of the Nicene and Post-Nicene Fathers of the Christian Church Series*, 8 vols. (Grand Rapids, Mich.: Eerdmans, 1955). On-line version at www.ccel.org.

27. Ibid.

28. Ibid. Vincent of Lerins offered a similar interpretation of Ham as the father of mockers and heretics in the church. See Lewis, *A Study of the Interpretation of Noah and the Flood*, 179.

29. "City of God," XVI: 2, in Schaff, *Select Library*. On-line version at www.ccel.org. The passage continues: "And therefore was Ham cursed in his son, he being, as it were, his fruit. So, too, this son of his, Canaan, is fitly interpreted 'their movement,' which is nothing else than their work. But Shem and Japheth, that is to say, the circumcision and uncircumcision, or, as the apostle otherwise calls them, the Jews and Greeks, but called and justified, having somehow discovered the nakedness of their father (which signifies the Saviour's passion), took a garment and laid it upon their backs, and entered backwards and covered their father's nakedness, without their seeing what their reverence hid. For we both honor the passion of Christ as accomplished for us, and we hate the crime of the Jews who crucified Him. The garment signifies the sacrament, their backs the memory of things past: for the church celebrates the passion of Christ as already accomplished, and no longer to be looked forward to, now that Japheth already dwells in the habitations of Shem, and their wicked brother between them. But the wicked

brother is, in the person of his son (i.e., his work), the boy, or slave, of his good brothers, when good men make a skillful use of bad men, either for the exercise of their patience or for their advancement in wisdom."

30. Lewis, *A Study of the Interpretation of Noah and the Flood,* 178. In the Carolingian era, Rabanus Marus interpreted Ham and his posterity as representing those who do not believe in Christ. See Jean Devisse, *The Image of the Black in Western Art,* vol. 2 part 1, trans. William Granger Ryan (Cambridge: Harvard University Press, 1976–79) 221 n. 175.

31. Sollors, *Neither Black nor White,* 84–85.

32. This view is expressed in *Genesis Rabbah.* In answer to the question, "should Ham be the one who sinned yet Canaan be cursed?" R Judah said, "It is because it is said, 'And God blessed Noah and his sons' (Gen. 9:1). Now there cannot be a cursing where there has been a blessing. Accordingly, he said, 'Cursed be Canaan' " (Neusner, *Genesis Rabbah,* 33).

33. See Justin Martyr, "Dialogue with Trypho," in *The Ante-Nicene Fathers,* vol. 1, 269; and Andrew Willet, *Hexapla in Genesin* (London: Tho. Creede, 1608), 104.

34. Ambrose concurs, writing that "the one who mocked him remained exposed to the shame of everlasting disgrace" (Lewis, *A Study of the Interpretation of Noah and the Flood,* 118). Charles Copher sees in Irenaeus the beginning of the influence of the Septuagint and rabbinic commentary on Gentile readings of the curse. See his "Three Thousand Years of Biblical Interpretation with Reference to Black Peoples," *Journal of the Interdenominational Theological Center* 13 (Spring 1986): 233.

35. Hannaford, *Race,* 95.

36. "Divine Institutes," ch. XIV, in *The Ante-Nicene Fathers,* vol. 7, 63.

37. Origen, "Genesis Homily XVI," in *Homilies on Genesis and Exodus,* 215.

38. "Recognitions of Clement," Book IV, ch. xxvii, in *Ante-Nicene Fathers,* vol, 8, 140. Pierre Bayle ascribes to John Cassian (ca. 360–435) the view that Ham, not daring to bring his magic books with him in the ark, carved their main dogmas on very hard bodies that could resist the waters of the Flood.

39. "Recognitions of Clement," Book I, chs. xxx–xxxi, in *Ante-Nicene Fathers,* vol. 8, 85–86.

40. Allen, *Legend of Noah,* 77.

41. According to some patristic readings, the curse on Ham's descendants was removed in the conversion of the Ethiopian eunuch to Christianity (Acts 8:26–40). See Devisse, *The Image of the Black in Western Art,* vol. 2, part I, 21.

42. Andrew Horn's *Mirror of Justices* (late thirteenth century) recorded that "serfage, according to some, comes from the curse which Noah pronounced against Canaan, the son of his son Ham, and against his issue." In David Brion Davis, *The Problem of Slavery in Western Culture* (Ithaca, N.Y.: Cornell University Press, 1966), 97.

43. Sollors, *Neither Black nor White,* 83.

44. Ibid., 85.

45. In Albert B. Friedman, " 'When Adam Delved . . . ': Contexts of an Historic Proverb," in Larry D. Benson, ed., *The Larned and the Lewed: Studies in Chaucer and Medieval Literature,* Harvard English Studies 5 (Cambridge: Harvard University Press, 1974), 227–229. The matter of how an African Ham could be the progenitor of European servants was addressed by *The Boke of St. Albans* (1486), which declared that after cursing Ham, Noah assigned him the northern part of the world, Japheth Asia, and Shem Africa (229).

46. Ibid., 228.

47. Allen, *Legend of Noah,* 139.

48. Ibid., 73.

49. See Francis Lee Utley, "Noah's Ham and Jansen Enikel," *Germanic Review* (1941): 241–49.

50. Cited in ibid., 241. An expanded, more fanciful version of the legend occurs in Jansen Enikel's *Weltcrhonik* (ca. 1276). The theme of Ham's inability to remain celibate on the ark was part of medieval Jewish midrashic collections and seems to have come into Christian tradition fairly early. According to Louis Ginzberg, the story was used by Philo Judaeus, Origen, the Ethiopic *Book of Adam,* and Ephraem Syrus, among others. (See ibid., 243.)

51. Ibid., 248. Utley continues: "Magicians themselves encouraged the belief in order to give their art the sanction of antiquity. Ham's role as preserver of the tradition appears in the widely circulated *Sefer-ha-Yashar* (probably written by a Spanish Jew in the Twelfth Century) and in Clement of Alexandria, who attributes to Ham a *Book of Prophecies* on the authority of the Gnostic Isidore. . . . Ham's magic, like the command to continence on the ark, goes back to Jewish tradition. . . ."

52. Cited in Benjamin Braude, "The Sons of Noah and the Construction of Ethnic and Geographical Identities in the Medieval and Early Modern Periods," *William and Mary Quarterly* 54, no. 1 (1997): 117.

53. "Lectures on Genesis, Chapter IX," in *Luther's Works,* 55 vols., ed. Jaroslav Pelikan (St. Louis: Concordia, 1955), 2:165. Despite his high regard for the patriarch, Luther does not defend Noah's lapse into drunkenness as the result of inexperience with wine. In fact, Luther thinks "Noah was not unfamiliar with the nature of this juice and, together with his family, often made use of wine before this. . . ." Noah's inebriated state Luther "simply cannot excuse." However, Luther finds it odd that, given Noah's "outstanding achievements over the course of so many years," Moses records only "this . . . silly and altogether unprofitable little story" of Noah's drunkenness. At this point in his commentary, Luther sounds a theme that would become common parlance among interpreters influenced by the Reformation: "But the intention of the Holy Spirit [in prompting Moses to record this story] is familiar from our teaching. He wanted the godly, who know their weakness and for this reason are disheartened, to take comfort in the offense that comes from the account of the lapses among the holiest and most perfect patriarchs" (166).

54. Luther's emphasis on Ham's laughter extends to his descendants, who "laugh at the punishment [announced in the curse] and make a joke of the threats that they hear from their parent Noah" (ibid., 220).

55. Ibid., 172, 186.

56. Ibid., 175. See also 180, 212.

57. Ibid., 185. Interestingly, Luther interprets Ham's name this way: "I believe that this name was given to him by his father because of the great hope he had formed about his youngest son, as though in comparison with him the other two were cold."

58. Ibid., 176. For a discussion of Luther's role in perpetuating racist readings of Genesis 9, see L. Richard Bradley, "The Curse of Canaan and the American Negro," *Concordia Theological Monthly* 42 (Fall 1971): 100–110.

59. John Calvin, *Commentaries on the First Book of Moses Called Genesis,* 2 vols., trans. John King (Grand Rapids, Mich.: Eerdmans, 1948), 1:302.

60. Ibid., 304.
61. Ibid., 301.
62. Ibid., 304.
63. Ibid., 301.
64. Andrew Willet, *Hexapla in Genesin* (London: Tho, Creede, 1608), 105–06. Raphael Holinshed (d. ca. 1580), drawing on an anthology of the "missing volumes" of Berossus published at the end of the fifteenth century, claimed Britain had been settled by the giant Albion, a descendant of Ham. Ham himself Holinshed described as a sorcerer and giant descended from Cain. The Hamites taught witchcraft, sorcery, and buggery and were wiped out by the Trojan leader Brutus. See Hannaford, *Race*, 163–64.
65. Abraham Rosse, *An Exposition on the Fourteene First Chapters of Genesis, by Way of Question and Answere, Collected Out of Ancient and Recent Writers: Both Briefely and Subtilly Propounded and Expounded* (London: B. A. and T. F., 1626), 54.
66. Ibid., 58. Meanwhile, Rosse casts Noah's sons as types of the pious and infidel: As Shem and Japheth covered Noah's nakedness, so Joseph and Nicodemus covered Christ's body; as Ham was cursed for scorning his father, the Jews are accursed for killing their savior. Also in keeping with tradition is Rosse's rendering of Noah as a picture of industry, chastity, and temperance; he did "not sinne in drinking . . . [since] he was exceeding olde and weake at this time, therefore was quickly ouercome."
67. Ibid., 61.
68. See Devisse, *The Image of the Black in Western Art*, 217. The map is part of Schledel's *Nuremberg Chronicle* (1493).
69. Cited in Sollors, *Neither Black nor White*, 93.
70. Benjamin Braude argues that there are more white Cushites in medieval art than black. See his forthcoming *Sex, Slavery, and Racism: The Secret History of Noah and His Sons*.
71. See Schledel's *Nuremberg Chronicle* (1493) in Devisse, *The Image of the Black in Western Art*, 220.
72. Allen, *Legend of Noah*, 77–78.
73. In Braude, "The Sons of Noah," 132.
74. Allen, *Legend of Noah*, 78. See also Gene Rice, "The Curse That Never Was (Genesis 9:18–27)," *Journal of Religious Thought* 29, no. 1 (1972): 23 n. 98.
75. Winthrop D. Jordan, *White over Black: American Attitudes Toward the Negro, 1550–1812* (Chapel Hill: University of North Carolina Press, 1968), 36.
76. In Sollors, *Neither Black nor White*, 97–98.
77. Recall Luther's assertion that Ham went to Babylon and established himself as "lord of all Asia." In the seventeenth century, Andrew Willet cited Berrosus's claim that Ham "was cast out from his father and dwelt in Egypt, where he was a God under the name of Saturne, and they built him a citie called Chemmin, that is, the citie of Cham, the inhabitants whereof were called Chemenita" (Willet, *Hexapla in Genesin*, 106).
78. Davis, *The Problem of Slavery*, 452.
79. In the seventeenth-century Spanish comedy *El arca de Noe*, Ham is a ne'er-do-well who is infatuated with his brother's bride-to-be. He betrays wedding guests into playing a wicked game of fortune. A demon tempts Nacor and Ham to destroy Noah's ark with fire and convinces Ham that the flood is not universal. Ham then

accuses Noah of inventing the story for his own glory. The same demon reveals the drunken and naked Noah to Ham, who summons his brothers and says, "Here's your crazy father." The play concludes with the cursing of Ham and the division of the world. Noah was the subject of three plays written in the last half of the seventeenth century, including *El arca de Noe*. Joost Vondel's *Noah, of ondergang der eerste weerelt* (1667) presents Ham as a salacious buffoon (Allen, *Legend of Noah*, 149, 151–52).

80. *La Seconde Sepmaine*, in *The Works of Guillaume De Salluste Sieur Du Bartas*, vol. 3 (Chapel Hill: University of North Carolina Press, 1940). Translation by James Vest.

81. Ibid., "Deuxieme Jour," lines 85–95, passim.

82. Ibid., "L'Arche," lines 521–48.

83. Ibid., "L'Arche," lines 549–60.

84. John Milton, *Paradise Lost* (New York: Norton, 1975), 266.

85. Ibid. The context indicates that the term *race* should be taken to refer to humanity as a whole rather than to the descendants of Ham in particular.

86. *Dictionaire Historique et Critique par Mr. Pierre Bayle; avec la vie de l'auteur, par Mr. Des Maizeaux* (Amsterdam: Par la Compagnie des Libraires, 1734). English translation by Lawrence de Bartolet.

87. Ibid., 403–4.

88. Ibid., 404.

89. See Augustin Calmet, *Calmet's Dictionary of the Bible As Published by the Late Mr. Charles Taylor, with the Fragments Incorporated. The Whole Condensed and Arranged in Alphabetical Order, Seventh Edition, Revised, with Large Additions, by Edward Robinson* (Boston: Crocker and Brewster, 1835), 476. See also Thomas V. Peterson, *Ham and Japheth in America: The Mythic World of Whites in the Antebellum South* (Metuchen, N.J.: American Theological Library Association, 1978), 43–44. Benjamin Braude opines that "the article on Ham in Calmet's *Dictionary* was the single most important statement on the curse ever published, because of the authoritative character and longevity of the book" ("How Did Ham Become a Black Slave?: Reexamining the Noahides in the Abrahamic Tradition," presentation at the annual meeting of the Middle Eastern Studies Association, San Francisco, November 1997, 4). Braude's article will be part of the forthcoming book *Sex, Slavery, and Racism: The Secret History of Noah and His Sons*. Other eighteenth-century encyclopedias, though less influential than Calmet's, also cataloged traditional tales concerning Ham and his transgression. Among them was Johann Heinrich Zelder's *Universallexikon* (1732–54).

90. This connection fails to appear in the revised American edition of Calmet's *Dictionary of the Holy Bible* (1832), beyond the initial claim that Ham's name means "black." As Benjamin Braude has shown, the American and English abridgments of Calmet, "responding to the rising tide of abolitionism, removed the slavery-justifying passages, while retaining those which linked Ham to Africans and other people of color" (Braude, "How Did Ham Become a Black Slave?" 8). Nor does the original 1722 edition of the *Dictionary* associate Ham with either blackness or Africa. Yet the 1728 supplementary edition included a reference to "the author of the Tharik-Thabari, [who] teaches that Noah directed his curse to Ham and Canaan. The effect of this curse was not only that their posterity was enslaved to their brothers, and thus born into slavery, but also that with one stroke the color

of their skin became black" (in Braude, "How Did Ham Become a Black Slave?" 7). Braude concludes that "the turning point in Western Christendom [for connecting the curse of Ham with the enslavement of Black Africans] occurred in the eighteenth century with a revised edition" of Calmet's dictionary, in which Calmet cited a Muslim source ("How Did Ham Become a Black Slave?" 2).

91. Thomas Newton, *Dissertations on the Prophecies, Which Have Remarkably Been Fulfilled, and at This Time Are Fulfilling in the World*, vol. 1 (New York: William Durell, 1794), 13.

92. According to Peterson, Newton was dependent on Calmet for this insight. Newton (*Dissertations*, 18–19) goes on to observe that Vatablus and other interpreters read "Canaan" to mean "the father of Canaan," and to argue that "if we regard the metre, this line 'Cursed be Canaan,' is much shorter than the rest, as if something was deficient." Based on this evidence, may we not suppose, Newton asks, "that the copyist by mistake wrote only *Canaan* instead of *Ham the father of Canaan*, and that the whole passage was originally thus?: 'And Ham the father of Canaan saw the nakedness of his father, and told his two brethren without—And Noah awoke from his wine, and knew what his younger son had done unto him. And he said, Cursed be Ham the father of Canaan; and servant of servants shall he be unto his brethren. And he said, Blessed be the Lord God of Shem; and Ham the father of Canaan shall be servant to them. God shall enlarge Japheth; and he shall dwell in the tents of Shem; and Ham the father of Canaan shall be servant to them.' "

93. Thomas Peterson notes that Newton's *Dissertations* was one of the few sources cited by Southern advocates of the curse (*Ham and Japheth*, 43). Joseph C. Addington is an American proslavery writer who cited the "Arabic version" of the biblical text, apparently under Newton's influence. See *Reds, Whites and Blacks, or the Colors, Dispersion, Language, Sphere and Unity of the Human Race, as Seen in the Lights of Scripture, Science and Observation* (Raleigh, N.C.: Strother & Marcom, 1862), 29, where the author places the "English" and "Arabic" versions of Genesis 9 in parallel columns.

94. *Matthew Henry's Commentary on the Whole Bible, Wherein Each Chapter, Is Summed Up in Its Contents: The Sacred Text Inserted at Large in Distinct Paragraphs; Each Paragraph Reduced to its Proper Heads: The Sense Given, and Largely Illustrated with Practical Remarks and Observations, Vol. 1, Genesis to Deuteronomy* (New York: R. Carter and Brothers, 1880), 73.

95. Ibid.

96. Adam Clarke, *The Holy Bible Containing the Old and New Testaments, The Text Carefully Printed from the Most Correct Copies of the Present Authorized Translation, Including the Marginal Readings and Parallel Texts, With a Commentary and Critical Notes; The Old Testament, Vol. 1, Genesis to Deuteronomy* (1810; reprint, New York: Abingdon-Cokesbury, 1977), 83.

97. According to Clarke, "it is very probable that this was the first time the wine was cultivated; and it is as probable that the strength or intoxicating power of the expressed juice was never before known. Noah, therefore, might have drunk it at this time without the least blame, as he knew not till this trial the effects it would produce." Clarke relates a similar case he himself had witnessed: A fatigued traveler stopped for refreshment at a Somersetshire farmer's house and innocently drank half a pint of cider to quench his thirst, only to become intoxicated. "This I

presume to have been precisely the case with Noah," he concludes. Thus, no one can "can attach any blame to the character of Noah on this ground" unless he is known to have repeated the act. Clarke is adamant on this point and has no patience with "expositors [who] seem to be glad to fix on a fact like this, which by *their distortion* becomes a *crime*; and then, in a strain of sympathetic tenderness, affect to deplore 'the failings and imperfections of the *best of men*;' when, from the interpretation that *should* be given of the place, neither *failing* nor *imperfection* can possibly appear" (ibid., 82).

98. Ibid., 82–83.

Chapter 3

1. According to Benjamin Braude, this is "the first example in the iconography of Ham in Jewish, Christian, and Muslim art in which Noah's son is blackened or racialized in any way" (letter to the author, 16 January 2001). See Braude's forthcoming *Sex, Slavery, and Racism: The Secret History of Noah and His Sons*.

2. For biographical information on Priest, see Winthrop Hillyer Duncan, "Josiah Priest, Historian of the American Frontier: A Study and Bibliography," *Proceedings of the American Antiquarian Society* 44 (1934): 45–102. I am indebted to Benjamin Braude for bringing this article to my attention.

3. Umberto Cassuto, *A Commentary on the Book of Genesis, Part II: From Noah to Abraham, Genesis 5:19 to 11:32* (Jerusalem: Magnes Press, 1949).

4. Ibid., 200. Cassuto notes that "such quotations introduced from epic poetry into registers of important personages are likewise found in Mesopotamian writings." Like Gilgamesh and Enkidu, it is related that Nimrod demonstrated his prowess by fighting "fearsome animals and terrifying monsters." Because the Bible reports that Nimrod was a mighty hunter before Yahweh, we can conclude that the epic poem from which these verses are cited was a purely Israelite work (202). It is also possible that Nimrod's name suggests a connection with Ninurri in *The Epic of Gilgamesh*, who is called a "hunter."

5. All references here are to Louis Ginzberg, *The Legends of the Jews*, Vol. 1, *Bible Times and Characters from the Creation to Jacob*, trans. Henrietta Szold. (Philadelphia: Jewish Publication Society of America, 1968), 174–80.

6. Ibid., 174.

7. Robert Graves and Raphael Patai, *Hebrew Myths: The Book of Genesis* (New York: Greenwich House, 1983), 125.

8. Ibid.

9. Ginzberg, *Legends of the Jews*, 177.

10. Ibid.

11. Ibid.

12. Graves and Patai, *Hebrew Myths*, 126.

13. Ginzberg, *Legends of the Jews*, 179.

14. Ibid., 180. According to the same tradition, "the punishment inflicted upon the sinful generation of the tower is comparatively lenient ... [for they were] preserved in spite of their blasphemies and all their other acts offensive to God."

15. Graves and Patai, *Hebrew Myths*, 127.

16. Ibid., 134.

17. Ibid., 134–37.

18. Ibid., 140, 141.
19. Ibid., 194, 127.
20. See Josephus, *Complete Works of Josephus, in Ten Volumes, a New and Revised Edition Based on Havercamp's Translation*, Vol. 1, *Antiquities of the Jews, Books I– III* (Cleveland: World, 1940), Book I, ch. iv, 19ff.
21. Ibid., 20.
22. Ibid., 21.
23. Graves and Patai note that in Jewish legend, the Nimrod tradition became attached to the myth of Samael's rebellion against El (*Hebrew Myths*, 128).
24. "Augustine, City of God, XVI: 3 in Philip Schaff, ed. *A Select Library of the Nicene and Post-Nicene Fathers of the Christian Church*, 8 vols. (Grand Rapids, Mich.: Eerdmans, 1955). Augustine acknowledges that "some interpreters have misunderstood this phrase, being deceived by an ambiguity in the Greek, and consequently translating it as 'before the Lord,' instead of 'against the Lord.' . . . [But] it is in the latter sense that we must take it in the description of Nimrod; that giant was 'a hunter against the Lord.' "
25. See Jean Devisse, *The Image of the Black in Western Art*, Vol. 2, part 1, trans. William Granger Ryan (Cambridge: Harvard University Press, 1976–79) 220 n. 158. Devisse notes that some Muslim authors make Nimrod an ancestor of Goliath, who was said to have taken refuge in North Africa after he was defeated.
26. Cited in James L. Kugel, *The Bible as It Was* (Cambridge: Harvard University Press, 1997), 128.
27. Ibid., 578. In light of Numbers 13:32–33, where *Nephilim* appears to denote men of great stature, early Bible readers interpreted the term in Genesis 6:4 as "giants," a reading that is reflected in the Septuagint.
28. Although there is no direct evidence that the Christian image of Nimrod was influenced by *1 Enoch*, it is interesting that the book's portrayal of the prediluvian giants "as a race of tyrannical and oppressive creatures who terrorize humanity, deplete the earth's resources, and spread violence and death everywhere" is a fair description of the way Nimrod and his associates came to be viewed among European Bible readers. As Kugel (ibid., 709, 110–11) notes, ancient interpreters routinely associated these giants with arrogance and rebellion.
29. "But those things that are here [on earth] are against those things which are there [in heaven]. For this reason it is not ineptly said [that Nimrod was] 'a giant *before* God' which clearly [means] *in opposition to* the Deity" (Philo, *Questions and Answers in Genesis*, cited in ibid., 126).
30. "City of God," in Schaff, *Select Library*, XVI: 3.
31. Ibid.
32. Ibid.
33. Ibid.
34. Cited in Kugel, *The Bible as It Was*, 127.
35. "Recognitions of Clement," Book I, chs. xxx–xxxi, in *The Ante-Nicene Fathers*, Vol. 8 (New York: Charles Scribner's Sons, 1926), 85–86. Clement remarks that in the ancient world Ham was also known as Zoroaster. In another place, however, he says it is Ham's descendant Nebrod (Nimrod) who was called Zoroaster (172, 186).
36. Devisse, *The Image of the Black in Western Art*, Vol. 2, part 1, 224 n. 231.
37. The quotations are from Isidore of Seville (ca. 560–636) and Ambrose. See ibid., 221 n. 175, 224 n. 231.
38. Ibid., 18.

39. Agapius al-Manbiji, cited in ibid., part 2, 268 n. 148.
40. See Stephen Gero, "The Legend of the Fourth Son of Noah," *Harvard Theological Review* 73 (1980); 321–30.
41. Ibid., 324.
42. Ibid., 326. *The Book of the Cave of Treasures* also claims that Nimrod sent emissaries to Balaam "the priest of Mount Se'ir" upon learning that he was an expert in reading the signs of the Zodiac.
43. According to Stephen Gero, one function of the Yonton story, which probably had a Mesopotamian origin, was to transmit useful knowledge and skills to Nimrod, "a culture-hero of eastern Syria and Mesopotamia" (328). Gero also believes that the origin of the rabbinic view that Ham castrated his father, Noah, may have been official concern with a popular form of Judaism that held up Nimrod and Yonton as heroes. This theory would help explain the vilification of Nimrod in Jewish sources: While Noah's fourth son could be eliminated with a stroke of Ham's knife, Nimrod had to be "denigrated as a senseless tyrant and an idolater" (329).
44. Charles Homer Haskins, "Nimrod the Astronomer," in *Studies in the History of Mediaeval Science* (New York: Frederick Ungar, 1924), 336–45.
45. Ibid., 336. The text is Philip de Thaon's *Li Cumpoz* (1119), "the earliest monument of Anglo-Norman literature." Astronomical tables under Nimrod's name are known to have been current in Arabic, and Nimrod received mention in the twelfth century by Hugh of St. Victor and William of Conches and in the thirteenth-century *Speculum astronomie* (337).
46. Ibid.
47. Ibid., 338. The treatise is still extant in two manuscripts, MS. Lat. VIII 22 of St. Mark's at Venice and MS. Pal. Lat. 1417 of the Vatican.
48. Ibid.
49. According to Haskins (ibid., 343), "the dialogue [between Nimrod and Jonathan] bears clear traces of Syrian origin, for the disciple Ioathon or Ioanton can be none other than the fourth son of Noah. . . . Unknown in Hebrew tradition, he is found in works of Syrian origin and in these only, and is there brought into direct relation to Nimrod. Thus in the *Cave of Treasure,* which in its Syrian form is probably of the sixth century, Ionton is visited by Nimrod in the land of Nod and teaches him that wisdom and learning of the stars which the Persians call the oracle and the Romans astronomy."
50. Cited in Benjamin Braude, "The Sons of Noah and the Construction of Ethnic and Geographical Identities in the Medieval and Early Modern Periods," *William and Mary Quarterly* 54, no. 1 (1997): 117.
51. Ibid., 131. Braude writes: "The section in Comestor's *Historia Scholastica* on Genesis 10 that deals with what modern critics have mislabeled 'The Table of Nations' is entitled in the manuscript and all editions I have consulted 'De Dispersione filiorum Noe et Nemrod' ('On the dispersion of the Sons of Noah and Nimrod'). In the authoritative sixteenth-century commentary of Pererius, Nimrod and his realm in Babylonia gain more attention than any other figure in the entire Noachic genealogy. Nimrod's role as the master builder of the Tower of Babel earned him repeated attention from medieval and early modern artists."
52. Ibid., 132. Braude writes that "in the mid-fourteenth century the genealogy of the House of Luxembourg placed Ham and Nimrod at its origins, and the Habsburg

ruler Maximilian I (1459–1519), also drawn to these images, claimed similar descent." In another paper, Braude notes the irony that the representative of a presumably cursed race built such a powerful kingdom: "In Mandeville's account Ham
is identified with mastery and tyranny not slavery and subjection. . . . Luther's *Sermons on Genesis* similarly set Ham in Asia and identify him with wealth and power.
Some Curse!" ("How Did Ham Become a Black Slave? Reexamining the Noahides
in the Abrahamic Tradition," paper presented at the annual meeting of the Middle
Eastern Studies Association, San Francisco, November 1997, 4). In the sixteenth
century, Sir Walter Raleigh commented on the irony that a presumably cursed
race held such sway over the world in earlier times: "Indeed the great masters of
nations, so far as we can know, were in that age of the issues of Ham; the blessing
of God given by Noah to Shem and Japhet taking less effect, until divers years
were consumed. . . ." See *The Works of Sir Walter Ralegh, Kt., Now First Collected:
To Which are Prefixed The Lives of the Author, by Oldys and Birch, In Eight Volumes,*
Vol. 2, *The History of the World* (Oxford: University Press, 1829), book I, chapter
viii, section ii, 253.
53. *The Divine Comedy of Dante Alighieri, 1: Inferno,* trans. John D. Sinclair (New
York: Oxford University Press, 1961), XXXI: 46–66.
54. Ibid., 67–75.
55. These references include *Purgatory* XII: 34–36: "Mine eyes beheld Nimrod, beneath
his dire/ High handiwork, look stunned upon the men/ That shared in Shinar his
proud heart's desire" (*The Comedy of Dante Alighieri, the Florentine,* trans. Dorothy
L. Sayers, 3 vols. [New York: Basic Books, 1962]) and *Paradiso* XXVI: 124–127: "The
tongue I spoke was all extinct before Nimrod's race gave their mind to the un-
accomplishable task; for no product whatever of reason—since human choice is
renewed with the course of heaven—can last forever" (trans. Sinclair, 3:379).
56. Luther, *Lectures on Genesis,* in *Luther's Works,* 55 vols., ed. Jaroslav Pelikan (St.
Louis: Concordia, 1955), ch. IX, 175.
57. Ibid., 210.
58. Ibid., 212.
59. Ibid., 219. In his view of Ham's activities following this episode with Noah, Luther
seems to have been influenced by several of the church fathers. For instance, he
alludes to the patristic notion that Ham "later on filled the world with idolatry,"
claims that after being cursed Ham went to Babylon where he "engage[d] in building a city and a tower . . . establish[d] himself as lord of all Asia," and developed
"a new government and a new religion" and even adopts Augustine's suggestion
that Ham's name means "hot."
60. John Calvin, *Commentaries on the First Book of Moses Called Genesis,* 2 vols., trans.
John King (Grand Rapids, Mich.: Eerdmans, 1948), 1:316–320.
61. *La Seconde Semaine,* "Babylon," lines 39–92. In *The Works of Guillaume Salluste
Sieur Du Bartas,* Vol. 3 (Chapel Hill: University of North Carolina Press, 1940).
Translation by James Vest.
62. Ibid. Summary of lines 93–104 by James Vest; quotation from line 105.
63. Raleigh, *History of the World,* book I, chapter viii, section ii, 251.
64. Ibid., 252.
65. Ibid., 353.
66. Ibid., 355.
67. According to Merritt Y. Hughes, "Milton was acquainted with the discourse on

tyranny with which Du Bartas introduces his account of Nimrod in *Babalon*, and in Du Bartas' applications to French politics he had an example for his suggestion in *Eikonoklastes*, xi, that the bishops might have told King Charles 'that Nimrod, the first that hunted after faction, is reputed by ancient tradition the first that founded monarchy.' " See Milton, *Paradise Lost*, ed. Merritt Y. Hughes (New York: Odyssey Press, 1962), 390 n. 24.

68. Ibid., XII: 24–62. In the notes to this section of Book XII, Hughes guides us toward some of the sources for Milton's picture of Nimrod: "From Josephus (*Antiquities*, I, iv, 2) came the belief which prevailed in the seventeenth century that 'the secret design of *Nimrod* was to settle unto himself a place of dominion and . . . the beginning of his kingdom was *Babel*' (Sir Thomas Browne, *Vulgar Errors*, VII, vi)." See *Paradise Lost* I: 694 for another reference to Babel: "And here let those/ Who boast in mortal things, and wondr'ing tell/ Of *Babel*, and the works of *Memphian* Kings,/ Learn how thir greatest Monuments of Fame,/ And Strength and Art are easily outdone/ By spirits reprobate, and in an hour/ What in an age they with incessant toil/ And hands innumerable scarce perform."

69. Hughes observes that "Milton's epigram is an echo of Du Bartas' statement that Nimrod 'Leaves hunting Beasts, and hunteth Men' ('The Divine Weekes,' 120)." See ibid., 390 n. 30.

70. Milton's connection of Nimrod with the building of the Tower of Babel "had patristic authority as well as that of Josephus and the example of Dante's vision of Nimrod at the foot of his tower (*Purgatorio*, XII, 34; compare *Inferno*, XXXI, 77)." See ibid., 390 n. 38.

71. Milton scholarship has long sought to trace the sources for *Paradise Lost*. In the case of Nimrod, the influence of several sixteenth-century authors has been confirmed, among them Sir Walter Raleigh and Robert Stephanus (d. 1559). The association of Nimrod's name with rebellion may have come to Milton from Stephanus's *Thesaurus*. It is important to note, however, what Milton did not adopt from Stephanus, including the description of Nimrod as a giant ten cubits tall. See Dewitt T. Starnes and Ernest William Talbert, *Classical Myth and Legend in Renaissance Dictionaries: A Study of Renaissance Dictionaries in Their Relation to the Classical Learning of Contemporary English Writers* (Chapel Hill: University of North Carolina Press, 1955), 264–268.

72. In another textual note, Hughes writes that "from Josephus comes the idea that the brick in the Tower of Babel was 'cemented together with mortar, made of bitumen' (*Antiquities*, I, iv, 3)."

73. Irene Samuel, *Dante and Milton: The* Commedia *and* Paradise Lost (Ithaca, N.Y.: Cornell University Press, 1966), 118–19.

74. *The Works of the Right Reverend Father in God, Gervase Babington, Late Bishop of Worcester. Containing Comfortable Notes Upon the First Bookes of Moses* (London: Miles Flesher, 1637), 35.

75. Abraham Rosse, *An Exposition on the Fourteene First Chapters of Genesis, by Waye of Question and Answere, Collected Out of Ancient and Recent Writers: Both Briefely and Subtilly Propounded and Expounded* (London: B.A. and T.F., 1626), 87–88.

76. Andrew Willet, *Hexapla in Genesin* (London: Tho. Creede, 1608), 117.

77. Ibid., 124.

78. Augustin Calmet, *Calmet's Dictionary of the Bible, As Published by the Late Mr. Charles Taylor, with the Fragments Incorporated. The Whole Condensed and Ar-*

ranged in Alphabetical Order, Seventh Edition, Revised, with Large Additions, by Edward Robinson (Boston: Crocker and Brewsler, 1835), 705. As did most intellectuals of his time, Calmet tried to place the biblical patriarchs in the context of classical history and mythology: "The name Nebrodeus, or Nebrodus, given to Bacchus, is perhaps derived from Nembrod, or Nimrod, though the Greeks derive it from a goat-skin, with which they pretend Bacchus was clothed. The same Bacchus may also be derived from Bar-chus, 'son of Cush;' because Nimrod was indeed the son of Cush. The Greeks gave to Bacchus the name of hunter, just as Moses gives it to Nimrod. The expeditions of Bacchus into the Indies are formed on the wars of Nimrod in Babylonia and Assyria."

79. Calmet also refers to an aspect of Nimrod's biography that was ignored by most Christian interpreters—his encounter with Abraham. In his article "Babylon," Calmet quotes Ibn Haukal: "There are two heaps [at Babylon], one of which is in a place called Koudi Ferik, the other Koudi Derebar: in this the ashes still remain; and they say that it was the fire of Nimrod into which Abraham was cast; may peace be on him!" (ibid., 126).

80. Henry's words would indicate that he supports the antiquity and legitimacy of monarchy, if not its divine origin.

81. *Matthew Henry's Commentary on the Whole Bible, wherein each chapter, is summed up in its contents: The sacred text Inserted at Large in Distinct Paragraphs; Each Paragraph Reduced to its Proper Heads: The sense given, and largely illustrated with practical remarks and observations,* Vol. 1, Genesis to Deuteronomy (New York: R. Carter and Brothers, 1880), 76–77.

82. Adam Clarke, *The Holy Bible containing the Old and New Testaments, The text carefully printed from the Most Correct Copies of the Present Authorized Translation, including the Marginal Readings and Parallel Texts, with a Commentary and Critical Notes; The Old Testament,* Vol. 1, *Genesis to Deuteronomy* (1810; reprint, New York: Abingdon-Cokesbury, 1977) 86.

83. Ibid.

84. Alexander Hislop, *The Two Babylons, or Papal Worship Proved to be the Worship of Nimrod and His Wife* (1858; reprint, New York: Loizeaux Brothers, 1953). According to the Library of Congress on-line catalog, the book was republished twice in the late 1990s: Brooklyn: A&B Publishers, 1999; Chicago: Research Associates School Times Publications, 1996.

85. Ibid., 23. Hislop says that "it was by inuring his followers to the toils and dangers of the chase, that [Nimrod] gradually formed them to the use of arms, and so prepared them for aiding him in establishing his dominions."

86. Ibid.

87. Ibid., 50.

88. Ibid., 50–51. Hislop goes on to cite commentators who contend that Nimrod was the first to gather humankind into communities, the first mortal to reign, and the first to offer idolatrous sacrifices.

89. Ibid., 52.

90. Ibid., 53, 55.

91. Ibid., 67.

92. Ibid., 55, 63.

93. Ibid., 34. Indebted to Hislop on this point are a number of European and American thinkers who in the twentieth century have spun bizarre racial theories as-

sociated with Cain, Ham, and Nimrod. Ellen Bristowe's *Sargon the Magnificent* (London: Covenant, 1927)—an attempt to reconstruct Cain's life after his arrival in the "land of Nod"—is among the works influenced by *The Two Babylons*. As Hislop identifies Nimrod with the Babylonian king Ninus, Bristowe conflates Cain with "the great Babylonian monarch Sargon of Akkad." Like Hislop's Nimrod, Bristowe's Cain is a confederate of Satan who is responsible for the birth of idolatry and establishes a Babylonian cult based upon cannibalism. See Michael Barkun, *Religion and the Racist Right: The Origins of the Christian Identity Movement*, rev. ed. (Chapel Hill: University of North Carolina Press, 1997), 165ff.

Although Hislop was not overtly concerned with racial distinctions, Bristowe was, and she exercised considerable influence on leaders of the American Christian Identity movement, whose preoccupation with race is notorious. Her focus on Cain rather than the Hamite Nimrod has allowed Christian Identity thinkers to apply her theories directly to "Jews," who represent the chief racial threat in their worldview. Africans and other nonwhite peoples are seen in the dominant Identity paradigm as pawns in a Jewish racial plot to undermine white society. A significant exception to this generalization is the use of Nimrod and his Babylonian cult in the theology of the Missouri-based Identity group, Covenant, Sword and Arm of the Lord. According to Barkun, the CSA has been influenced in their view of Nimrod by Des Griffin, *Fourth Reich of the Rich* (South Pasadena, Calif: Emissary Publications, 1978). See also C. Lewis Fowler, *O House of Israel and Thou Judah* (New York: Maranatha Publishers, 1941). Fowler was an American proponent of British Israelism who placed Noah's sons in an imminent end-of-days scenario he believed was unfolding in World War II: "Three new, distinct races began with Ham, Shem, and Japheth. Read Genesis, the tenth chapter. Two of these boys yielded at once to Satan, to Lucifer, the fallen angel of light. They were self-centered, wise in their own conceits. They would not listen to God at all . . . Then came Nimrod in the Ham line, the grandson of Ham, who listened to Satan and was inspired by him in all he did. Satan had worked out and perfected a complete system of social, economic, religious and governmental organization. Both Ham and Japheth accepted the Satan system. Babylon—or Babel—was built. . . . Ham loves gold and down to that 'god' he also bows. From the beginning Ham worshipped gold. He built the golden image upon the plains of Shinar and required all, both small and great, to come, fall down and worship it" (54, 60).

94. Hislop, *The Two Babylons*, 28. Relying on an intricate and unlikely series of linguistic connections, Hislop associates Cush with "division" and "confounding." He concludes that Cush must have been "the DIVIDER of the speeches of men" (26).

95. Ibid., 25. Later, Cush is referred to as "the great soothsayer or false prophet worshipped at Babylon"(34).

Chapter 4

1. Ronald G. Walters, *The Anti-Slavery Appeal: Abolitionism after 1830* (Baltimore: Johns Hopkins University Press, 1976), 74.

2. Apparently, the connection between slavery and the Southern culture of honor was being made by opponents of the peculiar institution as early as the 1840s.

Slavery apologist James Henry Hammond acknowledged that "it is true that the point of honor is recognized throughout the slave region, and the disputes of certain classes are frequently referred for adjustment to the 'trial by combat.' " But Hammond averred that whatever evils may arise from these practices "cannot be attributed to slavery, since the same notion and custom prevails both in France and England." See *Gov. Hammond's Letters on Southern Slavery: Addressed to Thomas Clarkson, the English Abolitionist* (Charleston, S.C.: Walker & Burke, 1845), Letter Two, 7.

3. Ralph L. Moellering, *Christian Conscience and Negro Emancipation* (Philadelphia: Fortress, 1965), 52: "The favorite argument used by those seeking a religious sanction for slavery was to refer to the curse which Noah pronounced on his grandson Canaan. . . ."

4. See Andrew E. Murray, *The Presbyterian and the Negro—A History* (Philadelphia: Presbyterian Historical Society, 1966), where the author summarizes the biblical proslavery argument this way: "The chain of scriptural argument began with the original divine decree in Genesis, which fixed the racial patterns of mankind by ordaining that Canaan should be a servant to his brothers as punishment for his sin against his father, Noah"(69). There are no textual warrants, of course, for regarding Noah's curse as "divine," or for viewing Canaan (the grandson, not the son, of Noah) as the perpetrator of any "sin."

Another striking example of apparent ignorance of the biblical text appears in Bertram Wyatt-Brown's *Honor and Violence in the Old South* (New York: Oxford University Press, 1986), where the author on several occasions refers to the "expulsion" (25) or "banish[ment]" (34) of Ham. Wyatt-Brown seems to have confused Noah's curse on Ham or Canaan with the punishment of Cain related in Genesis 4. Although "it is not unlikely that the force 'banned' is the basic denotation of [the Hebrew term] *'arur* in the pronouncemnt of Noah," all standard English translations render the Hebrew "cursed be Canaan." See Herbert C. Brichto, *The Problem of "Curse" in the Hebrew Bible*, Journal of Biblical Literature Monograph Series 13 (Philadelphia: Society of Biblical Literature and Exegesis, 1963), 86–87.

For a synopsis of the story that imaginatively fills textual gaps without acknowledging doing so, see Donald G. Mathews, *Religion in the Old South* (Chicago: University of Chicago Press, 1977), where the author refers to "the curse of the drunken Noah upon the descendants of his son, Ham (Africans) because of an invasion of the patriarch's privacy"(171).

5. "These divines were intelligent, learned, and well trained, not only in theology but in history, political economy, political theory, and the natural sciences. . . . They were neither demagogues nor ignoramuses nor bigots." See Eugene D. Genovese and Elizabeth Fox-Genovese, "The Social Thought of Antebellum Theologians," in William B. Moore Jr. and Joseph F. Tripp, eds., *Looking South: Chapters in the Story of an American Region*, Contributions in American History 136 (Westport, Conn.: Greenwood, 1989), 31.

6. Benjamin Braude, "The Sons of Noah and the Construction of Ethnic and Geographical Identities in the Medieval and Early Modern Periods," *William and Mary Quarterly* 54, no. 1 (1997): 133.

7. Randall C. Bailey, "They're Nothing but Incestuous Bastards: The Polemical Use of Sex and Sexuality in Hebrew Canon Narratives," in Fernando F. Segovia and

Mary Ann Tolbert, eds., *Reading from This Place,* Vol. 1 *Social Location and Biblical Interpretation in the United States* (Minneapolis: Fortress, 1994), 134.

8. Ibid. Braude maintains that the sexual understanding of Genesis 9 that dominated Christian and Jewish interpretation through the sixteenth century is "manifest most strikingly in Michelangelo's depiction of Ham and the drunkenness of Noah in the ceiling frescoes of the Sistene Chapel ("How Did Ham Become a Black Slave?" Reexamining the Noahides in the Abrahamic Tradition," paper presented at annual meeting of the Middle Eastern Studies Association, San Francisco, November 1997, 7).

9. Laurence Turner identifies the beginning of the Flood narrative as an interpretive cue for Genesis 9: "Verses 6.1–4, whatever else they might convey, are concerned with illicit sexual liaisons that occurred immediately before the flood and provide (at least part of) the motivation for God's sending the Flood. . . . In fact, whether [9:20–27] refers to homosexual rape, castration, incest or Ham's simple viewing of Noah exposed in his tent . . . the story carries sexual connotations to a greater or lesser degree. The semantic range of *érwâ* (nakedness) contains significant sexual connotations, so that 'to see nakedness' is used as a euphemism for sexual offenses (e.g. Lev. 20.17). Just as the 'sons of God' take the initiative, but humanity is punished (6.3), so Ham committed the offense but his offspring (Canaan) is cursed (9.25–27)." See Laurence A. Turner, *Genesis,* (Sheffield: Sheffield Academic Press, 2000), 56.

10. See Curtis Brown Watson, *Shakespeare and the Renaissance Concept of Honor* (Princeton, N.J.: Princeton University Press, 1960).

11. Both authors are cited in Winthrop Jordan, *White over Black: American Attitudes toward the Negro, 1550–1812* (Chapel Hill: University North Carolina Press, 1968), 54.

12. Thomas V. Peterson, *Ham and Japheth in America: The Mythic World of Whites in the Antebellum South* (Metuchen, N.J.: American Theological Library Association, 1978), 48.

13. In reviewing more than fifty primary documents from the antebellum period— all of which cite Noah's curse as a central if not exclusive justification for slavery— I have discovered no explicit references to sexual misconduct on the part of Ham (or Canaan). According to Thomas Peterson, many proslavery writers hinted that the sin depicted in Genesis 9 was somehow sexual in nature. He cites as examples William Stringfellow's use of the phrase "beastly wickedness," Nathan Lord's reference to an "unnatural crime" that represented Ham's "obscene" nature, and James Sloan's "indecency." But Peterson provides no rationale for a sexual interpretation of such language. Nevertheless, when he is analyzing the curse, Peterson himself refers to Ham's act as "lewd and sensual" (*Ham and Japheth,* 79) or a "heinous sexual crime" (118), speaks of "slavery as the result of Ham's sexual crime" (119), and affirms that "Ham commits an indecent, sexual act and is condemned" (117, 118).

14. John Bell Robinson, *Pictures of Slavery and Anti-Slavery. Advantages of Negro Slavery and the Benefits of Negro Freedom. Morally, Socially and Politically Considered* (Philadelphia, 1863), 20.

15. In Werner Sollors, *Neither Black nor White yet Both: Thematic Explorations of Interracial Literature* (New York: Oxford University Press, 1997), 98–99.

16. Priest asks his readers to imagine a scene in which Noah explains to Ham just why his malediction is justified: "Oh Ham, my son, it is not for this one deed

alone which you have just committed that I have, by God's command, thus condemned you and your race, but the Lord has shown me that all your descendants will, more or less, be like *you* their father, on which account, it is determined by the Creator that you and your people are to occupy the lowest condition of all the families among mankind, and even be enslaved as brute beasts, going down in the scale of human society, beyond and below the ordinary exigencies of mortal existence, arising out of war, revolutions, and conflicts, for you *will*, and *must* be, both in times of peace and war, a despised, a degraded, and an oppressed race." See Josiah Priest, *Slavery as it Relates to the Negro or African Race* (1843; reprint, New York: Arno, 1977), 75–80 passim.

17. According to Winthrop Hillyer Duncan, Priest's *Slavery as It Relates to the Negro or African Race* was printed three times in Albany, New York, between 1843 and 1845 and was republished in Kentucky in the 1850s as *Bible Defence of Slavery.* Duncan describes six editions of the text published between 1852 and 1864 in either Glasgow or Louisville, Kentucky, the first two of which identified the author as "Rev. Josiah Priest, A.M." See Duncan, "Josiah Priest, Historian of the American Frontier: A Study and Bibliography," *Proceedings of the American Antiquarian Society* 44 (1934), 98ff. It is possible that this fallacious appellation stemmed from simple confusion, because the author had a son of the same name who became a noted Presbyterian divine. It is more likely, however, that the title "Rev." was conferred to bolster Priest's authority among Southern readers. At least one Southern proslavery intellectual cited "the Rev. J. Priest." See Eugene D. Genovese, *"Slavery Ordained of God," The Southern Slaveholders' View of Biblical History and Modern Politics,* twentieth-fourth annual Fortenbaugh Memorial Lecture (Gettysburg, Pa.: Gettysburg College, 1985), 13.

18. See Peterson, *Ham and Japheth,* 76–77.

19. James Smylie, *Review of a Letter from the Presbytery of Chillicothe, to the Presbytery of Mississippi, on the Subject of Slavery* (Woodville, Miss.: Wm. A. Norris, 1836), 16. It is interesting that, despite withholding any hint as to the nature of the transgression for which Hamites have been cursed, Smylie emphasizes in his discussion of Paul's teaching that slaves owe their masters honor, as well as obedience, hard work, and loyalty. See Randy J. Sparks, "Mississippi's Apostle of Slavery: James Smylie and the Biblical Defense of Slavery," *Journal of Mississippi History* 51 (May 1989): 103.

20. Cited in Peterson, *Ham and Japheth,* 45. Baptist J. B. Thrasher also belongs in this category. Although he opines that "it was, perhaps, Canaan who first saw the nakedness of his grand father, Noah, and told his father of it," Thrasher is interested in the curse and its aftermath, not in the events that precipitated it. See his *Slavery A Divine Institution, by J. B. Thrasher of Port Gibson, A Speech, Made before the Breckinridge and Lane Club, November 5th, 1860* (Port Gibson, Miss.: Southern Reveille Book and Job Office, 1861), 7ff.

21. George D. Armstrong, *The Christian Doctrine of Slavery* (1857; reprint, New York: Negro Universities Press, 1969), 111. Even abolitionists did not deny Ham's "sin" but attacked the story on other grounds, particularly whether the curse applied to all of Ham's descendants or was limited to "Canaanites." Thus, John Gregg Fee, while attempting to overturn the curse, referred vaguely to the "act of Ham." See his *An Anti-Slavery Manual* (1848; reprint, New York: Arno Press and New York Times, 1969), 18.

22. J. L. Dagg, *The Elements of Moral Science* (New York: Sheldon, 1860).

23. Ibid., 344. See also Mark E. Dever, "John L. Dagg," in Timothy George and David S. Dockery, eds., *Baptist Theologians*, (Nashville: Broadman, 1990), 165–87.

24. Frederick Dalcho, *Practical Considerations Founded on the Scriptures Relative to the Slave Population of South-Carolina* (Charleston, S.C.: A. E. Miller, 1823).

25. Ibid., 8, 10.

26. John Fletcher, *Studies on Slavery, In Easy Lessons, Compiled into Eight Studies, and Subdivided into Short Lessons for the Convenience of Readers* (1852; reprint, Miami: Mnemosyne, 1969), 446. For Fletcher, the curse came upon Ham not only for his "ill-manners . . . toward his father" but also for marrying into the line of Cain.

27. Robert L. Dabney, *A Defence of Virginia and Through Her, of the South, in Recent and Pending Contests against the Sectional Party* (1867; reprint, New York: Negro Universities Press, 1969), 90, 102.

28. This term and its application to slave societies is adapted from Orlando Patterson, *Slavery and Social Death: A Comparative Study* (Cambridge: Harvard University Press, 1982). Proslavery speculations that "Canaan" means "the submissive one" or "submissive knee-bender" reflect the conviction that the slave lives without honor and must derive his or her very life from submission to the master, confirming Patterson's observation that "the dishonor of slavery . . . came in the primal act of submission" (78).

29. In Peterson, *Ham and Japheth,* 144–45.

30. Ibid.

31. Samuel Davies Baldwin, *Dominion; or, the Unity and Trinity of the Human Race; With the Divine Political Constitution of the World, and the Divine Rights of Shem, Ham, and Japheth* (Nashville: Stevenson and F. A. Owen, 1858).

32. Ibid., 60, 61, 62.

33. James A. Sloan, *The Great Question Answered; or, Is Slavery a Sin in Itself (Per Se) Answered According to the Teaching of the Scriptures* (Memphis: Hutton, Gallaway, 1857), chap. 4, "The Origin of Color and Slavery."

34. Ibid., 66. The reference to "unseemly enjoyment" hints at sexual offense, yet Sloan rules out an assault on Noah when he writes that the patriarch could not have known of the "indecent and sinful conduct of his son Ham from any other source" than the Holy Spirit (67).

35. Ibid., 74–75. Sloan writes: "So that, according to the law of God, Ham deserved death for his unfilial and impious conduct. But the Great Lawgiver saw fit, in his good pleasure, not to destroy Ham with immediate death, but to set *a mark of degradation* on him, as he had done with the first murderer, Cain, that all coming generations might know and respect the laws of God. Slavery was, properly, a *commutation* or a change of punishment."

36. H. O. R., *The Governing Race: A Book for the Time, And for All Times* (Washington, D.C.: Thomas McGill, 1860), 5–7.

37. Howell Cobb, *A Scriptural Examination of the Institution of Slavery in the United States; with Its Objects and Purposes* ([Perry?], Ga.: printed for the author, 1856), 27.

38. Leander Ker, cited in Peterson, *Ham and Japheth,* 74; "The Mark of Cain and the Curse of Ham," *Southern Presbyterian Review* (January 1850): 415–26; Joseph C. Addington, *Reds, Whites and Blacks, or the Colors, Dispersion, Languages, Sphere and Unity of the Human Race, as Seen in the Lights of Scripture, Science and Observation* (Raleigh, N.C.: Strother & Marcom, 1862), 30. A military man stationed

in Kansas, Ker spent a good deal of time in the South: "During my residence in the South, which was several years, I for the most part spent my time on large cotton and sugar plantations, on which were hundreds of negroes; and I went there with the prejudice and feelings of the North in reference to slavery, and I looked in vain for those scenes of horror and cruelty of which I had read and heard in my childhood; but I saw them not." See *Slavery Consistent with Christianity*, 3d ed. (Weston, Mo.: Finch & O'Gormon, 1853), 32.

39. Robinson, *Pictures of Slavery and Anti-Slavery*, 23.

40. Ibid.

41. Ibid., 22.

42. Ibid., 26.

43. John Henry Hopkins, D.D., LL.D., *A Scriptural, Ecclesiastical, and Historical View of Slavery, from the Days of the Patriarch Abraham, to the Nineteenth Century, Addressed to the Right Rev. Alonzo Potter, D.D., Bishop of the Prot. Episcopal Church, in the Diocese of Pennsylvania* (1864; reprint, New York: Negro Universities Press, 1968).

44. Ibid., 71–72.

45. Ibid., 7. Italics in the original.

46. Priest's is a very interesting case, for his interpretation of Genesis 9 actually falls into several of the categories I am describing here. At some points of his rather lengthy treatment of the text, he is cautious in describing Ham's transgression. For instance, he writes that "why, or on what account, *Ham* came to intrude on the sacredness of his father's rest is not known; but so it was. . . ." In the next paragraph, Priest mentions the "the awful conduct of Ham," which his brothers considered a "crime of the deepest dye; a transaction if perpetrated at the present time, would mark the actor as a character of the basest and lowest kind." Yet Priest does not describe the act. A few paragraphs later, he characterizes Ham's sin as an "unchaste, unfilial, and unholy deed."

47. Joseph P. Thompson, *Teachings of the New Testament on Slavery* (New York: Joseph H. Ladd, 1856), 9.

48. The claim that biblical defenders of slavery were literalists, though misleading, is frequently advanced. For example, Clement Eaton writes that "one of the most powerful arguments in the pro-slavery dialectic was the alleged support of the Bible, for the overwhelming majority of Southern people were firmly indoctrinated in a belief in the sacredness of the literal word of the Bible." See *A History of the Old South* (New York: Macmillan, 1949), 386.

49. According to Bayle (*Dictionaire Historique et Critique par Mr. Pierre Bayle; avec la vie de l'auteur, par Mr. Des Maizeaux* [Amsterdam: Par La Compagnie des Libraries, 1734], 403), Rabbi Samuel related that Ham "did a thing so vile and abominable that I want to say nothing about it for fear that I should hurt chaste ears."

50. Andrew Murray, *Presbyterians and the Negro*, 75. Particularly during Reconstruction, the potential for sexual aggression and desire for amalgamation attributed to blacks by Southern whites were chief arguments in the defense of racial segregation.

51. Randall C. Bailey shows that this process can be detected in Hebrew Bible texts (including Genesis 9), where "the difference between 'in' and 'out' is expressed in labeling the other as one who practices a taboo sexual act" ("They're Nothing but Incestuous Bastards: The Polemical Use of Sex and Sexuality in Hebrew Canon

Narratives," in Fernando F. Segovia and Mary Ann Tolbert, eds., *Reading from This Place*, Vol. 1, *Social Location and Biblical Interpretation in the United States* [Minneapolis: Fortress, 1994], 124).

52. "Whenever, wherever, race relations are discussed in the United States, sex moves arm in arm with the concept of segregation." See Lillian Smith, *Killers of the Dream* (New York: W. W. Norton, 1949), 102.

53. In private correspondence, Eugene D. Genovese has emphasized the likely influence of Calvin on proslavery divines such as Baptist John L. Dagg and Presbyterian Benjamin Palmer. Because American advocates of the curse almost never cited sources, it is difficult to gauge the extent of this influence. But if Calvin's comments on Genesis did influence professed Calvinists, one would expect them to invoke him as an authority.

54. Bertram Wyatt-Brown observes, "Middle Eastern cultures, then and now, have been partly based upon rigid rules of honor and heightened fears of disgrace and humiliation. In Holy Scripture, the worship of God was conceptualized in terms of that code. The prophets' jeremiads denounced the wayward Israelites for the dishonoring offense of impugning the blamelessness of God. They took from God due honor and glory—two interconnected modes of praise rendered in the one Hebrew word *kabod*. . . . Southern Protestants had no difficulty in adopting such an approach." See "Church, Honor, and Secession," in Randall M. Miller, Harry S. Stout, and Charles Reagan Wilson, eds., *Religion and the American Civil War* (Oxford and New York: Oxford University Press, 1998), 101–2.

55. Julian Pitt-Rivers, "Honor," in David L. Sills, ed., *International Encyclopedia of the Social Sciences*, 18 vols. (New York: Macmillan, 1968), 505.

56. Wyatt-Brown, "Church, Honor, and Secession," 89–109, 101–2.

57. John Hope Franklin, *The Militant South: 1800–1861* (Cambridge: Harvard University Press, 1956), 34–35.

58. Wyatt-Brown, *Honor and Violence in the Old South*, 75; Patterson, *Slavery and Social Death*, 94.

59. Clement Eaton, "The Role of Honor in Southern Society," *Southern Humanities Review* 10 (1976, supplement): 52. In 1986, Wyatt-Brown confirmed this view, noting that "it was threat of honor lost, no less than slavery, that led [Southerners] to secession and war" and that "whites in the antebellum South were a people of honor who would not subject themselves to the contempt of a ruthless enemy, as the Yankee supporters of Abraham Lincoln and abolitionists were thought to be" (*Honor and Violence in the Old South*, 5, viii). Charles Reagan Wilson points out that by 1830 the formerly liberal South "had developed a new image of itself as a chivalric society, embodying many of the agrarian and spiritual values that seemed to be disappearing in the industrializing North. The cult of chivalry developed, focusing on manners, women, military affairs the idea of the Greek democracy, and Romantic oratory." See *Baptized in Blood: The Religion of the Lost Cause 1865–1920* (Athens: University of Georgia Press, 1980), 3.

60. Michael P. Johnston, "Planters and Patriarchy: Charleston, 1800–1860," *Journal of Southern History* 46, no. 1 (1980): 33.

61. Ibid., 46.

62. Bertram Wyatt-Brown, "Modernizing Southern Slavery: The Proslavery Argument Reinterpreted," in J. Morgan Kousser and James M. McPherson, eds., *Religion, Race and Reconstruction: Essays in Honor of C. Vann Woodward* (New York: Oxford

University Press, 1982), 30. In this article, Wyatt-Brown identifies three stages in the evolution of Southern slavery: (1) crude chattel bondage, characteristic of the colonial period; (2) state racial regulation requiring civil bureaucracies and legal professionalization, which made only limited progress before 1861; and (3) the patriarchal model, a form that became prominent in the early national years, largely as a result of Christian evangelicalism.

63. Ibid., 30, 36. According to Wyatt-Brown, the domestic view of slavery was "intimately connected with evangelical and indeed scriptural reverence for familial government." For those Wyatt-Brown calls the "Southern church fathers," slavery was a condition rather than a moral evil and, as such, "resembled the family, civil government, hierarchies, all elements of social organization with which God had forever equipped his fallen, self-seeking creatures" (32).

64. Wyatt-Brown, *Honor and Violence in the Old South*, viii, 33; Kenneth S. Greenberg, *Honor and Slavery: Lies, Duels, Noses, Masks, Dressing as a Woman, Gifts, Strangers, Humanitarianism, Death, Slave Rebellions, the Proslavery Argument, Baseball, Hunting, and Gambling in the Old South* (Princeton, N.J. Princeton University Press, 1996), 7, 9. Greenberg writes that in the Old South "the man of honor was the man who had the power to prevent his being unmasked. Anyone could unmask the dishonored. For those who aspired to honor, what you wore mattered less than whether you could and would risk your life to repel any man who tried to remove what you wore"(25).

65. Pitt-Rivers, "Honor," 508.

66. Greenberg, *Honor and Slavery*, 14.

67. Patterson, *Slavery and Social Death*, 80.

68. Ted Ownby notes both the centrality of alcohol in Southern male culture and the way it served as a stimulant to aggressive behavior. He describes the "drinking establishment as a setting for the typically masculine combination of drink, profanity and violence." See *Subduing Satan: Religion, Recreation and Manhood in the Rural South, 1865–1920* (Chapel Hill: University of North Carolina Press, 1990), 53.

69. Wyatt-Brown, *Honor and Violence in the Old South*, 59, 33. Franklin, *The Militant South*, 202–3.

70. Eaton, "The Role of Honor in the Old South," 47, 48; Steven M. Stowe, *Intimacy and Power in the Old South: Ritual in the Lives of the Planters* (Baltimore: Johns Hopkins University Press, 1987), 49. According to Stowe, "The affair [of honor] was theatre and ideology; it happened and it explained what happened. . . . Particular affairs inevitably developed into stories about the social meaning of a man's personal morality" (47).

71. "The central concern of Southern men was to have their words treated with respect. . . . Words of masters had to be respected because they were the words of a man of honor" (Greenberg, *Honor and Slavery*, 7, 11).

72. Greenberg, *Honor and Slavery*, 41. Wyatt-Brown, *Honor and Violence in the Old South*, 31.

73. Wyatt-Brown, *Honor and Violence in the Old South*, 39; John Hope Franklin, *The Militant South*, 202–03, and Pitt-Rivers, "Honor," 506.

74. Wyatt-Brown, *Honor and Violence in the Old South*, 74.

75. Greenberg, *Honor and Slavery*, 107–11.

76. Armstrong, *The Christian Doctrine of Slavery*, 110.

77. Patterson, *Slavery and Social Death*, 100; Eaton, "The Role of Honor in Southern

Society," 49; Wyatt-Brown, *Honor and Violence in the Old South,* vii; Christine
Leigh Heyrman, *Southern Cross: The Beginnings of the Bible Belt* (Chapel Hill and
London: University of North Carolina Press, 1997), 249.

78. Ownby, *Subduing Satan,* 12.

79. Ibid., 14.

80. Bertram Wyatt-Brown, "God and Honor in the Old South," *Southern Review* 25
(April 1989): 283. In *Honor and Violence in the Old South,* Wyatt-Brown distinguished the "primal honor" derived from the Indo-European system of ethics and
the "gentility" that arose from the English Deists. "Ancient largesse became, under
Stoic influence, Aristotelian magnanimity, which in turn grew into Christian charity" (38). The South's concern with the classics, Wyatt-Brown said, "reflected the
continued relevance of Stoic traditions of honor and virtue" (47). "During the
eighteenth century, under the influence of the rationalism of the Enlightenment,
the Southern model of honorable conscience conformed with the classical heritage.
... By the 1830s, however, religious precept, somewhat democratic in character,
transformed Southern gentility" (51, 53).

81. Wyatt-Brown, "God and Honor in the Old South," 285.

82. Ibid., 289.

83. Ibid., 295.

84. Ibid. Wyatt-Brown comes closer than any other scholar to clarifying the link between the biblical defense of slavery and the culture of honor. He even notes that
the traditional ethic of honor was readily incorporated by Southern clergy, in part
because of the "narratives and codification of honor to be found in Scripture,
particularly in the Old Testament" (ibid., 284).

85. Edward R. Crowther, "Holy Honor: Sacred and Secular in the Old South," *Journal
of Southern History* 58, no. 4 (1992): 619–636.

86. Ibid., 620.

87. Ibid.

88. Ibid., 631.

89. John H. Hopkins's reading of the story, in which "eminen[ce]" and "piety" are
connected in Noah, slavery and "the abominations of heathen idolatry" in Ham,
provides another glimpse of holy honor at work.

90. H.O.R., *The Governing Race,* 7–9.

91. Significantly, a similar interpenetration of honor and righteousness is evident in
Calvin's comments on Genesis 9:20–27, which may have influenced some proslavery divines. In Calvin, the language of holiness ("piety," "impious," "abominable,"
"divine judgment," "divine blessing," "ungodly," "depraved," "wicked," "reprobate," "grace," "mercy") is thoroughly integrated with the language of honor and
shame ("modesty," "dignity," "honor," "polluted," "disgraced," "impure," "shameful"). See John Calvin, (*Commentaries on the First Book of Moses Called Genesis,* 2
vols., trans. John King (Grand Rapids, Mich.: Eerdmans, 1948), 1: 300–307.

92. Wyatt-Brown, *Honor and Violence in the Old South,* 24.

93. C. E. McLain, *Place of Race* (New York: Vantage, 1965), 25. Biblical commentaries
and devotional aids published during the first half of the twentieth century often
intimated that Ham's transgression had a sexual component. For instance, Keil
and Delitzsch, though they do not characterize the offense, cite the view that the
"chief characteristic" of the Hamitic race is sexual sin. See C. F. Keil and F. Delitzsch, *Biblical Commentary on the Old Testament,* Vol. 1, *The Pentateuch,* trans.
James Martin (Grand Rapids, Mich.: Eerdmans, 1949), 157.

94. Carey Daniel, "God the Original Segregationist: The Bible Basis of Racial Segregation," in *God the Original Segregationist and Seven Other Segregation Sermons* (n.p, n.d.), 9. This sermon was originally delivered 23 May 1954.

95. Ibid., 32.

96. During the Civil Rights era, sexual readings of Genesis 9 could be found among antisegregationists as well. Writing in 1959, T. B. Maston offered a familiar retelling of the tale of Noah and his sons: "After the Flood Noah planted a vineyard, made some wine, drank too much, and got drunk. While drunk he became uncovered, or literally uncovered himself. One of his sons, Ham, saw his nakedness and reported it to the other sons, possibly ridiculing his father or making immodest statements concerning him. When Noah awoke from his stupor, he found out about the incident and pronounced a curse upon Canaan, the youngest son of Ham." The references in Maston's text to ridicule and immodesty seem to place it within the American tradition of nonsexual readings of Genesis 9. But on the following page, Maston explains that Canaan may have been the object of Noah's curse because he "was already walking in the sensual footsteps of his father." See T. B. Maston, *The Bible and Race* (Nashville: Broadman, 1959), 109, 110.

Chapter 5

1. James McBride Dabbs, *Who Speaks for the South?* (New York: Funk & Wagnalls, 1964), 130–138, 131.

2. Ibid., 135, 137.

3. James Oscar Farmer Jr., *The Metaphysical Confederacy: James Henley Thornwell and the Synthesis of Southern Values* (Macon: Ga.: Mercer University Press, 1986), 155.

4. Thomas V. Peterson, *Ham and Japheth in America: The Mythic World of Whites in the Antebellum South* (Metuchen, N.J.: American Theological Library Association, 1978), 113.

5. Ibid., 83.

6. Joseph C. Addington, *Reds, Whites and Blacks, or the Colors, Dispersion, Language, Sphere and Unity of the Human Race, as Seen in the Lights of Scripture, Science and Observation* (Raleigh, N.C.: Strother & Marcom, 1862), 28.

7. "The Black Race in North America: Why Was Their Introduction Permitted?" *Southern Literary Messenger* (1855), 658.

8. See Peterson, *Ham and Japheth*, 81–84.

9. James A. Lyon, "Slavery, and the Duties Growing out of the Relation," *Southern Presbyterian Review* 16, no. 1 (1863): 14.

10. *Slavery Ordained of God*, in Kristen E. Kvam, Linda S. Schearing, and Valarie H. Ziegler, eds., *Eve and Adam: Jewish, Christian, and Muslim Readings on Genesis and Gender* (Bloomington: Indiana University Press, 1999), 325.

11. *Slaveholding Not Sinful* (1856), in Kvam et al., *Eve and Adam*, 327. See also Eugene D. Genovese and Elizabeth Fox-Genovese, "The Social Thought of Antebellum Southern Theologians," in *Looking South: Chapters in the Story of an American Region*, ed. Willam B. Moore Jr. and Joseph F. Tripp, Contributions in American History 136 (Westport, Conn.: Greenwood, 1989), 38ff.

12. See Steven A. Channing, *Crisis of Fear: Secession in South Carolina* (New York: W. W. Norton, 1970), 59. Harper wrote in 1837.

13. See Peterson, *Ham and Japheth*, 37–41.

14. Leander Ker, *Slavery Consistent with Christianity*, 3d ed. (Weston, Mo.: Finch & O'Gormon, 1853), 32.

15. "Hammond's Letters on Slavery," in *The Proslavery Argument as Maintained by the Most Distinguished Writers of the Southern States, Containing the Several Articles on the Subject by Chancellor Harper, Governor Harper, Dr. Simms and Professor Dew* (1852; reprint, New York: Negro Universities Press, 1968), 143.

16. William Gilmore Simms, "The Morals of Slavery, in *The Proslavery Argument*, 201–2.

17. Thomas R. Dew, "Professor Dew on Slavery," in *The Proslavery Argument*, 463.

18. In Peterson, *Ham and Japheth*, 68–69.

19. Dew, in *The Proslavery Argument*, 326.

20. From Fitzhugh's pamphlet *Slavery Justified* (1851), cited in C. Vann Woodward, "George Fitzhugh, Sui Generis," in Fitzhugh, *Cannibals All!, or Slaves Without Masters*, ed. C. Vann Woodward (Cambridge, Mass.: Belknap Press, 1960), xvi.

21. Ibid., 85.

22. Ibid., xix.

23. Ibid., 244.

24. Ibid., 35.

25. Ibid., xxxix.

26. Genovese and Genovese, "The Social Thought of Antebellum Southern Theologians," 37. On the association of abolitionism with fanatacism, see Genovese, "*Slavery Ordained of God": The Southern Slaveholders' View of Biblical History and Modern Politics*, twenty-fourth annual Fortenbaugh Mermorial Lecture (Gettysburg, Pa.: Gettysburg College, 1985), 21 and 29 n. 55.

27. Lyon, "Slavery, and the Duties Growing out of the Relation," 4, 18, 21, 34, 8–9. The link between slavery and order is reflected in Lyon's opposition to the slave trade on the grounds that it introduces a "savage and barbarous element" among semicivilized slaves.

28. John B. Adger and John L. Girardeau, eds., *The Collected Writings of James Henley Thornwell, D.D., LL.D.*, 4 vols. (Richmond, Va.: Presbyterian Committee of Publication, 1873), 4:434.

29. Charles Reagan Wilson, *Baptized in Blood: The Religion of the Lost Cause 1865–1920* (Athens: University of Georgia Press, 1980), 106; see 102ff.

30. "The Colored Man in the South," *Southern Presbyterian Review* (January 1877): 85, passim.

31. Robert L. Dabney, *A Defence of Virginia and through Her, of the South, in Recent and Pending Contests agaisnt the Sectional Party* (1867; reprint, New York: Negro Universities Press, 1969), 101–2.

32. Ker, *Slavery Consistent with Christianity*, 10.

33. Josiah Priest, *Slavery as It Relates to the Negro or African Race* (1843; reprint, New York: Arno, 1977), 70, 75.

34. See *The New Interpreter's Bible: General Articles & Introduction, Commentary and Reflections for Each Book of the Bible, including the Apocryphal Deuterocanonical Books*. Vol. 1 (Nashville: Abingdon, 1994), 405.

35. Priest writes: "Noah was born but 178 years after the death of Adam, whose father was the Patriarch Lamech, born 182 years before Adam's death, there being but one intermediate Patriarch between Noah and Adam; of necessity, therefore, how intimate must the mind of Noah have been with all that appertained to the knowl-

edge of God and his providences from the beginning till his own time, and how capable he must have been of instructing his own house in all true knowledge, as well as the arts, after the flood, as he lived 350 years after that event" (*Slavery as It Relates to the Negro or African Race,* 69).

36. Josephus, *Antiquities* I: 6, in *Complete Works of Josephus, In Ten Volumes, A New and Revised Edition Based on Havercamp's Translation* (Cleveland: World, 1940), 25. The laughter theme may have originated in Jewish rabbinic commentary. According to one tradition, Canaan castrated his father and Ham responded by "smiling as if it were a jest for idlers in the marketplace." See Robert Graves and Raphael Patai, *Hebrew Myths: The Book of Genesis* (New York: Greenwich, 1983), 121. Josiah Priest, who quoted approvingly from Josephus's *Antiquities* and capitalized the word "LAUGHING" for emphasis, may have been a proximate source for the proslavery theme of Ham's laughter, although the reluctance of slavery apologists to cite their sources makes it difficult to know for sure. Priest explains that "when Ham had been within the tent, and had seen the condition of his father, he was noticed by them to rush out in a state of very great excitement, yelling and exploding with laughter" (*Slavery as It Relates to the Negro or African Race,* 76–77).

37. On Ambrose, see Jean Devisse, *The Image of the Black in Western Art,* Vol. 2, part 1 William Granger Ryan (Cambridge: Harvard University Press, 1976–79), 55. Origen describes Ham's progeny as people who are "prone to a degenerate life and quickly sink to slavery of the vices. Look at the origin of the race and you will discover that their father Cham, who had laughed at his father's nakedness, deserved a judgment of this kind . . ." ("Genesis Homily XVI," in *Homilies on Genesis and Exodus,* trans. Ronald E. Heine [Washington, D.C.: Catholic University of America Press, 1982], 215). In his *Chronicle,* Sulpicius Severus writes: "But Ham, who laughed at his father drunk with wine, earned a curse from his father. His son, Chus by name, gave birth to the giant Nebroth [Nimrod], by whom it is said the city of Babylon was constructed" (in Devisse, *The Image of the Black in Western Art,* Vol. 2, part 1, 221 n. 173).

38. Christian receptivity to the laughter theme may have been rooted in patristic comparisons of Noah and the suffering Christ. As was noted in chapter 2, the church fathers saw in the drunkenness of Noah a prefiguration of Christ's passion. Following this typological take on the story, because Ham represented those who ridiculed the suffering Christ, his irreverence was interpreted as mockery. See Sally Fisher, *The Square Halo and Other Mysteries of Western Art: Images and the Stories That Inspired Them* (New York: Harry N. Abrams, 1995), 17–18.

39. Adam Clarke, *The Holy Bible Containing the Old and New Testament, The Text Carefully Printed from the Most Correct Copies of the Present Authorized Translation, Including the Marginal and Parallel Texts, with a Commentary and Critical Notes; The Old Testament,* Vol. 1, *Genesis to Deuteronomy* (1810; reprint, New York: Abingdon-Cokesbury, 1977), 82–83.

40. Even contemporary scholars have been known to valorize the tradition that Ham "made sport" of his father. See Latta R. Thomas, *Biblical Faith and the Black American* (Valley Forge, Pa: Judson, 1974), 33. For an example in the Muslim tradition, see the story "The Man of Al-Yaman and His Six Slave-Girls" in *Thousand and One Nights* (in Werner Sollors, *Neither Black nor White yet Both: Thematic Explorations of Interracial Literature* (New York: Oxford University Press, 1997), 96.

41. In premodern traditions of interpretation, Ham's laughter was often tied to sexuality: Ham mocks Noah upon seeing his "natural member" or after Noah discovers his scheme to have relations with his wife on the ark. The sexual element in this laughter tradition is evident in European visual art, where the laughing Ham is sometimes portrayed as luridly peering through the curtains of Noah's tent.

42. In Peterson, *Ham and Japheth,* 49.

43. Forrest G. Wood, *The Arrogance of Faith: Christianity and Race in America from the Colonial Era to the Twentieth Century* (Boston: Northeastern University Press, 1991), epigraph at the beginning of the chapter titled "The Curse." Another example of the laughter theme's internalization is provided by slave creation legends, which often explain Ham's black skin and subservience as "punishment for laughing at his father's nakedness." See Deborah McDowell, in the annotations to Nella Larsen, *Passing* (New Brunswick, N.J.: Rutgers University Press, 1986), cited in Sollors, *Neither Black nor White,* 455.

44. *Jefferson Davis Constitutionalist: His Letters, Papers and Speeches,* Vol. 4, ed. Dunbar Rowland (Jackson: Mississippi Department of Archives and History, 1923), 230–31: "Remarks of Jefferson Davis on the bill for the benefit of schools in the District of Columbia. April 12, 1860."

45. Bertram Wyatt-Brown, *Honor and Violence in the Old South* (New York: Oxford University Press, 1986), 156.

46. "A South Carolinian," *A Refutation of the Calumnies Circulated against the Southern and Western States, Respecting the Institution and Existence of Slavery Among Them, to Which is Added a Minute and Particular Account of the Actual State and Condition of Their Negro Population, Together With Historical Notices of all the Insurrections That Have Taken Place Since the Settlement of the Country* (1822; reprint, New York: Negro Universities Press, 1996), 61.

47. Charles Grier Sellers Jr., "The Travail of Slavery," in *The Southerner as American,* ed. Charles Grier Sellers Jr. (Chapel Hill: University of North Carolina Press, 1960), 69.

48. Wyatt-Brown, *Honor and Violence in the Old South,* 161, 164, 167.

49. Although Peterson does not elucidate the theme of order (or the subtheme of impudence) in antebellum readings of Genesis 9, he does note that the story of Noah and his sons pictured blacks as "mirthful" (*Ham and Japheth,* 101).

50. Given their assumption that blacks were ill prepared by experience and character to exercise freedom, following emancipation many Southern whites were convinced that liberty would spell blacks' ruin as a people, and some went so far as to predict their literal extinction. When census data in 1870 and 1880 appeared to contradict this "retrogression theory" (i.e., that left to their own devices the black race would swiftly degenerate and disappear), some Southerners remolded their argument and contended that it was precisely Negro success, and the racial conflict it would engender, that portended the demise of African Americans. Some even called for the mass deportation of blacks as an expedient to forestall conflict. See Guion Griffis Johnson, "The Ideology of White Supremacy, 1876–1910," in *Essays in Southern History* ed. Fletcher Melvin Green (Chapel Hill: University of North Carolina Press, 1949), 139ff.

51. "The Black Race in North America," 658.

52. Frederick Dalcho, *Practical Considerations Founded on the Scriptures Relative to the Slave Population of South-Carolina* (Charleston, S.C.: A.E. Miller, 1823), 33–36.

53. Ibid.
54. Ibid., 4.
55. Ibid., 5.
56. Samuel A. Cartwright, *Essays, Being Inductions Drawn from the Baconian Philosophy Proving the Truth of the Bible and the Justice and Benevolence of the Decree Dooming Canaan to be Servant of Servants: And Answering the Question of Voltaire: "On demande quel droit des etrangers tels que les Juifs avaient sur le pays de Canaan?" in a Series of Letters to the Rev. William Winans* (Vidalia, La.: n.p., 1843), 12.
57. "Sandell had been an officer in a Mississippi infantry regiment during the Civil War, and during the last days of the conflict he came to see the resemblances between it and the prophecies recorded in the biblical books of Daniel and Revelation. He continued pondering the similarities for forty years, publishing his conclusions after the turn of the century" (Wilson, *Baptized in Blood*, 64).
58. J.W. Sandell, *The United States in Scripture. The Union Against the States. God in Government* (Magnolia, Miss., 1907), 41.
59. Ibid.
60. Ibid., 44.
61. According to Sethian doctrine, two angels had intercourse with Eve, producing Cain and Abel. The divine mother sent a flood to destroy this corrupt brood, but other angels frustrated her plan by ensuring that Ham, one of the race she wished to destroy, was taken into the ark. In this way, the seed of malice survived to fill the earth. See Jack P. Lewis, *A Study of the Interpretation of Noah and the Flood in Jewish and Christian Literature* (Lerden: E.J. Brill, 1968), 109.
62. See also Priest, *Slavery as it Relates to the Negro or African Race,* 72 (although Fletcher does not appear to be dependent upon him): "It cannot be supposed for a moment, that Noah would allow the three distinct complexions, or races of his family to mingle or amalgamate, for he knew it was God who had produced for a wise purpose, these very characters; amalgamation, therefore, would certainly have destroyed what God so evidently had ordained and caused to exist. The amazing fact of the existence of three complexions, of his own sons, by the same mother, was to Noah, a sufficient reason, even without a Divine revelation on the subject, that these were to be kept sacredly asunder, and pure from each other's blood forever. That this view of the subject was held as binding upon these families for many ages, we have no doubts—each dreading to break over a barrier which the creator had evidently placed between them; amalgamation therefore, during the 350 years of Noah's life after the flood, it is not likely often happened among them." In *The Arrogance of Faith,* Forrest Wood ascribes a similar view to Fletcher's contemporary Nathan Lord, president of Dartmouth College, who in 1860 spoke of Ham's "forbidden intermarriage with the previously wicked and accursed race of Cain." The intermarriage theme is also prominent in the two-seed line fantasies of the late-twentieth-century Christian Identity Movement. See Michael Barkun, *Religion and the Racist Right: The Origins of the Christian Identity Movement,* rev. ed. (Chapel Hill: University of North Carolina Press, 1997), chaps. 7–9.
63. John Fletcher, *Studies on Slavery, In Easy Lessons, compiled into Eight Studies, and subdivided into Short Lessons for the Convenience of Readers* (1852, reprint, Miami: Mnemosyne, 1969), 250.
64. The explanation that Ham's sin was his marriage to "Naamah, the daughter of Lamech, of the race of Cain," conveniently allowed Fletcher to attach Cain's mark—which he interpreted as black skin—to the descendants of Ham (ibid.,

449). Linking the curse of slavery to Cain's physical and symbolic stigmata was not an original contribution. Particularly in colonial South America, many defenders of slavery and the inferiority of blacks had argued that black Africans were descendants of Cain. The association was also common in eighteenth-century North America. See David Brion Davis, *The Problem of Slavery in Western Culture* (Ithaca, N.Y.: Cornell University Press, 1966), 171, 236, 459. Cf. Elihu Coleman, *Testimony against that Anti-Christian Practice of Making Slaves of Men, Wherein it is Shewed to be Contrary to the Dispensation of the Law and Time of the Gospel, and Very Opposite Both to Grace and Nature* (1733; reprint, New Bedford, Mass.: Adam Shearman, 1825), 16: "But some may object, as I myself have heard them, that there was a mark set upon Cain, and they do believe that these negroes are the posterity of Cain, because of their hair, and their being so black, differing from all others, and that Canaan was to be a servant of servants to his brethren, whom they take to be of the same lineage. . . ."

In the 1830s, Joseph Smith, founder of Mormonism, wrote that the mark placed upon Cain was dark skin and that when Ham married a woman of Cain's lineage, he and Canaan were cursed with servitude and with Cain's mark. See Naomi Felicia Woodbury, "A Legacy of Intolerance: Nineteenth Century Pro-Slavery Propaganda and the Mormon Church Today" (master's thesis, University of California at Los Angeles, 1966), 70. Just before the Civil War, Samuel Cartwright took a similar position with regard to Cain and Ham. But Fletcher's version of the parallel between Cain's mark and Ham's curse was less vulnerable to the observation—made by abolitionists as far back as Coleman in 1733—that Negroes could not be of the line of Cain because his descendants perished in the Flood.

65. Fletcher, *Studies on Slavery,* 446.
66. Ibid., 433.
67. "Ariel" [Buckner H. Payne], *The Negro: What Is His Ethnological Status: Is He the Progeny of Ham? Is He a Descendant of Adam and Eve? Has He a Soul? Or Is He a Beast in God's Nomenclature? What Is His Status as Fixed by God in Creation? What Is His Relation to the White Race?* 2d ed. (Cincinnati: n.p., 1867), 48. Emphasis in the original.
68. Ibid., 47–48. Emphasis in the original.
69. The practice of unlocking meanings from obscure Hebrew words is as old as Bible reading itself, and it was applied to Ham early in the interpretive tradition. Recall that Augustine surmised that because "Ham" means "hot," Noah's son represented "the tribe of heretics, hot with the spirit, not of patience, but of impatience."
70. Priest, *Slavery as it Relates to the Negro or African Race,* 33. Emphasis in the original.
71. Ibid.
72. The complex link between honor and order in the proslavery imagination may be evident in the fact that "impudence"—a term crucial for comprehending proslavery affirmations of Ham's laughter—literally means "shamelessness."
73. James A. Sloan *The Great Question Answered; or, Is Slavery a Sin in Itself (Per Se) Answered According to the Teaching of the Scriptures* (Memphis: Hutton, Gallaway, 1857), chap. 4, "The Origin of Color and Slavery."
74. Ibid., 75. Emphasis in the original.
75. Ker, *Slavery Consistent with Christianity,* 10.
76. In Peterson, *Ham and Japheth,* 145. Peterson observes that antebellum slavery apologists viewed Ham's misdeed as "an attack against the authority of the family and thereby against God's chosen institution for governing the human race"(49).

77. Kenneth S. Greenberg, *Honor and Slavery: Lies, Duels, Noses, Masks, Dressing as a Woman, Gifts, Strangers, Humanitarianism, Death, Slave Rebellions, the Proslavery Argument, Baseball, Hunting, and Gambling in the Old South* (Princeton, N.J.: Princeton University Press, 1996) 123.

78. Wyatt-Brown, *Honor and Violence in the Old South*, 39.

79. Cited in Ernest Trice Thompson, *Presbyterians in the South*, Vol. 2, *1861–1890* (Richmond, Va.: John Knox, 1973), 61–62.

80. In the rare instances when it was cited, Noah's curse no longer carried the burden of defending racial slavery per se. For instance, the four-page section on "The Curse upon Canaan" in Dabney's *A Defence of Virginia* (1867) rehearsed many of the claims advanced by antebellum proponents of the curse but included the unusual admission that it was not essential to link Noah's curse to present-day Africans. In fact, Dabney concluded, "this passage of Scripture is not regarded, nor advanced, as of prime force and importance in this argument. Others more decisive will follow" (104).

81. Humphrey K. Ezell, *The Christian Problem of Racial Segregation* (New York: Greenwich, 1959).

82. Ibid., 13.

83. Ibid., 14.

Chapter 6

1. Cited in Cain Hope Felder, "Race, Racism and the Bible Narratives," in Felder, ed., *Stony the Road We Trod: African American Biblical Interpretation* (Minneapolis: Fortress, 1991), 134.

2. Many who applied Genesis 9–11 to American history asserted that Nimrod was master builder at the Tower of Babel. They failed, however, to cite Josephus, Luther, Milton, or any other ancient authority in support of this identification. This raises the possibility that the nexus between Ham, Nimrod, and the tower evolved naturally from the proslavery association of Ham and his posterity with rebellion and disorder.

3. Josiah Priest, *Slavery as it Relates to the Negro or African Race* (1843; reprint, New York: Arno, 1977), 210. See also 212: "[Ham] laughed at his holy father and despised his religion and doctrine. After he had separated from his father . . . he established both a new government and a new religion. His grandson Nimrod likewise sinned against both the government and the church. He did not cultivate the true religion; and he practiced unjust tyranny on his cousins, whom he expelled from their paternal lands."

4. An intriguing example of Priest's influence in the South is Joseph Henry Lumpkin, chief justice of the Supreme Court of Georgia. In 1853, while considering a case involving manumission of a slave, Lumpkin read Priest's *Slavery*. Soon afterward, he wrote to a friend that the book "should be in the house and hands of every southern slaveholder. It agrees with and fully confirms all of my previous notions as to the Bible doctrine of slavery. Which in short are neither more nor less than this—that the tribe of Ham are cursed. That they are judicially condemned to perpetual bondage. Did you ever suspect that Jezebel was a Negro wench with a black skin and wooly head? And that Nimrod was a big Negro fellow? Priest proves this incontestably." The letter is cited in Timothy S. Huebner, "The Southern

Judicial Tradition: Southern Appellate Judges and American Legal Culture in the Nineteenth Century" (Ph.D. dissertation, University of Florida, 1993), 136.

5. Priest, *Slavery as it Relates to the Negro or African Race,* 48.

6. Ibid., 233.

7. Ibid., 234.

8. Ibid., 319. As Priest seems to be aware, the association of Nimrod with "rebellion against Noah and Shem's religion" is founded on Jewish tradition. Priest is unusual among antebellum proslavery writers in his obvious dependence upon Jewish sources, especially Josephus, from whom he adopts the notion that the tower was built to withstand a second flood. See especially 320.

9. Ibid., 321.

10. Ibid., 56.

11. See, e.g., Joseph C. Addington, *Reds, Whites and Blacks, or the Colors, Dispersion, Language, Sphere and Unity of the Human Race, as Seen in the Lights of Scripture, Science and Observation* (Raleigh, N.C.: Strother & Marcom, 1862), 23. Addington believes that following the Babel episode each "color" had its own peculiar language.

12. Priest, *Slavery as it Relates to the Negro or African Race,* 39. Priest writes that it was the policy of Nimrod and "his coadjutors to draw a line of separation between his people and those who adhered to the religion of Noah" (237). In Priest's portrait of Nimrod, there is obvious tension between the religious schismatic and the great consolidator.

13. Ibid., 237. Departing from the typical American view of "Hamites," Priest asserts that Nimrod possessed the sort of knowledge upon which civilizations are built. The tower "was wholly of Negro invention, who had the requisite geometrical knowledge at the time, derived from the house of Noah, who brought this knowledge with all other from beyond the flood. On this account, for some hundred years, the first people of those countries had more scientific knowledge than the nations, many of them, had a thousand years afterwards" (319).

14. Jerome B. Holgate, *Noachidae: or, Noah and His Descendants* (Buffalo: Breed, Butler, 1860), 25. See also 90–91, 143, 147.

15. According to Robert Graves and Raphael Patai, "the Persians called the constellation Orion 'Nimrod'; thus linking him with the rebel angel Shemhazai, and with the Greek hero Orion, also 'a mighty hunter' who offended his god" (*Hebrew Myths: The Book of Genesis* [New York: Greenwich, 1983], 128). See also Alexander Hislop, who identifies Nimrod with Orion (*The Two Babylons* [1858; reprint, New York: Loizeaux Brothers, 1953], 13).

16. Holgate, *Noachidae,* 171–73.

17. *Noachidae* provides Orion-Nimrod many opportunities to demonstrate his legendary physical prowess: He crushes a serpent with his bare hands, forces a boulder "the size of a boy's head" down the throat of a ravenous lion, brings down a tiger with one thrust of his spear, raises a horse on his shoulder, and grinds stones to powder.

18. Holgate, *Noachidae,* 262.

19. Ibid., 254.

20. Ibid., 287.

21. Ibid., 294. One of the novel's more dramatized scenes is an encounter between Nimrod and Noah. When the aged patriarch arrives to inspect the Tower of Babel,

Orion exhibits no respect. Rather, "stretching out his brawny arms, and expanding his chest to its utmost limits," he says simply, "I am potent." Noah responds that if he were as potent spiritually as physically there should be reason to rejoice. "Spiritually!... what's that?" is Nimrod's predictable answer. As the interview ends, Noah gives Orion a new name: "NIMROD!" he exclaims, "with peculiar vehemence, which made the entire assemblage start, for the word signifies REBEL, and could not have been applied to him previous to this time. . . ." Ibid., 281–82.

22. According to Jewish legend, earth and fire from heaven each destroyed a third of the tower, while a third remained standing (Graves and Patai, *Hebrew Myths*, 126).

23. Holgate, *Noachidae*, 297.

24. Ibid., 262. Cf. Matthew Henry, who writes that "the builders were scattered abroad upon the face of the whole earth . . . to the several countries and places allotted to them in the division that had been made, which they knew before, but would not go to take possession of till now that they were forced to it" (*Matthew Henry's Commentary on the Whole Bible, Wherein Each Chapter Is Summed up in Its Contents: The Sacred Text Inserted at Large in District Paragraph Reduced to its Proper Heads: The Sense Given, and Largely Illustrated with Practical Comments, and Observations*, Vol. 1, *Genesis to Deuteronomy* [New York: R. Carter, 1880], 81).

25. Holgate, *Noachidae*, 272.

26. Frederick Dalcho, *Practical Considerations Founded on the Scriptures Relative to the Slave Population of South-Carolina* (Charleston, S.C.: A.E. Miller, 1823), 8, 10, 12.

27. J. Wm. Flinn, ed., *Complete Works of Rev. Thomas Smyth, D.D.*, Vol. 8 (Columbia, S.C.: R. L. Bryan, 1910), 125, 112. Smyth cites a Mr. Faber, who "pursues at great length" the view that the triple division of the earth by the sons of Noah is reflected in extrabiblical myths. He does so by "an illustration of the primitive dominion secured by Nimrod and his Cushites over their brethren, as manifested in the existence of distinct castes or races, and in other customs found among nations in every quarter of the globe" (114). In a note, Smyth instructs the reader to "See the authorities given by Faber, vol. iii, 475–498." See also Samuel Davies Baldwin, *Dominion: or, the Unity and Trinity of the Human Race; with the Divine Political Constitution of the World, and the Divine Rights of Shem, Ham, and Japheth* (Nashville: Stevenson and F. A. Owens, 1858), where the author alludes to "Nimrod the apostate" (378).

28. At least one antebellum writer invoked the legend of Nimrod without any mention of Ham. In a sermon delineating the doctrine of "Bible slavery," W. T. Hamilton of Alabama noted that "Nimrod, the mighty hunter, is often asserted to have been the first slaveholder, Gen. 10:9." See W. T. Hamilton, *The Duties of Masters and Slaves Respectively: or Domestic Servitude as Sanctioned by the Bible: A Discourse, Delivered in the Government-Street Church, Mobile, Ala., on Sunday Night, December 15, 1844* (Mobile: F. H. Brooks, 1845), 9.

29. In 1838, Sara Grimké wrote that the first effect of the Fall was "the lust of dominion." But while woman was its first victim, this lust for dominion was afterwards "exhibited by Cain in the murder of his brother, by Nimrod in his becoming a mighty hunter of men, and setting up a kingdom over which to reign." See "Letters on the Equality of the Sexes and the Condition of Woman," in Kristen E. Kvam, Linda S. Schearing, and Valarie H. Ziegler, eds., *Eve and Adam: Jewish, Christian, and Muslim Readings on Genesis and Gender* (Bloomington: Indiana State University Press, 1999), 344.

30. Joseph P. Thompson, *Teachings of the New Testament on Slavery* (New York: Joseph H. Ladd, 1856), 8.
31. William Henry Brisbane, *Slaveholding Examined in the Light of the Holy Bible* (Philadelphia, 1847), 20.
32. James W. C. Pennington, *A Text Book of the Origin and History &c. &c. of the Colored People* (Hartford: L. Skinner, 1841), 32.
33. "Ariel" [Bucker H. Payne], *The Negro: What is His Ethnological Status: Is He the Progeny of Ham? Is He a Descendant of Adam and Eve? Has He a Soul? Or is He a Beast in God's Nomenclature? What is His Status as Fixed by God in Creation? What is His Relation to the White Race?* 2d ed. (Cincinnati 1867), 32.
34. Ibid., 33.
35. Ibid., 31. "Ariel" cites other biblical traditions as well: "This view of Nimrod as a *mighty* hunter, will be sustained, not only by the facts narrated in our Bible, of what he did, but to the mind of every Hebrew scholar, it will appear doubly strong by the sense of the original. We see that God, by his prophets, gives the name *hunter* to *all tyrants*, with manifest reference to Nimrod as its originator. In the Latin Vulgate, Ezekiel xxxii: 30, plainly shows it." Emphasis in the original.
36. "Ariel" opines that the "daughters of men" referred to in Genesis 6 were Negroes who married "sons of God," i.e., children of Adam and Eve.
37. "Ariel," *The Negro,* 31.
38. Ibid., 32.
39. J. W. Sandell, *The United States in Scripture. The Union Against the States. God in Government* (Magnolia, Miss., 1907), 41, 44. About the same time, Pauline Hopkins wrote that "Nimrod first arose to national greatness as a monarch so that until this day his name is great among the princes of the earth. He was the founder of the great Assyrian Empire . . . Previous to this time the people were governed by patriarchs." See Pauline E. Hopkins, *A Primer of Facts Pertaining to the Early Greatness of the African Race and the Possibility of Restoration by its Descendants—with Epilogue* (Cambridge, Mass.: P. E. Hopkins, & Co., 1905), 10.
40. Sandell, *The United States in Scripture,* 48. Sandell perceives a similar force at work in America's "tendency to the centralization of power even at the sacrifice of the rights of the States and the people."
41. According to H. C. Leupold, "the tendency of this Cushite must have been to rise up against, and to attempt to overthrow, all existing order." See H. C. Leupold, *Exposition of Genesis* (Grand Rapids, Mich.: Baker, 1950), 366.
42. See W. H. Griffith, *Genesis: A Devotional Commentary* (1946; reprint, Grand Rapids, Mich.: Kregel, 1988), 103: "It would seem as though Nimrod represented a revival of the antediluvian spirit of independence and rebellion with its disregard of God and His authority." Interestingly, a few of these commentaries cite archeological evidence in support of the tradition. For instance, the architectural ruins near modern Babylon (known as Birs Nimrud) are said to represent the remains of the failed tower (a fact that presumably confirms Nimrod's role in its construction).
43. The assumption that Nimrod tyrannized men, though unsupported by the biblical text, was shared by popular and critical commentaries alike during the first half of the twentieth century. In *A Critical and Exegetical Commentary on Genesis* (New York: Charles Scribner's Sons, 1925), John Skinner wrote that Nimrod was "famous as the originator of the idea of the military state, based on arbitrary force" (207).

According to Paul E. Kretzmann's *Popular Commentary of the Bible, The Old Testament*, Vol. 1, *The Historical Books of he Old Testament: Genesis to Esther* (St. Louis: Concordia, 1923), Nimrod's work was undertaken "over against God, in opposition to Jehovah, in the haughtiness and pride of his own mind, a fact which also made him a tyrant toward men" (24).

44. Joseph S. Exell, *The Biblical Illustrator*, Vol. 1, *Genesis* (Grand Rapids, Mich.: Baker, 1956), 504.

45. See Arthur W. Pink, *Gleanings in Genesis* (Chicago: Moody, 1950), 131–32.

46. Ibid., 135. Emphasis in the original.

47. Harry Lacey, *God and the Nations* (New York: Loizeaux Brothers, 1947), 25.

48. Ibid., 23.

49. Ibid., 23, 25.

50. Ibid., 26. Of course, as Regina M. Schwartz has noted, "the Bible itself describes the origins of the nations as a punishment, the punishment for challenging the sovereign power of the heavenly deity, the punishment for building an idol heavenward." See *The Curse of Cain: The Violent Legacy of Monotheism* (Chicago: University of Chicago Press, 1997), 38.

51. Lacey, *God and the Nations*, 23.

52. *Congressional Record*, 88th Cong., 2d sess., 1964, 110, pt. 10:13207. Byrd also invoked Genesis 1, Leviticus 19, Matthew 20, and Acts 17 in his case against the civil rights bill. See Taylor Branch, *Pillar of Fire: America during the King Years 1963–65* (New York: Simon and Shuster, 1998), 336.

53. In the same genre are the following works: T. B. Maston, *The Bible and Race* (Nashville: Broadman, 1959); and *Segregation and Desegregation: A Christian Approach* (New York: Macmillan, 1959); Everett Tilson, *Segregation and the Bible* (New York and Nashville: Abingdon, 1958); James O. Buswell III, *Slavery, Segregation and Scripture* (Grand Rapids, Mich.: Eerdmans, 1964); Ralph L. Moellering, *Christian Conscience and Negro Emancipation* (Philadelphia: Fortress, 1965); and Alan P. Grimes, *Equality in America: Religion, Race, and the Urban Majority* (New York: Oxford University Press, 1964).

54. Cited in Latta R. Thomas, *Biblical Faith and the Black American* (Valley Forge, Pa.: Judson, 1974), 27–28.

55. See, e.g., Maston, *Segregation and Desegregation*, in which the author laments that "the only reason to give any space to 'the curse of Ham' is the fact that so many people are using it today to justify the present racial pattern, just as their forefathers used it to defend slavery" (99).

56. A notable exception is Buswell, who in *Slavery, Segregation and Scripture* writes that "the all-important case [of supposed segregation in the Old Testament] is that of the 'segregation' in Genesis of Noah's three sons who are supposed to be the progenitors of the three races" (58–59). To his credit, Buswell notes the tower's association with "the sinful and 'rebellious' character of Ham" and the connection of both with nineteenth-century racism.

57. G. T. Gillespie, *A Christian View of Segregation. An Address Made Before the Synod of Mississippi of the Presbyterian Church in the U. S., November 4, 1954* (Greenwood: Association of Citizens' Councils of Mississippi, 1954), 16.

58. Ibid., 9.

59. Gillespie's debt to readings of Genesis that stress the maintenance of order is evident in his claims that forced integration of the schools will lead either to

intermarriage or to "a state of constant friction and tension . . . which would greatly complicate the problem of discipline and administration" and will "imperil the stability of the social order and the future welfare of the race" (ibid., 4, 11).

60. Kenneth R. Kinney, "The Segregation Issue," *Baptist Bulletin* (October 1956): 9–10.

61. Ibid., 9.

62. Ibid. Emphasis in the original.

63. Finnis Jennings Dake, ed., *Dake's Annotated Reference Bible* (Lawrenceville, Ga.: Dake Bible Sales, 1991), 9.

64. Ibid., 159.

65. Dake refers to Genesis 9:24ff as a "great racial prophecy" dealing with a "servile posterity" and claims that "the three sons of Noah were to produce 3 distinct classes of people."

66. This phrase appears throughout a 1960 prosegregation address by Bob Jones Sr. See *Is Segregation Scriptural?* (Greenville, S.C.: Bob Jones University, 1960), 12.

67. Carey Daniel, "Segregation's Archenemy Hiss' United Nations, Or, Let's Get the U.S. Out of the U.N.," in *God the Original Segregationist and Seven other Segregation Sermons* (n.p, n.d.), 53–54.

68. According to Daniel (ibid., 15): "If we are to trace the Scriptural doctrine of Segregation to its origin we must go back even behind the tenth chapter of Genesis to the first chapter and the story of Creation. There in that opening passage of the Bible we are told repeatedly for the sake of emphasis—NO LESS THAN TEN TIMES IN FIVE VERSES—that God made each of His creatures 'after his kind.' . . . This means that the Lord made each creature with a gregarious instinct so that it would associate only with its own kind and reproduce only after its own kind. . . . Segregation is therefore a Divine Principle that operates throughout all nature, and mongrelization is a sinful and satanic mockery of it. . . . So the Lord pronounced His original creation, this highly segregated creation of His, to be VERY GOOD— not bad. It is the Devil who would have us believe that segregation is bad."

69. Ibid., 17.

70. Ibid.

71. "When later [the Canaanites] dared to violate God's sacred law of segregation by moving into and claiming the land farther east [from the land allotted them along the Mediterranean coast], so that the Hebrew territory became known as 'the land of Canaan,' the Lord justly commanded His chosen people to wage war upon them and 'utterly destroy them' (Deut. 7:1, 2)" (ibid., 9).

72. Ibid.

73. Ibid., 18. Daniel translates the verse thus: "He (God) stood, and measured the earth: he beheld, and DROVE ASUNDER THE NATIONS; and the everlasting mountains were scattered, the perpetual hills did bow: HIS WAYS ARE EVERLASTING. I saw the tents of Cushan in affliction. . . ." Daniel comments: "We might almost say that the Old Testament begins and ends with the doctrine of racial segregation. In the last chapter of Habakkuk, one of the last short books of the Old Testament, we find that inspired prophet referring to the Lord's 'scattering' of the 'nations' at the Tower of Babel recorded in the tenth and eleventh chapters of Genesis, the first book of the Old Testament. . . . The Bible word for 'race' is 'nation.' So when it says that God has 'driven asunder the nations,' it means that He has forcibly separated and segregated the races of this earth, and that He means for them to STAY that way at least as long as this present world shall last" (53–54).

74. Ibid., 53ff.

75. Ibid., 54.

76. Ibid. Daniel goes on to say: "That comparison between the ancient and modern towers of Babel must have been one of the things that Christ had in mind when He said, 'As the days of Noe were, so shall also the coming of the Son of man be' (Matt. 24:37). This text is generally used in making comparisons between present-day conditions and those just before the great flood. But Noah lived many years after the flood, and the conditions that gave rise to the building of Babel began to take shape during his lifetime. It was undoubtedly in the days of Noah that God gave His first command for racial segregation (sadly, unheeded) that by Noah's three sons should the nations be divided in the earth after the flood (Gen. 10:32)" (55).

77. The source for this connection may be Alexander Hislop, who linked Nimrod with the "Giants [who] rebelled against Heaven." But the link goes deep into the history of interpretation, perhaps as far as 1 Enoch (third century B.C.E.).

78. C.E. McLain, *Place of Race* (New York: Vantage, 1965), 35. The 1936 edition of Hislop's *The Two Babylons* is cited in a note. McLain reveals Hislop's influence also in his claim that "the pagan religions of the world had their inception on this occasion [the building of the tower]—'Mystery, Babylon the great, the mother of harlots and abominations of the earth' (Rev. 17:5)" (37).

79. See Griffith, *Genesis*, 110–11: "When outward unity is attempted, the result will be, as in this case [the Tower of Babel], separation, dispersion, confusion. What a lesson we have here in connection with all attempts at church unity."

Chapter 7

1. See Ernest Trice Thompson, *Presbyterians in the South,* Vol. 2, *1861–1890* (Richmond, Va.: John Knox, 1963). Even African American divines were known to refer to Palmer's sermons. In 1862, Edward W. Blyden cited Palmer's words "in the famous sermon of this distinguished divine on *Slavery a Divine Trust,*" where Palmer had acknowledged the fruits of black labor on Southern soil. See "The Call of Providence to the Descendants of Africa in America," in Howard Brotz, ed., *Negro Social and Political Thought 1850–1920: Representative Texts* (New York: Basic Books, 1966), 121.

2. James Oscar Farmer Jr., *The Metaphysical Confederacy: James Henley Thornwell and the Synthesis of Southern Values* (Macon, Ga.: Mercer University Press, 1986), 10.

3. Eugene D. Genovese emphasizes that many Southern Presbyterian divines—including Thomas H. Thornwell, Robert L. Dabney, George Howe, John Adger, and Joseph L. Wilson—failed to invoke the Noahic curse with specific reference to blacks. See *A Consuming Fire: The Fall of the Confederacy in the Mind of the White Christian South,* Mercer University Lamar Memorial Lectures 41 (Athen and London: University of Georgia Press, 1998), 4, 81, 160 n. 7.

4. Ibid., 96.

5. Noll, "The Bible and Slavery," 47. Noll notes three principles that were constitutive of the Reformed approach to scripture so prevalent in America before 1860: *scriptura sola* (the Bible as a unique authority), the "regulative principle" (the requirement to do what the Bible commands and not do those things about which the

Bible is silent), and the "Third Use of the Law" (the view that the moral teaching of Scripture provided a blueprint for life). Mark A. Noll, "The Bible and Slavery," in *Religion and the American Civil War*, ed. Randall N. Miller, Harry S. Stout, and Charles Reagan Wilson (New York: Oxford University Press, 1998), 43–73.

6. Ibid., 63.

7. See especially C. Vann Woodward, *The Strange Career of Jim Crow*, 3d ed. (New York: Oxford University Press, 1974).

8. See, e.g., "National Responsibility before God," in *God's New Israel: Religious Interpretations of American Destiny*, ed. Conrad Cherry (Englewood Cliffs, N.J.: Prentice-Hall, 1971); and Wayne C. Eubank, "Benjamin Morgan Palmer's Thanksgiving Sermon, 1860," in *Antislavery and Disunion, 1853–1861: Studies in the Rhetoric of Compromise and Conflict*, ed. J. Jeffery Auer (New York: Harper and Row, 1963), 291–309.

9. Thompson, *Presbyterians in the South*, 2:41.

10. Palmer, "The Import of Hebrew History," *Southern Presbyterian Review* 9 (April 1856): 582–610.

11. Ibid., 591.

12. Ibid., 595.

13. Palmer, *Our Historic Mission, An Address Delivered before the Eunomian and Phi-Mu Societies of La Grange Synodical College, July 7 1858* (New Orleans: True Witness Office, 1859).

14. Ibid., 4–5.

15. Ibid., 7.

16. Schlegel's actual statement is: "Even America . . . occupies here a comparatively subordinate rank; and it is only in latter ages, and since its discovery, that it can be said to belong to history. . . . America may be regarded as a remote dependency [of Europe], and, as it were, a continuation of old Europe on the other side of the Atlantic." See James Burton Robertson, ed., *The Philosophy of History: In a Course of Lectures Delivered at Vienna by Frederick von Schlegel, Translated from the German with a Memoir of the Author* (London: H. G. Bohn, 1852), 109.

17. Palmer, *Our Historic Mission*, 8.

18. Ibid., 10. According to Palmer, these "problems of the historical calculus" are *political* (the possibility of self-government), *ecclesiastic* (the proper relationship of church and state), *educational*, and *economic*.

19. Ibid., 30.

20. Schlegel took seriously the early chapters of Genesis as he sketched his "historical land chart of civilization." However, his view of human origins diminished the influence he was to have upon Palmer. Specifically, Schlegel's biblically derived dualism—in which an original conflict between Cain and Seth is reflected throughout subsequent history—did not suit Palmer's purposes, in that it provided no firm textual basis for assigning the relative destinies of Anglo-Saxons and African Americans. Thus, before it could inform Palmer's conception of American history and destiny, Schlegel's notion of historic peoples had to be fused with Rougemont's conviction that with the Flood human history had begun again, and according to a novel pattern: The postdiluvian age features three rather than two historical antagonists, and each is prepared by Providence and by their distinctive characters for a unique role in the history of redemption. For Rougemont, as for Palmer, the interrelationships between the descendants of Noah's sons are clarified in the prophecy of their common ancestor.

21. Schlegel's influence on Palmer can be traced to the "cultural nationalism" that burgeoned in South Carolina during his years in Columbia (1843–56). As he interacted with notable theorists of Southern values including Joseph LeConte and James Henley Thornwell, Palmer imbibed both European Romanticism and the native sociology of LeConte, in which human societies were perceived as "organisms" subject to natural laws of development. See Farmer, *The Metaphysical Confederacy*, 106–9; and Charles Reagan Wilson, *Baptized in Blood: The Religion of the Lost Cause, 1865–1920* (Athens, Ga: Univ. of Georgia, 1980), 3.

22. Farmer, *The Metaphysical Confederacy*, 31–2.

23. Thomas Carey Johnson, *The Life and Letters of Benjamin Morgan Palmer* (1906; reprint, Edinburgh and Carlisle, Pa.: Banner of Trath Trust, 1987), 187–88. Johnson writes that Palmer "took quickly and easily the very first place not only in his city and Presbytery, but in his Synod and in the vast section of the Southwest" (191).

24. H. Shelton Smith, *In His Image, But . . . : Racism in Southern Religion, 1780–1910* (Durham, N.C.: Duke University Press, 1972), 173. See also Samuel Wilson Jr., *The First Presbyterian Church of New Orleans* (Louisiana Landmarks Society, 1988), 36; Johnson, *Life and Letters*, 219, 237; James W. Silver, *Confederate Morale and Church Propaganda* (New York: Norton, 1957), 17, 95.

25. Smith, *In His Image, But . . .* , 175.

26. Mitchell Snay, *Gospel of Disunion: Religion and Separatism in the Antebellum South* (Cambridge: Cambridge University Press, 1993), 175.

27. In a letter of December 20, 1860, J. H. McHuaine of Princeton, New Jersey wrote to his cousin Jos. S. Copes, M.D., that "we in these parts are all grieved at Dr. Palmer's sermon. Did you hear it? It has utterly destroyed our confidence in him as a man of large and capacious mind." Letter in Howard-Tilton Memorial Library, Tulane University, Manuscripts Division, "Palmer, Dr. B. M." personnel folder.

28. "Review of a Discourse Delivered in the First Presbyterian Church, New Orleans, Nov. 29, 1860, by Rev. B. M. Palmer, D.D.," *Boston Atlas and Bee*, 12 January 1861, 1. The review occupies four of seven columns on the paper's front page.

29. According to Eugene Genovese's *A Consuming Fire*, the language of "trust" was popular among proslavery writers in the antebellum period, particularly Presbyterians and Episcopalians. Note that in the "Thanksgiving Sermon" the language of instinct, interest, and duty prominent in Palmer's writings from the 1850s has been displaced and greater stress placed on "providence." See also Palmer's "Secession and the South,"*Southern Presbyterian Review* 14, no. 1 (1861): 156: "It is therefore the duty of the South, in the discharge of a great historic trust, to conserve and transmit [slavery]."

30. See Johnson, *Life and Letters*, 215, where Palmer refers to the abolitionist threat, saying "we have seen the trail of the serpent five and twenty years in our Eden," and 218, where he invokes the story of Abraham's separation from Lot as a model for peaceful secession.

31. "Abstract of a Discourse Delivered in the First Presbyterian Church before the Crescent Rifles, on Sabbath Morning, May 26," *New Orleans Sunday Delta*, 2 June 1861, 1.

32. Johnson, *Life and Letters*, 237–38. Palmer maintained this view of the conflict until at least December 1862, when he asserted that "no nation was ever called to conduct a great struggle so completely under the shadow of Jehovah's throne. . . . The sanctity of our war is found in the fact that in its issue the supremacy and prerogatives of the Divine Ruler of the world are distinctly implicated. . . . To the

people of our Confederacy the sublime mission is assigned of standing guard for the Divine supremacy." See *Address Delivered at the Funeral of General Maxcy Gregg, in the Presbyterian Church, Columbia, S.C., December 20, 1862* (Columbia, S.C.: Southern Guardian Steam-Power Press, 1863), 10.

33. Ibid.

34. Eubank, "Benjamin Morgan Palmer's Thanksgiving Sermon," in Auer, *Antislavery and Disunion*, 308.

35. See Cherry, *God's New Israel*, 177–94. In this sermon, Palmer laments that "eleven tribes sought to go forth in peace from the house of political bondage: but the heart of our modern Pharaoh is hardened, that he will not let Israel go. In their distress, with the untried sea before and the chariots of Egypt behind, ten millions of people stretch forth their hands before Jehovah's throne, imploring him to 'stir up his strength before Ephraim and Benjamin and Manasseh, and come and save them.' "

36. Ibid., 179.

37. Ibid., 179–80. The "accordingly" that begins the second sentence in this passage signals the way biblical and historical "facts" have been assimilated in Palmer's perception of the African "race." Increasingly throughout his subsequent career, Palmer would utilize the "evidence" of history to undergird the authority of Noah's prophecy.

38. Ibid., 180.

39. See, e.g., C. Vann Woodward, ed., *Mary Chesnut's Civil War* (New Haven: Yale University Press, 1981), 644, 674, 677, 703, 730; Virginia Ingraham Burr, ed., *The Secret Eye: The Journal of Ella Gertrude Clanton Thomas, 1848–1889* (Chapel Hill: University of North Carolina Press, 1990), 196, 210; and Earl Schenk Miers, ed., *When the World Ended: The Diary of Emma LeConte* (Lincoln: University of Nebraska Press, 1957), 26, 77, 95. Chesnut and LeConte relate hearing Palmer preach in Columbia, South Carolina, Thomas in Augusta, Georgia.

40. On Southern Presbyterians' attitude toward slavery during the war, see Smith, *In His Image, But*, 205: "The plain truth is that the white ruling class in the Confederate South was bent upon maintaining Negro servitude, even though the slave code fell short of 'the Gospel standard.' By and large, the Confederacy's religious leaders were equally determined to perpetuate it. We have a striking exhibition of this determination in the 'Narrative on the State of Religion,' which was adopted by the General Assembly of the Presbyterian Church in the Confederate States at Charlotte, North Carolina, in the spring of 1864. Said the Narrative: 'The long-continued agitations of our adversaries have wrought within us a deeper conviction of the divine appointment of domestic servitude, and have led to a clearer comprehension of the duties we owe to the African race. We hesitate not to affirm that it is the peculiar mission of the Southern Church to conserve the institution of slavery, and to make it a blessing both to master and slave.' "

41. *The Rainbow Round the Throne; or Judgment Tempered with Mercy: A Discourse Before the Legislature of Georgia, Delivered on the Day of Fasting, Humiliation and Prayer, Appointed by the President of the Confederate States of America, March 27th, 1863* (Milledgeville, Ga.: Doughton, Nisbet & Barnes, 1863), 39.

42. Ibid., 31.

43. Ibid., 31–32. The passage continues: "The explanation of all this lies upon the face of the story. Having covenanted with Noah that he would not a second time destroy mankind with a deluge, God must restrain human depravity that it may

not rise again to the gigantic proportions of the Antediluvians. This is done by the institution of civil government; the germ of which was planted in the Death penalty, 'whoso sheddeth man's blood, by man shall his blood be shed,' and that human magistrates [could make an] effective restraint against wickedness, the race is distributed into sections, each living under its own constitution, government and laws. These communities in their turn, check and restrain each other: and it has been by balancing nation against nation, and kingdom against kingdom, that God has held under a measure of restraint the super-abounding wickedness of the world."

44. Ibid., 32.

45. Palmer also uses the Babel image in this address to justify the South's departure from the stream of American history. He acknowledges that "we have sinned against God in the idolatry of our history. We have looked out from our palaces and towers and said, 'Is not this great Babylon that we have built for the house of the kingdom, by the might of our power for the honor of our majesty.' " Palmer also opines that "the South will not cower beneath the hardships by which a truly historic people proves itself worthy of a truly historic mission" (32).

46. *A Discourse before the General Assembly of South Carolina, on December 10, 1863, Appointed by the Legislature as a Day of Fasting, Humiliation and Prayer* (Columbia, S.C.: Charles P. Pelham, 1864), 3. Palmer's text mistakenly refers to the passage as Psalm 55.

47. Ibid., 5.

48. Ibid., 21.

49. Ibid., 15.

50. Ibid., 7.

51. Ibid., 6, 8.

52. Ibid., 14.

53. The *New Orleans Daily True Delta*, 11 July 1865 noted: "The Rev. Dr. Palmer, formerly pastor of the First Presbyterian Church, arrived in the city last Saturday, from Mobile. The arrival of this eminent divine, whose eloquence is only equaled by his piety, and his learning by his benevolence and the practice of all Christian virtues, will be hailed with unalloyed satisfaction by numerous friends. We do not know what the intentions of the Doctor are in regard to the future, but we are much mistaken in our estimate if he is not called upon to adorn some pulpit in New Orleans ere long" (4).

54. Johnson, *Life and Letters,* 310. According to an advertisement appearing in a New Orleans newspaper in 1870, Palmer was president of the school's board of directors. Johnson writes: "There can be little question that Dr. Palmer's labors in the [Larned] institute, as well as his influence in its behalf, contributed much to its success. . . . Once established he gave the [school] his church specially fathered not a little valuable service." This service included a series of lectures on history Palmer delivered to students at the institute.

55. It is interesting to note that sometime in the early 1870s, when the white citizens of New Orleans rallied "to denounce the contact of the races in school relations," the event was held in Lafayette Square, the location of First Church. See George Washington Cable, "My Politics," in Arlin Turner, ed., *The Negro Question: A Selection of Writings on Civil Rights in the South* (Garden City, N.Y.: Doubleday, 1958), 13.

56. Palmer, "George Washington and Robert E. Lee" (1870) in Thomas McCaleb, ed.,

The Louisiana Book: Selections from the Literature of the State (New Orleans: R. F. Straughan, 1894), 165–67.

57. Palmer, *The Present Crisis and its Issues, an Address Delivered before the Literary Societies of Washington and Lee University, Lexington, Va., 27ᵗʰ June, 1872 by Rev. B. M. Palmer, D.D.* (Baltimore: John Murphy, 1872). Palmer's biographer refers to the address as "The Present Crisis and its Issue," which is the title used herafter.

58. Wilson, *Baptized in Blood,* 158.

59. "The Present Crisis and its Issue," 20.

60. Ibid., 18.

61. Ibid., 18–19.

62. A turning point may be discerned in Palmer's Fast Day addresses in March and December 1863. In March, the dispersion of peoples after the Flood is described as part of God's providential organization of the world; by December, the same phenomenon is depicted as God's intervention in human affairs to prevent sin and conquest. Surely much of the change is attributable to the inexplicable decline in Southern fortunes during the middle of 1863—the period of Stonewall Jackson's death and the defeats at Gettysburg and Vicksburg.

63. It is possible that the source for the association in Palmer's mind between Nimrod and the tower was *Paradise Lost*; tradition reports that when Palmer was a child his mother read Milton to him.

64. Recall that in 1856 Palmer had taken the view "that society is broken up into these small and independent communities, where the human will is first subdued, and obedience to authority enforced, under the mild despotism of the family. Hence, in the original formation of society, the Patriarchal rule must be held as preceding every other . . ." ("The Import of Hebrew History," 595). For Palmer, as for commentators in earlier ages, Nimrod seems to represent the establishment of despotism on the ruins of patriarchy.

65. "The Present Crisis and its Issue," 19.

66. The overture had originated the previous year in a committee Palmer chaired for the Synod of Mississippi. See Smith, *In His Image, But,* 241–42: "In 1874, widespread pressure from the lower judicatories prompted the General Assembly to take more decisive action on the tantalizing subject [of the establishment of separate churches for Blacks]. When the assembly of that year convened at Columbus, Mississippi, overtures from the Presbytery of Memphis (Tennessee), South Carolina, and Mississippi urged the high court to set the freedmen apart in a completely independent African communion. The most impressive overture came from the Synod of Mississippi, in the form of a lengthy paper which had been adopted by that body in November, 1873, upon the recommendation of a committee headed by Benjamin Morgan Palmer."

67. Ibid. Palmer's words "instinct of race" are reminiscent of a phrase popularized by Senator Albert Beveridge around the turn of the century in his famous "March of the Flag" address. Beveridge spoke of a God whose "great purpose [is] made manifest in the instincts of our race" (Forrest G. Wood, *The Arrogance of Faith: Christianity and Race in American from the Colonial Era to the Twentieth Century.* [Boston: Northeastern, University Press, 1991], 226.)

68. In Johnson, *Life and Letters,* 472. Note that the language used by Palmer to describe divine action has shifted once again: The relatively benign terms *distribution* and *separation* Palmer utilized in the 1860s are now absent. Rather, he writes of a God

who "divided the human race into several distinct groups, for the sake of keeping them apart." The apocalyptic note of the immediate postwar period is gone, but God's action is decisive and clear in intent.

69. Ibid., 472.

70. Ibid., 472–73.

71. The Southern Historical Society was reorganized and moved to Richmond in 1873. The United Confederate Veterans organized in New Orleans in 1889. In 1900, in an address before the Confederate Reunion in Louisville, Kentucky, Palmer uttered these words: "It is about five and thirty years since the Confederate War was closed, and about thirty-nine years since it was begun, and it is sometimes asked why we should stir the ashes of that ancient feud? Why should we not bury the past in its own grave, and turn to the living issues of the present and the future? To this question, comrades, we return the answer with a voice loud as seven thunders, because it is history, because it is our history and the history of our dead heroes who shall not go without their fame. As long as there are men who wear the gray, they will gather the charred embers of their old campfires and in the blaze of these reunions tell the story of the martyrs who fell in the defense of country and of truth. [The remote origin of the war] explains how we of the South, convinced of the rightfulness of our cause can accept defeat without the blush of shame mantling the cheek of a single Confederate of us all; and while accepting the issue of the war as the decree of destiny, openly appeal to the verdict of posterity for the final vindication of our career."

72. Testimonial signed by J. D. Hill, Jos. McConnell, and H. Yinder, Howard-Tilton Memorial Library, Tulane University, Manuscripts Division, Louisiana Historical Archives, "Confederate Personnel, 1861–" Collection.

73. "Address of Rev. Dr. B. M. Palmer," *Southern Historical Society Papers*, Vol. 10 (Richmond, Va.: n.p., 1882): 251.

74. "Discourse of Rev. B. M. Palmer, D.D.," *Southern Historical Society Papers*, Vol. 18 (Richmond, Va.: n.p., 1890): 210–17. Palmer observes that the "Divine rule is extended over the whole breadth of history through all ages. . . . Thus, we find men distributed into races and nations, each enclosed within corporate limits, under such environment and acted upon by such influences as to evolve a composite character."

75. Ibid., 214.

76. Ibid.

77. Ibid.

78. Ibid.

79. Johnson, *Life and Letters*, 570.

80. *The Address of Rev. B. M. Palmer, D.D. LL.D. Delivered On the First Day of the New Year and Century in The First Presbyterian Church, New Orleans, La., at the Request of Citizens, And Members of the Church, of Which He Has Been Pastor Since December 30, 1856* (New Orleans: Brotherhood of the First Presbyterian Church, n.d.), 2.

81. Ibid.

82. Thomas V. Peterson, *Ham and Japheth in America: The Mythic World of Whites in the Antebellum South* (Metuchen, N.J.: American Theological Library Association, 1978), 8; see also 97ff.

83. Palmer writes: "Then put your hands next upon the tenth chapter of Genesis,

immediately following that prophetic outline; and there you have the most ancient
and the only reliable historic chart by which you may recognize the genealogy of
the nations of the earth as they were distributed in their respective portions of
territory; for, as was said by the great apostle, in that marvelous address which he
made from Mars Hill before the men of Athens: 'God hath made of one blood
all nations of men, for to dwell on all the face of the earth, and hath determined
the times before appointed and the bounds of their habitation' " (*The Address . . .
Delivered On the First Day of the New Year*, 3).

84. Ibid., 10. An anonymous article appearing in the *Southern Literary Messenger* in
January 1856 included a passage strikingly similar to this section of Palmer's sermon: "[The white man] has . . . subdued the wilderness, and made those vast sol-
itudes, hitherto unbroken save by the war-whoop of the Indian and the scream of
the eagle, vocal with the hum of industry and songs of Christian praise. . . . " See
"The Black Race in North America: Why Was Their Introduction Permitted?" 2.

85. *The Address . . . Delivered On the First Day of the New Year*, 10–11. In a foreshad-
owing of the "Century Sermon," Palmer wrote in "Our Historic Mission" that "by
its quiet and silent force, [the Anglo-Saxon race] has . . . built a mighty empire in
the bosom of a once unbroken wilderness—it has substituted commerce for conquest, and supplanted the sword and spear of the warrior by the plow and the axe
of the colonist" (9). Palmer's words here and in the "Century Sermon" are remarkably similar to those of Andrew Jackson, who in 1830 had asked: "What good
man would prefer a country covered with forests and ranged by a few thousand
savages to our extensive Republic, studded with cities, towns, and prosperous
farms, embellished with all of the improvements which art can devise or industry
execute, occupied by more than 12,000,000 happy people and filled with the blessings of liberty, civilization and religion[?]. See Wood, *Arrogance of Faith*, 226–27.
Similarly, in 1846 Thomas Hart Barton argued that "the Red race has disappeared
from the Atlantic coast: the tribes that resisted civilization, met extinction. This is
a cause of lamentation with many. For my part, I cannot murmur at what seems
to be the effect of divine law. I cannot repine that this Capitol has replaced the
wigwam—this Christian people, replaced the savages—white matrons the red
squaws—and that such men as Washington, Franklin and Jefferson, have taken
the place of Powhattan, Opechanecanough, and other red men, howsoever respect-
able they may have been as savages." See *Congressional Globe* (28 May 1846).

86. This attitude of whites toward the fate of the Native American can be traced as
far back as the colonial response to the great massacre of Good Friday, 1622. It
became common in the seventeenth century, in fact, for Puritan writers to argue
that as God had expelled the Canaanites before the ancient Israelites, he was driving the Indian tribes out of "New Canaan" before the Puritans. See Wood, *Arrogance of Faith*, 19, 210, passim. Palmer himself had proclaimed in 1861 that God
had "emptied out [the continent's] former inhabitants who melted away as the
Canaanites before Israel"("National Responsibility before God," in Cherry, *God's
New Israel*, 185).

87. Historical readings of the blessing viewed Japheth as representing the nations that
at one time or another had invaded and occupied the land of Israel and, for a
time at least, "dwelt in the tents of Shem." That is, the biblical phrase was regarded
as a prediction of one or more historical triumphs over the Hebrew descendants
of Shem. This tradition was adapted by American abolitionists such as John Ran-

kin, who in 1830 wrote that Noah's prediction regarding Japhet "was doubtless accomplished when the Greeks and Romans, who were descendants of Japhet, by conquest took possession of the tents of Shem." See William H. Pease and Jane H. Pease, eds., *The Antislavery Argument* (Indianapolis: Bobbs-Merrill, 1965), 120. Proslavery writers also historicized the reference to Japheth's enlargement. For instance, Josiah Priest saw the rule of Japheth over Shem and Ham fulfilled in the establishment of a Greek colony in Africa "in the very first ages"(*Slavery as it Relates to the Negro or African Race* [1843; reprint, New York: Arno, 1977], 239). Other American interpreters saw Japheth's "enlargement" as a reference to an as-yet-unaccomplished European colonial expansion into formerly "Semitic" lands. In the 1840s, Hollis Read interpreted this concept to include "an enlargement eastward, the discovery of the great East, by the Cape of Good Hope." See *The Hand of God in History; or, Divine Providence Historically Illustrated in The Extension and Establishment of Christianity* (Hartford: H. E. Robins, 1849), 85–86.

Alongside this historicizing tradition there developed a series of spiritual readings that took Japheth as a symbol of the Gentile nations that, as Noah foresaw through divine inspiration, would inherit Shem's blessings at the appearance of Jesus. For instance, Augustine asked, "is it not also in the houses of Christ, that is, in the churches, that the 'enlargement' of the nations dwells? For Japheth means 'enlargement' "(*City of God* XVI: 2, in Philip Schaff, ed. *A Select Library of the Nicene and Post-Nicene Fathers of the Church*, 8 vols. [Grand Rapids, Mich.: Eerdmans, 1955]). Calvin interpreted the text to mean "God shall gently bring back, or incline Japheth," until both sons "again coalesce in one body and have a common home" at the coming of Christ (*Commentaries on the First Book of Moses Called Genesis*, 2 vols. trans. John King [Grand Rapids, Mich: Eerdmans, 1948] 1: 308–09). This tradition also appeared in America, for instance, in the work of Samuel Davies Baldwin, a rough contemporary of Palmer, who in 1858 opined that Japheth's enlargement, "it is accorded by all, relates especially to the reception of Christianity by the Japhethites" and that Japheth received Shem's birthright when the latter "spurned" Christianity from his "tents"(*Dominion; or, the Unity and Trinity of the Human Race; with the Divine Political Constitution of the World, and the Divine Rights of Shem, Ham and Japheth* [Nashville: Stevenson and F. A. Owen, 1858], 67, 118–19).

It is possible that Palmer was influenced by Louisianan Samuel Cartwright's explication of the phrase "tents of Shem," which appeared in 1843: "The prophecy, 'God shall enlarge Japheth, he shall dwell in the tents of Shem and Canaan shall be his servant,' remained to be fulfilled. But how was Japheth, cooped up in Europe, the smallest division of the earth, to be enlarged? . . . At length, in the fullness of time, Japheth unexpectedly discovered an unknown hemisphere, thinly inhabited by the race of Shem, and hastened to take possession of it and to dwell in the tents of Shem. . . . By the discovery of America Japheth became enlarged, as had been foretold three thousand eight hundred years before. He took the whole continent. He literally dwelt in the tents of Shem in Mexico and South America. At this day, in our own country, he is dwelling in the wilderness, which constituted, a few years ago, the tents of Shem. No sooner did Japheth begin to enlarge himself, and to dwell in the tents of Shem, than Canaan left his fastnesses in the wilds of Africa, where the white man's foot had never trod, and appeared on the beach to get passage to America, as if drawn thither by an impulse of his nature to fulfill his destiny of becoming Japheth's servant"(*Essays, Being Inductions Drawn from the Baconian Philosophy Proving the Truth of the Bible and the Justice and Benevolence of the Decree Dooming Canaan to be Servant of Servants: And Answering the Question of Voltaire: "On demands quel droite des erangers tels que les juifs avaient surle pays de Cannan?" in a Series of Letters to the Rev. William Winans* [Vidalia, La.: n.p. 1843], 9–10). See also Peterson, *Ham and Japheth*, 91–96.

88. Palmer invoked this Canaanite ideology in his "National Responsibility before God" sermon of 1861, when he claimed that God gave the American nation "a broad land and full of springs—He emptied out its former inhabitants who melted away as the Canaanites before Israel and His gracious providence was a wall of fire around their armies through a long and painful war" (Cherry, *God's New Israel*, 185).

Chapter 8

1. *New Orleans Daily Delta*, 30 November 1860, 1; "Dr. Palmer's Sermon on Thanksgiving Day,"*New Orleans Sunday Delta*, 2, December 1860, 1.

2. Bertram Wyatt-Brown, "Church, Honor, and Secession," in *Religion and the American Civil War*, ed. Randall M. Miller, Harry S. Stout, and Charles Reagan Wilson (New York: Oxford University Press, 1998), 103.

3. Ibid., 101.

4. Ibid.

5. Ibid., 100.

6. Ibid., 101.

7. Conrad Cherry, ed., *God's New Israel: Religious Interpretations, of American Destiny* (Englewood Cliffs, N.J.: Prentice-Hall, 1971), 190.

8. Ibid., 156.

9. See, e.g., "The Southern Church's Role in the Rebellion," in Robert L. Stanton's *The Church and the Rebellion: A Consideration of the Rebellion against the Government of the United States; and the Agency of the Church, North and South, in Relation Thereto* (New York: Derby & Miller, 1864).

10. Julia Cobbs McGowan, "The Presbyterian Churches in New Orleans during Reconstruction"(master's thesis, Tulane University, 1937), 6.

11. Palmer, Review of Robert J. Breckenridge, *Discourse Delivered by Rev. Dr. R. J. Breckenridge, on the Day of National Humiliation, January 4th, 1861, at Lexington, Ky; and Our Country: Its Peril and its Deliverance. From Advance Sheets of the Danville Quarterly Review for March, 1861, Southern Presbyterian Review* 14 (April 1861): 134–177.

12. Ibid., 141.

13. Ibid., 144.

14. Ibid., 146, 175.

15. Ibid., 149.

16. Ibid., 175.

17. Ibid., 160.

18. Palmer, *Address Delivered at the Funeral of General Maxcy Gregg, in the Presbyterian Church, Columbia, S.C., December 20, 1862* (Columbia, S.C: Southern Guardian Steam-Power Press, 1863), 8.

19. B. M. Palmer, "Oath of Allegiance," Louisiana Historical Association Collection, Manuscripts Division, Howard-Tilton Memorial Library, Tulane University, New Orleans.

20. *The Pastoral Letter of 1870: A Historical and Official Document Setting Forth Three "Great Principles" that "Our Church Has Declared in the Most Solemn and Emphatic Manner" to be "Among the Fundamental Principles of our Organization,"* 12; Caroliniana Library, University of South Carolina.

21. Ibid., 13.

22. The diary of Robert H. Catmell, entry of 10 September 1902, 4. Robert H. Catmell papers, Tennessee State Library and Archives, Nashville.

23. J. Treadwell Davis, "The Presbyterians and the Sectional Conflict," *Southern Quarterly* 8, no. 2 (1970): 124.

24. Thomas Carey Johnson, *The Life and Letters of Benjamin Morgan Palmer* (1906; reprint, Edinburgh and Carlisle, Pa.: Banner of Truth Trust, 1987), 49–50.

25. Ibid., 50.

26. This version of the story appears in the diary of Robert H. Catmell, entry of 10 September 1902, 6–7. The account seems to be a paraphrase of newspaper stories that circulated after Palmer's death that May. Robert H. Catmell Papers, Tennessee State Library and Archives, Nashville.

27. Johnson, *Life and Letters*, 51.

28. Letter to Dr. Charles Hodge, 13 June 1860. Presbyterian Department of History, Montreat, North Carolina. In a letter to his congregation written in May 1864, Palmer assured his parishioners that "the ties which bind me to New Orleans are not only those of affection, but of honor"(Johnson, *Life and Letters*, 279).

29. Christine Leigh Heyrman, *Southern Cross: The Beginnings of the Bible Belt* (Chapel Hill and London: University of North Carolina Press, 1997), 252.

30. Ibid., 249.

31. B. M. Palmer, *An Address at the One Hundredth Anniversary of the Organization of the Nazareth Church and Congregation in Spartanburg, S.C.* (Richmond, Va.: Shepperson, 1872), 35.

32. "Thanksgiving Sermon"(1860), in Johnson, *Life and Letters*, 211.

33. Ibid.

34. B. M. Palmer, *The Family, in Its Civil and Churchly Aspects, An Essay, in Two Parts* (1876; reprint, Harrisonburg, Va.: Sprinkle, 1981), 123–24.

35. Ibid., 133, 134. Later, Palmer writes, "So long as this remains a sinful world, where man is under discipline for a holier and happier life hereafter, just so long must servitude, in some one of its diversified forms, continue to be a permanent relation; and in the Family, where human authority is first enforced, must the conditions of servitude first be regulated"(148).

36. Johnson, *Life and Letters*, 214.

37. Conrad Cherry, *God's New Israel: Religious Interpretations of American Destiny*, rev. ed. (Chapel Hill and London: University of North Carolina Press, 1998), 194–95.

38. See *Minutes of the General Assembly of the Presbyterian Church in the Confederate States of America, 1861–1864* (Augusta, Ga: The Assembly, 1865–).

39. Johnson, *Life and Letters*, 218.

40. According to Thomas Peterson, it was common for proslavery authors to raise "the specter of emancipated blacks engaged in massacres and barbarism by depicting the situation in Santo Domingo"(*Ham and Japheth in America: The Mythic*

World of Whites in the Antebellum South [Metuchen, N.J.: American Theological Library Association, 1978] Theological Library 37). Thomas R. Dew discusses Haiti in "Professor Dew on Slavery," in *The Proslavery Argument, as Maintained by the Most Distinguished Writers of the Southern States, Containing the Several Essays, on the Subject, of Chancellor Harper, Governor Hammond, Dr. Simms, and Professor Dew* (1852; reprint, New York: Negro Universities Press, 1968), 430–31. See also J. B. Thrasher's reference to "the bloody scenes in St. Domingo—the destruction of the white race, and the relapsing into barbarism of the black race"(*Slavery A Divine Institution, by J.B. Thrasher of Port Gibson, A Speech Made before the Breckinridge and Lane Club, November 5th, 1860)* [Port Gibson, Miss.: Southern Reveille Book and Job Office, 1861], 5).

41. In Johnson, *Life and Letters,* 207.

42. In Cherry, ed., *God's New Israel,* rev. ed., 191.

43. Peterson, *Ham and Japheth,* 15.

44. Ibid., 38.

45. In Johnson, *Life and Letters,* 207.

46. Ibid., 212.

47. In Cherry, ed., *God's New Israel,* rev. ed., 188.

48. Ibid., 183. According to Thomas Smyth, a contemporary and friend of Palmer, the South's vision had been sharpened so that it could see that the war was God's judgment on the North for its abolitionist fanaticism. Smyth cited the "principles substantially recognised by our fathers in framing the Constitution—but ultimately subverted by the infidel maxims of the Declaration of Independence [i.e., the absolute freedom and equality of all men] and their demoralizing influence on the increasing mass of ignorant foreign citizens: the result—liberty lost, the Union broken up, and war, subjugation, and lawless tyranny"(cited in Thompson, *Presbyterians in the South,* 2: 59). Here Smyth links disorder and servitude to argue that those fighting to end slavery are wreaking on American society precisely the sort of disorder ("lawless tyranny") that thralldom was instituted to prevent. In an article published in the *Southern Presbyterian Review* in 1861 Smyth described the Federal government as being "without law or constitution—fanatical, remorseless and tyrannical" (Ernest Trice Thompson, *Presbyterians in the South,* 3 vols. [Richmond, Va.: John Knox, 1963–73], 2:70). Similarly, when Robert L. Dabney published *A Defence of Virginia* in 1867, he claimed that slavery had been forced upon Virginia by the tyranny of England. See Thompson, *Presbyterians in the South,* 2:196.

49. William H. Pease and Jane H. Pease, eds. *The Antislavery Argument* (Indianapolis: Bobbs-Merrill, 1965), 128–142.

50. Ibid., 12.

51. Ibid., 12–13. Palmer's mentor, James Henley Thornwell, wrote in "The Christian Doctrine of Slavery" that "the parties in this conflict [over slavery] are not merely Abolitionists and Slaveholders; they are Atheists, Socialists, Communists, Red Republicans, Jacobins on the one side, and the friends of order and regulated freedom on the other." See John B. Adger and John L. Girardeau, eds., *The Collected Writings of James Henley Thornwell, D.D., L.L.D.,* 4 vols. (Richmond, Va.: Presbyterian Committee of Publication, 1871–73), 4:405.

52. Ibid., 15.

53. In Johnson, *Life and Letters,* 472.

54. Ibid., 473.
55. It is not clear whether Palmer's reading of Nimrod's "primary rebellion" was influenced by one of the many Bible interpreters—from Josephus to Milton—who viewed the tower as a tribute to Nimrod's vanity or by American proslavery writer Josiah Priest.
56. In Doralyn J. Hickey, "Benjamin Morgan Palmer: Churchman of the Old South"(Ph.D. Dissertation, Duke University, 1962), 6.
57. Ibid., 17.
58. In Ibid., 8. It is important to place this morbid prediction in the context of nineteenth-century child mortality. As one commentator has noted, parents in former centuries could not "allow themselves to become too attached to something that was regarded as a probable loss." See Robert W. Lynn and Elliott Wright, *The Big Little School: Sunday Child of American Protestantism* (New York: Harper & Row, 1971), 43.

Chapter 9

1. It is possible that Gillespie, who was born about 1885, knew Palmer, who died in 1902. He certainly would have been familiar with the racial views of the great nineteenth-century Presbyterian divine.
2. See Thomas Carey Johnson's *The Life and Letters of Benjamin Morgan Palmer* (1906; reprint, Edinburgh and Carlisle, Pa.: Banner of Truth Trust, 1987); Douglas Kelly, *Preachers with Power* (Edinburgh and Carlisle, Pa.: Banner of Truth Trust, 1992); and the website of Presbyterian Heritage Publications, Dallas, which posts Palmer's "The Warrant and Nature of Public Worship, a Sermon Preached on 9 October 1853 in Columbia, South Carolina." One may order photocopies of Palmer's *The Family in Its Offices of Instruction and Worship* (1876) and *Husbands, Wives, and Parents: Their Biblical Place and Duties* (1876) from http://www.swrb.com/puritan-books.htm.
3. The Palmer Memorial Tablet, Palmer Hall, Rhodes College.
4. It was widely assumed during the antebellum period that Noah's words contained a message for the young American nation. For instance, in 1856 an anonymous writer in the *Southern Literary Messenger* dramatized the history of settlement in North America by casting the sons of Noah as the eponymous ancestors of the various races. The writer opined that when the first African slaves arrived at Jamestown in 1620, "for the first time, the white man, the black man, and the red man stood face to face, and gazed upon each other in the New World." They were destined to "fulfil upon a large scale that remarkable prophecy uttered thousands of years before by the Patriarch Noah, when, standing upon the mount of inspiration, and looking down the course of future time, he proclaimed: 'God shall enlarge Japheth, and he shall dwell in the tents of Shem, and Canaan shall be his servant.'" See "Africa in America,"*Southern Literary Messenger* (22 January 1856): 1. In the November 1855 issue of the periodical, an article presumably by the same author "The Black Race in North America: Why Was Their Introduction Permitted?" imagined "a conference between two of the better informed of either race as the ship which bore these unhappy beings first drew up near the Virginia shore"(657). Such dramatic inventions involving Noah's sons were common in the

1850s, and the author's notion that "standing upon the mount of inspiration," Noah looked "down the course of future time" is strikingly similar to Palmer's image of Noah's prophecy as a lens for taking in the landscape of human history.

5. Jerome B. Holgate, *Noachidae: or, Noah and his Descendants* (Buffalo: Breed, Butler, 1860). Holgate indicates in his preface that this was the first of a planned two-volume study: "In this volume we bring the reader down to the dispersion at Babel; in the second we shall take up that branch of dispersion which settled Canaan and Egypt, and unfold the rise of exceedingly interesting kingdoms in those countries"(viii).

6. Ibid., 25. See also 90–91, 143, 147.

7. Ibid., 155.

8. Ibid., 156.

9. Ibid., 160.

10. Ibid., 162–63.

11. On the other hand, Ham is depicted again and again with a "dark" look or expression, and the brothers get a good laugh when Ham is aped by an orangutan. See, e.g., 250, 260, 278.

12. Ibid., 53–54. Cf. Adam Clarke, quoting "Dr. Hales": "The chief renown of Shem was of a spiritual nature"(*The Holy Bible Containing the Old and New Testaments, The Text Carefully Printed from the Most Correct Copies of the Present Authorized Translation Including the Marginal Readings and Parallel Texts, with a Commentary and Critical Notes; The Old Testament,* Vol. 1, *Genesis & Deuteronomy* [1810; reprint, New York: Abingdon-Cokesbury, 1977], 83).

13. Blyden, "The Call of Providence to the Descendants of Africa in America," in Howard Brotz, ed., *Negro Social and Political Thought, 1850–1920: Representative Texts* (New York: Basic Books, 1966), 121.

14. Thomas V. Peterson, *Ham and Japheth in America: The Mythic World of Whites in the Antebellum South* (Metuchen, N.J.: American Theological Library Association, 1978), 47.

15. Cited in Theopus H. Smith, *Conjuring Culture: Biblical Formations of Black Culture* (New York: Oxford University Press, 1994), 236–37. Cf. Marcus Garvey's statement, "As by the action of the world, as by the conduct of all the races and nations it is apparent that not one of them has the sense of justice, the sense of love, the sense of equity, the sense of charity, that would make men happy, and God satisfied. It is apparent that it is left to the Negro to play such a part in human affairs. . . . " See Leonard E. Barrett, *The Rastafarians* (Boston: Beacon, 1997), 78.

16. In Alonzo Potter Burgess Holly, *God and the Negro: Synopsis of God and the Negro or the Biblical Record of the Race of Ham* (Nashville: National Baptist Publishing Board, 1937), 150–51.

17. Ibid., 122.

18. Even white supremacists could view Noah's curse as predicting a dominant role for Ham at some future date. In 1879, Richard Taylor wrote that "all the armies and all the humanitarians can not change [the white race's rule] until the appointed time arrives for Ham to dominate Japhet."*Destruction and Reconstruction: Personal Experiences of the Late War,* cited in Claude H. Nolen, *The Negro's Image in the South: An Anatomy of White Supremacy* (Lexington: University of Kentucky Press, 1967), 42.

19. See, e.g., *Concordia Theological Monthly* 15, no. (1944): 346, where the editor ac-

knowledges that "frequently in our publications the view that 'the Bible has put a curse upon the Negro race' has been expressed and defended."

20. Not surprisingly, these commentaries maintain remarkable conformity with the orthodox interpretive paradigm established centuries before: Ham's "wickedness," though typically undefined, is denounced in the strongest terms. His behavior is "contumacious," "unnatural," "a very great sin," "a sensual act rightly punished"; it demonstrates "moral impurity" and "shameless sexuality"; it is "an exhibition of juvenile depravity." Ham's failure to honor his father is "evidence of a heart thoroughly depraved." He is said to have reported to his brothers with "malignant pleasure," to have "mocked at his father and despised him." "Like all fools, he made a mock of sin." Judging from his "sin against filial respect and honor," Ham possessed "no sense of filial love or even of common decency." By enjoying his father's shame and making it "a matter of scornful joking," he evinced "a bold and impious disposition of mind." Canaan no doubt emulated Ham in his "sinful, wicked disposition" and shared his "inclination to the unclean."

Meanwhile, the behavior of Shem and Japheth is characterized as loving, chaste, respectful, and honorable. These men of "pure mind" go about their task of covering their father with "silent sorrow," doing "what filial reverence demanded." They approach Noah with "filial love, true purity, and . . . profound sorrow." Their deed manifests their "childlike reverence as truly as their refined purity and modesty" and makes them types of "servants of Christ and ministers of the Gospel."

21. E.g., Marcus Dods, *The Book of Genesis, The Expositor's Bible, Series One*, Vol. 2 (New York: A. C. Armstrong, 1901), 71. See also Arthur W. Pink, *Gleanings in Genesis* (Chicago: Moody, 1950), 119–20, where the author discerns a "tenfold correspondence or likeness" between Adam and Noah.

22. W. H. Griffith, *Genesis: A Devotional Commentary* (1946; reprint, Grand Rapids, Mich.: Kregel, 1988), 94. Though atypical in this regard, Pink identifies Noah as a type of Christ, elaborating sixteen points where he finds Noah's typological status compelling. See *Gleanings in Genesis*, chap. 12, "Noah a Type of Christ," and chap. 13, "The Typology of the Ark."

23. Ibid., 119.

24. Dods, *The Book of Genesis*, 78. Dods writes that "Noah's sin brought to light the character of his three sons—the coarse irreverence of Ham, the dignified delicacy and honour of Shem and Japheth. . . . They are the true descendants of Ham, whether their faces be black or white, and whether they go with no clothes or with clothes that are the product of much thought and anxiety, who find pleasure in the mere contemplation of deeds of shame."

25. Pink, *Gleanings in Genesis*, 123.

26. H. C. Leupold, *Exposition of Genesis* (Grand Rapids, Mich.: Baker, 1950), 349; Pink, *Gleanings in Genesis*, 128.

27. See, e.g., Lewis Fowler, *O House of Israel and Thou Judah* (New York: Maranatha Publishers, 1941), an interpretation of the historical roles of Noah's sons by a proponent of British Israelism. Since in Fowler's typology Americans are descendants of Shem rather than Japheth, Shem's blessing is considered to be both material and spiritual. Fowler perceives the various characters of Noah's sons in the antagonists of Second World War: "Under the leader of fascism, the Babylonian-Hamitic peoples will make a great bid for power. . . . It will be at this time that

Japheth—The Dragon—Russia, and Prussia—Stalin and Hitler—will rise up against Ham—the Beast—and they will finally be completely destroyed" (56). "The Beast is Ham, and Ham is, today—the papacy. Mussolini, the Fascist, is truly Hamitic" (57). "Ham is intrigue, mental manipulation, spiritual perversion, political confusion, social enslavement, and total human exploitation. It is all that is the antithesis of God and His Kingdom and Truth. As a principle it must be burned out of racial consciousness" (62). "The final conflict will be between the forces of Ham, Japheth and Shem . . . that is between good and evil, godliness and ungodliness" (102). Fowler explicitly rejects the traditional racial view of Noah's sons: "There are those who seem to believe that Japheth is the yellow race and that Ham is the negro race. This is untrue since Ham, Shem, and Japheth were brothers, sons of Noah; as far as we know, of one mother. They were all white. . . . It is true that Ham married into the negro race and is responsible for a major portion of all dark races apart from the negro today. But Ham and all Hamites were and are white people" (69).

28. Basil C. Atkinson, *The Pocket Commentary of the Bible: The Book of Genesis* (Chicago: Moody, 1957), 99. See also Joseph S. Exell, *The Biblical Illustrator*, Vol. 1, *Genesis* (Grand Rapids, Mich.: Baker, 1956), 495: "Such as abuse sonship in the Church, may justly look to be made slaves unto it."

29. William Ballman writes that "the Negro is the leading living descendant of Ham and Canaan, and history shows that the Negro has been the slave of the world." See *Why Do I Believe the Bible Is God's Word?* (St. Louis: Concordia, 1946), 11. Arthur Pink simply observes that "the negroes who were for so long the slaves of Europeans and Americans, also claim Ham as their progenitor" (*Gleanings in Genesis*, 126).

30. C. F. Keil and F. Delitzsch, *Biblical Commentary on the Old Testament*, Vol. 1, *The Pentateuch*, trans. James Martin (Grand Rapids, Mich.: Eerdmans, 1949), 157.

31. Ham's laughter at his father is another element of the tradition that sometimes appears in these commentaries.

32. See Benjamin E. Mays, *Seeking to Be Christian in Race Relations* (New York: Friendship, 1957), 44–46; and L. Richard Bradley, "The Curse of Canaan and the American Negro," *Concordia Theological Monthly* 42 (Fall 1971): 109.

33. John C. Whitcomb Jr. in "The Prophecy of Noah's Sons," *Freedom Now* (August-September 1966): 7–8; Thomas O. Figart, *A Biblical Perspective on the Race Problem* (Grand Rapids, Mich.: Baker, 1973); John H. Hewett, "Genesis 2:4b–3:31; 4:2–16; 9: 20–27; 19:30–38," *Review and Expositor* 86 (1989): 237–41; Leon Kass, "Seeing the Nakedness of the Father," *Commentary* (June 1992): 43–45.

Figart includes a ten-page excursus on "the Noahic curse on Canaan" (53–64) in which he emphasizes that because the curse has no bearing on "Negroid peoples," it cannot be applied to "the American slavery question nor to the segregation issue today" (62). Nevertheless, his analysis of Genesis 9 conforms to the interpretive tradition that nurtured racist readings of the Bible for centuries.

Hewett writes that Ham's dishonor toward his father constituted a double outrage—he should neither have gazed upon his father's nakedness nor reported it to his brothers. "What he should have done was simply cover his father" (239). Kass declares that "Ham's viewing—and telling—is, metaphorically, an act of patricide and incest, of overturning the father as a father. Without disturbing a hair on Noah's head, Ham engages in father-killing." In response, Noah quite appropriately "unfathers" Ham. Kass also cites approvingly Robert Sacks: "Anticipating the various paganisms that will soon be founded by his descendants, Ham, 'the father of Canaan,' gives primacy to the merely temporal and amoral beginnings" (44). Kass adds that "as the stance of Ham points downward toward Canaanite paganism, so the stance of Shem points upward to the sacred" (47).

34. Arthur C. Custance, *Noah's Three Sons, The Doorway Papers*, Vol. 1 (Grand Rapids, Mich.: Zondervan, 1975), 12. Custance interprets Hamite servitude as rendering "extraordinary service to mankind from the point of view of the physical developments of civilization."

35. See also Clyde T. Francisco, "The Curse on Canaan," *Christianity Today* (24 April 1964): 9, 10. Acknowledging that Genesis 9 is "often used even today to defend segregation by earnest, Bible-loving Christians," Francisco insists that "this passage in no way relates to the present tensions between the races." Despite his disclaimer, however, Francisco's comments adhere strictly to the parameters of orthodox interpretation. On Noah's drunkenness, he writes that "perhaps the temptation to taste the product of his own labor was too strong for Noah and he soon became quite drunk, revealing that he was not accustomed to the habit. A man who gets drunk only once is not a drunkard." On Ham: "What did Ham do to his father? He disgraced him by exposing his shame to the world. . . . What his brothers did he should have done: he should have covered his father."

36. Robert Brow, "The Curse of Ham—Capsule of Ancient History," *Christianity Today* (26 October 1973): 8.

37. Figart, *A Biblical Perspective on the Race Problem*, 59; Whitcomb "The Prophecy of Noah's Sons," 7.

38. Allen P. Ross, "The Curse of Canaan," *Bibliotheca Sacra* 137 (July–September 1980): 223. Ross's reading of the story strikes many prominent themes in the history of interpretation. As a transgression of sexual morality, the action of Ham was an affront to the dignity of his father. "Because of this breach of domestic propriety, Ham could expect nothing less than the oracle against his own family honor. . . . [Ham's] seeing is the disgusting thing. Ham's frivolous looking, a moral flaw, represents the first step in the abandonment of a moral code. Moreover, this violation of a boundary destroyed the honor of Noah" (231). Ross contrasts Ham's hubris with the sensitivity and piety of his brothers and suggests that Ham "completed" Noah's nakedness by bringing the garment to his brothers. Because he disregarded both patriarchal honor and the sanctity of family, Ham deserves Noah's malediction, which "was in harmony with God's will for the preservation of moral purity" (235). The Canaanites were doomed to perpetual slavery for acting as their ancestor did, and thus becoming "enslaved sexually."

39. Ibid., 224. The relationship between Noah's oracle and the episode recorded in Genesis 9 is described thus: Shem acted in good taste and was blessed with knowledge of the true God. Japheth also acted properly and was promised geographical expansion. Ham acted wrongly, and as a result some of his descendants were cursed with subjugation.

40. Students in my Religion and Racism course have discovered this fact in interviews with local pastors. When asked how they explain human diversity, clergy from a variety of Christian denominations cite the Tower of Babel story.

41. Ibid., 41. Although this account of Babel's aftermath has a scientific ring, the American readings of Genesis 11 detailed in chapters 5 and 6 force us to consider the

possibility of regression to more sinister interpretations of the story. Particularly when Figart dates the tower to the generation of Noah's descendant Peleg (whose name connotes "division"), the unconscious link with segregationist readings of Genesis 11 becomes visible. See Figart, *A Biblical Perspective on the Race Problem*, 22, 35.

42. Ibid., 24.

43. Custance, *Noah's Three Sons*, 120.

44. Kass, "Seeing the Nakedness of His Father," 44.

45. In James Morrow, *Bible Stories for Adults* (New York: Harcourt Brace, 1996), 61–84.

46. Ibid., 78.

47. Ibid., 83.

48. Cain Hope Felder, ed., *The Original African Heritage Study Bible, King James Version, with Special Annotations Relative to the African/Edenic Experience* (Nashville: James C. Winston, 1993), 15.

49. Brooklyn: A&B Publishers, 1999; Chicago: Research Associates School Times Publications, 1996. In *The Trick* (Chino, Calif.: Chick Publications, n.d.), a Bible tract published by infamous anti-Catholic crusader Jack T. Chick, a character described as a former witch provides a brief history of Halloween: "It came from an ancient Druid custom set up for human sacrifices on Halloween night. Druids offered children in sacrifices. They believed that only 'the fruit of the body' offered to Satan was for the 'sin of the soul'." The note reads: "Paraphrased from *The Two Babylons* by Hislop, page 232."

50. William F. S. Miles, "Hamites and Hebrews: Problems in 'Judaizing' the Rwandan Genocide," *Journal of Genocide Research* 2:1 (March, 2000): 107–115; 108.

51. Ibid., 109.

52. Ibid., 113.

53. John Hanning Speke, *Journal of the Discovery of the Source of the Nile* (Mineola, N.Y.: Dover, 1996), xvii, 495–96. See also 241–42.

54. Saul Dubow, *Scientific Racism in South Africa* (Cambridge: Cambridge University Press, 1995), 84. "Napolean's invasion of Egypt in 1798 was the catalyst for a new twist to the Hamitic myth: the discovery that Egyptian civilisation predated the classical world of the Greeks and Romans had to be squared with the established view that Egyptians were "Negroid." One way out of the problem . . . was to re-interpret the Bible. By the early decades of the nineteenth century many authorities declared that only Canaan-son-of-Ham had been cursed. Thus the Egyptians re-emerged as the uncursed progeny of Ham by way of his other son, Mizraim." One revision of the biblical typology yielded the concept of the "caucasoid Hamite," an idea that enabled white theorists to maintain Negro inferiority while affirming that "development could come to him only by mediation of the white race" (Ibid., 85).

55. Johnson, *Life and Letters*, 211 and 217.

56. Palmer, *The Rainbow Round the Throne: or Judgment Tempered with Mercy: A Discourse Before the Legislature of Georgia Delivered on the Day of Fasting, Humiliation and Prayer, Appointed by the President of the Confederate States of America, March 27th, 1863* (Milledgeville, Ga.: Doughton, Nisbet & Barnes, 1863), 36.

57. Ibid, 38.

58. Ibid. See also Palmer's December 1863 Fast Day sermon, where he opined that the

North's "false philanthropy" threaten the Negro's "early and inevitable extermination" (12). In 1843, Josiah Priest had already alluded to the fate of ancient Canaanites as a precedent for his own time: "The destruction of the Old Canaanites by the Jews was a judicial act of God, who straightly commanded them, by the ministration of Moses, see Deut. vii, 2, that they should not spare them, nor show mercy or pity toward them. . . . That dreadful affair, the exterminating decree of God against the negroes of old Canaan, was not by the will of man, but of God. . . ." See Josiah Priest, *Slavery as it Relates to the Negro or African Race,* (1843; reprint, New York: Arno, 1977), 86.

59. "Address of Rev. Dr. B. M. Palmer," *Southern Historical Society Papers,* Vol. 10 (Richmond, Va., 1882), 251.

60. "Discourse of Rev. B. M. Palmer, D.D.," *Southern Historical Society Papers,* Vol. 18 (Richmond, Va., 1890), 212.

Chapter 10

1. Louis Ginzberg, *Legends of the Jews,* Vol. 1, *Bible Times and Characters from the Creation to Jacob,* trans. Henrietta Szold (Philadelphia: Jewish Publication Society, 1968), 1:159.

2. Louis Ginzberg, *Legends of the Bible* (Philadelphia: Jewish Publication Society of America, 1956), 79.

3. The rabbis go so far as to claim that Noah's drunkenness caused exile for himself and his descendants. See Jack P. Lewis, *A Study of the Interpretation of Noah and the Flood in Jewish and Christian Literature* (Leiden: E. J. Brill, 1968), chap. 6, "The Rabbinic Noah."

4. Although the fathers could not avoid the question of Noah's drunkenness, they attempted to explain it naturally: "Origen explains that Noah did not know the potency of wine, and Epiphanius excuses Noah on the grounds of his advanced years. Chrysostom thinks that he did not know how to qualify his wine. . . ." See Don Cameron Allen, *The Legend of Noah: Renaiseance Rationalism in Art, Science and Letters* (Urban: University of Illinois Press, 1963), 73.

5. Augustine, "City of God" XVI: 2, in Philip Schaff, ed., *A Select Library of the Nicene and Post-Nicene Fathers of the Christian Church,* 8 vols. (Grand Rapids, Mich.: Eerdmanss, 1955).

6. Examples include the Cathedral of Bourges, the palace of the Doges at Venice, Ulm an der Donau, Sainte Chapelle at Paris, the Florence Campanile, the carved wood of the lectern in the cloister at Maulbronn, and various miniatures. See Allen, *Legend of Noah,* 162–63.

7. Ibid., 173.

8. Guillaume Du Bartas, *La Seconde Sepmaine,* "L'Arche," lines 511–20, passim. Translation by James Vest.

9. Ibid., lines 561–70. Translation by James Vest.

10. John Calvin, *Commentaries on the First Book of Moses Called Genesis,* 2 vols., trans. John King (Grand Rapids, Mich.: Eerdmans, 1948), 1:300–1.

11. Ibid., 1:301. Emphasizing the grave consequences of Noah's transgression, Calvin adds that "such a debasing alienation of mind in the prince of the new world, and the holy patriarch of the Church, could not less astonish [Shem and Japheth],

than if they had seen the ark itself broken, dashed in pieces, cleft asunder, and destroyed"(302).

12. Calvin is confident that after awaking the patriarch repented from his grievous sin: "We ought not to doubt, that the holy man was truly humbled (as he ought to be) under a sense of his fault, and honestly reflected on his own deserts. . . ." This presumed repentance lends credibility to Noah's role as "the herald of Divine judgment." Noah assumed this role reluctantly; being "one of the best of parents, he would pronounce his sentence upon his son with the most bitter grief of mind"(ibid., 304).

13. *The Works of the Right Reverend Father in God, Gervase Babington, Late Bishop of Worcester. Containing Comfortable Notes Upon the First Bookes of Moses* (London: Miles Flesher, 1637) 33.

14. Babington warns: "And could [excess wine] so disfigure *Noah*, a man of such goodnesse, so highly commended before, and not disfigure us that are a thousand degrees behind him? . . . Think of it, and if you shame in *Noahs* behalfe to thinke how unseemingly hee lay, take heed to your selfe . . ." (ibid., 33–34; emphasis in the original).

15. Andrew Willet, *Hexapla in Genesin* (London: Tho. Creede, 1608), 105. See also 110.

16. Ibid.

17. Matthew Henry's, *Commentary on the Whole Bible, Wherein Each Chapter, Is Summoned Up in Its Contents: The Sacred Text Inserted at Large in Distinct Paragraphs; Each Paragraph Reduced to its Proper Heads: The Sense Given, and Largely Illustrated with Practical Remarks and Observations,* Vol. 1, *Genesis to Deuteronome* (New York: R. Carter, 1880), 73.

18. Thomas Newton, *Dissertations on the Prophecies, Which Have Remarkably Been Fulfilled, and at This Time are Fulfilling in the World* (New York: William Durell, 1794), 15.

19. Marcus Dods, *The Book of Genesis, The Expositor's Bible, Series 1,* Vol. 2 (New York: A. C. Armstrong, 1901), 75

20. Ibid., 76.

21. In Werner Sollors, *Neither Black nor White yet Both: Thematic Explorations of Interracial Literature* (New York: Oxford University Press, 1997).

22. "Certain it is," Bolingbroke continues, "that no writer but a Jew could impute to the economy of Divine Providence the accomplishment of such a prediction, nor make the Supreme Being the executor of such a curse." See "Letters on the Study and Use of History," Letter III, in *The Works of Lord Bolingbroke in Four Volumes* (Philadelphia: Carey and Hart, 1841), 2:209–10.

23. Ibid., 209.

24. Ibid., 210.

25. Ibid.

26. David Brion Davis, *The Problem of Slavery in Western Culture* (Ithaca, N.Y.: Cornell University Press, 1966), 316–17. Examples include William Edmunson and Elihu Coleman.

27. Samuel Sewall, *The Selling of Joseph: A Memorial,* ed. Sidney Kaplan (Amherst: University of Massachusetts Press, 1969). See also Theopus H. Smith, *Conjuring Culture: Biblical Formations of Black Culture* (New York: Oxford University Press, 1994), 84ff.

28. Sewall, *The Selling of Joseph*, 12.

29. Ibid., 13.

30. Ibid., 12–14. Can the Ethiopian change his skin? Sewall asks rhetorically. "This shows Black Men are the Posterity of *Cush*: Who time out of mind have been distinguished by their Colour."

31. See Theodore Dwight Weld, *The Bible Against Slavery: An Inquiry into the Patriarchal and Mosaic Systems on the Subject of Haman Rights* (New York: Anti-Slavery Society, 1838.)

32. Caroline L. Shanks, "The Biblical Anti-Slavery Argument of the Decade 1830–1840," *The Journal of Negro History* 15, no. 2 (1931): 132.

33. William Henry Brisbane, *Slaveholding Examined in the Light of The Holy Bible* (Philadelphia, 1847), 25. See also John Bell Robinson, *Pictures of Slavery and Anti-Slavery. Advantages of Negro Slavery and the Benefits of Negro Freedom. Morally, Socially and Politically Considered* (Philadelphia, 1863), 19.

34. Shanks writes that "most of the abolitionists who questioned this genealogy at all contented themselves with demanding proof that the Africans were indeed the offspring of Canaan and not of some other son" ("The Biblical Anti-Slavery Argument," 137).

35. For instance, John Rankin. See ibid., 138.

36. This view is succinctly expressed by Thornton Stringfellow, who declares that when Noah said "cursed be Canaan," he was speaking "in God's stead." See "A Scriptural View of Slavery," in *Slavery Defended: The Views of the Old South*, ed. Eric L. McKitrick, (Englewood Cliffs, N.J.: Prentice-Hall, 1963), 86.

37. This claim has enjoyed a long life in American interpretive history. It was used in 1900 by Charles Carroll, who denied that the drunken Noah had authority to call down a divine curse on his son. See *"The Negro, A Beast" or "In the Image of God"; The Reasoner of the Age, the Revelator of the Century! The Bible as it is! The Negro and His Relation to the Human Family* (1900; reprint, Miami. Minemosyne, 1969). Ironically, Carroll resurrected this abolitionist strategy to deny the equality of the races. It surfaced again in the writings of Christian advocates of racial integration in the 1950s and 1960s. See, e.g., L. Richard Bradley, "The Curse of Canaan and the American Negro," *Concordia Theological Monthly* 42 (Fall 1971): 110.

38. Brisbane, *Slaveholding Examined in the Light of The Holy Bible*, 19–20.

39. Sollors cites Charles W. Gordon (1887) and John W. Tyndall (1927) as examples of abolitionist writers who adopt this approach. See *Neither Black nor White*, 104.

40. "John Rankin Asserts That Religious Teaching Is against Slavery," in William H. Pease and Jane H. Pease, eds., *The Anti-Slavery Argument* (Indianapolis: Bobbs-Merrill, 1965), 120.

41. In 1848, John Gregg Fee wrote that "a mere form of prophecy never justifies those who fulfil it; otherwise the Egyptians who *oppressed the Hebrews*—Judas who betrayed Christ, and the Jews who crucified him, were innocent. For it was foretold that they would do these things." See *An Anti-Slavery Manual* (1848; reprint, New York: Arno and New York Times, 1969), 20. See also George Bourne, *Picture of Slavery in the United States of America* (Boston: I. Knapp, 1838), 70: "God has emphatically attested, that his wrath shall be effused upon Babylon; but the persons who shall execute the judgment will doubtless perform the grand design, from selfish and ambitious views. Christians will mark the progress of the ven-

geance, and rejoice in the destruction, but they will not actively participate in the horrors of the tremendous overthrow." Albert Barnes (*An Inquiry into the Scriptural Views of Slavery*, 86) emphasized that "the prediction of the Saviour that he would be betrayed by Judas, and even the command to him to do 'what he was about to do' *quickly*, (John xiii.27,) did not justify the act of the traitor." See also Brisbane, *Slaveholding Examined in the Light of The Holy Bible*, 22.

42. Brisbane, *Slaveholding Examined in the Light of the Holy Bible*, 20.

43. "John Rankin Asserts that Religious Teaching is Against Slavery," in William H. Pease and Jane H. Pease, eds., *The Anti-Slavery Argument*, 120.

44. J. L. Stone, *Slavery and the Bible; or, Slavery as Seen in its Punishment* (San Francisco: B. F. Sterett, 1863), 11.

45. Ibid.

46. Ibid., 12.

47. George B. Cheever, *God against Slavery: and the Freedom and Duty of the Pulpit to Rebuke It, As a Sin Against God* (1857; reprint, New York: Arno, 1969), 100–102.

48. Ibid., 102.

49. For example, William Henry Brisbane argued at length that Noah's curse did not justify slavery of any kind and that the entire argument as advanced by slavery's supporters was a non sequitur. Nevertheless, he acknowledged that in the story "Ham was the offender." See *Slaveholding Examined in the Light of The Holy Bible*, chap. 2, "Canaan's Curse" (19ff).

50. Eliku Coleman, *Testimony against that Anti-Christian Practice of Making Slaves of Men, Wherein it is Shared to be Contrary to the Dispensation of the Law and Time of the Gospel, and Very Opposite Both to Grace and Nature* (1733; reprint, New Bedford, Mass.: Adam Shearman, 1825), 16.

51. Seeking to drive a wedge between the curse and American slavery, Isaac Allen wrote: "Canaan thus became the servant (not slave) of Shem; and when afterward Israel was oppressed and rendered tributary to other nations, the Canaanites became thus not only 'servants,' but 'servants of servants.' " See *Is Slavery Sanctioned by the Bible?* (Boston: American Tract Society, 1860), 5. Similarly, Presbyterian George Bourne, while insisting that Ham's other posterity were excluded from the curse's purview, averred that "the denunciation of Noah has been remarkably verified in the history of the Canaanites, who from the period when the iniquity of the Amorites was full, have seldom been released from the exactions of foreign tyrants." See *Picture of Slavery in the United States of America*, 69.

52. James W. C. Pennington, *A Text Book of the Origin and History, &c. &c of the Colored People* (Hartford: L. Skinner, 1841), chap. 1. This problem—endemic to any approach that is limited to a proper exegesis of Genesis 9:20–27—became evident again during the 1950s, when Christian opponents of segregation energetically refuted the curse's application to contemporary race relations. For instance, in *The Bible and Race* (Nashville: Broadman, 1959), T. B. Maston argued that the "curse of Ham" could not be used to justify American segregation because it was not Ham but Canaan who was cursed, the latter being quite deserving of Noah's malediction. See chap. 8, " 'Cursed Be Canaan,' " 105–17. Similarly, in "The Curse of Canaan and the American Negro" (1970), L. Richard Bradley asserted that the curse could not be utilized to justify de facto segregation because "the curse applied only to Canaan and his descendants and

therefore three-fourths of the descendants of Ham are exempt from the curse" (100). The implication, of course, is that the "Canaanites," whoever they may be, are not exempt.

53. An exception is Stephen M. Vail, who in 1864 wrote that Ham had "just opened his eyes and then turned away as any pure minded man would." See *The Bible against Slavery, with Replies to the "Bible View of Slavery," by John H. Hopkins, D.D., Bishop of the Diocese of Vermont; and to "A Northern Presbyter's Second Letter to Ministers of the Gospel," by Nathan Lord, D.D., Late President of Dartmouth College; and to "X," of the New-Hampshire Patriot* (Concord, N. H.: Fogg, Hadley, 1864). Cited in Sollors, *Neither White nor Black*, 96.

54. Significantly, Albert Barnes's 1857 tract of nearly 400 pages devoted only one footnote to the malediction upon Ham-Canaan. Barnes called the argument from Noah's curse "weak," observing that it was pronounced on Canaan rather than on Ham and adding that, in any case, Noah's words were a mere prediction of what would be and thus "no justification of wickedness." With a note of disdain, Barnes concluded "it is surprising that [this argument] was ever used" (*An Inquiry into the Scriptural Views of Slavery*, 86).

55. Adrianus Van Selms offers further historical-critical observations on this text: (1) that Canaan is described as a son of Ham to make a political rather than a genealogical point (i.e., that Canaan is part of the Egyptian empire); (2) that the blessings pronounced on Shem and Japheth must be post-Mosaic in origin because they contain the divine name YHWH; (3) that the "tents of Shem" indicate nomadic invaders from the east; (4) that the name "Japheth" is probably related to "Iapetos," regarded as an ancestor of the human race in Greek mythology; (5) and that the blessing of Shem and Japheth and cursing of Canaan reflect "a program of cooperation between the Hebrew invaders from the East and the Pessagic invaders from the West against the settled population of Canaan." See "The Canaanites in Genesis," *Oudtestamentische Studiën* 12 (1958): 182–213. See also Frederick W. Bassett, "Noah's Nakedness and the Curse of Canaan: A Case of Incest? *Vetus Testamentum* 21 (1971): 232.

56. Randall C. Bailey, "They're Nothing But Incestuous Bastards: The Polemical Use of Sex and Sexuality in Hebrew Canon Narratives," in *Reading from This Place*, Vol. 1, *Social Location and Biblical Interpretation in the United States*, ed. Fernando F. Segovia and Mary Ann Tolbert (Minneapolis Fortress, 1994). 135–36. Bailey summarizes: "In effect, the Priestly school says: Why venerate Hamites? They're nothing but sexual deviants, destined to be slaves to Shemites. And if there is any question about it, listen to what YHWH has to say about them in Leviticus 18 and 20"(137).

57. Gene Rice, "The Curse That Never Was (Genesis 9:18–27)," *Journal of Religious Thought* 29 no. 1 (1972): 7. See Rice for a list of scholars who have maintained this understanding of the story, a list that indicates that "after its introduction in the 1870s the interpretation presented [here] quickly won the assent of the majority of authorities and has maintained that position to the present"(8). Rice notes, however, that a number of biblical scholars have defended the unity of Genesis 9:18–27.

58. Ibid., 16.

59. Gunther Wittenberg, "Let Canaan Be His Slave" (Genesis 9:26). Is Ham Also Cursed?" *Journal of Theology for Southern Africa* 74 (March 1991): 49, 52.

60. Umberto Cassuto, *A Commentary on the Book of Genesis, part 2, From Noah to Abraham, Genesis 5:19 to 11:32* (Jerusalem: Magnes, 1949), 149.

61. Ibid., 155.

62. Nonetheless, Cassuto emphasizes that the received text indicates Ham's sin was in seeing only (150).

63. Albert I. Baumgarten, "Myth and Midrash: Genesis 9:20–29," in *Christianity, Judaism and Other Greco-Roman Cults*, ed. Jacob Neusner, Vol 12, part 3, *Studies in Judaism in Late Antiquity* (Leiden: E. J. Brill, 1975), 63.

64. Ibid., 64. Noting that the earliest hints of Ham doing more than looking on his father appear in second-century translations of the text by Aquila, Symmachus, and Theodotion; that the first appearance of the castration story is in the work of Theophilus of Antioch (late second century C.E.); and that the first datable rabbinic allusion to castration is early third century C.E., Baumgartner concludes that the castration tradition was not preexisting but was created by the rabbis in the second century to explain textual difficulties, particularly those dealing with transfer of the curse (67).

65. Frederick W. Bassett, "Noah's Nakedness and the Curse of Canaan: A Case of Incest? *Vetus Testamentum* 21 (1971): 232–37; Anthony Phillips, "Uncovering the Father's Skirt," *Vetus Testamentum* 30, no. 1 (1980): 38–43. Phillips argues that the case of Ham and Noah explains the Deuteronomistic prohibition against sexual relations between father and son in Deut. 27:20, which he translates, "Cursed be he who lies with the wife of his father for he has uncovered the skirt of his father."

66. Bailey, "They're Nothing but Incestuous Bastards," 134.

67. C. F. Keil and F. Delitzsch, *Biblical Commentary on the Old Testament*, Vol. 1, *The Pentateuch*, trans. James Martin (Grand Rapids, Mich: Ferdmans, 1949), cited in Bradley, "The Curse of Canaan and the American Negro," 103 n. 21.

68. Cassuto, *A Commentary on the Book of Genesis*, 153.

69. Robert Graves and Raphael Patai, *Hebrew Myths: The Book of Genesis* (New York: Greenwich, 1983), 122. Graves and Patai do not find plausible Canaan's use of a cord to castrate his grandfather. Rather, they suggest the original instrument may have been a pruning knife from Noah's vineyard.

70. Wittenberg, "Let Canaan Be His Slave," 55–56.

71. Rice, "The Curse That Never Was," 18.

72. Thomas V. Peterson, *Ham and Japheth in America: The Mythic World of Whites in the Antebellum South* (Metuchen, N.J.: American Theological Library Association, 1978), 131.

73. Howard Eilberg-Schwartz, *God's Phallus and Other Problems for Men and Monotheism* (Boston: Beacon, 1994), 97.

74. H. Hirsch Cohen, *The Drunkenness of Noah* (Tuscaloosa: University of Alabama Press, 1974), 8, 12.

75. Ibid., 18.

76. Ibid., 19.

77. Ibid., 29.

78. Arthur Frederick Ide, *Noah and the Ark: The Influence of Sex, Homophobia and Heterosexism in the Flood Story and Its Writing* (Las Colinas, Tex: Monument, 1992).

79. Ibid., 19.

80. One example will suffice: "Covertly introduced, [the story] probes the darkest

recesses of the mind, exposing the raw erection of ideas that impregnate the world's most erotic literature. Dramatically it massages the imagination until the moist poignant details erupt in a jet of emotions that leave the reader panting" (*Noah and the Ark*, 42).

81. Ibid., 44.

82. Ibid., 44–45.

83. Ibid., 51.

84. Ibid., 49. To strengthen his case that Ham should be viewed as the story's hero, Ide observes that he is the only one of Noah's sons after whom a country is named (cf. the biblical description of Egypt as "the land of Ham").

85. Ibid., 33.

86. Ide's reading is also dangerously anti-Jewish. It blames suppression of the sodomy incident on "the priests of Shiloh," who wished to spiritually enslave people so they could devote their time to the Temple. Like some feminist rereadings of the Bible, Ide assigns to "male-dominated" Israelites responsibility for "mysogynistic attitude[s] toward women."

87. Regina M. Schwartz, *The Curse of Cain: The Violent Legacy of Monotheism* (Chicago: University of Chicago Press, 1997), 106.

88. Ibid., 112.

89. Ibid., 115.

90. Ibid., 108.

91. Ibid.

92. Ibid., 110.

93. Schwartz regards the pattern in Israelite narrative in which siblings compete with one another instead of with their father as "another expression of the priestly interest in protecting the preserve of divinity" (ibid. 115).

94. In Sollors, *Neither Black nor White*, 105.

95. Mark Twain, *Letters from the Earth*, ed. Bernard Devoto (New York: Harper, 1991), 35.

96. *The Short Fiction of Charles W. Chesnutt*, ed. Sylvia Lyons Render (Washingon, D. C.: Howard University Press, 1981), 177–82. See Sollors, *Neither Black nor White*, 108.

97. Cited in Sollors, *Neither Black nor White*, 451. Sollors also quotes a statement of Baldwin describing his sentiments on the curse: "I realized that the Bible had been written by white men. I knew that, according to many Christians, I was a descendant of Ham, who had been cursed, and that I was therefore predestined to be a slave. This had nothing to do with anything I was, or contained, or could become; my fate had been sealed forever, from the beginning of time" (*Neither Black nor White*, 95–96).

98. Zora Neale Hurston, "The First One: A Play in One Act," in *Ebony and Topaz: A Collectanea*, ed. Charles Spurgeon Johnson (1927; reprint, Freeport, N.Y.: Books for Libraries Press, 1971), 53–57.

99. Pauline Hopkins is a black author who does not affirm the curse per se but perpetuates many views of Noah's family, color differentiation, and geographical dispersion that were associated with the curse in the nineteenth century. See Pauline E. Hopkins, *A Primer of Facts Pertaining to the Early Greatness of the African Race and the Possibility of Restoration by its Descendants—with Epilogue* (Cambridge: P. E. Hopkins, 1905), chaps. 1–3.

100. Walker and Douglass are cited in Sollors, *Neither Black nor White*, 105–7.

101. See ibid., 107. See also Charles B. Copher, "Three Thousand Years of Biblical Interpretation with Reference to Black Peoples," in Gayraud S. Wilmore, ed., *African American Religious Studies: An Interdisciplinary Anthology* (Durham: Duke University Press, 1989), 121–23.

102. Peterson, *Ham and Japheth*, 46–7.

103. See Charles B. Copher, "Three Thousand Years of Biblical Interpretation with Reference to Black Peoples," *Journal of the Interdenominational Theological Center* 13 (Spring 1986): 242. From the reference to Nimrod in Genesis 10, Copher concludes that an ancient Hebrew writer believed that civilization in Mesopotamia owed its origins to a son of Cush. Copher, "The Black Presence in the Old Testament," in Cain Hope Felder, ed., *Stony the Road We Trod: African American Biblical Interpretation* (Minneapolis: Fortress, 1991), 153–54.

104. Copher, "Three Thousand Years of Biblical Interpretation with Reference to Black Peoples; in *African American Religious Studies*, ed. Wilmore, 167–68.

105. Alonzo Potter Burgess Holly, *God and the Negro: Synopsis of God and the Negro or the Biblical Record of the Race of Ham* (Nashville: Nation Baptist Publishing Board, 1937), 122. In chapter 2 "The Curse of Noah," Holly affirms that Canaan is the ancestor of the Negro "race" but, following Exodus 20:5 (in which God is said to punish only to the third and fourth generation), claims that Noah's curse remained in effect for no more than one hundred years.

106. Copher's writings have been particularly influential for a generation of African American scholars seeking to reassess and recapture the black presence in the Bible.

107. See Latta R. Thomas, *Biblical Faith and the Black American* (Valley Forge, Pa.: Judson, 1974). Thomas stresses the ego needs of white Bible readers and the etiological dimensions of the original biblical text. In an attempt to "unmask the hermeneutical distortions of White Christians," Katie Geneva Cannon attacks the mythology of black inferiority rooted in "the metonymical curse of Ham." See Cannon, "Slave Ideology and Biblical Interpretation," in Randall C. Bailey and Jacquelyn Grant, eds., *The Recovery of Black Presence: An Interdisciplinary Exploration: Essays in Honor of Dr. Charles B. Copher* (Nashville: Abingdon, 1995), 119, 121.

108. Felder, "Race, Racism and the Bible Narratives," in *Stony the Road We Trod*, 127.

109. Ibid., 131.

110. P. K. McCary, *Black Bible Chronicles: From Genesis to the Promised Land* (New York: African American Family Press, 1993).

111. Some advocates of the new Hamite hypothesis regard Cush as an exception to this generalization. But the fundamental point is that because sub-Saharan Africans were not within the purview of the biblical writers, none of the persons mentioned in Genesis 9–11 should be regarded as black. See Felder, ed., *Stony the Road We Trod*, 150–51; and Copher, "Blacks and Jews in Historical Interaction: The Biblical/African Experience," *Journal of the Interdenominational Theological Center* 3 (Fall 1975): 9–10.

112. See Copher, "Three Thousand Years of Biblical Interpretation," 244.

113. See, e.g., the photograph entitled "Noah and his Sons" in Cain Hope Felder, ed., *The Original African Heritage Study Bible, King James Version, with Special Annotations Relative to the African/Edemic Experience* (Nashville: James C. Winston,

1993), following 47; and George W. Gentry, *Black Madonna, Infant Jesus* (Okolona, Ark.: n.p., 1999), 3: "Japheth, Shem & Ham were all Black as the Bible makes so explicitly clear."

114. Jeanette Winterson and James Morrow are among the contemporary authors who irreverently revisit the story of Noah and the Flood. The characters in Winterson's *Boating for Beginners* (London: Methuen, 1985) include Noah's sons Japheth, Ham, and Shem, along with "their lovely wives Sheila, Desi and Rita." Japheth is a "jewellery king, Ham the owner of that prestigious pastrami store, More Meat, and Shem, once playboy and entrepreneur, now a reformed and zealous pop singer" (21). Yet despite her satirical treatment of the history behind the Genesis flood story and her portrayal of Noah as Yahweh's inventor, Winterson ignores the tale of Noah and his sons narrated in Genesis 9. Morrow's "Bible Stories for Adults, No. 17: The Deluge" is a "deconstruction of the Flood legend" in which Noah and his sons rescue a sinful survivor of the Deluge named Sheila. While Morrow does not refer to the tale of Noah's drunkenness, he characterizes Ham as "low and slithery," a merciless man who votes to murder "the whore" and agrees to be her executioner (*Bible Stories for Adults* [New York: Harcourt Brace, 1996], 1–14).

115. Frederick Buechner, *Peculiar Treasures: A Biblical Who's Who* (San Francisco: Harper, 1979), 46–47. Buechner's commentary is critical of the story's misuse, noting that for generations certain preachers have regarded it as "biblical sanction for whatever form of white supremacy happened to be going on at the time all the way from literal slavery to separate but equal schools, segregated toilet facilities, and restricted housing." Nevertheless, by ignoring the role of Canaan, Buechner's retelling places the curse less ambiguously upon Ham.

116. Julian Barnes, *A History of the World in 10½ Chapters* (New York: Knopf, 1989), 8, 16–17. Among the modern authors who refer to Noah's fondness for wine is G. K. Chesterton, who has Noah say: "It looks like rain . . . But I don't care where the water goes if it doesn't get into the wine." See Allen, *Legend of Noah*, 154–55.

117. Alicia Suskin Ostriker, *The Nakedness of the Fathers: Biblical Visions and Revisions* (New Brunswick, N.J.: Rutgers University Press, 1994), 15.

118. Ibid., 43–44.

119. In *The First One*, Zora Neale Hurston writes that while "Mrs. Ham" gazes in horror at the dead who float in the receding waters of the deluge, Noah seeks the "juice of the grape to make us forget." "Drink wine, forget water—it means death, *death!*," he cries. Biblical commentator Leon Kass opines that "given his ordeal upon the waters, one can perhaps understand Noah's turn to drink. He may well have sought solace in the grape, or even forgetfulness." Commenting on the role of wine in the biblical story, Kass notes that it causes not only drunkenness but also "the erosion of the ability to make distinctions, of chaos." See Kass, "Seeing the Nakedness of His Father," *Commentary* (June 1992): 43–44.

120. Kass, "Seeing the Nakedness of His Father," 43.

121. In the Hebrew Bible, fermented drink functions as an ambiguous symbol. On one hand, the grape harvest symbolizes God's blessings of life and fertility. See *The New Interpreter's Bible*, Vol. 1 (Nashville: Abingdon, 1994), 403. On the other hand, passages such as Proverbs 31:4–5 indicate a keen awareness of the consequences of human intoxication: "It is not for kings, O Lemuel, / it is not for kings to drink wine, / or for rulers to desire strong drink; / or else they will drink

and forget what has been decreed, / and will pervert the rights of all the afflicted." Some texts even connect fermented drink with nakedness and shame; for instance, Habbakuk 2:15: " 'Alas for you who make your neighbors drink, / pouring out your wrath until they are drunk, / in order to gaze on their nakedness!' "; and Lamentations 4:21: "Rejoice and be glad, O daughter Edom, / you that live in the land of Uz;/ but to you also the cup shall pass;/ you shall become drunk and strip yourself bare." The temporary effects of intoxication—nakedness and exposure—are prophetic images of Israel's apostasy (*New Interpreter's Bible*, 1:404). And the Apocryphal book of 3 *Baruch* identifies the "forbidden fruit" of Adam and Eve as excessive wine drinking. See Kristen E. Kvam, Linda S. Schearing, and Valarie H. Ziegler, eds., *Eve and Adam: Jewish, Christian, and Muslim Readings on Genesis and Gender* (Bloomington: Indiana University Press, 1999), 43–4. It is interesting that in the New Testament, violence and wine are related. See, for instance, 1 Timothy 3:1–5; Titus 1:7.

122. Ginzberg, *Legends of the Bible*, 79.

123. Jacob Neusner, ed., *Genesis Rabbah: The Judaic Commentary to the Book of Genesis, a New American Translation*, 30.

124. Anbraham Rosse, *An Exposition on the Fourteene First Chapters of Genesis, by Way of Question and Answere, Collected Out of Ancient and Recent Writers: Both Brifely and Subtilly Propounded and Expounded* (London: B. A. T. F., 1626), 60. Rosse may have been infuenced by the rabbinic notion that wine was responsible for the sin of "Adam, whose fall had also been due to wine, for the forbidden fruit had been the grape, with which he had made himself drunk" (Ginzberg, *Legends of the Bible*, 79).

125. I am indebted to René Girard for this understanding of the *pharmakon*. According to Girard, "the word *pharmakon* in classical Greek means both poison and the antidote for poison, both sickness and cure—in short, any substance capable of perpetrating a very good or very bad action, according to the circumstances and the dosage. The *pharmakon* is thus a magic drug or volatile elixir, whose administration best be left by ordinary men in the hands of those who enjoy special knowledge and exceptional powers—priests, magicians, shamans, doctors, and so on." See *Violence and the Sacred*, trans. Patrick Gregory (Baltimore: Johns Hopkins University Press, 1977), 95.

Chapter 11

1. In 1867, "Ariel" gave this stark, but simple advice: "Subdue the negro as we do the other animals, and like them, teach them all we can; then turn them loose, free them entirely from the restraints and control of the white race, and, just like all other animals or beasts so treated, back to his native nature and wildness and barbarism and the worship of daemons, he *will* go" (*The Negro: What is His Ethnological Status: Is He The Progency of Ham? Is He a Descendant of Adam and Eve? Has He a Soul? Or is He a Beast in God's Nomenclature? What is His Status as Fixed by God in Creation? What is His Relation to the White Race?* 2d ed. (Cincinnati n.p. 1867), 44).

2. American Bible readers have utilized traditional readings of Genesis to combat the polygenetic version of human origins propagated by American racists from "Ariel" to Charles Carroll to the preachers of Christian Identity.

3. The compulsion to defend the Christian notion of human unity helps explain the remarkable popularity of Acts 17:26 as a proof-text in Christian discussions of race relations. While preaching in Athens, Paul proclaimed that "From one ancestor [God] made all nations to inhabit the whole earth, and he allotted the times of their existence and the boundaries of the places where they would live." While progressives have tended to cite the first half of this verse as evidence for the "brotherhood of man," conservatives from Benjamin Palmer to Bob Jones Sr. have seen in Paul's message the felicitous combination of two ideas—the unity of humankind and God's active role in separating peoples. See Jones, *Is Segregation Scriptural?* (Greenville, S.C.: Bob Jones University, 1960), 4–6.

4. On this point, Regina Schwartz's critique of proslavery Bible readings is misleading. She writes that "the more people were victimized by the institution of slavery in the United States, the more persistent became the cultural effort to imagine them as another 'race,' that is, another 'family of man,' and often worse, as a subhuman species" (*The Curse of Cain: The Violent Legacy of Monotheism* [Chicago: University of Chicago Press, 1997], 103). Antebellum Christians who developed a consistent proslavery ideology never wavered in their conviction of blacks' humanity.

5. *The New Interpreter's Bible,* Vol. 1 (Nashville: Abingdon, 1994), 1:405. See also Laurence A. Turner, *Genesis,* (Sheffield: Sheffield, Academic Press, 2000). 54–56. Terry J. Prewitt notes these parallels between the genealogies of Adam, Noah, and Terah: "Each had three sons, all of whom figure more or less prominently in the narrative texts of Genesis. Cain's opposition to his brother Abel is similar to the opposition of Ham, the 'father of Canaan,' to his brothers Shem and Japheth." See *The Elusive Covenant: A Structural-Semiotic Reading of Genesis* (Bloomington: Indiana University Press, 1990), 5.

6. The prophecy that an elder brother will serve a younger is a leitmotif in the Pentateuch. It is operative in the relationship of Abraham's eldest son, Ishmael, and his younger brother, Isaac, and is especially prominent in the story of Isaac's sons by Rebekah, Jacob and Esau. Genesis 25:22–23 says of Rebekah when she is pregnant with Esau and Jacob: "The children struggled together within [Rebekah]; and she said, 'If it is to be this way, why do I live?" So she went to inquire of the LORD. And the LORD said to her, 'Two nations are in your womb,/ and two peoples born of you shall be divided;/ the one shall be stronger than the other,/ the elder shall serve the younger.' " Note, however, the differences between this passage and Genesis 9. The prediction of the brothers' relationship is made before their birth; it is a statement of fact rather than a punishment; instead of a father announcing that one of his adult sons will serve the other two, God responds to a mother's query with the observation that one of her contending sons will be subdued by the other. The prediction is fulfilled later in the same chapter when Esau convinces a famished Jacob to trade his birthright for stew. In chapter 27 we read of a second fulfillment of the reversal, when Isaac, old and blind, asks Esau to hunt game for him in exchange for a paternal blessing. While he is gone, Rebekah schemes with Jacob to impersonate Esau and usurp the dying father's blessing. The plan is successful. Adumbrations of Genesis 9 in this text include the fact that both Jacob and Esau enter into Isaac's tent and that Isaac cannot see them (27:18), that Jacob is concerned with the possibility that Rebekah's scheme may elicit a curse from his father rather than a blessing (27:12), that Isaac is given wine to increase the likelihood that the ruse will work (27:25), and that the blessing and curse pro-

nounced on Jacob and Esau, respectively, emphasize that one brother will serve the other.

7. James G. Williams, *The Bible, Violence, and the Sacred: Liberation from the Myth of Sanctioned Violence* (Valley Forge, Pa.: Trinity, 1995), 60.

8. Turner, *Genesis,* 56.

9. Prewitt, *The Elusive Covenant,* 74.

10. This theme is "the keynote of the dominant priestly version of the story: the earth, once described as 'good' (Genesis 1.31), is seen to be corrupt owing to human violence or willful, lawless deeds, beginning with rebellion in the garden." See *The New Oxford Annotated Bible with the Apocryphal/Deuterocanonical Books* ed. Bruce M. Metzger and Roland E. Murphy (New York: Oxford University Press, 1991), annotation to Genesis 6:11–12.

11. "The Surrogate Victim," in René Girard, *The Girard Reader,* ed. James G. Williams (New York: Crossroad, 1996), 29.

12. According to Girard, the Flood and Tower of Babel are metaphors of crisis that belong to the first moments in the origin of culture. In *Things Hidden since the Foundation of the World: Research Undertaken in Collaboration with Jean-Michel Oughourlian and Guy Lefort* (Stanford, Calif.: Stanford University Press, 1987), Girard includes several brief references to Noah and the Flood: "Since the single victim brings reconciliation and safety by restoring life to the community, it is not difficult to appreciate that a sole survivor in a world where all others perish can, thematically, amount to the same thing as a victim extracted from a group in which no one, save the victim, perishes. Noah's Ark, which alone is spared by the Flood, guarantees that the world will begin all over again. . . . For Noah, the final reorganization [of order] is implied not only in the Covenant after the Flood, but also in the confinement of prototypes of all species within the Ark; here we have something like a floating system of classification, on the basis of which the world will repeople itself in conformity with the norms of God's will" ("The Bible's Distinctiveness and the Gospel," in *The Girard Reader,* 147–48). "The Flood also results from an escalation that involves the monstrous dissolution of all differences: giants are born, the progeny of a promiscuous union between the sons of the gods and the daughters of men. This is the crisis in which the whole of culture is submerged, and its destruction is not only a punishment from God; to almost the same extent it is the fatal conclusion of a process which brings back the violence from which it originally managed to get free, thanks to the temporary benefits of the founding murder" (ibid., 151).

13. I have been encouraged in the application of Girardian analysis to Genesis 9 by James Williams, Robert Hamerton-Kelly, and Gil Baillie, who have employed mimetic theory in rereading other biblical stories that have been generative of violence.

14. "The Scapegoat as Historical Referent," in *The Girard Reader,* 105.

15. Editor's introduction to "Stereotypes of Persecution," in *The Girard Reader,* 107.

16. "Stereotypes of Persecution," in *The Girard Reader,* 108.

17. Ibid., 113.

18. Ibid., 110.

19. Ibid.

20. Leo Kuper, Foreword to Robert Melson's *Revolution and Genocide: On the Origins of the Armenian Genocide and the Holocaust* (Chicago: University of Chicago Press, 1992), x.

21. Editor's introduction to "Triangular Desire," in *The Girard Reader*, 33.
22. Ibid., 38.
23. *The Girard Reader*, 271.
24. Editor's introduction to "Sacrifice as Sacral Violence and Substitution," in *The Girard Reader*, 69.
25. *The Girard Reader*, 12.
26. "The Surrogate Victim," in *The Girard Reader*, 28.
27. *The Girard Reader*, 11.
28. In *Violence and the Sacred* (trans. Patrick Gregory [Baltimore: Johns Hopkins University Press, 1977]) Girard discusses the story of Cain and Abel (Genesis 4) as well as that of Jacob and Isaac (Genesis 27). He comments that "a frequent motif in the Old Testament, as well as in Greek myth, is that of brothers at odds with one another. Their fatal penchant for violence can only be diverted by the intervention of a third party" ("Sacrifice as Sacral Violence and Substitution," in *The Girard Reader*, 74).
29. Randall C. Bailey, "They're Nothing but Incestuous Bastards: The Polemical Use of Sex and Sexuality in Hebrew Canon Narratives," in *Reading from This Place*, Vol. 1, *Social Location and Biblical Interpretation in the United States*, ed. Fernando F. Segovia and Mary Ann Tolbert (Minneapolis: Fortress, 1994), 134.
30. "Mimesis and Violence," in *The Girard Reader*, 12.
31. To the extent that he accuses Noah of all manner of crimes, Arthur Frederick Ide challenges this paradigm. But like other modern readers who foreground the dynamics of desire, he ignores its imitative nature.
32. See, e.g., figures 23 and 24 in Dom Cameron Allen, *The Legend of Noah: Renaissance Rationalism in Art, Science and Letters* (Urbana: University of Illinois Press, 1963). These are illustrations from the Cologne Bible and Lubeck Bible (both fifteenth century) that depict one of the brothers covering Noah's nakedness while the other two watch.
33. Umberto Cassuto, *A Commentary on the Book of Genesis*, Part 2, *From Noah to Abraham*, *Genesis 5:19 to 11:32* (Jerusalem: Magnes, 1949), 163. Randall Bailey intimates the brothers' rivalry and its dire consequences for the community when he writes that "the narrator . . . spends meticulous details in describing how carefully and awkwardly the other two sons place a robe on their shoulders (which is generally an idiom for burdens that only the deity can remove), walk backward (which is generally associated with death), and without seeing, cover their father" ("They're Nothing but Incestuous Bastards," 134).
34. Figure 23 in Allen, *Legend of Noah*.
35. John Calvin, *Commentaries on the First Book of Moses called Genesis*, 2 vols., trans. John King (Grand Rapids, Mich.: Eerdmans, 1948), 1:309.
36. Cf. Robert Hamerton-Kelly, "Mimesis and Mirror Images in History," paper delivered at the annual conference of the Colloquium on Violence and Religion, Stanford University, 27 June 1996.
37. Schwartz, *The Curse of Cain*, xi, 115.
38. Marcus Dods raised this possibility in 1901: "Many questions must have arisen in [Noah's] mind regarding the relation of the new to the old. Was there to be any connection with the old world at all, or was all to begin afresh? Were the promises, the traditions, the events, the genealogies of the old world of any significance now?" (*The Book of Genesis*, *The Expositor's Bible*, series 1, Vol. 2 [New York: A.C. Armstrong, 1901], 71–72).

39. The brothers are typically referred to as "Shem, Ham and Japheth" (Gen. 5:32; 6: 10; 7:13; 9:18; 10:1; 1 Chron. 1:4). But if Ham is Noah's "youngest son" (Gen. 9:24), why is he listed as the middle child? Adding to the confusion, Genesis 10:21 can be read so that Shem is designated "the brother of Japheth the elder." Biblical commentators have suggested many solutions to the enigma of birth order—for instance, that Shem and Ham are listed in succession because their descendants live in proximity, or that the arrangement Shem, Ham, and Japheth is "euphonic rather than chronological." See J. Ernest Shufelt, "Noah's Curse and Blessing: Gen. 9:18–27," *Concordia Theological Monthly* 17 (1946): 737; and Clyde T. Francisco, "The Curse on Canaan," *Christianity Today* (24 April 1964): 9.

40. "Triangular Desire, in *The Girard Reader*, 40.

41. "Mimesis and Violence," in *The Girard Reader*, 13.

42. According to Girard, "the unity of novelistic conclusions consists in the renunciation of metaphysical desire. The dying hero repudiates his mediator" ("Desire and the Unity of Novelistic Conclusions," in *The Girard Reader*, 48). In Genesis 9, Noah denounces the brothers' rivalry, uttering on their behalf "words which clearly contradict their former ideas"(47).

43. Generative violence must remain hidden; thus, the theme of chance recurs in folklore, myth, and fable: "The motif of chance has its origin in the arbitrary nature of the violent resolution. . . . The selection is not made by men, but left to divine Chance, acting through violence"("The Surrogate Victim," in *The Girard Reader*, 24, 26).

44. According to Girard, this differentiation is the effect rather than the cause of the scapegoat's misdeed: "The mythical sequence is a scapegoat inspired reversal of cause and effect." See "Python and His Two Wives: An Exemplary Scapegoat Myth," in *The Girard Reader*, 118.

45. Ibid., 119.

46. *Violence and the Sacred*, 7. Girard writes that those who sacrifice the *pharmakos* "are striving to produce a replica, as faithful as possible in every detail, of a previous crisis that was resolved by means of a spontaneously unanimous victimization. All the dangers, real and imaginary, that threaten the community are subsumed in the most terrible danger that can confront a society: the sacrificial crisis. The rite is therefore a repetition of the original, spontaneous 'lynching' that restored order in the community by reestablishing, around the figure of the surrogate victim, that sentiment of social accord that had been destroyed in the onslaught of reciprocal violence. Like Oedipus, the victim is considered a polluted object, whose living presence contaminates everything that comes in contact with it and whose death purges the community of its ills—as the subsequent restoration of public tranquility clearly testifies. That is why the *pharmakos* was paraded about the city. He was used as a kind of sponge to sop up impurities, and afterward he was expelled from the community or killed in a ceremony that involved the entire populace" (94–95).

47. Walter Burkert, "The Problem of Ritual Killing," in *Violent Origins: Walter Burkert, René Girard, and Jonathan Z. Smith on Ritual Killing and Cultural Formation*, ed. Robeert G. Hamerton-Kelly (Stanford, Calif.: Stanford University Press, 1987), 172.

48. See Bailey, "They're Nothing But Incestuous Bastards."

49. More than one modern writer has noted that sacrificial themes overflow into Genesis 9. Leon Kass observes that Noah's voluntary sacrifice of "scores of his former ark-mates" immediately after leaving the ark is evidence of his "suscepti-

bility to Dionysian chaos" and reveals his "lust for meat—or, at the very least, his blood lust, his willingness to shed blood." Kass also criticizes Noah's act of revenge as a "willingness to 'sacrifice' his grandson, Canaan, to Molech" (Kass, "Seeing the Nakedness of the Father," *Commentary,* [June 1992]: 43, 47).

50. Girard, "Sacrifice as Sacral Violence and Substitution," in *The Girard Reader,* 76–77.

51. Ibid., 77–78.

52. Ibid., 81.

53. In the canonical Gospels, Jesus is presented as "an innocent victim of a group in crisis, which, for a time at any rate, is united against him" (The Bible's Distinctiveness and the Gospel," in *The Girard Reader,* 165).

54. Girard writes that "in the first books of the Bible, the founding mechanism [of human culture] shows through the texts here and there, sometimes strikingly but never completely and unambiguously.... Throughout the Old Testament, a work of exegesis is in progress, operating in precisely the opposite direction to the usual dynamics of mythology and culture." In the Prophets, Girard believes, there is an increasing tendency for the victim to be brought to light, along with a subversion of the pillars of primitive religion, including "the primitive conception of the law as a form of obsessive differentiation, a refusal of mixed states that looks upon in differentiation with horror"("The Bible's Distinctiveness and the Gospel," in *The Girard Reader,* 154, 55, 57).

55. *The Girard Reader,* 17, 18.

56. Ibid., 18.

57. Girard writes that "Abel is only the first in a long line of victims whom the Bible exhumes and exonerates: 'The voice of your brother's blood cries to me from the ground' "("The Bible's Distinctiveness and the Gospel," in *The Girard Reader,* 151). Girard goes on to observe that instead of corroborating the accusation that Joseph has acted inappropriately with the Egyptian's wife, Genesis declares that the accusation is false. This supplies quite a contrast, of course, with the narrator's role in the story of Ham.

58. Williams, *The Bible, Violence and the Sacred,* 183, 184.

59. Ibid., 14–15.

60. Ibid.

61. Ibid.

62. William Stringfellow was an antebellum slavery apologist who presumed to speak for Ham. In a proslavery tract published in 1861, Stringfellow had a son of Japheth approach a son of Ham in Africa to offer him the role of servant. Pondering the history of his people, the young Hamite acknowledged that "Ham, my father, was a compound of beastly wickedness" while "the descendants of Ham, the beastly and degraded sons of Noah, were subjected to a degraded servitude to Shem and Japheth" (in Thomas V. Peterson, *Ham and Japheth in America: The Mythic World of Whites in the Antebellum South* [Metuchen, N.J.: American Theological Library Association, 1978], 130).

63. Williams, *The Bible, Violence and the Sacred,* 187.

64. While I am generally uncomfortable with the typological mode of interpretation that Christians have utilized to exploit the riches of the "Old Testament," I am emboldened to treat Ham as a type of Christ by the fact that readers of the Hebrew Bible have not regarded him as a treasure.

65. Du Bois's "Jesus Christ in Texas," in *Darkwater: Voices from within the Veil* (New

York: Harcourt, Brace and Howe, 1920), 123–33. Cullen's "The Black Christ" is anthologized in *My Soul's High Song: The Collected Writings of Countee Cullen, Voice of the Harlem Renaissance*, ed. Gerald Early (New York: Doubleday, 1991). For American artistic depictions of lynching as crucifixion, see "Christmas in Georgia, A.D., 1916," *Crisis* (December 1916); "Not Kultur, but Americans Passed This Way," *Richmond Planet* (22 November 1919); and Prentiss Taylor, "Christ in Alabama"(1932). See also Kelly Brown Douglas, *The Black Christ* (Maryknoll, N.Y.: Orbis, 1994).

66. See David Novak, *The Image of the Non-Jew in Judaism: An Historical and Constructive Study of the Noahide Laws* (New York and Toronto: Edwin Mellen, 1983).

67. Canonical antidotes for segregationist uses of the Babel story include Zephaniah 3:9–11 and Isaiah 66:18–23, texts in which Yahweh promises that when the process of salvation is fulfilled, the curse of Babel will be reversed. See Douglas Bax, "The Bible and Apartheid 2," in *Apartheid Is a Heresy*, ed. John W. DeGruchy and Charles Villa-Vicencio (Grand Rapids: Eerdmans, 1983), 124. The story of Pentecost can also be read as a reversal of Babel.

68. Desmond Tutu, *The Rainbow People of God: The Making of a Peaceful Revolution* (New York: Doubleday, 1994), 61. See also Allister Sparks, *The Mind of South Africa* (New York: Knopf, 1990), 289–91.

Chapter 12

1. Elisabeth Young-Bruehl, *The Anatomy of Prejudices* (Cambridge: Harvard University Press, 1996), 34.

2. See, e.g., Forrest G. Wood, *The Arrogance of Faith: Christianity and Race in America from the Colonial Era to the Twentieth Century* (Boston: Northeastern University Press, 1991).

3. This exegetical tradition, which entered popular lore in Islamic culture, is reflected in the tale of "The Man of Al-Yaman and His Six Slave-Girls" in *Thousand and One Nights*: "And indeed it is told in certain histories, related on the authority of devout men, that Noah (on whom be peace!) was sleeping one day, with his sons Cham and Shem seated at his head, when a wind sprang up and, lifting his clothes, uncovered his nakedness; whereat Cham looked and laughed and did not cover him: but Shem arose and covered him. Presently, their sire awoke and learning what had been done by his sons, blessed Shem and cursed Cham. So Shem's face was whitened and from him sprang the prophets and the orthodox Caliphs and Kings; whilst Cham's face was blackened and he fled forth to the land of Abyssinia, and of his lineage came the blacks. All people are of one mind in affirming the lack of understanding of the blacks, even as saith the adage, 'How shall one find a black with a mind?' " In Werner Sollors, *Neither Black nor White yet Both: Thematic Explorations of Interracial Literature* (New York: Oxford University Press, 1997), 91.

On the evolution of the Hamitic myth in the Muslim world, see William McKee Evans, "From the Land of Canaan to the Land of Guinea: The Strange Odyssey of the 'Sons of Ham,' " *American Historical Review* 85, no. 1 (1980): 15–43.

Bibliography

Aaron, Daniel. "The 'Inky Curse': Miscegenation in the White American Literary Imagination." *Social Science Information* 22, no. 2 (1983): 169–90.

Aaron, David H. "Early Rabbinic Exegesis on Noah's Son Ham and the So-Called 'Hamitic Myth.'" *Journal of the American Academy of Religion* 63, no. 4 (1995): 721–59.

Addington, Joseph C. *Reds, Whites and Blacks, or the Colors, Dispersion, Language, Sphere and Unity of the Human Race, as Seen in the Lights of Scripture, Science and Observation.* Raleigh, N.C.: Strother & Marcom, 1862.

Adger, John B., and John L. Girardeau, eds. *The Collected Writings of James Henley Thornwell, D.D., LL.D.,* 4 vols. Richmond: Presbyterian Committee of Publication, 1871–73.

"Africa in America." *Southern Literary Messenger* 22, no. 1 (1856): 1–14.

Aikman, William. *The Future of the Colored Race in America: Being an Article in the Presbyterian Quarterly Review, of July, 1862.* New York: Anson D. F. Randolph, 1862.

Allen, Dom Cameron. *The Legend of Noah: Renaissance Rationalism in Art, Science and Letters.* Urbana: University of Illinois Press, 1963.

Allen, Isaac. *Is Slavery Sanctioned by the Bible?* Boston: American Tract Society, 1860.

The Ante-Nicene Fathers. 10 vols. New York: Charles Scribner's Sons, 1926.

"Ariel" [Buckner H. Payne]. *The Negro: What is His Ethnological Status: Is He the Progeny of Ham? Is He a Descendant of Adam and Eve? Has He a Soul? Or is He a Beast in God's Nomenclature? What is His Status as Fixed by God in Creation? What is His Relation to the White Race?* 2d ed. Cincinnati, n.p.: 1867.

Armstrong, George D. *The Christian Doctrine of Slavery.* 1857. Reprint, New York: Negro Universities Press, 1969.

Atkinson, Basil C. *The Pocket Commentary of the Bible: The Book of Genesis.* Chicago: Moody Press, 1957.

Auer, J. Jeffery, ed. *Antislavery and Disunion, 1853–1861: Studies in the Rhetoric of Compromise and Conflict.* New York: Harper and Row, 1963.

"Augustus B. Moran, v. Gardner Davis." *Annals of Supreme Court of Georgia.* August
    Term, 1855.
Babington, Gervase. *The Works of the Right Reverend Father in God, Gervase Babington,
    Late Bishop of Worcester. Containing Comfortable Notes Upon the First Bookes of
    Moses.* London: Miles Flesher, 1637.
Bailey, Randall C. "They're Nothing but Incestuous Bastards: The Polemical Use of Sex
    and Sexuality in Hebrew Canon Narratives." In *Reading from This Place.* Vol 1,
    Social Location and Biblical Interpretation in the United States, edited by Fernando
    F. Segovia and Mary Ann Tolbert. Minneapolis: Fortress, 1994.
Baldwin, Samuel Davies. *Dominion; or, the Unity and Trinity of the Human Race; with
    the Divine Political Constitution of the World, and the Divine Rights of Shem, Ham,
    and Japheth.* Nashville: Stevenson and F. A. Owen, 1858.
Ballman, William. *Why Do I Believe the Bible Is God's Word?* St. Louis: Concordia,
    1946.
Barkun, Michael. *Religion and the Racist Right: The Origins of the Christian Identity
    Movement.* Rev. ed. Chapel Hill: University of North Carolina Press, 1997.
Barnes, Albert. *An Inquiry into the Scriptural Views of Slavery.* 1857. Reprint, New York:
    Negro Universities Press, 1969.
Barnes, Julian. *A History of the World in 10½ Chapters.* New York: Knopf, 1989.
Barrett, Leonard E. *The Rastafarians.* Boston: Beacon, 1997.
Bassett, Frederick W. "Noah's Nakedness and the Curse of Canaan: A Case of Incest?"
    Vetus Testamentum 21 (1971): 232–37.
Baumgarten, Albert I. "Myth and Midrash: Genesis 9: 20–29." In *Christianity, Judaism
    and Other Greco-Roman Cults: Studies for Morton Smith at Sixty,* edited by Jacob
    Newsner. Vol. 12, pt. 3, *Studies in Judaism in Late Antiquity,* Leiden: E. J. Brill,
    1975.
Bax, Douglas. "The Bible and Apartheid 2." In *Apartheid Is a Heresy,* edited by John
    W. DeGruchy and Charles Villa-Vicencio. Grand Rapids, Mich.: Eerdmans, 1983.
Ben-Judah, H. *When? A Prophetical Novel of the Very Near Future.* Vancouver, B.C.
    British Israel Association of Greater Vancouver, 1944.
Benson, Larry D., ed. *The Larned and the Lewed: Studies in Chaucer and Medieval
    Literature.* Harvard English Studies 5. Cambridge: Harvard University Press,
    1974.
"The Black Race in North America: Why Was Their Introduction Permitted?" *Southern
    Literary Messenger* 21 no. 11 (1855): 641–84.
Blassingame, John W. *The Slave Community: Plantation Life in the Antebellum South.*
    New York: Oxford University Press, 1972.
Bohlen, Anne, Kevin Rafferty, and James Ridgeway. *Blood in the Face.* Right Thinking
    Productions, 1986.
Bolingbroke, Henry. *The Works of Lord Bolingbroke in Four Volumes.* Philadelphia:
    Carey and Hart, 1841.
Bourne, George. *Picture of Slavery in the United States of America.* Boston: I. Knapp,
    1838.
Bradley, L. Richard. "The Curse of Canaan and the American Negro." *Concordia The-
    ological Monthly* 42 (Fall 1971): 100–110.
Branch, Taylor. *Pillar of Fire: America during the King Years 1963–65.* New York: Simon
    and Schuster, 1998.
Braude, Benjamin. "How Did Ham Become a Black Slave?: Reexamining the Noahides
    in the Abrahamic Tradition." Paper presented at the annual meeting of the Middle

Eastern Studies Association, San Francisco, November 1997. To be included in forthcoming book *Sex, Slavery, and Racism: The Secret History of Noah and His Sons*. New York: Knopf.

————. "The Sons of Noah and the Construction of Ethnic and Geographical Identities in the Medieval and Early Modern Periods." *William and Mary Quarterly* 54, no. 1 (1997): 103–42.

Brichto, Herbert C. *The Problem of "Curse" in the Hebrew Bible*. Journal of Biblical Literature Monograph Series 13. Philadelphia: Society of Biblical Literature and Exegesis, 1963.

Brisbane, William Henry. *Slaveholding Examined in the Light of The Holy Bible*. Philadelphia, 1847.

Bristowe, Ellen. *Sargon the Magnificent*. London: Covenant, 1927.

Brotz, Howard, ed. *Negro Social and Political Thought 1850–1920: Representative Texts*. New York: Basic Books, 1966.

Brow, Robert. "The Curse of Ham—Capsule of Ancient History." *Christianity Today* (26 October 1973): 8–10.

Buechner, Frederick. *Peculiar Treasures: A Biblical Who's Who*. San Francisco: Harper, 1979.

Burkert, Walter. "The Problem of Ritual Killing." In *Violent Origins: Walter Burkert, René Girard, and Jonathan Z. Smith on Ritual Killing and Cultural Formation*. Edited by Robert G. Hamerton-Kelly. Stanford, Calif.: Stanford University Press, 1987.

Burr, Virginia Ingraham, ed. *The Secret Eye: The Journal of Ella Gertrude Clanton Thomas, 1848–1889*. Chapel Hill: University of North Carolina Press, 1990.

Burrow Library Archive, Rhodes College, Memphis, Tenn.

Buswell, James O., III. *Slavery, Segregation and Scripture*. Grand Rapids, Mich.: Eerdmans, 1964.

Calmet, Augustin. *Calmet's Dictionary of the Bible As Published by the Late Mr. Charles Taylor, with the Fragments Incorporated. The Whole Condensed and Arranged in Alphabetical Order, Seventh Edition, Revised, with Large Additions, by Edward Robinson*. Boston: Crocker and Brewster, 1835.

Calvin, John. *Commentaries on the First Book of Moses Called Genesis*. Translated by John King. 2 vols. Grand Rapids, Mich.: Eerdmans, 1948.

Cannon, Katie Geneva. "Slave Ideology and Biblical Interpretation." In *The Recovery of Black Presence: An Interdisciplinary Exploration: Essays in Honor of Dr. Charles B. Copher*, edited by Randall C. Bailley and Jacqueline Grant. Nashville: Abingdon, 1995.

Carroll, Charles. *"The Negro a Beast" or "In the Image of God"; The Reasoner of the Age, the Revelator of the Century! The Bible as it is! The Negro and His Relation to the Human Family!, etc.* 1900. Reprint, Miami: Mnemosyne, 1969.

————. *The Tempter of Eve; Or, The Criminality of Man's Social, Political, and Religious Equality with the Negro, and the Amalgamation to Which These Crimes Inevitably Lead. Discussed in the Light of the Scriptures, the Sciences, Profane History, Tradition, and the Testimony of the Monuments*. St. Louis: Adamic, 1902.

Cartwright, Samuel, A. *Essays. Being Inductions Drawn from the Baconian Philosophy Proving the Truth of the Bible and the Justice and Benevolence of the Decree Dooming Canaan to be Servant of Servants: And Answering the Question of Voltaire: "On demande quel droit des etrangers tels que les Juifs avaient sur le pays de Canaan?" in a Series of Letters to the Rev. William Winans*. Vidalia, La.: n.p., 1843.

Cassuto, Umberto. *A Commentary on the Book of Genesis, Part 2: From Noah to Abraham, Genesis 5:19 to 11:32.* Jerusalem: Magnes, 1949.

Channing, Steven A. *Crisis of Fear: Secession in South Carolina.* New York: W. W. Norton, 1970.

Cheever, George B. *God against Slavery: and the Freedom and Duty of the Pulpit to Rebuke It, As a Sin Against God.* 1857. Reprint, New York: Arno, 1969.

Cherry, Conrad, ed. *God's New Israel: Religious Interpretations of American Destiny.* Englewood Cliffs, N.J.: Prentice-Hall, 1971.

——. *God's New Israel: Religious Interpretations of American Destiny.* Rev. ed. Chapel Hill and London: University of North Carolina Press, 1998.

Chick, Jack T. *The Trick.* Chino, Calif.: Chick Publications, n.d.

Clarke, Adam. *The Holy Bible Containing the Old and New Testaments, The Text Carefully Printed from the Most Correct Copies of the Present Authorized Translation, Including the Marginal Readings and Parallel Texts, with a Commentary and Critical Notes; The Old Testament.* Vol. 1, *Genesis to Deuteronomy.* 1810. Reprint, New York: Abingdon-Cokesbury, 1977.

Cobb, Howell. *A Scriptural Examination of the Institution of Slavery in the United States; with Its Objects and Purposes.* [Perry?], Ga, 1856.

Cohen, H. Hirsch. *The Drunkenness of Noah.* Tuscaloosa: University of Alabama Press, 1974.

Coleman, Elihu. *Testimony against that Anti-Christian Practice of Making Slaves of Men, Wherein it is Shewed to be Contrary to the Dispensation of the Law and Time of the Gospel, and Very Opposite Both to Grace and Nature.* 1733. Reprint, New Bedford, Mass.: Adam Shearman, 1825.

Congressional Record, Proceedings and Debates of . . . Congress. 150 Volumes. Washington: Supt. of Docs., U. S. G. P. O., 1873-.

"The Colored Man in the South." *Southern Presbyterian Review* (January 1877): 83–102.

The Constitution of the Presbyterian Church (U.S.A.). Part 1, *The Book of Confessions.* Louisville, Ky.: Office of the General Assembly, 1996.

Cooper, W. Raymond. *Southwestern at Memphis 1848–1948.* Richmond, Va.: John Knox, 1949.

Copher, Charles B. "Blacks and Jews in Historical Interaction: The Biblical/African Experience." *Journal of the Interdenominational Theological Center* 3 (1975): 9–16.

——. "Three Thousand Years of Biblical Interpretation with Reference to Black Peoples." In *African American Religious Studies: An Interdisciplinary Anthology,* edited by Gayraud S. Wilmore. Durham, N.C.: Duke University Press, 1989. First published in *Journal of the Interdenominational Theological Center* 13 (Spring 1986): 225–46.

Crowther, Edward R. "Holy Honor: Sacred and Secular in the Old South." *Journal of Southern History* 58, no. 4 (1992): 619–36.

Cullen, Countee. *My Soul's High Song: The Collected Writings of Countee Cullen, Voice of the Harlem Renaissance.* Edited by Gerald Early. New York: Doubleday, 1991.

Custance, Arthur C. *Noah's Three Sons, The Doorway Papers.* Vol. 1 Grand Rapids, Mich.: Zondervan, 1975.

Dabbs, James McBride. *Who Speaks for the South?* New York: Funk & Wagnalls, 1964.

Dabney, Robert L. *A Defence of Virginia and through Her, of the South, in Recent and Pending Contests against the Sectional Party.* 1867. Reprint, New York: Negro Universities Press, 1969.

Dagg, J. L. *The Elements of Moral Science*. New York: Sheldon, 1860.

Dake, Finnis Jennings, ed. *Dake's Annotated Reference Bible*. Lawrenceville, Ga.: Dake Bible Sales, 1991.

Dalcho, Frederick. *Practical Considerations Founded on the Scriptures Relative to the Slave Population of South-Carolina*. Charleston, S.C.: A. E. Miller, 1823.

Dalhouse, Mark Taylor. *An Island in the Lake of Fire: Bob Jones University, Fundamentalism, and the Separatist Movement*. Athens and London: University of Georgia Press, 1996.

Daniel, Carey. *God the Original Segregationist and Seven other Segregation Sermons*. n.p, n.d.

Dante Alighieri. *The Comedy of Dante Alighieri, the Florentine*. Translated by Dorothy L. Sayers. Illustrated with a selection of William Blake's drawings. 3 vols. New York: Basic Books, 1962.

———. *The Divine Comedy of Danted Alighieri*. 3 vols. Translated by John D. Sinclair. New York: Oxford University Press, 1961.

Davis, David Brion. *The Problem of Slavery in Western Culture*. Ithaca, N.Y.: Cornell University Press, 1966.

Davis, J. Treadwell. "The Presbyterians and the Sectional Conflict." *Southern Quarterly* 8, no. 2 (1970): 117–34.

Devisse, Jean. *The Image of the Black in Western Art*. Translated by William Granger Ryan. 2 vols. Cambridge: Harvard University Press, 1976–79.

Dictionaire Historique et Critique par Mr. Pierre Bayle; avec la vie de l'auteur, par Mr. Des Maizeaux. Amsterdam: Par la Compagnie des Libraires, 1734.

Dods, Marcus. *The Book of Genesis, The Expositor's Bible, Series One*. Vol. 2. New York: A. C. Armstrong, 1901.

Douglas, Kelly Brown. *The Black Christ*. Maryknoll, N.Y.: Orbis, 1994.

Du Bartas, Guillaume. *The Works of Guillaume De Salluste Sieur Du Bartas*. Vol. 3. Chapel Hill: University of North Carolina Press, 1940.

DuBois, W. E. B. *Darkwater: Voices from within the Veil*. New York: Harcourt, Brace and Howe, 1920.

Dubow, Saul. *Scientific Racism in South Africa*. Cambridge: Cambridge University Press, 1995.

Duncan, Winthrop Hillyer. "Josiah Priest, Historian of the American Frontier: A Study and Bibliography." *Proceedings of the American Antiquarian Society* 44 (1934): 45–102.

Eaton, Clement. *The Mind of the Old South*. Baton Rouge: Louisiana State University, 1964.

———. *The Growth of Southern Civilization, 1790–1860*. New York: Harper Brothers, 1961.

———. "The Role of Honor in Southern Society." *Southern Humanities Review* 10 (1976, supplement): 47–58.

———. *A History of the Old South*. New York: Macmillan, 1949.

Eilberg-Schwartz, Howard. *God's Phallus and Other Problems for Men and Monotheism*. Boston: Beacon, 1994.

Evans, William McKee. "From the Land of Canaan to the Land of Guinea: The Strange Odyssey of the 'Sons of Ham.' " *American Historical Review* 85, no. 1 (1980): 15–43.

Exell, Joseph S. *The Biblical Illustrator* Vol. 1, *Genesis*. Grand Rapids, Mich.: Baker, 1956.

Ezell, Humphrey K. *The Christian Problem of Racial Segregation*. New York: Greenwich, 1959.

Farmer, James Oscar, Jr. *The Metaphysical Confederacy: James Henley Thornwell and the Synthesis of Southern Values*. Macon, Ga.: Mercer University Press, 1986.

Fee, John Gregg. *An Anti-Slavery Manual*. 1848. Reprint, New York: Arno and New York Times, 1969.

Felder, Cain Hope, ed., *The Original African Heritage Study Bible, King James Version, with special Annotations Relative to the African/Edenic Experience*. Nashville: James C. Winston, 1993.

———. *Stony the Road We Trod: African American Biblical Interpretation*. Minneapolis: Fortress, 1991.

Figart, Thomas O. *A Biblical Perspective on the Race Problem*. Grand Rapids, Mich.: Baker, 1973.

Fisher, Sally. *The Square Halo and Other Mysteries of Western Art: Images and the Stories That Inspired Them*. New York: Harry N. Abrams, 1995.

Fletcher, John. *Studies on Slavery, In Easy Lessons, Compiled into Eight Studies, and Subdivided into Short Lessons for the Convenience of Readers*. 1852. Reprint, Miami: Mnemosyne, 1969.

Flinn, J. Wm., ed. *Complete Works of Rev. Thomas Smyth, D.D.*, Vol. 8. Columbia, S.C.: R. L. Bryan, 1908–1912.

Fowler, C. Lewis. *O House of Israel and Thou Judah*. New York: Maranatha Publishers, 1941.

Francisco, Clyde T. "The Curse on Canaan,"*Christianity Today* (24 April 1964): 9–10.

Franklin, John Hope. *The Militant South: 1800–1861*. Cambridge: Harvard University Press, 1956.

Freedman, David Noel, ed. *The Anchor Bible Dictionary*. 6 vols. New York: Doubleday, 1992.

Freedman, Paul. *Images of the Medieval Peasant*. Stanford, Calif.: Stanford University Press, 1999.

Genovese, Eugene D. *A Consuming Fire: The Fall of the Confederacy in the Mind of the White Christian South*. Mercer University Lamar Memorial Lectures 41. Athens and London: University of Georgia Press, 1998.

———. *"Slavery Ordained of God": The Southern Slaveholders' View of Biblical History and Modern Politics*. Twenty-fourth annual Fortenbaugh Memorial Lecture. Gettysburg, Pa.: Gettysburg College, 1985.

Genovese, Eugene D., and Elizabeth Fox-Genovese. "The Social Thought of Antebellum Theologians." In *Looking South: Chapters in the Story of an American Region*, edited by William B. Moore Jr. and Joseph F. Tripp. Contributions in American History 136. Westport, Conn.: Greenwood, 1989.

Gentry, George W. *Black Madonna, Infant Jesus*. Okolona, Ark.: n.p., 1999.

George, Timothy, and David S. Dockery, eds. *Baptist Theologians*. Nashville: Broadman, 1990.

Gero, Stephen. "The Legend of the Fourth Son of Noah." *Harvard Theological Review* 73 (1980): 321–30.

Gillespie, G. T. *A Christian View of Segregation. An Address Made Before the Synod of Mississippi of the Presbyterian Church in the U. S., November 4, 1954*. Greenwood: Association of Citizens' Councils of Mississippi, 1954.

Ginzberg, Louis. *The Legends of the Bible*. Philadelphia: Jewish Publication Society of America, 1956.

———. *The Legends of the Jews*. Vol. 1, *Bible Times and Characters from the Creation to Jacob*. Translated by Henrietta Szold. Philadelphia: Jewish Publication Society of America, 1968.

Girard, René. *The Girard Reader*. Edited by James G. Williams. New York: Crossroad, 1996.

———. *Things Hidden since the Foundation of the World: Research Undertaken in Collaboration with Jean-Michel Oughourlian and Guy Lefort*. Stanford, Calif.: Stanford University Press, 1987.

———. *Violence and the Sacred*. Translated by Patrick Gregory. Baltimore: Johns Hopkins University Press, 1977.

Gov. Hammond's Letters on Southern Slavery: Addressed to Thomas Clarkson, the English Abolitionist. Charleston, S.C. Walker & Burke, 1845.

Graves, Robert, and Raphael Patai. *Hebrew Myths: The Book of Genesis*. New York: Greenwich, 1983.

Green, William Scott. "The Difference Religion Makes." *Journal of the American Academy of Religion* 62, no. 4: 1191–1207.

Greenberg, Kenneth S. *Honor and Slavery: Lies, Duels, Noses, Masks, Dressing as a Woman, Gifts, Strangers, Humanitarianism, Death, Slave Rebellions, the Proslavery Argument, Baseball, Hunting, and Gambling in the Old South*. Princeton, N.J.: Princeton University Press, 1996.

Griffin, Des. *Fourth Reich of the Rich*. South Pasadena, Calif.: Emissary, 1978.

Griffith, W. H. *Genesis: A Devotional Commentary*. 1946, Reprint, Grand Rapids, Mich.: Kregel, 1988.

Grimes, Alan P. *Equality in America: Religion, Race, and the Urban Majority*. New York: Oxford University Press, 1964.

H. O. R. *The Governing Race: A Book for the Time, And for All Times*. Washington, D.C.: Thomas McGill, 1860.

Hamerton-Kelly, Robert G. "Mimesis and Mirror Images in History." Paper presented at the conference of the Colloquium on Violence and Religion, Stanford University, June 1996.

Hamilton, W. T. *The Duties of Masters and Slaves Respectively: or Domestic Servitude as Sanctioned by the Bible: A Discourse, Delivered in the Government-Street Church, Mobile, Ala., on Sunday Night, December 15, 1844*. Mobile, Ala.: F. H. Brooks, 1845.

Hannaford, Ivan. *Race: The History of an Idea in the West*. Baltimore: Johns Hopkins University Press, 1996.

Haskins, Charles Homer. "Nimrod the Astronomer." In *Studies in the History of Mediaeval Science*. New York: Frederick Ungar, 1924.

Haynes, Stephen R. *Reluctant Witnesses: Jews and the Christian Imagination*. Louisville, Ky.: Westminster John Knox, 1995.

Hesseltine, W. B. "Some New Aspects of the Pro-Slavery Argument." *Journal of Negro History* 21, no. 3 (1936): 1–14.

Hewett, John H. "Genesis 2:4b–3:31; 4:2–16; 9:20–27; 19:30–38." *Review and Expositor* 86 (1989): 237–41.

Heyrman, Christine Leigh. *Southern Cross: The Beginnings of the Bible Belt*. Chapel Hill and London: University of North Carolina Press, 1997.

Hickey, Doralyn J. "Benjamin Morgan Palmer: Churchman of the Old South." Ph.D. D. diss. Duke University, 1962.

Hislop, Alexander. *The Two Babylons*. 1858. Reprint, New York: Loizeaux Brothers, 1953.

Holgate, Jerome B. *Noachidae: or, Noah and his Descendants*. Buffalo: Breed, Butler, 1860.

Holly, Alonzo Potter Burgess. *God and the Negro: Synopsis of God and the Negro or the Biblical Record of the Race of Ham*. Nashville: National Baptist Publishing Board, 1937.

Hopkins, John Henry. *A Scriptural, Ecclesiastical, and Historical View of Slavery, from the Days of the Patriarch Abraham, to the Nineteenth Century, Addressed to the Right Rev. Alonzo Potter, D.D., Bishop of the Prot. Episcopal Church, in the Diocese of Pennsylvania*. 1864. Reprint, New York: Negro Universities Press, 1968.

Hopkins, Pauline E. *A Primer of Facts Pertaining to the Early Greatness of the African Race and the Possibility of Restoration by its Descendants—with Epilogue*. Cambridge, Mass.: P. E. Hopkins, 1905.

Huebner, Timothy S. "The Southern Judicial Tradition: Southern Appellate Judges and American Legal Culture in the Nineteenth Century." Ph.D. diss. University of Florida, 1993.

Hughes, Richard T., and C. Leonard Allen. *Illusions of Innocence: Protestant Primitivism in America, 1630–1875*. Chicago: University of Chicago Press, 1988.

Human Relations and the South African Scene in the Light of Scripture. Cape Town: Dutch Reformed Church Publishers, 1976.

Hurston, Zora Neale. "The First One: A Play in One Act." In *Ebony and Topaz: A Collectanea*. Edited by Charles Spurgeon Johnson. 1927. Reprint, Freeport, N.Y.: Books for Libraries Press, 1971.

Ide, Arthur Frederick. *Noah and the Ark: The Influence of Sex, Homophobia and Heterosexism in the Flood Story and Its Writing*. Las Colinas, Tex.: Monument, 1992.

Jefferson Davis Constitutionalist: His Letters, Papers and Speeches. Vol. 4. Edited by Dunbar Rowland. Jackson, Mississippi Department of Archives and History, 1923.

Johnson, Guion Griffis. "The Ideology of White Supremacy, 1876–1910." In *Essays in Southern History*. Edited by Fletcher Melvin Green. Chapel Hill: University of North Carolina Press, 1949.

Johnson, Thomas Carey. *The Life and Letters of Benjamin Morgan Palmer*. 1906. Reprint, Edinburgh and Carlisle, Pa.: Banner of Truth Trust, 1987.

Johnston, Michael P. "Planters and Patriarchy: Charleston, 1800–1860." *Journal of Southern History* 46, no. 1 (1980): 45–72.

Jones, Bob, Sr. *Is Segregation Scriptural?* Greenville, S.C.: Bob Jones University, 1960.

Jordan, Winthrop D. *White over Black: American Attitudes toward the Negro, 1550–1812*. Chapel Hill: University of North Carolina Press, 1968.

Josephus. *Complete Works of Josephus, In Ten Volumes, A New and Revised Edition Based on Havercamp's Translation*. Vol. 1, *Antiquities of the Jews, Books I–III*. Cleveland: World, 1940.

Kass, Leon. "Seeing the Nakedness of His Father." *Commentary* (June 1992): 41–47.

Keil, C. F., and F. Delitzsch. *Biblical Commentary on the Old Testament*. Vol. 1, *The Pentateuch*. Translated by James Martin. Grand Rapids, Mich.: Eerdmans, 1949.

Kelly, Douglas. *Preachers with Power*. Edinburgh and Carlisle, Pa.: Banner of Truth Trust, 1992.

Ker, Leander. *Slavery Consistent with Christianity*. 3d ed. Weston, Mo.: Finch & O'Gormon, 1853.

Kinney, Kenneth R. "The Segregation Issue." *Baptist Bulletin* (October 1956): 9–10.

Kretzmann, Paul E. *Popular Commentary of the Bible, The Old Testament* Vol. 1, *The Historical Books of the Old Testament: Genesis to Esther*. St. Louis: Concordia, 1923.

Kugel, James L. *The Bible as It Was*. Cambridge: Harvard University Press, 1997.

Kvam, Kristen E., Linda S. Schearing, and Valarie H. Ziegler, eds. *Eve and Adam: Jewish, Christian, and Muslim Readings on Genesis and Gender*. Bloomington: Indiana University Press, 1999.

Lacey, Harry. *God and the Nations*. New York: Loizeaux Brothers, 1947.

Larsen, Nella. *Passing*. New Brunswick, N.J.: Rutgers University Press, 1986.

Letters of the Late Bishop England to The Hon. John Forsyth, on the Subject of Domestic Slavery: To Which are Prefixed Copies, in Latin and English, of the Pope's Apostolic Letter, concerning the Atlantic Slave Trade, with Some Introductory Remarks, Etc. New York: Negro Universities Press, 1969.

Leupold, H. C. *Exposition of Genesis*. Grand Rapids, Mich.: Baker, 1950.

Lewis, Jack P. *A Study of the Interpretation of Noah and the Flood in Jewish and Christian Literature*. Leiden: E. J. Brill, 1968.

Luther's Works. 55 vols. Edited by Jaroslav Pelikan. St. Louis: Concordia, 1955–86.

Lynn, Robert W., and Elliott Wright. *The Big Little School: Sunday Child of American Protestantism*. New York: Harper & Row, 1971.

Lyon, James A. "Slavery, and the Duties Growing out of the Relation." *The Southern Presbyterian Review* 16, no. 1 (1863): 1–37.

Mamdani, Mahmood. *When Victims Become Killers: Colonialism, Nativism, and the Genocide in Rwanda*. Princeton, N.J.: Princeton University Press, 2001.

Martin, Philip. "Interracial Marriage Ban." "NPR's Morning Edition." April 15, 1999.

"The Mark of Cain and the Curse of Ham." *Southern Presbyterian Review* (January 1850): 415–26.

Maston, T. B. *The Bible and Race*. Nashville: Broadman, 1959.

———. *Segregation and Desegregation: A Christian Approach*. New York: Macmillan, 1959.

Mathews, Donald G. *Religion in the Old South*. Chicago: University of Chicago Press, 1977.

Matthew Henry's Commentary on the Whole Bible, Wherein Each Chapter, Is Summed Up in Its Contents: The Sacred Text Inserted at Large in Distinct Paragraphs; Each Paragraph Reduced to its Proper Heads: The Sense Given, and Largely Illustrated with Practical Remarks and Observations. Vol. 1, *Genesis to Deuteronomy*. New York: R. Carter, 1880.

Mays, Benjamin E. *Seeking to Be Christian in Race Relations*. New York: Friendship, 1957.

McCaleb, Thomas, ed. *The Louisiana Book: Selections from the Literature of the State*. New Orleans: R. F. Straughan, 1894.

McCary, P. K. *Black Bible Chronicles: From Genesis to the Promised Land*. New York: African American Family Press, 1993.

McGowan, Julia Cobbs. "The Presbyterian Churches in New Orleans during Reconstruction." Master's thesis, Tulane University, 1937.

McKenzie, Steven L. "Response: The Curse of Ham and David H. Aaron." *Journal of the American Academy Religion* 65, no. 1. (1997): 183–86.

McLain, C. E. *Place of Race*. New York: Vantage, 1965.

Mellinkoff, Ruth. *The Mark of Cain*. Berkeley: University of California Press, 1981.

Melson, Robert. *Revolution and Genocide: On the Origins of the Armenian Genocide and the Holocaust.* Chicago: University of Chicago Press, 1992.

Miers, Earl Schenk, ed. *When the World Ended: The Diary of Emma LeConte.* Lincoln: University of Nebraska Press, 1957.

Miles, William F. S. "Hamites and Hebrews: Problems in 'Judaizing' the Rwandan Genocide." *Journal of Genocide Research* 2, no. 1 (2000): 107–15.

Miller, Randall M., Harry S. Stout, and Charles Reagan Wilson, eds. *Religion and the American Civil War.* Oxford and New York: Oxford University Press, 1998.

Milton, John. *Paradise Lost.* Norton Critical Edition. New York: Norton, 1975.

———. *Paradise Lost.* Edited by Merritt Y. Hughes. New York: Odyssey, 1962.

Minutes of the General Assembly of the Presbyterian Church in the Confederate States of America, 1861–1864.

Moellering, Ralph L. *Christian Conscience and Negro Emancipation.* Philadelphia: Fortress, 1965.

Morrow, James. *Bible Stories for Adults.* New York: Harcourt Brace, 1996.

Murray, Andrew E. *The Presbyterian and the Negro—A History.* Philadelphia: Presbyterian Historical Society, 1966.

Neusner, Jacob, ed. *Genesis Rabbah: The Judaic Commentary to the Book of Genesis, a New American Translation.* Vol. 2. Atlanta: Scholars Press, 1985.

The New Interpreter's Bible. Vol. 1. Nashville: Abingdon, 1994.

The New Oxford Annotated Bible with the Apocryphal/Deuterocanonical Books. Edited by Bruce M. Metzger and Roland E. Murphy. New York: Oxford University Press, 1991.

Newby, I. A., ed. *The Development of Segregationist Thought.* Homewood, Ill.: Dorsey, 1968.

Newton, Thomas. *Dissertations on the Prophecies, Which Have Remarkably Been Fulfilled, and at This Time are Fulfilling in the World.* New York: William Durell, 1794.

Nolen, Claude H. *The Negro's Image in the South: An Anatomy of White Supremacy.* Lexington: University of Kentucky Press, 1967.

Noll, Mark A. "The Bible and Slavery," in Randall M. Miller, Harry S. Stout and Charles Reagan Wilson, eds., *Religion and the American Civil War* (New York: Oxford University Press, 1998), 43–73.

Novak, David. *The Image of the Non-Jew in Judaism: An Historical and Constructive Study of the Noahide Laws.* New York and Toronto: Edwin Mellen, 1983.

Origen. *Homilies on Genesis and Exodus.* Translated by Ronald E. Heine. Washington: Catholic University of America Press, 1982.

Osofsky, Gilbert. *The Burden of Race: A Documentary History of Negro-White Relations in America.* New York: Harper & Row, 1967.

Ostriker, Alicia Suskin. *The Nakedness of the Fathers: Biblical Visions and Revisions.* New Brunswick, N.J.: Rutgers University Press, 1994.

Ownby, Ted. *Subduing Satan: Religion, Recreation and Manhood in the Rural South, 1865–1920.* Chapel Hill: University of North Carolina Press, 1990.

Palmer, Benjamin M. "Abstract of a Discourse Delivered in the First Presbyterian Church before the Crescent Rifles, on Sabbath Morning, May 26." *New Orleans Sunday Delta,* 2 June 1861.

———. *An Address at the One Hundredth Anniversary of the Organization of the Nazareth Church and Congregation in Spartanburg, S.C.* Richmond, Va.: Shepperson, 1872.

———. *Address Delivered at the Funeral of General Maxcy Gregg, in the Presbyterian Church, Columbia, S.C., December 20, 1862*. Columbia, S.C.: Southern Guardian Steam-Power Press, 1863.

———. "Address of Rev. Dr. B. M. Palmer." In *Southern Historical Society Papers*. Vol. 10. Richmond, Va., 1882.

———. *The Address of Rev. B. M. Palmer, D.D. LL.D. Delivered On the First Day of the New Year and Century in The First Presbyterian Church, New Orleans, La., at the Request of Citizens, And Members of the Church, of Which He Has Been Pastor Since December 30, 1856*. New Orleans: Brotherhood of the First Presbyterian Church, n.d.

———. *A Discourse before the General Assembly of South Carolina, on December 10, 1863, Appointed by the Legislature as a Day of Fasting, Humiliation and Prayer*. Columbia, S.C.: Charles P. Pelham, 1864.

———. "Discourse of Rev. B. M. Palmer, D.D." *Southern Historical Society Papers*. Vol. 18. Richmond, 1890.

———. *The Family, in its Civil and Churchly Aspects, An Essay, in Two Parts*. 1876. Reprint, Harrisonburg, Va.: Sprinkle, 1981.

———. "The Import of Hebrew History." *Southern Presbyterian Review* 9 (April, 1856): 582–610.

———. "Oath of Allegiance." Louisiana Historical Association Collection, Manuscripts Division, Howard-Tilton Memorial Library, Tulane University, New Orleans.

———. *Our Historic Mission, An Address Delivered Before the Eunomian and Phi-Mu Societies of La Grange Synodical College, July 7 1858*. New Orleans: True Witness Office, 1859.

———. *The Pastoral Letter of 1870: A Historical and Official Document Setting Forth Three "Great Principles" that "Our Church Has Declared in the Most Solemn and Emphatic Manner" to be Among the Fundamental Principles of our Organization*. Caroliniana Library, University of South Carolina.

———. *The Present Crisis and Its Issues, an Address Delivered Before the Literary Societies of Washington and Lee University, Lexington, Va., 27ᵗʰ June, 1872 by Rev. B. M. Palmer, D.D*. Baltimore: John Murphy, 1872.

———. *The Rainbow Round the Throne; or Judgment Tempered with Mercy: A Discourse Before the Legislature of Georgia, Delivered on the Day of Fasting, Humiliation and Prayer, Appointed by the President of the Confederate States of America, March 27th, 1863*. Milledgeville, Ga.: Doughton, Nisbet & Barnes, 1863.

———. "Sesession and the South" Review of Robert J. Breckenridge, *Discourse Delivered by Rev. Dr. R. J. Breckenridge, on the Day of National Humiliation, January 4th, 1861, at Lexington, Ky*; and *Our Country: Its Peril and its Deliverance. From Advance Sheets of the Danville Quarterly Review for March, 1861. Southern Presbyterian Review* 14 (April 1861): 134–77.

Patterson, Orlando. *Slavery and Social Death: A Comparative Study*. Cambridge: Harvard University Press, 1982.

Pease, William H., and Jane H. Pease, eds. *The Antislavery Argument*. Indianapolis: Bobbs-Merrill, 1965.

Pennington, James W. C. *A Text Book of the Origin and History &c. &c. of the Colored People*. Hartford: L. Skinner, 1841.

Peterson. Thomas V. *Ham and Japheth in America: The Mythic World of Whites in the Antebellum South*. Metuchen, N.J.: American Theological Library Association, 1978.

Phillips, Anthony. "Uncovering the Father's Skirt." *Vetus Testamentum* 30, no. 1 (1980): 38–43.

Pink, Arthur W. *Gleanings in Genesis.* Chicago: Moody, 1950.

Pitt-Rivers, Julian. "Honor." In *International Encyclopedia of the Social Sciences*, edited by David L. Sills. 18 vols. New York: Macmillan, 1968.

Prewitt, Terry J. *The Elusive Covenant: A Structural-Semiotic Reading of Genesis.* Bloomington: Indiana University Press, 1990.

Priest, Josiah. *Slavery as It Relates to the Negro or African Race.* 1843. Reprint, New York: Arno, 1977.

The Proslavery Argument, as Maintained by the Most Distinguished Writers of the Southern States, Containing the Several Essays, on the Subject, of Chancellor Harper, Governor Hammond, Dr. Simms, and Professor Dew. 1852. Reprint, New York: Negro Universities Press, 1968.

Raleigh, Walter. *The Works of Sir Walter Ralegh, Kt., Now First Collected: To Which are Prefixed The Lives of the Author, by Oldys and Birch.* 8 vols. Oxford: University Press, 1829.

Read, Hollis. *The Hand of God in History; or, Divine Providence Historically Illustrated in The Extension and Establishment of Christianity.* Hartford: H. E. Robins, 1849.

Render, Sylvia Lyons, ed. *The Short Fiction of Charles W. Chesnutt.* Washingon, D.C.: Howard University Press, 1981.

"Review of A Discourse Delivered in the First Presbyterian Church, New Orleans, Nov. 29, 1860, by Rev. B. M. Palmer, D.D.," *Boston Atlas and Bee*, 12 January, 1861, 1.

Rice, Gene. "The Curse That Never Was (Genesis 9:18–27)." *Journal of Religious Thought* 29, no. 1 (1972): 5–27.

Richardson, Cyril., ed. *Early Christian Fathers*, Vol. 1. The Library of Christian Classics. Philadelphia: Westminster, 1953.

Robertson, James Burton, ed. *The Philosophy of History: In a Course of Lectures Delivered at Vienna by Frederick von Schlegel, Translated from the German with a Memoir of the Author.* London: H. G. Bohn, 1852.

Robinson, John Bell. *Pictures of Slavery and Anti-Slavery. Advantages of Negro Slavery and the Benefits of Negro Freedom. Morally, Socially and Politically Considered.* Philadelphia, 1863.

Ross, Allen P. "The Curse of Canaan." *Bibliotheca Sacra* 137 (July-September 1980): 223–40.

Rosse, Abraham. *An Exposition on the Fourteene First Chapters of Genesis, by Way of Question and Answere, Collected Out of Ancient and Recent Writers: Both Briefely and Subtilly Propounded and Expounded.* London: B. A. and T. F., 1626.

Ruchames, Louis, ed. *Racial Thought in America.* Vol. 1, *From the Puritans to Abraham Lincoln.* Boston: University of Massachusetts Press, 1969.

Ruprecht, Ferdinand. *Bible History References: Explanatory Notes on the "Advanced Bible History."* Vol. 1, *Old Testament Stories.* St. Louis: Concordia, 1947.

Salzman, Jack, and Cornel West, eds. *Struggles in the Promised Land: Toward a History of Black-Jewish Relations in the United States.* New York: Oxford University Press, 1997.

Samuel, Irene. *Dante and Milton: The Commedia and Paradise Lost.* Ithaca, N.Y.: Cornell University Press, 1966.

Sandell, J. W. *The United States in Scripture. The Union Against the States. God in Government.* Magnolia, Miss., 1907.

Sawyer, John F. A. *The Fifth Gospel: Isaiah in the History of Christianity.* New York: Cambridge University Press, 1996.

Sayce, A. H. *The Races of the Old Testament.* London: Religious Tract Society, 1925.

Schaff, Philip, ed. *A Select Library of the Nicene and Post-Nicene Fathers of the Christian Church.* 8 vols. Grand Rapids, Mich.: Eerdmans, 1955.

Schwartz, Regina M. *The Curse of Cain: The Violent Legacy of Monotheism.* Chicago: University of Chicago Press, 1997.

Sellers, Charles Grier, Jr., ed. *The Southerner as American.* Chapel Hill: University of North Carolina Press, 1960.

Sewall, Samuel. *The Selling of Joseph: A Memorial.* Edited by Sidney Kaplan. Amherst: University of Massachusetts Press, 1969.

Shanks, Caroline L. "The Biblical Anti-Slavery Argument of the Decade 1830–1840." *Journal of Negro History* 15, no. 2 (1931): 132–57.

Shufelt, J. Ernest. "Noah's Curse and Blessing: Gen. 9:18–27." *Concordia Theological Monthly* 17 (1946): 737–42.

Silver, James W. *Confederate Morale and Church Propaganda.* New York: Norton, 1957.

Skinner, John. *A Critical and Exegetical Commentary on Genesis.* New York: Charles Scribner's Sons, 1925.

Sloan, James A. *The Great Question Answered; or, Is Slavery a Sin in Itself (Per Se) Answered According to the Teaching of the Scriptures.* Memphis: Hutton, Gallaway, 1857.

Smith, H. Shelton. *In His Image, But . . . : Racism in Southern Religion, 1780–1910.* Durham, N.C.: Duke University Press, 1972.

Smith, Lillian. *Killers of the Dream.* New York: W. W. Norton, 1949.

Smith, Theopus H. *Conjuring Culture: Biblical Formations of Black Culture.* New York: Oxford University Press, 1994.

Smylie, James. *Review of a Letter from the Presbytery of Chillicothe, to the Presbytery of Mississippi, on the Subject of Slavery.* Woodville, Miss.: Wm. A. Norris, 1836.

Snay, Mitchell. *Gospel of Disunion: Religion and Separatism in the Antebellum South.* Cambridge: Cambridge University Press, 1993.

Sollors, Werner. *Neither Black nor White yet Both: Thematic Explorations of Interracial Literature.* New York: Oxford University Press, 1997.

"A South Carolinian." *A Refutation of the Calumnies Circulated against the Southern and Western States, Respecting the Institution and Existence of Slavery Among Them, to Which is Added a Minute and Particular Account of the Actual State and Condition of Their Negro Population, Together With Historical Notices of all the Insurrections That Have Taken Place Since the Settlement of the Country.* 1822. Reprint, New York: Negro Universities Press, 1996.

Sparks, Allister. *The Mind of South Africa.* New York: Knopf, 1990.

Sparks, Randy J. "Mississippi's Apostle of Slavery: James Smylie and the Biblical Defense of Slavery." *Journal of Mississippi History* 51 (May 1989): 89–106.

Speke, John Hanning. *Journal of the Discovery of the Source of the Nile.* Chiefly Illustrated from Drawings by James Grant. 1863. Reprint, Mineola, N.Y.: Dover, 1996.

Stanton, Robert L. *The Church and the Rebellion: A Consideration of the Rebellion against the Government of the United States; and the Agency of the Church, North and South, in Relation thereto.* New York: Derby & Miller, 1864.

Starnes, Dewitt T., and Ernest William Talbert. *Classical Myth and Legend in Renaissance Dictionaries: A Study of Renaissance Dictionaries in Their Relation to the*

Classical Learning of Contemporary English Writers. Chapel Hill: University of North Carolina Press, 1955.

Stone, J. L. *Slavery and the Bible; or, Slavery as Seen in its Punishment*. San Francisco: B. F. Sterett, 1863.

Stowe, Steven M. *Intimacy and Power in the Old South: Ritual in the Lives of the Planters*. Baltimore: Johns Hopkins University Press, 1987.

Stringfellow, Thornton. "A Scriptural View of Slavery." In *Slavery Defended: The Views of the Old South*, edited by Eric L. McKitrick. Englewood Cliffs, N.J.: Prentice-Hall, 1963.

Thomas, Latta R. *Biblical Faith and the Black American*. Valley Forge, Pa.: Judson, 1974.

Thompson, Ernest Trice. *Presbyterians in the South*. 3 vols. Richmond: John Knox, 1963–73.

Thompson, Joseph P. *Teachings of the New Testament on Slavery*. New York: Joseph H. Ladd, 1856.

Thornwell, James Henley. "The Christian Doctrine of Slavery." In *The Collected Writings of James Henley Thornwell, D. D., LL.D.* Vol. 4. Edited by John B. Adger and John L. Girardeau. Richmond, Va.: Presbyterian Committee of Publication, 1873.

Thrasher, J. B. *Slavery A Divine Institution, by J. B. Thrasher of Port Gibson, A Speech, Made before the Breckinridge and Lane Club, November 5ᵗʰ, 1860*. Port Gibson, Miss.: Southern Reveille Book and Job Office, 1861.

Tilson, Everett. *Segregation and the Bible*. New York and Nashville: Abingdon, 1958.

Turner, Arlin, ed. *The Negro Question: A Selection of Writings on Civil Rights in the South*. Garden City, N.Y.: Doubleday, 1958.

Turner, Laurence A. *Genesis*. Sheffield: Sheffield Academic Press, 2000.

Tutu, Desmond. *The Rainbow People of God: The Making of a Peaceful Revolution*. New York: Doubleday, 1994.

Twain, Mark. *Letters from the Earth*. Edited by Bernard Devoto. New York: Harper, 1991.

———. *Life on the Mississippi by Mark Twain. Illustrated by Thomas Hart Benton. With an Introduction by Edward Wagenknecht, and a Number of Previously Suppressed Passages, Now Printed for the First Time, and Edited with a Note by Willis Wager*. New York, Heritage Press, 1959.

Utley, Francis Lee. "Noah's Ham and Jansen Enikel." *Germanic Review* 16 (1941): 241–49.

Vail, Stephen M. *The Bible against Slavery, with Replies to the "Bible View of Slavery," by John H. Hopkins, D. D., Bishop of the Diocese of Vermont; and to "A Northern Presbyter's Second Letter to Ministers of the Gospel," by Nathan Lord, D. D., Late President of Dartmouth College; and to "X," of the New-Hampshire Patriot*. Concord, N.H.: Fogg, Hadley, 1864.

Van Selms, Adrianus. "The Canaanites in Genesis." *Oudtestamentische Studien* 12 (1958): 182–213.

Vorster, Willem. "The Bible and Aparteid 1." In *Apartheid is a Heresy*, edited by John W. DeGruchy and Charles Villa-Vicencio. Grand Rapids, Mich.: Eerdmans, 1983.

Walters, Ronald G. *The Anti-Slavery Appeal: Abolitionism after 1830*. Baltimore: Johns Hopkins University Press, 1976.

Watson, Curtis Brown. *Shakespeare and the Renaissance Concept of Honor*. Princeton, N.J.: Princeton University Press, 1960.

Weld, Theodore Dwight. *The Bible Against Slavery: An Inquiry into the Patriarchal and Mosaic Systems on the Subject of Human Rights.* New York: American Anti-Slavery Society, 1838.

Whitcomb, John C., Jr. "The Prophecy of Noah's Sons." *Freedom Now* (August–September 1966): 7–8.

Willet, Andrew. *Hexapla in Genesin.* London: Tho. Creede, 1608.

Williams, James G. *The Bible, Violence, and the Sacred: Liberation from the Myth of Sanctioned Violence.* Valley Forge, Pa.: Trinity, 1995.

Willis, John Ralph, ed. *Slaves and Slavery in Muslim Africa,* 2 vols. London: F. Cass, 1985.

Wilson, Charles Reagan. *Baptized in Blood: The Religion of the Lost Cause, 1865–1920* (Athens: University of Georgia Press, 1980).

Wilson, Samuel, Jr., *The First Presbyterian Church of New Orleans.* New Orleans: Louisiana Landmarks Society, 1988.

Winterson, Jeanette. *Boating for Beginners.* London: Methuen, 1985.

Wittenberg, Gunther. "Let Canaan Be His Slave" (Genesis 9:26). Is Ham Also Cursed?" *Journal of Theology for Southern Africa* 74 (March 1991): 46–56.

Wood, Forrest G. *The Arrogance of Faith: Christianity and Race in America from the Colonial Era to the Twentieth Century.* Boston: Northeastern University Press, 1991.

Woodbury, Naomi Felicia. "A Legacy of Intolerance: Nineteenth Century Pro-Slavery Propaganda and the Mormon Church Today." Master's Thesis, University of California at Los Angeles, 1966.

Woodward, C. Vann. "George Fitzhugh, Sui Generis." In *Cannibals All!, or Slaves Without Masters,* edited by C. Vann Woodward. Cambridge, Mass.: Belknap Press, 1960.

———. *The Strange Career of Jim Crow* 3d ed. New York: Oxford University Press, 1974.

Wyatt-Brown, Bertram. "God and Honor in the Old South." *Southern Review* 25 (April 1989): 283–96.

———. *Honor and Violence in the Old South.* New York: Oxford University Press, 1986.

———. "Modernizing Southern Slavery: The Proslavery Argument Reinterpreted." In *Religion, Race and Reconstruction: Essays in Honor of C. Vann Woodward,* edited by J. Morgan Kousser and James M. McPherson. New York: Oxford University Press, 1982.

———. *Southern Honor: Ethics and Behavior in the Old South.* New York: Oxford University Press, 1982.

Woodward, C. Vann, ed. *Mary Chesnut's Civil War.* New Haven: Yale University Press, 1981.

Young-Bruehl, Elisabeth. *The Anatomy of Prejudices.* Cambridge: Harvard University Press, 1996.

Index

abolitionism, 8, 11, 66, 77, 79, 90, 91, 96, 103, 111, 116, 135, 148, 156, 181–84, 202
  and anarchy, 91
  and fanaticism, 155
  and infidelity, 91, 154
abolitionists. *See* abolitionism
Abraham, 27, 111
Abram, 4, 43, 44
Adam, 15, 31, 37, 69, 93, 95, 102, 152, 172, 178, 190, 192, 194, 199, 201
Addington, Joseph C., 89
Africa, 3, 5, 6, 7, 12, 23, 26, 27, 28, 34, 48, 77, 117, 141, 142, 153, 163, 164, 185
African Americans
  divines, 164
  extinction, 173
African Servitude, 72, 85, 102
Africans, 8, 9, 132
  and heathenism, 92
  and savagery, 141
  and servitude, 126
Afrocentrism, 196
alcohol, 80
Alcuin, 5
Allen, Don Cameron, 31, 34
amalgamation. *See* intermarriage
Ambrose of Milan, 7, 29, 48, 94
America
  antebellum period, 9, 10, 12, 65, 66, 69
  colonial period, 8

  postbellum period, 13, 14, 100–01, 126, 127
  and racial discourse, 6
Amherst College, 151, 159
Andover Seminary, 159
apartheid, 18, 19
Appomatox, 139
"Ariel." *See* Buckner H. Payne
Ararat, 18, 93, 108
ark, 27, 31, 35, 93, 197, 215
Armstrong, George D., 71, 82
Army of Tennessee, 128
Asia, 5, 6, 28, 49, 117, 141, 142
Asshur, 109
Assyria, 42, 57
Atlas, 49
Augustine, 7, 28, 29, 30, 46, 47, 55
Azurara, Gomes Eanes de, 34

Babel. *See* Tower of Babel
Babington, Gervase, 55, 179
Babylon, 18, 42, 44, 47, 48, 50, 56, 57, 58, 61, 113, 183, 195
Bailey, Randall, 185, 195
Baldwin, James, 192
Baldwin, Samuel Davies, 73, 85
Barkun, Michael, 16
Barnes, Julian, 196
Bassett, Frederick W., 186–87
Battle of Shiloh, 128

Baumgarten, Albert I., 186
Bayle, Pierre, 37–8
Bede, Venerable 30, 48
Beecher, Henry Ward, 151
Belus, 56, 58
Berossus, 26, 34, 35
Best, George, 35, 36
biblical criticism, 184
Black Bible Chronicles, 195
black "race," 132
blackness, 7, 11, 12, 36, 48, 61, 95, 99, 180,
    192, 198
    and evil, 86
blacks
    and animality, 98
    as children, 89
    and disorder, 104
    as emotional, 98
    as savages, 90, 93
    as ungovernable, 97–99
Blassingame, John W., 10
Blyden, Edward Wilmot, 164
Bob Jones University, 3, 4
Bolingbroke, Henry St. John, 180
Book of Adam and Eve, The, 26
Book of Enoch, 189
Book of Jubilees, 26
Book of the Cave of Treasures, The, 48
Book of the Generations of Adam, 189
Boston, Massachusetts, 130
Brackenridge, Hugh Henry, 191
Braude, Benjamin, 49, 67
Breckenridge, Robert J., 147, 148
Brisbane, William H., 111, 182
Bristowe, Ellen, 15
British-Israelism, 16
Brooks, Iveson, 82
brother stories, 204, 206
Brow, Robert, 168
Brown v. Board of Education, 116
Brown, John, 96, 102
Browne, Sir Thomas, 180
Buechner, Frederick, 196
Butler, Benjamin, 149
Byrd, Robert, 116

Cain, 15, 16, 30, 34, 74, 99, 100, 194, 204,
    205, 211, 214
Calhoun, John C., 90, 155
Calmet, Augustin, 38, 56
Calvin, John, 33, 39, 51, 68, 77, 178–79,
    210
Calvinism, 13

Canaan, 7, 8, 12, 24, 25, 26, 27, 28, 29, 30,
    36, 38, 39, 40, 41, 67, 68, 71, 72, 74, 75,
    77, 88, 95, 99, 143, 159, 163, 167, 180,
    181, 184, 185, 194, 202, 211
    and sexual assault on Noah, 186–87, 190
Canaanites, 5, 6, 12, 16, 24, 29, 30, 68, 76,
    100, 144, 181, 185, 192, 202
    and sexual perversion, 188
Cannon, Katie Geneva, 195
Carroll, Charles, 15
Cartwright, Samuel, 82, 98
Cash, W. J., 9, 77
Cassian, John, 30
Cassuto, Umberto, 42, 185, 187, 209
Chartres Cathedral, 30
Cheever, George B., 183
Chesnutt, Charles W., 192
China, 141
Christ. *See* Jesus
Christian Identity, 16
Christians, 8
Chrysostom, 29, 30
Church Fathers, 7, 27–30, 31, 33, 44, 46, 47,
    51, 67, 77, 178
Chus. *See* Cush
Civil Rights Movement, 86, 201
Civil War, 8, 9, 10, 12, 14, 69, 79, 88, 92,
    102, 126, 138, 150
Clarke, Adam, 40, 57
Clement, 29, 33, 47, 88
Cobb, Howell, 74, 89
Cohen, H. Hirsch, 188–89
Coke, Sir Edward, 68
Coleman, Elihu, 184
Cologne Bible, 210
Columbia Seminary, 152
Columbia, South Carolina, 133, 147
Comestor, Peter, 5, 31, 32
Confederacy, 83, 128, 131, 135, 136, 154
confusion of tongues, 150
Copher, Charles B., 195
covenant, 205
creation, 203
Crowther, Edward R., 84
Crummel, Alexander, 194
Cullen, Countee, 218
curse of Canaan. *See* Ham, curse
Cursor Mundi, 30
Cush, 7, 35, 36, 41, 43, 46, 48, 58, 61, 109,
    194
    and Tower of Babel, 59
Cushan, 120
Custance, Arthur C., 167, 169

Dabbs, James McBride, 88
Dabney, Robert L., 71, 93
Dagg, J. L., 71
Dake, Finis Jennings, 118
Dalcho, Frederick, 71, 97, 111
Daniel, Carey, 86, 119
Dante, 31, 47, 55
    on Nimrod, 49
Dathan, 35
David, 31, 185, 194
Davis, Jefferson, 79, 83, 95, 140
de la Peyere, Isaac, 15
Debow, Saul, 173
Delitzsch, Franz, 187
Deluge. *See* Flood
demons, 30, 31
desire, 188–191; 209
Devil. *See* Satan
Dew, Thomas Roderick, 82, 90
differentiation, 4–6
disorder
    and African character, 96
    and white fear, 101
dispersion, 4–6, 44, 45, 55, 126
Dods, Marcus, 179
Douglass, Frederick, 194
Du Bartas, Guillaume De Salluste Sieur, 36–
    7, 54, 178
    on Nimrod, 52–53
Dubois, W. E. B., 218
Dutch Reformed Church, 18

Early Modern Period, 34–37
Eaton, Clement, 9, 79, 82
Eber, 5
Eden, 16, 43, 90, 94, 109, 192, 204
Egypt, 132, 183, 184, 195
Eilberg-Schwartz, Howard, 188
Elam, 186
Emancipation, 14, 92, 113, 162
Enlightenment, 37–40, 155
Enoch, 27
Ephrem of Nisibis, 7
Esau, 44
Ethiopia, 172, 181
Eubank, Wayne C., 131
Europe, 5, 6, 28, 117, 141, 142
Eve, 15, 16–17, 37, 90, 94, 110
    Ham's wife, 193
Exell, Joseph, 114
Exploration, Age of, 6, 35
Ezell, Humphrey K., 103

Fall, the 28; second, 94
Felder, Cain Hope, 187, 195
Figart, Thomas, 169
Filaster, 46
Fitzhugh, George, 91
Fletcher, John, 17, 71, 99, 112
Flood, 5, 12, 16, 17, 30, 34, 38, 42, 44, 48,
    53, 72, 100, 108, 110, 115, 129, 133, 142,
    143, 150, 153, 167, 172, 180, 188, 197,
    199, 210, 214
    and biblical narrative, 205, 212
    and dispersion, 137
    and wickedness, 137
Franklin, John Hope, 9, 78, 81, 82
French Revolution, 154, 155, 156
Freud, Sigmund, 191, 220

Gale, William Potter, 17
Garrison, William Lloyd, 91, 156
Generations of Noah, The, 189
Genesis Rabbah, 24
genocide, 171
Genovese, Eugene D., 11, 12, 13, 14, 112, 126,
    174
Gillespie, Thomas G., 116, 161
Girard, René, 206–15
Gnosticism, 99
Governing Race, The, 74, 84, 95
Graves, Robert 186–89
Grayson, William J., 82
Greenberg, Kenneth, 9, 79, 80, 81, 102
Gregg, Maxcey, 149
Gregory of Tours, 30
Grimké, Sara, 90
Gunkel, Hermann, 185

Ham, 3, 5, 6, 8, 16, 24, 26, 29, 30, 31, 32, 34,
    41, 43, 126, 141
    and black "race," 12, 24, 25, 89, 101, 162,
    193
    and castration, 67, 167, 189
    curse of, 6, 8, 47, 66, 78, 94, 103, 165, 166
    and degradation, 102
    and deicide, 67
    and dishonor, 33, 34, 39, 40, 67, 68, 74,
    75, 76, 78, 80, 84, 102, 178, 211
    and disorder, 101
    and disrespect, 163
    eponymous ancestor of Africans, 9, 23,
    71, 80, 98, 106, 172, 181
    and Ethiopia, 164
    failure to sexualize his transgression, 69,
    71, 74

"father of Canaan," 207
gaze upon Noah, 67
and greed, 36
and heresy, 69
and impiety, 72, 76, 85
and impropriety, 166
and incest, 35, 38, 67, 69, 186, 191
and incontinence at sea, 24, 31, 35–6, 38, 67
and infidelity, 162
and intermarriage, 99
and irreverence, 36, 68, 163
and Jesus, 206
laughter, 24, 26, 29, 31, 32, 33, 87, 94, 95, 96, 97, 193
and magic, 29, 31, 32, 34, 38, 69
meaning of his name, 101
and mischievous behavior, 10
and mockery, 32, 51, 96, 106, 193
Noah's youngest son, 204
and paganism, 167
and physicality, 167
and rebellion, 68, 69
and scapegoating mechanism, 215
and seduction of Noah, 186
and servitude, 132, 133, 158;
and sexual assault, 24, 25, 30, 67, 69, 77, 205, 209
and social death, 72, 73, 74
and sodomy, 190
and territorial expansion, 32
and theft of Noah's potency, 18
his transgression, 25, 70, 73, 84, 86, 93, 99, 146, 180, 195, 201
as type of Christ, 217
as type of heretics, 28
and vice, 74
as victim, 203, 206, 212, 215, 217
and voyeurism, 187, 189
and wickedness, 71
Hamites, 6, 27, 43, 47, 51, 182, 201, 203
and ambition, 163
and astrology, 67
and "Bantus," 171
and barbarism, 135
and cannibalism, 101
and covetousness, 163
and degradation, 71, 76
and disorder, 88, 99, 106, 107, 118, 157
and divine plan, 195
and idolatry, 67, 75
and inventive genius, 167
and lewdness, 69

and rebellion, 10, 117, 169;
savage condition of, 129, 132, 133
and sensuality, 86
and servitude, 14, 73, 87, 103, 133
and sexual sin, 187
their prophetic mission, 165
and Tower of Babel, 167
and violence, 101
and wickedness, 97
and witchcraft, 67
Hamitic hypothesis, 171–74
Hammond, William Henry, 90
Harper, William, 82, 90
Haskins, Charles Homer, 48
hell, 54, 55
Henry, Matthew, 39, 57, 179
Heyrman, Christine Leigh, 82, 152, 157
Hilary, 28, 30
Hislop, Alexander, 58, 106, 171
Hodge, Charles, 151, 152
Holgate, Jerome, 107, 108, 162
Holly, Alonzo Potter Burgess, 195
Holly, James Theodore, 164
Honor
    and Christianity, 82
    in Noah's family, 70
    and order, 101–02
    and shame, 78
    and slavery 73
    Southern, 8, 9, 11, 12, 66
Honorarius of Autun, 30
Hopkins, John H., 75
How, Samuel B., 89
human diversity, 73
Hurston, Zora Neale, 193
Hutus, 172, 173

Iapheth. See Japheth
Ide, Arthur Frederick, 189
idolatry, 30, 33, 44
India, 128
Indians. See Native Americans
integration, 103
intermarriage, 4, 17, 103, 118, 157, 194
    and antediluvian corruption, 99
    and disorder, 100
    and divine punishment, 100
    and white fears, 137
intertextuality, 6, 213
Irenaeus, 29
Isidore of Seville, 28
Islam, 7, 8, 95, 221

Jackson, Stonewall, 83
Japhet. *See* Japheth
Japheth, 5, 24, 28, 30, 32, 36, 40, 41, 42, 70,
    72, 73, 74, 75, 80, 97, 129, 132, 133, 143,
    158, 163, 164, 182, 184
    and Anglo-Saxons, 166
    as conspirator in Ham's transgression,
        190
    and enlargement, 144
    and Romans, 165
    and white "race," 89, 99, 100, 103, 117,
        141, 162, 209, 210
Japhethites, 43
Jerome, 30, 47
Jesus, 28, 156, 194
    as innocent victim, 214
Jews, 8, 16, 28, 35, 183
Jim Crow, 10
Jobson, Richard, 36
Johnson, Thomas Carey, 151
Johnston, Michael P., 79
Joktan, 42
Jonathan, fourth son of Noah, 48, 49, 214
Jordan, Winthrop, 35
Joseph, 214
Josephus, 26, 33, 44, 45, 47, 51, 55, 94

Kafka, Franz, 208
Kass, Leon, 169
Keil, C. F., 187
Ker, Leander, 90, 93, 95, 102
Kinney, Kenneth R., 117
Ku Klux Klan, 17, 92
Kugel, James L., 17
Kuper, Leo, 208

Lacey, Harry, 115
Lactantius, 27, 29
Landrith, James, 3, 4
Lee, Robert E., 83, 136, 140
Lincoln, Abraham, 83
Lost Cause, 92, 140, 141
Luther, Martin, 32, 33, 68, 88
    on Nimrod, 50–52
lynching, 218
Lyon, James A., 89, 92

M'Causland, Dominick, 15
McKenzie, Steven L., 187
McLain, C. E., 86, 120
Magi, 5, 48
male gaze, 188
Mardon, 43
Mars, 49, 52

Martyr, Justin, 27
Maston, T. B., 116
Maurus, Rabanus, 30
Mengele, Josef, 191
Michelangelo, 178
Middle Ages, 45, 48–50
Midrash, 26, 42
Miles, William F. S., 172
Milton, John, 36, 37, 45, 56
    on Nimrod, 54–55
mimetic crisis, 208
mimetic rivalry, 207, 209, 211
miscegenation. *See* intermarriage
Mongols, 32
Morrow, James, 170
Moses, 51
myth, 207

Nat (slave stereotype), 10
National Broadcasting Corporation, 3, 4
National Public Radio, 3
Native Americans
    as Canaanites, 144–45
    extermination as judgment, 144, 145
    as Hamites, 145
    as "lost tribes" of Israel, 144
    as Semites, 144–45
    their practical extinction, 143
Nebuchadnezzar, 149
negroes, 12, 14, 36
    and barbarism, 96, 156
    and disorder, 87
    and immorality, 92
    as pre-Adamite beasts
    and rebellion, 87
    and sensuality, 77, 88
    stereotypes of, 10
    white views of, 70
Nephilim, 17, 59, 120
New Hamite Hypothesis, 196
New Orleans, 13, 125, 127, 128, 133, 135, 140,
    147, 152
New York City, 151
Newton, Thomas, 38–9, 40, 179
Nimrod, 5, 6, 10, 14, 16, 36, 41–61, 104, 126,
    195
    and Adonis, 59
    and alcohol, 110
    and ambition, 48, 51, 54, 57, 61, 170
    and anarchy, 119
    and animal passions, 107
    and anti-Christ, 56, 115
    as anti-Noah, 45
    as apostate, 59, 60

and asceticism, 53
and Assyria, 111
and astrology, 44
and astronomy, 48, 50
and Baal, 111
and Bacchus, 60
and Belus
blackness of, 106, 107
as builder of Tower of Babel, 49, 50, 51,
  54, 56, 57, 58, 60, 61, 107, 108, 109, 114,
  119, 133, 158, 159, 168, 170, 171
as challenger of patriarchal rule, 53, 58,
  60
and Charles Darwin, 121
as child and young man, 52
as city builder, 44, 61
clothing of, 43, 44, 56, 60
club of, 108
and confusion, 47, 50, 55, 60, 119
and consolidation, 138
and corruption, 110
death of, 59
and demons, 49
and desire for fame, 115
as dictator, 120
dominion of, 43
empire of, 49, 51, 52, 57, 61
and establishment of Babylonian
  monarchy, 54, 115
and Ethiopia, 111
and expulsion of Semites, 51–52
and false religion, 118
and fire worship, 47, 56
gigantic stature of, 46, 47, 49, 50, 56, 58,
  59, 60, 108
as grandson of Ham, 49, 50, 56, 60, 106,
  108, 158, 159, 182
and greed, 56
and heathenism, 111
and Hercules, 52, 60, 108
and hidden knowledge, 48, 60
and human sacrifice, 59
as hunter (oppressor) of men, 46, 53, 54,
  56, 61, 114, 115, 120
as hunter of wild beasts, 42, 43, 46, 52,
  57, 58, 60, 61, 108, 109, 170
and idolatry, 44, 46, 47, 56, 57, 60, 68,
  69, 107, 109, 114
and impiety, 43, 51
and insurrection, 158
and integration, 120
and intermarriage, 112, 113
and Karl Marx, 121
legend of, 42, 48

and magic, 45
meaning of his name, 58, 59, 114, 118
messianic prophecy of, 48
mystery cult of, 59, 61
negro, 59, 61, 112
and Northern aggression, 154
and Osiris, 59, 60
as prideful, 46, 47
and proslavery argument, 111
and prostitution, 59
and rebellion, 43, 45, 49, 50, 54, 57, 60,
  61, 106, 107, 110, 111, 113, 114, 118, 119,
  121, 138, 149
and resistance to postdiluvial dispersion,
  45, 47, 60, 108, 109, 110, 111, 113, 115
and Satan, 59, 61, 107, 109, 115, 120
self-divination of, 43
and sensual pleasure, 59
and slaughter of innocents, 44
as son of Cush, 170
as son of God, 49
and sovereignty, 49, 51, 54, 57, 58, 60, 107
and statecraft, 48, 61
and sun worship, 109
and Tammuz, 59
and territorial expansion, 42, 47, 61, 158
throne of, 43, 44
and Tower of Babel, as protection
  against second flood, 43, 45, 46, 53,
  60, 112
turning men from God, 43, 45
and tyranny, 45, 47, 49, 50, 51, 52, 54, 55,
  56, 57, 58, 60, 106, 112, 114, 118, 138,
  170
veneration of, 43, 46, 57, 58
and violence, 45, 110
nineteenth century, 40
Ninevah, 182
Ninus, 58
Noah, 4 , 18, 129, 139
  alcohol, 188, 197, 199
  birth of, 204
  blessing of, 75, 132
  curse of, 7, 34, 75, 76, 77, 78, 81, 82, 83,
    85, 96, 108, 125, 131, 132, 134, 143, 154,
    157, 159, 162, 171
  and discrimination among his sons, 116
  and dishonor, 72
  drunkenness of, 4, 5, 24, 28, 32, 34, 65,
    67, 71, 80, 86, 94, 146, 152, 163, 165, 178–
    80, 183, 190, 193, 198, 214
  fall of, 165, 179
  and genocide, 190
  as governor of postdiluvian world, 72

Noah (continued)
    as head of human family, 72
    and his nakedness, 30, 192, 193, 195, 205
    and homosexual desire, 190
    and honor, 72
    and intemperance, 179
    legend of, 30, 35
    paternal blessing of, 210
    as patriarch, 75
    and plantation life, 69
    as planter, 134
    prophecy of, 6, 11, 13, 14, 70, 73, 74, 75,
        81, 99, 125, 127, 132, 133, 143, 144, 145,
        146, 148, 159, 164, 165, 166, 180, 182, 211
    righteousness of, 24, 31, 36, 69, 177, 206,
        209
    as second Adam, 93, 134, 165, 204
    and shame, 72, 75, 79, 80, 102, 179
    sons of, 66, 68
    as type of Christ, 27, 28, 31, 178
    as victim, 206
Noahides, 218
Noll, Mark, 126
Northerners
    as meddlers in South, 98

Oedipus, 212
Old South, 66, 77, 88, 99
1 Enoch, 46
order, 8
    and honor, 101–02
    and the Southern mind, 88–93
Origen, 7, 27, 29, 94
Orion. See Nimrod
Ostriker, Alicia Suskin, 197
Ownby, Ted, 83, 84

Palmer, Benjamin M., 13–15
    address before Crescent Rifles, 131
    address before General Assembly of
        South Carolina, 133–35
    address before Legislature of Georgia,
        133–34
    address before Washington Artillery, 131
    and America's mission, 129, 130
    "Century Sermon," 128, 142, 173
    and confusion of tongues, 137, 139
    and dispersion at Babel, 134, 135
    Family, in Its Civil and Churchly Aspects,
        The, 153
    and holy war, 131
    and honor, 147–52
    "Import of Hebrew History, The" 128

    and language of genocide, 173–74
    and law of separation, 128, 133, 134, 136,
        137, 139, 142, 145
    legacy of, 161
    and Lost Cause, 136
    and mastery, 157
    and national character, 131, 132, 133
    "National Responsibility before God,"
        128, 132, 148, 155–56
    and necessity of servitude, 153
    on Nimrod, 137
    on Noah's curse and physical separation,
        133
    "Oath of Allegiance," 149
    and order, 152–55
    "Our Historic Mission," 129–131
    "Pastoral Letter of 1870, The" 150
    as patriarch, 159
    philosophy of history of, 129, 136
    as preacher, 127
    "Present Crisis and Its Issue, The" 136–
        38, 158
    and racial hierarchy, 141
    and racial purity, 137, 140
    and rebellion at Babel, 138
    relationship with his father, 159
    relationship with his son, 160
    and religious justification for slavery, 132
    and school segregation, 136
    and scientific racism, 140
    and segregation, 137
    and separation of races, 128
    and servitude as normal condition of
        blacks, 135
    and South's providential trust to
        preserve slavery, 131, 135
    "Thanksgiving sermon," 128, 130–131,
        147, 153, 155
    and the race problem, 136, 139
    and tripartite division of human race,
        129, 140, 143
    and tyranny, 153, 158
    and victimhood, 158, 159
    "Vindication of Secession and the South,
        A," 148
    and yellow fever epidemic of 1858, 130
Palmer, Edward, 159
Paradise, 93
Parham, Charles, 17
Patai, Raphael, 186–89
patristic writers. See Church Fathers
Patterson, Orlando, 9, 80, 81, 82
Payne, Buckner H., 17, 100, 112

Peleg, 5
Pennington, James W. C., 111, 184, 194
persecution texts, 207
Peter, 48
Peter of Riga, 31
Peterson, Thomas, 11, 143, 155, 187
pharmakon, 199, 200
pharmakos, 212
Phenech, 42
Philistines, 185
Phillips, Anthony, 186
Philo, 26, 46
Pink, Arthur, 115
Pitt-Reeves, Julian, 78, 81
polygenesis, 15, 202
Portugal, 7
pre-Adamism, 15–17, 202
prejudice, 220
Presbyterians, 13
    Northern, 139, 141, 150, 157, 158
    Presbyterian Church in Confederate
        States of America, 92, 102
    Southern, 77, 93, 125, 127, 138, 150, 154,
        157
Prewitt, Terry, 205
Priest, Josiah, 41, 42, 69, 76, 87, 101, 106,
    107
primordial violence, 207, 213
Princeton, New Jersey, 130
Princeton Seminary, 152
proslavery
    argument, 66, 70
    divines, 66
    intellectuals, 11, 65, 67, 69, 76, 77, 78
Protestant Episcopal Church, 97
Pseudo Methodius, 48
Purchas, Samuel, 35

rabbis, 7, 24–25, 28, 31, 42, 67, 77, 87, 177,
    198
racial hierarchy, 89, 99, 114, 126, 145, 165
racism
    intuitive, 126
    religious, 126
    scientific, 13, 103, 113, 126, 127, 174, 202
Raleigh, Sir Walter, 53
Rankin, John, 182–83
rebelliousness, 26, 44
Reconstruction, 126, 136, 137, 138
red "race," 132, 143
Reformation, 32–34, 50–56, 95
Renaissance, 50–56, 67
    and personal honor, 68

revivalism, 155
Rice, Gene, 106, 185
Robb, Thom, 17
Robinson, John Bell, 69, 75
Rogers, Gus "Jabbo," 95
Roman Catholic Church, 58
Romanticism, 81, 88, 127, 141
Ross, Allen P., 168
Ross, Fred A., 89
Rosse, Abraham, 34, 56, 199
Rougemont, F. de, 129
Ruffin, Edmund
Rwanda, 172, 173

sacrifice, 205, 208, 213, 214
Saffin, John, 8
Sahara, 129
Sambo (slave stereotype), 10, 193
Samson, 31
Sandell, J. W., 98, 113
Santo Domingo (Haiti), 154
Satan, 31, 32, 33, 51, 55, 69, 156, 198
scapegoating mechanism, 208, 211, 215
Schlegel, Friederich von, 126, 129, 130
Schwartz, Regina M., 191, 210
Scott, Sir Walter, 9, 88
secession, 78, 83, 84, 125, 130, 131, 134, 147
Second Great Awakening, 155
segregation, 86, 92, 103, 104, 114, 116, 127,
    162
    as providential, 117
    as scriptural principle, 118, 119
Semiramis, 59
Semites, 43, 132
Septuagint, 5, 39
servitude. *See* slavery
Sewall, Samuel, 8, 181
Shanks, Caroline L., 182
Shem, 5, 24, 28, 30, 32, 34, 36, 40, 42, 43,
    70, 72, 73, 74, 75, 80, 90, 97, 103, 117,
    129, 132, 133, 141, 143, 163, 164, 182, 184,
    188, 193, 209, 210
    as conspirator in Ham's transgression,
        190
    and Jews, 165
    and red "race," 89, 99, 162
    and spirituality, 167
    "tents" of, 143, 144, 145
Shinar, 6, 18, 43, 45, 53, 57, 61, 108, 111, 134,
    170
sibling rivalry, 192
Sibylline Oracles, 26
Simms, William Gilmore, 90

slavery, 6, 7, 8, 10, 30, 34, 65, 66, 71
  and Bible standard, 89, 92
  as civilizing influence, 93, 98
  as domestic, 89, 130, 131, 152
  and honor, 75, 81
  as patriarchal, 129, 135
  and rebellion, 77, 90, 92, 96, 97
  and slave impudence, 80, 97
  and social control, 91
  and subordination, 91
slaves, as children, 153
Sloan, James A., 73, 84, 102
Smith, H. Shelton, 130
Smith, Joseph, 15
Smith, Lillian, 77
Smith, William, 71
Smylie, James, 70
Smyth, Thomas, 111
Snay, Mitchell, 13
social death, 9, 77
Sodom, 30, 66, 86, 100
Solomon, 104
sons of Noah
  and unfolding of world history, 165–68
South Carolina, 3, 134, 151, 152, 159
Southern Historical Society Papers, 140
Southern Literary Messenger, 89
Southern mind, 78
  and conservatism, 88
  and honor, 78
  and nationalism, 141
Southerners, as rebels, 134, 138, 148
Spain, 7
Speke, John Hanning, 172
Spring Resolutions, 148
Stone, J. L., 183
subordination, 73
Sulpicius Severus, 94
superstition, 29
Swift, Wesley, 17
Sylvester Larned Institute, 136

Table of Nations (Genesis 10), 5, 12, 42, 46,
  106, 143, 168, 185
Taylor, Jeremy, 68
Terah, 44
Tertullian, 46
Thomas, Latta, 195

Thompson, Joseph P., 76, 111
Thornwell, James H., 92, 138
Tower of Babel, 4, 6, 10, 13, 18, 41, 43, 44,
  45, 113, 134, 140, 162, 187
  and city of Babylon, 6, 41, 100
  and dispersion, 114
  and human diversity, 169
  and human sin, 218–9
  as symbol of international
    confederation, 115
  as symbol of internationalism, 120
  as symbol of modern social ills, 121
Travels of Sir John Mandeville, 32, 49
Turner, Nat, 102
Tutsis, 172, 173
Tutu, Desmond, 218
Twain, Mark, 192
  Life on the Mississippi, 8, 9, 88

Uncle Remus, 10
Uncle Tom, 10
United States Constitution, 99, 147, 148,
  156

Virginia, 136
Von der Hardt, Hermann, 35
von Trimberg, Hugo, 30
Vulgate, 5

Walker, David, 194
Washington & Lee College, 136
Wayland, Francis, 71
Weld, Theodore, 11, 70, 177, 181
Wellhausen, Julius, 184–88
white domination, 127
white "race," 132
Willet, Andrew, 33, 34, 56, 179
Wilson, Charles Reagan, 92
Winchell, Alexander, 15, 17
Wittenberg, Gunther, 185, 187
Wyatt-Brown, Bertram, 9, 79, 80, 81, 82,
  83, 84, 85, 102, 147

Yonton. See Jonathan
Young-Bruehl, Elisabeth, 220

Zohar, 27, 88
Zoroaster, 30, 32

CPSIA information can be obtained at www.ICGtesting.com
Printed in the USA
BVOW02s0759061214

377543BV00004B/4/P

9 780195 313079